Managing Diversity

AN ASIAN AND PACIFIC FOCUS

Edited by
Margaret Patrickson
and
Peter OBrien

Contributors

Lynne Bennington, John Burgess, Janice Burns, Cheng Soo-May, Chung Yuen Kay, Helen De Cieri, Beverley Kitching, Mari Kondo, Robin Kramar, Jacqueline Landau, Sugumar Mariappanadar, Trudie McNaughton, Siva Muthaly, Mara Olekalns, Jean Renshaw, Niti D. Villinger

John Wiley & Sons Australia, Ltd

First published 2001 by
John Wiley & Sons Australia, Ltd
33 Park Road, Milton, Qld 4064

Offices also in Sydney and Melbourne

Typeset in 10.5/12 pt Berkeley

National Library of Australia
Cataloguing-in-publication data

Managing diversity: an Asian and Pacific focus.

Includes index.
ISBN 0 471 34234 3.

1. Labour laws and legislation — Asia. 2. Labour laws and legislation — Australasia 3. Diversity in the workplace — Asia. 4. Diversity in the workplace — Australasia.
5. Minorities — Legal status, laws, etc. — Asia.
6. Minorities — Legal status, laws, etc. — Australasia
7. Affirmative action programs — Asia. 8. Affirmative action programs — Australasia. I. Patrickson, Margaret. II. OBrien, Peter, 1944–.

331.133

Printed in Singapore

10 9 8 7 6 5 4 3 2 1

Contents

Preface

Increasing numbers of individuals in the Asia and Pacific region are expatriate managers and workers, and this has helped raise the profile of national and cultural differences between management practices and legitimised it as an area of research. This book is aimed at managers who move between countries in the Asia and Pacific region and need to understand and operate within the typical staff management practices that local managers in each country take for granted but that are unfamiliar to the expatriate. The area was chosen because it exhibits a greater range of diversity among its populations than any other region of the globe. Each country's managerial environment is a unique product of its individual history, geography, natural resources and ecology, economy, socio-cultural and political systems, none of which is independent of the others. Different practices between countries reflect the values and beliefs from the wider social environment that each is facing. It is these practices that form the broad focus for this book.

In particular the book addresses the issue of how each country manages differences between workers. Worker differences can arise in terms of type of task undertaken, educational level, skill level, years of service, earnings, categories of experience or in terms of gender, race, ethnicity, disability, or religion. Developmental variables, such as education, are subject to change with increasing experience and skill. Demographic variables, such as race and ethnicity, are either immutable or, like age and sex, difficult to change. Policies and practices that address worker differences are collectively referred to as diversity management. It is these largely immutable differences that form the substance of this book.

The book consists of 14 chapters. An introductory chapter looks at the field of diversity management, how it evolved, different research perspectives, and the different meanings of diversity. Next follow chapters directed at the legal and cultural environment of human resource management issues facing managers in each country. Each chapter has been especially commissioned and has been crafted by authors who have each spent considerable time in the country on which they have written. All chapters contain material on gender differences, some also address such issues as race, religion, caste, age, and child labour. A final chapter provides a comparative analysis of the various countries, looking at the plethora of influences that have led each to its present situation, the practices that have evolved, the legislative framework, the remedies (if any) available to an individual who has been the target of discrimination, and future trends.

It is a measure of the complexity of the topic that the issue of how to order the chapters on each country provided the editors with a series of dilemmas as we confronted the problems and challenges of various classification schemes. Size loomed as our first choice. How should size be measured? As population? Using population size would lead to chapters on the larger countries such as China, India, Indonesia and Japan appearing first, followed by medium-sized countries and economies such as Thailand, Taiwan, Malaysia and Australia with smaller countries and economies such as Hong Kong, New Zealand and Singapore last. We rejected this scheme as inappropriate given that our information showed poor correspondence between size and the treatment of minorities.

Should size be measured in terms of GDP? Our second choice was the level of economic development. This scheme could potentially mean chapters on Japan, Singapore, Taiwan, Australia, New Zealand and Hong Kong appearing first, followed by Malaysia, Thailand, and the Philippines then lastly India, Indonesia, and perhaps China. But we rejected this scheme also as we considered it inappropriate to use an economic classification to order countries on the issue of diversity management.

Ideally, it would have made sense to order the chapters on some scale of diversity management practice but this is far easier said than done. There is no agreed definition of the nature of diversity in Australia and it might well prove impossible to get an agreed definition across the variety of cultures in the Asia and Pacific region. What are the vital ingredients of diversity management? How do they order their contribution? Does this order vary between countries? Our evidence suggests that the perception of diversity so varies between cultures that arriving at a classification scheme that would be acceptable to all contributors would not be possible.

Finally, we opted to order the chapters in alphabetical order by country. This is not a cop-out but rather a reflection of the complexities posed by the issue. Nothing else would be universally acceptable. The choice reflects our firm belief that what constitutes best practice in diversity management is a matter of where, when, and who is being asked. All of us continue to learn from and about each other.

We recommend that readers choose the chapters in any order but always read the introductory and the concluding chapters in order to examine each with respect to the whole.

Margaret Patrickson

Peter OBrien

January 2001

Acknowledgements

The editors, Margaret Patrickson and Peter W. OBrien, wish to thank Rosemary Nicholls, who provided editorial assistance and whose keen editorial eye is greatly valued.

Mari Kondo wishes to thank Rosaly Marie Aquino for help with her chapter on the Philippines.

Lynne Bennington and Sugumar Mariappanadar wish to thank Ruth Wein, Shalini Goel and Catherine McCarthy for their assistance in the preparation of the chapter on India.

Lynne Bennington expresses appreciation to Ruth Wein who conducted detailed library searches and provided valuable comments on the draft chapter on Indonesia. She also thanks Wawan Putra, Wahdi Yudhi, Tan Johan, Phillip Joyce, Pat Miller, Greg Lee and Dr Prijono Tjiptoherijanto for their assistance. Appreciation is also expressed to those academics at IPMI, to the managers in Jakarta who participated in her research, and to her Indonesian graduate students who introduced her to their country.

Contributors

Lynne Bennington

Dr Bennington is an Associate Professor in the Graduate School of Management at La Trobe University. She has had more than 20 years' management experience in both the public and private sectors. Her lecturing is primarily in the areas of human resource management and international management, although she has published in the areas of services quality, public administration, benchmarking, age discrimination, recruitment and selection, change management, policy development, call centres, and partnerships.

John Burgess

John Burgess is Associate Professor at the Department of Economics, University of Newcastle. He previously held appointments at the University of Sydney and Charles Sturt University. His research interests include macroeconomic policy, labour market policy, gender and work, and workplace change.

Janice Burns

Janice Burns is a partner in a small consultancy company specialising in equity issues. She has held senior positions in the New Zealand Public Service and has contributed to many publications on EEO/diversity. Janice has acknowledged expertise in the analysis and design of pay equity initiatives.

Cheng Soo-May

Dr Cheng Soo-May is an Associate Professor in Management at the International Graduate School of Management, University of South Australia. Her primary research and teaching interests are in international and Asian business management, with Greater China, Southeast Asia and Australia as key areas of focus. She has published widely, edited a working paper series on Business in the Asia–Pacific, and is a reviewer for several journals and research grants bodies in Asia. Currently she teaches and supervises doctoral students in Australia and Asia with an interest in Asian management issues.

Chung Yuen Kay

Chung Yuen Kay is a sociologist who has variously worked as a school teacher, waitress, production operator, director of a women's organisation and researcher. Currently she teaches courses on human relations management and cultural diversity in ASEAN at the Faculty of Business Administration, National University of Singapore. She has published on feminist methodology, gender and workplace politics, and trade unions in Singapore.

Helen De Cieri

Helen De Cieri is an Associate Professor in the Department of Management, Monash University. Her teaching experience includes visiting appointments in China, Hong Kong, Malaysia and the USA. Her research interests focus on strategic and international aspects of human resource management. Helen is the editor of the *Asia Pacific Journal of Human Resources.*

Beverley Kitching

Dr Beverley Kitching currently lectures in International Business at Queensland University of Technology. Here she helped develop the new undergraduate and postgraduate programs in international business. She has published on Chinese science policy, Sino–Australian relations in science and technology and, most recently, on women in business in the People's Republic of China. She has also co-authored an international business textbook.

Mari Kondo

Professor Mari Kondo, a Japanese national, has lived in the Philippines since 1990. She is currently a program director of the Master of Business Management Program at the Asian Institute of Management. Here she teaches two core courses: Management Issues of Globalisation and Asian Business Systems. She has been researching extensively on cross-cultural management issues in Asia.

Robin Kramar

Dr Robin Kramar is an Associate Professor in Management at Macquarie University. She has more than 20 years' experience lecturing in universities and now teaches in Australia, Hong Kong and Singapore. Robin has published and researched internationally and in Australia in a range of areas such as human resource management, equal employment opportunity and diversity management, organisational change, and managing work and family issues.

Jacqueline Landau

Dr Jacqueline Landau was a Professor of Organisational Behaviour and Human Resource Management for 16 years. She has written over 20 articles and book chapters for leading publications, and is now a management consultant in the United States.

Sugumar Mariappanadar

Dr Mariappanadar is a Lecturer at Monash University. He has had broad management consulting experience in Indian public and private sector companies. His teaching and publications cover human resource management, organisational change and development, leadership and management, entrepreneurship and small business management, and organisational behaviour. His present interests are sustainable human resources management, employee motivational gratification, and spirituality and management.

Trudie McNaughton

Trudie McNaughton is currently Executive Director of the EEO Trust, New Zealand. The EEO Trust is an independent not-for-profit organisation helping workplaces achieve success through diversity. Here, Trudie has led a range of projects including the annual EEO Trust Work and Life Awards, the development of the annual EEO Trust Diversity Index and the development of the EEO Employers Group. Trudie is a member of Xchange, a global work and life forum.

Siva Muthaly

Dr Siva Muthaly is Assistant Dean International at the Faculty of Economics and Commerce, University of Newcastle. Dr Muthaly's research interests include Australian companies' involvement in the United States, United Kingdom, Malaysia, Indonesia and Thailand.

Peter OBrien

Peter W. OBrien is Associate Professor in International Management at the Adelaide University School of Commerce, and is an Adjunct Associate Professor at the University of South Australia's International Graduate School of Management. He has a particular interest in human resource management issues in international management, and his present research focuses on career issues of expatriate managers.

Mara Olekalns

Mara Olekalns is a Senior Fellow at the Melbourne Business School, where she teaches organisational behaviour and negotiation. She has lectured in organisational behaviour at the University of Otago and in the Department of Management at the University of Melbourne. She has also worked for the Australian Public Service in a range of human resource management positions. Her research focuses on communication processes in negotiation.

Margaret Patrickson

Margaret Patrickson is Associate Professor in Human Resource Management at the International Graduate School of Management at the University of South Australia. Her research interests are focused on the management of workforce change and the management of diversity. She is the author of four books and a number of articles in the field of human resource management.

Jean Renshaw

Jean R. Renshaw is a principal in the consulting firm, AJR International Associates, and a Professor of Management and Organisational Behaviour. She has lived and worked internationally in the Middle East, India, Europe, Latin America, Asia and the Pacific. Her work includes developing managers for the multicultural workforce; gender, culture and communications; strategic planning and organisational change projects; and the creation of adaptive organisations.

Niti Dubey-Villinger

Niti Dubey-Villinger is Assistant Professor of Management at Hawaii Pacific University. In addition to graduate studies at the Universities of Chicago and Cambridge, she has lectured at Wolfson College (Cambridge) and worked for a number of companies in Germany. Her research has focused on international management, and organisation and human resources issues pertaining to the investment strategies of Western multinationals in emerging markets.

Introduction to diversity

Margaret Patrickson

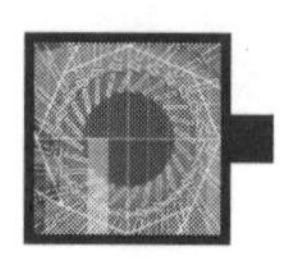

Introduction

There is no widely accepted definition of diversity. Most people would agree diversity refers to differences between individuals, but there is disagreement concerning which different attributes should be included within the ambit of the concept. Some differences between individuals are more or less immutable — these include race, gender, disability and age. These are the factors that underlie any legislative approach to the management of diversity within a society. Others, such as religion, culture, sexual orientation, education and socio-economic grouping, are either wholly or partially socially constructed and develop through social interaction. These latter seldom appear in legislation though they can be important influences on the differential treatment that individuals can receive in our society.

This book has its primary emphasis on examining the impact of immutable differences such as gender, race and ethnicity in the workplace with the aim of comparing policies and practices in a number of Asian and Pacific Rim countries. This is not to downplay the significant potential for disagreement that arises in socially constructed differences — simply to limit the comparison focus to primary differences such as those factors potentially covered by legislation. The region has been chosen for several reasons. First and foremost, given the racial variety among its indigenous people, its historical diversity, its plethora of languages and religious beliefs, and the breadth of its socio-economic divide, it offers perhaps the greatest range of differences of any regional area on the globe. Second, there is an opportunity to compare policies and practices within nation states, many of which have relatively short experience as global players, although they have long trading histories. Third, the area is among the world's most exciting cultural and social environments; little concerning localised labour force management is known to Western managers — and much needs to become known. It represents a microcosm of diversity management in which an understanding of how differences arise and how they can be harnessed can be a significant contributor to achieving greater international understanding and perhaps facilitate forms of competitive advantage.

Differences have always existed, as they are part of the human condition. They have an impact on how individuals perceive their environment, interpret information and resolve to act in problematic situations. Depending on how each is valued, differences between individuals can be seen either as assets or as liabilities. As liabilities they are likely to be viewed as a disruption to the development of homogeneity and hence something to be eliminated. As assets they may be experienced as a stimulus to expand the number of perspectives that can be harnessed to examine a common issue, and hence broaden an appreciation of the problem.

Until recently, differences were taken largely for granted and rarely became a focus for investigation or change. During the latter half of the twentieth century, however, as organisations have expanded the global nature of their operations and issues of human rights have become more widely debated, the management of diversity has emerged as a strategic issue for multinational firms. Globalisation's essential feature is that organisations manufacture, service, employ and market to populations with different laws, different religious and ethnic beliefs, and different levels of socio-economic development. Crossing international boundaries involves coming to terms with different customs for recruitment, training, work organisation, and other aspects of ongoing staff management.

To give some insight into the extent of internationalisation, one recent estimate (Deal & Kennedy 1999) suggested that 73 million people in today's global workforce now work for foreign owners. Twenty-five million people work for US corporations outside the United States and about 12 million are in the developing world. Approximately five million Americans work for foreign-owned companies operating in the United States. Bartlett and Ghoshal (2000) report that the annual revenue of some global companies exceeds the annual gross national product (GNP) of many smaller nations, citing the annual revenue of General Motors as equal to the GNP of Denmark.

Such international operations can succeed only if there is mutual respect, tolerance and reciprocal accommodation for the practices and beliefs of individuals from other countries. Cross-national management requirements impact on all aspects of a firm's operations both within and across national and international boundaries. Policies need to be determined with respect to internal staff management, marketing, and the conduct of international alliances to acknowledge difference and promote its benefits.

The area has become a minefield for both researchers and practitioners. Researchers are grappling with issues such as the selection and preparation of expatriate managers, comparative assessment of performance between countries and between managers, appropriate benchmarks for pay determination, the resolution of difficulties of inter-cultural miscommunication, and the creation of suitable structures to facilitate interaction and broaden the input of ideas. Expatriate practitioners are faced with the demands of having to obtain results in an unfamiliar environment, where the staff management practices honed during their early careers in their home country are likely to be ineffective. They need to learn new practices rapidly while maintaining high levels of proficiency.

The contents of this book are directed to this latter group, and to those responsible for their education and preparation. By bringing together information regarding typical workforce management practices in various countries in the Asia–Pacific region, the authors hope to enable educators and academics to better prepare practitioners. Information is provided which will introduce them to the situation they may encounter on arrival, assist them to operate more effectively once there, and help them to understand matters which need to be considered should they wish to initiate change. No matter what the origin of differences between people, or how immutable these differences may be, their consequences face global managers and challenge them to make the best use of the people available.

In tackling this issue we will follow a pathway which considers the history of diversity research and ends with the issues relevant to the twenty-first century — namely, how best to energise, maintain and combine the competencies of an international workforce to achieve competitive advantage in a globalised world.

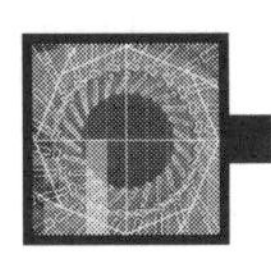

The beginnings

In the 1970s and 1980s writers adopted two main approaches to diversity. The first of these looked mainly at immutable differences, predominantly race and gender, and examined legislative barriers to discrimination and management practices aimed at promoting a more representative workforce at all organisational levels. The second approached the issue from the viewpoint of classifying cross-cultural values, beliefs

and customs, seeking ways to promote greater understanding and a more inclusive culture. Here, their methodologies were underpinned by the assumption that better understanding of each other's belief system would improve inter-cultural communication and this would lead in turn to more effective joint achievements.

The first approach is typified by the work of comparative industrial relations writers who examine the labour laws in different countries, seek to compare the forces which have led to the present differences and discuss their impact on the working environment. Frenkel and Royal (1997), for example, compare the degree to which International Labour Organisation (ILO) conventions have been ratified by different countries in the Asia–Pacific area, and evaluate the extent to which governments in the various countries regulate the role of unions. They suggest that the most frequent practice is to adopt the labour management practices of the host country while at the same time seeking to introduce workable corporate-wide initiatives. They comment that the implementation of labour laws in many countries is limited by resource constraints on expenditure, and workers are often vulnerable to exploitation by powerful employers.

In an eight-country comparison, Deery and Mitchell (1993) found three models of labour law predominated. The first resembled the British model, which is essentially voluntarist, emphasising collective bargaining, legal immunity for workers and unions taking industrial action, a non-interventionist system of union registration, and support mechanisms for conciliation and arbitration. The second was the American model, with a greater emphasis on institutionalised collective bargaining, and the third, common in Australia and New Zealand, emphasised compulsory arbitration. In many Asian countries with histories of British colonialism, the British model was adapted to suit local history and culture. In some others, such as Japan and Korea, which had experienced a period under US influence, the American model was adopted and subsequently modified.

However, neither Frenkel and Royal nor Deery and Mitchell specifically directed their attention to the management of workforce diversity. Adler and Israeli's (1994) comparison of the issues facing female managers was a landmark in such efforts, but their work was largely confined to the issues facing educated women and did not address the problems of other marginalised groups in the workforce. The book contains reports from 21 countries and looks at the broader social context in which women managers are increasingly trying to forge careers, and the social forces which help shape their opportunities, motivations and choices. They found a picture emerging in almost every country whereby men control the centres of political and economic power, and women face major barriers in their quest for managerial recognition. Women find themselves with fewer career choices and fewer promotional possibilities as a result of institutionalised discrimination that favours males. However, Adler's research found that in Asia expatriate managerial women often fare better than indigenous women. This is summarised by Adler and Israeli (1994: 35) as follows:

> Therefore the societal and cultural rules governing the behaviour of local women that limit their access to managerial positions and responsibility do not apply to foreign women.

Beneria (1998) comments on the situation facing indigenous women. He believes that as acceptance of women workers has increased in newly industrialised countries

(NICs), this has generally been followed by greater equality and a gradual breakdown of gender stereotypes. He suggests that many women are brought into the workforce through informal or casual channels as households rely on extended families and send more family members into the workforce.

However, it is the cultural barriers, particularly those not generally articulated, which are pervasive in their influence and sparked the desire of researchers to undertake comparison of national cultures, that characterised the second approach to diversity, which occurred in the 1980s. Initial efforts in this direction adopted methodologies from cultural anthropology and are generally acknowledged as gaining momentum with the work of Kluckhohn and Strodbeck (1961), who examined the extent to which values within a culture helped shape assumptions and perceptions. Their work was followed by Hofstede (1980), who believed language, media, the educational system and the political system were strong forces helping to cement and differentiate national cultures. His initial research gathered information on work values held mostly by IBM male employees worldwide and analysed the data to develop four, then later (Hofstede 1991) five dimensions on which national work cultures could be distinguished from each other. His research involved a total of 116 000 individuals from 50 countries in which IBM operated worldwide. The five dimensions are listed as power distance, individualism/collectivism, masculinity/femininity, uncertainty avoidance, and Confucian dynamism or long-term orientation.

Subsequent criticism of his work (e.g. Bangert & Pirzada 1992; Yeh & Lawrence 1997) has challenged his conclusions by commenting that the dimensions may have quite different meanings in different cultures and thus the variables may not equate across the sample. More important, it is becoming clear that values as measured are a function of research timing and Hofstede's data is no longer timely as we head into the twenty-first century. His major contribution, however, was not so much his findings but his initiative in tackling such a monumental piece of global research and directing subsequent research attention to this as a legitimate and timely area to investigate.

Hofstede's work was followed by that of Trompenaars (1994), who adopted a similar methodology by administering surveys to managers in several countries. His data led him to propose five cultural dimensions, some of which replicated the earlier work of Hofstede. His categories included universalism/particularism, individualism/collectivism, neutral/affective, specific/diffuse and achievement/ascription. Trompenaars also examined different understandings between cultures of the concept of time, concluding that differences ranged between tight adherence to prescribed appointments and honouring schedules, through to adopting a more flexible approach to time, placing higher value on relationships and viewing time as a flexible commodity.

Such approaches present useful tools for examining cultural differences but, because they tend to focus on the dominant culture of each country, they often give a false impression of cultural unity and underemphasise the existence of regional or subordinate cultures. Parker (1998) cites a Harvard study of global managers in 1991 which showed greater convergence of values among business leaders than differences. He has argued that these changes are largely superficial, and that movement is two-way. Within cultures there are growing pressures for homogeneity operating side by side with growing heterogeneity resulting from increased travel, Internet access and business collaboration.

The major contribution of these findings and similar cross-cultural research has been to highlight the difficulties in transporting home-grown management and human resource strategies from one socio-political entity to another. The major problems of inter-cultural communication occur in the perception and attribution of meaning. Even when managers are fluent in several languages, or there is a shared common language such as English, meanings are not necessarily identical across cultural divides. The approach has spawned a new research area seeking to discover new strategies for improving communication and facilitating the transfer of meanings across national boundaries. Typical people management activities such as recruitment, development and evaluation, for example, require policies to serve two masters — the global parent and the local subsidiary.

Together these two approaches to research summarise much of the recent writing in international diversity management. However, they represent a predominantly Western view of the issue. Few Asian writers have addressed the problems they encounter from their own perspective — an exception being the recent publication of Chu (1995). Yet even her work was written for the American market. In a recent review of publications in international management, Wong-Mingji and Mir (1997) found that the United States dominated publications, followed by other European nations. Most of their citations are also based on Western writers since the majority of authors are fluent only in English. They conclude:

> ... Too often discussions on workplace diversity are restricted to North American concerns and issues (e.g. affirmative action, the American women's movement) and fail to even address some challenges raised by managing globally diverse populations. Even when IM scholars look beyond North American boundaries, it is usually with an espoused view to improve cross-cultural communication and so on (p. 362).

It is difficult to pinpoint any single factor as an explanation for the differing approaches to diversity adopted by West and East. In the West, legislation promoting equal opportunity and affirmative action occurred mostly in the late 1970s and early 1980s, with the emphasis changing to diversity in the United States, then later elsewhere, following the publication of *Workforce 2000* in 1987 (Johnston & Packard 1987). In Asia the strong push towards economic growth which has characterised the area since the 1970s led to rising pressure to raise exports, which in turn drove the demand for escalating levels of female workforce participation. But the role of women in society changed far more slowly. Governments were devoted to providing stability to underpin the necessary economic expansion and were unaccustomed to prescribing how workers should be treated, unions experienced relatively low levels of political power and loyalty to family was too deeply embedded to be openly challenged.

Equality of treatment simply did not surface either as an industrial issue or as a societal one until globalisation became a decisive force in the 1980s with its internationalisation of production, consumption and distribution, which meant that national economies lost their ability to act independently. Munck (1999) claims that until the mid-1970s only about two-thirds of the global workforce was linked to international markets. He predicted that by the beginning of the twenty-first century, 90 per cent of the world's labour would be internationally connected. Such interdependence has implications for human resource management and strategy, and comparison becomes inevitable. Policies acknowledged in the home country must receive attention in the host environment.

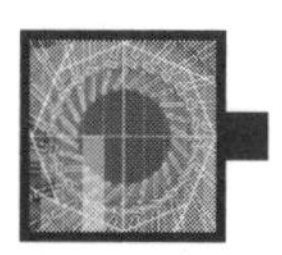

Key areas of international comparison

Managing across national boundaries requires practices to meet the twin expectations of parity and equity. Manager A in country X is compared with his/her counterpart in country Y. Both are charged with similar responsibilities, yet both have to achieve their respective goals under different economic conditions, with different labour constituencies, facing different market forces. New international divisions of labour emerged during the twentieth century. Developing countries have increasingly become sites for manufacturing activities and members of minority groups are commonly employed in the less desirable jobs with unattractive conditions and low pay.

The 1990s saw the publication of a number of comparative studies looking at differences in human resource management (HRM) practices. In Europe, Brewster and Hegwich (1994) distinguished the key challenges which face international HRM practice based on the Cranfield international survey of HRM practices as including pay and benefit systems, flexible working arrangements, equal opportunity options, training provision and employee relations. This survey has subsequently been administered throughout other countries but the results have yet to be published in full. Dowling, Schuler and Welch (1994) suggest key issues in international staff management are recruitment and selection, performance appraisal, training and development, compensation and labour relations. Their list has much in common with that of Brewster and Hegwich. In fact neither list contains any surprises. One would expect key staffing issues to be universal. Finding the 'right' people, keeping them, developing their talents, evaluating their activities and rewarding their efforts are fundamental tasks facing any management. Differences between countries are not likely to arise in terms of which tasks are to be tackled, only in how they are tackled.

Many factors can determine the different strategies, policies and practices which firms can adopt to respond to staffing demands abroad. Chief among these is likely to be the nature and timing of their overall global strategy, the beliefs of senior executives, their experience in staffing global operations, and the need to operate without time lost in labour disputes, all of which are related to profitability and consistency. As long as existing practices abroad are tolerable, they are likely to be incorporated in the operation of the foreign subsidiary and would result in a pragmatic approach to managing staff. In such a situation the customs of the host country would predominate provided that no serious comparative anomalies were to be uncovered which might indicate existing practices were unacceptable. Such is currently the case. Practices are not the same across countries. Their histories are different, their different geographic terrains are associated with different levels of agricultural and infrastructural development, their infrastructure facilitates different levels of education, their natural resources result in different levels of prosperity, and their religions foster different approaches to societal organisation, work and family. Thus staffing practices in each regional area operate within a unique set of parameters which are not identical to anywhere else.

The purpose of this book is to compare some of these differences — in particular those relating to the treatment of workforce diversity. Do differences in gender, age, race, ethnicity, religion or physical and mental ability affect the way members of each country's workforce gain access to jobs, promotion, training and salaries? Each

country will be examined in a separate chapter in terms of both its legislation and its typical practice. The aim is to determine:

- whether anti-discrimination legislation exists and if so what penalties are available to punish illegal behaviours
- the levels at which members of disadvantaged groups are represented in the workforce
- whether members of minorities have equivalent access to promotion paths and are employed in senior positions in management
- whether access to training is freely available
- the degree to which the earnings of minority group members reflect their education, and competencies.

Our purpose is not to act as judges but to inform global managers of existing practices; those practices that have developed within each country and that are congruent with the country's history and are likely to be encountered by the situation managers on arrival. Knowing what to expect will help avoid some of the obvious pitfalls of ignorance.

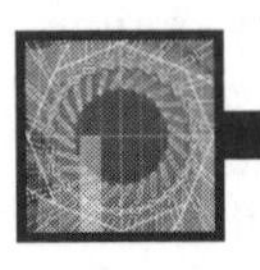

Options for treatment of minorities

Countries vary significantly in the degree to which they support making comparable opportunities available for all individuals. Providing equality of opportunity in employment, promotion, training and income to all potential members of the workforce is an expression of the dominant social values within a society. Depending on whether the area is covered by legislation, and how these laws are interpreted, the gates facing some individuals may open totally, partially or not at all. Furthermore, even when laws against discrimination do exist, they operate with varying degrees of force, and may not necessarily result in more than cosmetic changes in employment practice.

Lasserre and Schutte (1999) comment that the people management challenges presented in the Asia–Pacific region are more complex than in any other global region. In their opinion the entire Asia–Pacific region is typified by a shortage of skilled managers, a highly mobile managerial population, and a reluctance to work for foreign companies, all of which loom as major obstacles to change. Perceptions of fairness are an integral ingredient of any interpersonal relationship in the region and people management policies in most organisations reinforce the paternalistic type of family culture predominant through Asia. The authors list a number of characteristics which they believe typify the social structure, such as group reference for behaviour, conflict avoidance, face saving, respect for authority and seniority, paternalism, credentialism, nepotism, and a lower status for women. It is the latter which militates against women receiving equal treatment and seems to underpin much discriminatory practice within indigenous workplaces. According to Adler (Adler & Israeli 1994), discrimination against foreign women is rare. Nonetheless, many individuals simply do not believe that discriminatory behaviour (as defined through Western eyes) is unacceptable within their own societal structures. Rather, it is seen as reflecting and reinforcing deeply embedded social norms.

Personal relationships in Asia permeate all aspects of doing business. Family relationships are not distinct from business, and networks form intricate webs of reciprocity. Business is not a separate world but a replication of the extended family.

Thus one's family status is reflected in one's business status. Asian families tend to be patriarchal, and many women gain status through their position in the family rather than as individuals in their own right. Thus their ability to command respect to some extent is circumscribed by their family affiliation — a situation which many Westerners attribute to the dominance of Confucianism in Singapore, China and Hong Kong, given that one of its core values is a preference for sons rather than daughters.

It is this context which spills over into employment. Businesses have traditionally been seen as a man's world with women's roles reduced to support and assistance. Few women face barriers to gaining employment. But in many Asian countries access to certain types of employment is strongly gender segregated. In a comparison of Hong Kong, Taiwan and Singapore, Salaff (1990) concluded that it was the inexpensive labour of women, chiefly engaged in lower skill activities, which had financed much of the economic expansion of these newly industrialised countries. Any personal earned-income was used to contribute to family need rather than individual financial independence. Until the 1990s the issue of opportunities for women was seldom raised. Nowadays it is common to find items relating to women in business almost every day in the local English language press in most Asian countries. It is emerging into the public arena as an area for debate and concern.

One survey published in *Asian Business* (Abdoolcarim 1993) reported that Asian women rated Hong Kong as the most woman-friendly country followed by Singapore, and then the United States. Japan ranked twelfth after China yet before South Korea, India and Indonesia. Those few who reach managerial rank tend mainly to do so in industries considered female such as retail, cosmetic, fashion and education; they are rarely seen in engineering, medicine or construction.

Much of the discrimination is invisible, unremarked and unchallenged. Even women who privately believe their treatment to be unfair rarely directly confront any received injustice. To do so would be an isolating action in a society that places high value on harmony and cooperation. Change that has been achieved has largely been due to a minority of outstanding dedicated women, many highly educated, who work long hours to achieve their goals. As will be seen in the following chapters, large numbers work in the public service or in their own business.

Nonetheless, opportunities for women in Asia are opening, although more so in some countries than others. But for other minorities the future is less immediately favourable. Members of racial and ethnic minorities throughout Asia continue to be caught in a vicious circle of family poverty, lack of education and hence problems in accessing high-skill jobs which pay well.

It is only the more wealthy countries that can afford some kind of economic support for their ageing citizens. The number of older persons are expanding and they are generally found less onerous jobs in late working life. In Indonesia there are so few older workers that, except in a small number of individual cases, the issue does not arise. In countries with predominantly Chinese populations, such as Singapore and Hong Kong, Confucian values demand respect for older family members and it is normal practice for each family to take care of its ageing relatives. The problem of older worker discrimination looms larger in the West. Australia and New Zealand have been the arenas in which this issue has received the most attention. Economic restructuring and workforce downsizing have combined to increase the vulnerability of those over 50 years of age during the last decade.

On the other hand, it is the predominantly Asian economies where members of racial and ethnic minorities face the greatest barriers to employment opportunity. This does not necessarily arise as a consequence of prejudice but rather as a by-product of the strongly integrated system of family business networks. Unlike the West where individuals tend to leave their families, both physically and psychologically, as they mature to form families of their own, Asian families tend to maintain close ties and act as both an economic and a social unit throughout their life span. Often it is the family, rather than the individual, which finds employment for its members. Families tend to live together, work together and support other branches of their more extended family through establishing long-term buying and selling relationships so that each may prosper. Relationships, especially kinship ties, are the basis of economic prosperity and sharing.

Yet it is the very strength of this system that makes it difficult for individuals from outside the family to enter established industries, no matter how meritorious they may be. Family always comes first. An outsider would face barriers to entry and success, which could only be overcome by a combination of heavy financial investment, competitive technology, and a commitment to a long-term presence. Those without either connections or resources are thus limited in their capacity to secure patronage. It is this situation which confronts members of ethnic minorities and becomes self-perpetuating. Without resources, access to higher education is more limited. Without education, access to better jobs is more restricted. Without a good job, income is more likely to be reduced. Outsider families may thus be kept in a recurring cycle of poverty from which it is difficult to become extricated. Nowhere is this system clearer than in India where birth determines caste, which determines job possibilities, which determines income, and where poverty is perpetuated from one generation to the next. The extended family system of economic interdependence can act as a barrier that may be even stronger and more difficult to permeate than the traditional glass ceiling.

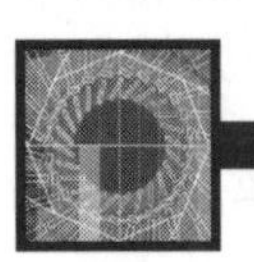

Factors influencing the management of diversity

Diversity is the product of so many interactive forces that it is impossible to disentangle the separate political, economic, racial, ethnic and religious influences that act to create and perpetuate minority groupings within society. Each country presents as a different melting pot of race, culture, language and religion. Multinational companies operating abroad can experience uncertainty and vulnerability, as their familiar knowledge base may no longer be appropriate.

Globalisation's inevitable pressures for international interdependence have led to an increased emphasis on international cooperation and raised the profile of diversity as a socially constructed phenomenon, which, once established in society, facilitates the development of power matrices embedded in social frameworks. Once a power base has been achieved it can be sustained through a series of interrelated activities which maintain the existing framework and help to disestablish alternatives. Established power elites can adopt practices that influence social and economic privileges to provide support for their own group members rather than respond to the demands of less powerful minorities.

Such a situation is not new. Society has always been stratified. Almost all societies have an established infrastructure which privileges some groups and marginalises

others. Managing across national borders may mean that managers must confront and perhaps challenge a different basis for stratification from the one with which they are already familiar. Stratification reflects society's core values and may act to reinforce differences between members of component factions. Core values define the fundamental beliefs, attitudes and acceptable behaviours that most precisely identify each group. Should group differences increase, the pressures that face those who move between them become more intense. It is these pressures which faces the international manager. The challenge is to treat all people one wants to understand and know as individuals, and at the same time to energise each different group towards the necessary cooperative effort to maximise the benefits for the organisation as a whole.

Successful initiatives in diversity management should allow an organisation to improve its performance. At the legislative level, the role of government appears to be limited to improving work conditions and eliminating discriminatory practices. However, not all nations have ratified ILO conventions. The Universal Declaration of Human Rights, proclaimed in 1994, aimed at creating a common standard and code for all nations, encompassing concerns such as child labour, working hours, safety at work, treatment of prisoners, and ethnic and gender equality, among other issues. International law thus recognises that the establishment of structures to prevent discrimination may be a valuable achievement. Yet, in some developing countries, discrimination appears to be more honoured in the breach than in the observance. The law will not work for minorities if the will of the people or the state does not support it.

Globalisation's effect on human rights is confusing, complex and contradictory and many countries in Asia have articulated negative attitudes to Western views. Onuma (1999), for example, states that the tendency of some Western countries to assume the superiority of their own system is often counterproductive and elicits resentment in Asia, where cultural norms are opposed to the high levels of violence and aggression observed in the West. Onuma believes Western views often miscast the human rights debate solely in terms of political and civil rights and largely ignore economic, social and cultural rights. These are the issues that are most relevant to developing countries. Social change cannot occur without raising global consciousness, and this is happening slowly.

Economic growth has raised standards of health, education and nutrition, facilitating equity of access to education and training, which remains chief among needed policy initiatives. Historically, minorities have experienced lower access to education and this subsequently reduces their access to higher paid and more responsible jobs. Additional skill development is the greatest single factor likely to impact on labour quality and hence provide minority members with the education needed to propel their upward movement. Global demand for staff with specialised technical and managerial skills is escalating at an exponential rate. In combination with people skills it may represent a force strong enough to overcome any prejudice due to minority membership. Know-how may thus challenge know-who to act as a powerful entry to senior responsibility, spurred on by the acute shortage of senior managerial talent.

At the corporate level there is much that organisations can do to foster recognition for minority members and promote respect for their contribution in a changing context. According to Ghai (1999), international corporations are gradually assuming the role of policy making within their jurisdictional spheres. In his view,

Asian values in the 1980s and 1990s seemed to fit with the imperatives of globalisation, with their emphasis on minimal state welfare, limited trade union rights, reliance on family, and restricted political participation. Yet these also have some negative aspects for corporate governance in the form of dynastic politics, nepotism, cronyism, lack of transparency and accountability, and the absence of or failure to enforce regulations. Some researchers (e.g. Yuen & Kee 1993) believe that multinational corporations need to decide for each country whether and to what degree to adapt home management processes. Similarly, indigenous companies need to explore alternatives to their current practices. Adjusting the demographics of workplace composition, both in total and at each managerial level, is only a beginning. Interventions need to consider extending beyond simply the task of proportional representation to overcoming cultural prejudices and instilling new values that celebrate difference. This may be a tall order in the light of historical practices that have previously existed in some areas.

Performance appraisal, for example, has a Western tradition of top-down staff evaluation facilitating control over staff activities and gatekeeping access to developmental experience. However, a recent four-nation study, Vance et al. (1992), found typical practices varied significantly across countries. In particular, negative feedback needs to be handled very sensitively in non-Western countries and can be highly inflammatory in Asia if given in a straightforward manner.

Willingness to change needs to occur in both directions. Bridging of languages can be addressed initially through training, exposure and goodwill. It should be supplemented by multilingual communication and additional time for validation to ensure that meaning is communicated as well as words. New creative practices need to be discovered to best utilise the demands of electronic communication. Similarly, realisation that existing hierarchical structures generally work well in their own context may help Western managers adjust to the limited egalitarianism they encounter in Asian companies.

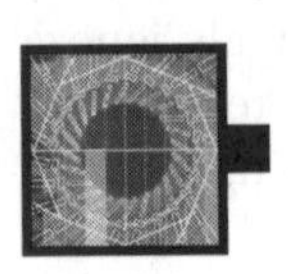

The focus of this book

The forthcoming chapters in this book examine how prevailing management practices respond to the situation in various Asian–Pacific countries in terms of variations in the gender, age, disability, race or ethnicity of the workforce. Given that diversity management and potential discrimination are less talked about in Asia than in Australia or New Zealand, it is a topic that has provided a greater challenge than originally envisaged by the editors. Not all countries publish detailed breakdowns of their employment statistics, neither are the practices by which they are collected strictly comparable. Though legislation exists in some countries to promote equal employment opportunity (e.g. Hong Kong and the Philippines), this is more frequently aimed at redressing injustice rather than more actively promoting Western notions of equality. Tribunals, in countries where they exist, are mostly complaint-based and citizens are generally reluctant to initiate confrontation against direct discriminatory practices. Consequently, these are seldom challenged. Moreover there are few significant deterrents for organisations that discriminate against minority group employees. One Japanese woman describes the consequences of early discrimination faced by many young women in their first job.

> Thousands of Japanese women hit the 'glass ceiling' two months after starting work. Hired in April, many seek psychiatric help in June for depression caused by discrimination, and the prospect of stultifying, dead-end assignments or the shame of quitting and looking for another job (Renshaw 1999: 19).

More recently, however, there have been signs this is beginning to change, partly triggered by the economic crisis of the late 1990s, which forced many Asian-based organisations to rethink their labour demands, and partly as a result of rising numbers of foreign-owned multinational corporations that are opening up within Asia. Two simultaneous strategies acted to increase the numbers of foreign-owned companies during this turbulent period. Many new ventures being established in Asia by foreign corporations were in greenfield sites as wholly foreign-owned subsidiaries, but others were more likely set up as some form of joint venture partnership in which the foreign company took up a proportion of the equity with local management. Haley (2000) comments on how the financial crisis highlighted the growing vulnerability of Asian organisations and led a number local managers to seek new owners for ailing parts of their business in a bid to ensure the survival of other enterprises within their consortium. Takeovers by Western-owned corporations significantly increased during this time and added to the growing numbers of wholly-owned foreign entities. Strong pressures on these foreign firms from their home base and global strategic positioning helped them to counterbalance the Asian downturn and facilitated their growth and survival. Their international operations reduced their vulnerability to the vicissitudes of the local economy, and rising numbers of employees increased their power base in the economic structure. Thus their influence grew and the majority rapidly became profitable concerns.

By the start of the twenty-first century, foreign corporations were strongly established in the business landscape of many Asian countries and this helped ensure that, rather than remaining a rarity, the management styles of the foreigners gradually became better known. Though many had found it difficult initially to attract good people away from locally-owned firms, as their presence increased, they began to employ local people in significant numbers. Necessity had earlier yielded a broad recruitment base and often resulted in higher levels of mixed workforce than their local counterparts. Within countries, multinationals often operated differently from local companies and in turn there were differences in their operations between countries. Under new ownership many former local organisations have been required to adopt a number of Western-style staff management practices that they had previously been able to ignore. While there is only a scattering of empirical evidence to suggest multinationals offer more equitable staff management practices than locally-owned firms, there are nonetheless a number of anecdotal comments that indicate members of minority groups find them more friendly and supportive.

This tightening of economic conditions in Asia in the late 1990s, coupled with an increasing presence of foreign management and increasing pressures being mounted by minorities for recognition in many world environments, impacted on staff management practices in two contradictory ways. On the one hand, pressure on the cost of labour highlighted the need in Western organisations to weigh the competency brought to the firm by each individual and thus added pressure to focus on contribution to overall performance as a key ingredient by which to measure individual worth. On the other hand, throughout many family-based firms in Asia, action was taken to promote the protection of one's own and to ensure that it was the minority or outgroup members who bore the brunt of the pain.

The next section of this chapter briefly summarises how each of the countries examined in this book has responded to these pressures and introduces the reader to the material to be covered in greater detail as the book unfolds.

The rationale for each chapter is first to address the specific environmental conditions facing the country, covering such issues as the prevailing social, political and economic variables that impact on the demand for labour, and whether labour laws exist to protect minorities. More important, the chapters report on typical managerial practices and a number raise key points for expatriate managers who may be involved in comparing operations between countries or may need to prepare themselves quickly for transfer to another location.

Renshaw's chapter, for example, asserts that Japan, more than any other Asian country, is often credited with giving priority to its own citizens and with operating a system of patronage within its corporate ranks. Its status as an island country and its former insularity contributed to the entrenchment of these practices. They were in turn reinforced by a social structure that meant being a 'real Japanese' was given pre-eminence and those who did not fit were either excluded or treated less favourably. In her experience many Japanese nationals not only hold a deeply shared belief in homogeneity but an equally strong belief in the supremacy of everything Japanese. Together these beliefs have led to diversity being a largely unacknowledged issue. Renshaw shows how this refusal to recognise that differences may generate a need for differential treatment puts pressure on staff who are different to assimilate into the prevailing culture and ideology, and makes it daunting to challenge existing ways of managing. She states that women, older workers, non-Japanese and disabled individuals tend to be viewed as 'outsiders' in the workplace. Even within the ranks of the Japanese themselves, gradations of caste remain as a relic of previous feudal systems that distinguished citizens on the basis of birth.

That such exclusiveness should operate in conjunction with Japan's economic success raises a number of interesting questions. Japan's high rate of literacy and the high levels of educational attainment achieved by its population make it impossible to equate the belief in exclusiveness with lack of education. She cites, as an example of how deeply ingrained is the belief in homogeneity, the fact that citizenship is not necessarily granted to those born in Japan to foreign parents. The system is repressive by Western standards, and is becoming more difficult to maintain as more residents are becoming exposed to Western ideas. It can only be sustained if the relatively powerless members continue to accept the constraints placed on their development by the dominant in-group and there are signs this is changing. Fewer women, especially younger women with less traditional values, are willing to accept the prevailing orthodoxy uncritically. Though their salaries continue to lag behind those of men, they are becoming more politically active, engaging in protests, forming networks, and starting up their own economic enterprises.

Hong Kong faced not only similar economic pressures but also significant political change as the reins of government passed from the British to the Chinese. As one of the more economically developed regions of Asia, and the site for large numbers of multinational regional offices, it commanded a strategic position within the region. Yet little legislation against discrimination existed in Hong Kong prior to the 1990s. Kramar's chapter cites a 1994 study by Cheung that refutes claims by the 1991 government that such legislation was unnecessary as there was little evidence of discrimination in practice. Cheung's research found discrimination in employment was still experienced by many women. Kramar's chapter shows how, since 1998, all

Hong Kong employers have been required to observe ordinances that make it unlawful to discriminate against another person in terms of recruitment, training, promotion or dismissal. An Equal Opportunities Commission (EOC) has been set up since 1996 to ensure the legislation is implemented.

Yet in Kramar's opinion, the path ahead will prove challenging given the strong stereotypes that reinforce a domestic role as the primary focus for women, and the potential conceptual and value clash between Western and Chinese understanding as to the exact nature of human rights. She suggests that the Hong Kong legislation is based on a more Western view of human rights that is alien to traditional Chinese thinking and thus may not reflect traditional Chinese concepts of what is fair.

Singapore is similar in many ways to Hong Kong. Both have experienced a period under British rule, have a legacy of British law on their statute books, are relatively small in area with large urbanised populations, and have high percentages of citizens who are ethnically Chinese. Furthermore, the use of English as the dominant language for commercial transactions has been in force for some years. Nonetheless, differences in their political and economic history have contributed to divergent practices with respect to the treatment of diversity. Singapore has been independent only since 1965, when it separated from Malaysia. Since then its government has been stable without change in political party. The economy has remained strong throughout and the country continues to be seen as a relatively secure site for investment. The government is active in directing funding into education to ensure a ready supply of skilled workers. One oft-repeated commercial objective in the media is to become the Asian hub for telecommunications.

Landau and Kay, in their chapter, report that the official policy of the Singapore government is committed to multiracialism and multiculturalism, and the population has been under political pressure to assimilate. However, there are no specific laws addressing gender or age discrimination. Educational programs have been the major practices aimed to change attitudes voluntarily, rather than force them through legislative intervention. Government-owned media (such as *The Straits Times*) frequently publish articles aimed at assisting employers to develop more positive attitudes to workers who are members of minorities. Landau and Kay suggest these have had only limited success and claim traditional sex roles remain deeply embedded in the psyche of the population. Though women experience little difficulty in being recruited into good professional postings, promotion to senior ranks remains as a challenge. Change is happening but its progress on these matters is perceived to be very slow.

By contrast, only 60 per cent of the population in Malaysia is urbanised. Unlike Singapore or Hong Kong, which have similar historical experiences, the main focus of diversity management in Malaysia is not gender but race. The chapter by Burgess and Muthaly shows how ethnic Malays have increased their representation in the non-agricultural sector since independence, as a consequence of strong government pressure to improve their share of economic benefits and underpinned by an affirmative action program aimed to help them open up new employment opportunities. No legislation exists to counteract discrimination against women, older workers or the disabled. Neither is there any strong pressure from minority groups or from trade unions to enact any such legislation. Until the economic crisis, growth in recent years has been strong, with many opportunities for those seeking work. Malaysia's recovery has been relatively rapid and growth is once again a feature of its economic performance. The authors suggest further developments in the management of diversity to ensure that women and children are less vulnerable will be inevitable before too long.

Taiwan is similar to Singapore in that it is economically progressive with a rapidly expanding set of hi-tech industries. The majority of its population is ethnically Chinese with a strong Confucian heritage, and the population is well educated. As a result of an alliance with the United States from 1950 until 1972, Taiwan developed the rudiments of a democratic political system that has flourished in recent years. Early trading with the US and Japan also led to the establishment of a massive export-oriented economy which has proven resilient during the recent Asian economic crisis.

However, unlike Singapore where multinationals have become significant players in the local economy, the Taiwanese economy continues to contain a large proportion of family-style enterprises. The pressure for economic restructuring and international competitiveness has mounted with increasing challenge from other newly industrialised economies. Cheng's chapter points out how the current labour shortages and recent changes in political direction present new opportunities for Taiwan. One consequence is a gradually changing approach to diversity towards a more inclusive system in which more opportunities are open and family-friendly practices are becoming more common.

Thailand, in common with many other countries in Asia, contains a high proportion of non-indigenous people, and residents from neighbouring countries seeking employment. As in Singapore, assimilation has been officially and publicly encouraged. Dubey-Villinger's chapter indicates that in recent decades education levels have risen noticeably, fluency in English as well as Thai is becoming more common, and the workforce is moving from being largely agriculturally based to becoming more professional. Though women comprise almost 50 per cent of the labour force, with reduced rates of promotion and comparatively lower earnings, discrimination has rarely appeared as an active issue in employment relations. The majority of women are employed in small-scale establishments, and many are self-employed in cottage-type industries, which may have contributed to their acceptance of their situation. A new constitution enacted in 1997, which aims to prevent discrimination against women in employment, and to promote equality before the law for all persons irrespective of race, religion, age, gender, origin, health, personal status, and general economic or social standing, was received with little dissent. Unlike the stronger economies of Hong Kong and Singapore, Thailand weathered the monetary crisis poorly, with a negative impact on the numbers of employed and in the education system. Members of minorities, especially women, have suffered in terms of job loss, reduced earnings and curtailment of educational opportunities.

China, as it emerges from a centrally planned, state-owned system into carving out a role in the global market, presents as a paradox in Kitching's chapter. China contains 54 officially recognised minority nationalities. Like other predominantly Chinese economies, the management of business affairs is modelled on the management of the family, underpinned by values of harmony, unity and conformity, with women playing a subordinate role (they enjoyed few legal rights until the 1950s when they were enshrined in the Maoist constitution). The Maoist Marriage Law of 1982 enabled women to inherit property, choose their marriage partner, initiate divorce, retain guardianship of their children, earn jobs outside the home, earn equal pay and assume political office.

By the end of the twentieth century there were around 400 million women in China aged over 15 years. Their participation rate in the labour force is 80 per cent,

and they earn 85.6 per cent of men's wages. Few are present in management athough many are exploring opportunities in new entrepreneurial ventures following the reforms that legalised private business activities in the late 1980s. Almost five per cent of people in the PRC are disabled and legislation has only recently addressed this issue by adopting laws to protect disabled individuals (in 1990) and guarantee their civil rights (in 2000).

The country is confronting large-scale change on a broad front as it tackles the economic and social changes associated with becoming a major player in the global market. Education has emerged as a major need, and the pace of change is among the fastest in the world, affecting more individuals than any other country in Asia. Unlike many other Asian societies, it has no recent history of colonial rule, thus its heritage and legal system have evolved from Confucianism without the influence of Western-style input.

Though Indonesia's history contains a period of colonisation by the Dutch, the country achieved independence in the 1940s. In spite of its motto — Unity in Diversity — Indonesia is the least unified of all the countries we are examining in this book. With over two hundred dialects, over two hundred ethnic groups, two hundred million people, and a workforce of over ninety million, the country's population is scattered over 13 000 islands with an urbanisation rate of less than 30 per cent. Such a situation ensures great difficulty in developing uniform policies and militates against a transparent and comparable jurisdiction. Added to these problems are high levels of unemployment, low levels of literacy, and many children working to supplement family income. Bennington's chapter captures the confusion, and the lack of comparative justice associated with the plethora of employment conditions, recognising the strong discrepancies between official policy and practices, between the formal and informal sectors in the employment arena, and between the public and private sectors of the economy. Discrimination is practised actively against members of racial minorities and, though legislation exists to promote the rights of women and children, cases continue to be reported which indicate such laws are rarely enforced unless the breaches are flagrant and well publicised. Change is happening but given Indonesia's more vulnerable international financial position, any changes that do occur tend to be slow and sometimes bitter.

The Philippines, like Indonesia, consists of several groups of islands and is heavily regionalised with a number of local dialects and languages, but there the similarity ends. Its predominantly Christian heritage, as a result of former colonisation by both Spain and the United States, has resulted in greater allegiance to a belief in individualism than in more collective societies. In addition, the influence of the United States has been active in promoting American ideas of workplace equality. Kondo's chapter points out that though women have continued to place higher value on their domestic role than their working role, there is a strong history of achievement by women in senior roles. Almost 10 per cent of employed women occupy professional jobs. Kondo cites Corazon Aquino as one of few women in Asia to become a head of government and affirms that gender equality has been on the statute books since 1987, with corporations likely to face penalties in the event of complaints being upheld. Sexual harassment has been illegal since 1995, again with penalties for transgression. Her chapter contains an interesting insight into a practice that has developed in Manila among women office workers, who take up selling to other staff informally to supplement their income.

India has a strong British heritage. However, although English is the language of commerce, as in Singapore, Hong Kong and the Philippines, it is only spoken by a small proportion of the population, many of whom are illiterate. Moreover, the degree of diversity in India is greater then anywhere else in the world. In addition to the traditional categories of gender, race, age and disability, another even stronger one is included — that of caste. In their chapter Bennington and Mariappanadar explain how caste, even when illegal, can heavily influence access to education and employment. They discuss the many improvements that women have experienced over the last three decades, but comment that the labour market remains segregated, with access to some jobs restricted, promotion paths below those of males and salaries generally lower than those of their male counterparts. Older individuals generally retire in their mid-50s, though many older educated people may continue to be employed in the peripheral workforce. Of particular relevance in India is the issue of child labour where, even though legislation exists to protect children against exploitation in employment, it is largely ignored in some industries.

Although differences exist between Australia and New Zealand when compared with Asia, there are similarities between these two countries and their Asian neighbours. In common with Hong Kong, Singapore, the Philippines, India and Malaysia, Australia and New Zealand are English-speaking countries, with a period under British rule, an indigenous population, a multi-ethnic population and an influential historical period of colonisation. But their histories also reflect persistent differences. English is the language of the education system as well as the commercial system in both New Zealand and Australia. It is spoken in the majority of home environments and the majority of the media. The period of British rule occurred at a time when the government and legal systems were being developed and left a powerful legacy deep in the infrastructure of socio-political affairs. The immigrant population rapidly triumphed over the indigenous inhabitants both numerically and economically and resulted in the dominance of the Caucasians, their values, their religions and their social frameworks.

It was not until the large-scale migration that followed the end of World War II that the British heritage in Australia and New Zealand began to incorporate other European values. An emergent culture that reflected growing Australian or New Zealand nationalism slowly began to materialise as the inhabitants grew to enjoy some of the benefits of multiculturalism. By the 1960s both countries were starting to seek greater equality for working women and by the 1970s legislation had been enacted that penalised discrimination against women in the work environment and outlawed sexual harassment. Since then, New Zealand has done more than Australia to assist its indigenous population experience equality of opportunity in education, employment and development, spurred on by the heritage of the Treaty of Waitangi, the greater numerical proportion of indigenous people in the population and the strength of their political voice. The chapters by De Cieri and Olekalns on Australia and Burns and McNaughton on New Zealand discuss these movements and their consequences in greater detail.

The book offers a rich picture to those readers interested in working and managing in the Asia–Pacific. It shows the impact on labour diversity as a result of the similarities and the differences, the problems and the solutions, the progress and the stalemates that have confronted each country as they emerge from a financial crisis late last century and enter the new millennium. In the final chapter these various situations are compared, trends extracted and broader movements summarised. A

number of writers — for example, Naisbitt (1997) — have predicted the twenty-first century will be the century for Asia and the Pacific. It is axiomatic that by the end of the century the Asia–Pacific Region will look very different from the way it looks now. However, in our opinion, the shape of the future remains elusive.

References

Abdoolcarim, Z. 1993. 'How Women Are Winning at Work: Asia's Business Culture as Corporate Women See It'. *Asian Business*. Hong Kong, Nov: 24–9.

Adler, N. J. & Israeli, D. N. 1994. *Competitive Frontiers: Women Managers in a Global Economy.* Cambridge Mass.: Basil Blackwell.

Bangert, D. C. & Pirzada, K. 1992. 'Culture and Negotiation'. *The International Executive* 34(1): 43–64.

Bartlett, C. A. & Gloshal, S. 2000. *Transnational Management: Text, Cases and Readings in Cross-border Management*. Third Edition. Chicago: Irwin McGraw-Hill.

Beneria, L. 1998. 'Gender and the Global Economy'. In Ackerman, F., Goodwin, N. R., Dougherty, L. & Gallagher, K. *The Changing Nature of Work*. Washington, DC: Island Press.

Brewster, C. & Hegwich, A. 1994. *Policy and Practice in European Human Resource Management: The Price-Waterhouse-Cranfield Survey.* London UK: Routledge.

Chu, Chin-Ning. 1995. *Thick Face, Black Heart: The Asian Path to Thriving, Winning and Succeeding*. London UK: Nicholas Brealey Publishing.

Deal, T. E. & Kennedy, A. A. 1999. *The New Corporate Cultures*. Reading Mass.: Persues.

Deery, S. & Mitchell, R. 1993. *Labour Law and Industrial Relations in Asia*. Melbourne: Longman Cheshire.

Dowling, P., Schuler, R. & Welch, D. 1994. *International Dimensions of Human Resource Management*. Second Edition. Belmont USA: Wadsworth.

Frenkel, S. J. & Royal, C. 1997. 'The Globalisation of Work'. *Research in the Sociology of Work*. Vol. 6. Greenwich Conn.: JAI Press.

Ghai, Yash. 1999. 'Rights, Social Justice and Globalisation in East Asia'. In Bauer, J. R. & Bell, D. A. *The East Asian Challenge for Human Rights*. New York: Cambridge University Press, 241–263.

Haley, U. C. V. 2000. *Strategic Management in the Asia Pacific*. Oxford UK: Butterworth Heinemann.

Hofstede, G. 1980. *Cultures Consequences: International Differences in Work-related Values*. Beverly Hills CA: Sage.

Hofstede, G. 1991. *Cultures and Organisations: Software of the Mind*. Maidenhead USA: McGraw Hill.

Johnston, W. B. & Packard, A. H. 1987. *Workforce 2000: Work and Workers for the Twenty-first Century.* Indianapolis USA: Hudson.

Kluckhohn, F. R. & Strodbeck, F. L. 1961. *Variations in Value Orientations*. New York: Row, Peterson & Company.

Lasserre, P. & Schutte, H. 1999. *Strategies for Asia Pacific*. Second Edition. Melbourne: MacMillan Education Australia.

Munck, R. 1999. 'Labour Dilemmas and Labour Futures'. In Munck, R. & Waterman, P. *Labour Worldwide in the Era of Globalisation*. New York: MacMillan Press: 3–26.

Naisbitt, J. 1997. *Megatrends Asia: The Eight Asian Megatrends that Are Changing the World*. London UK: Nicholas Brealey Publishing.

Onuma, Yasuaki. 1999. 'Towards an Intercivilisation Approach to Human Rights'. In Bauer, J. R. & Bell, D. A. *The East Asian Challenge for Human Rights*. New York USA: Cambridge University Press: 103–23.

Parker, B. 1998. *Globalisation and Business Practice*. London UK: Sage.

Renshaw, J. R. 1999. *Kimono in the Boardroom*. New York: Oxford University Press.

Salaff, J. W. 1990. 'Women, the Family and the State: Hong Kong, Taiwan Singapore — Newly Industrialised Countries in Asia'. In Stichter, S. & Papart, J. L. *Women, Employment and the Family in the International Division of Labour*. Basingstoke UK: The MacMillan Press: 98–136.

'Transcending Business Boundaries: 12 000 World Managers View Change'. 1991. *Harvard Business Review* May/June: 151–64.

Trompenaars, A. 1994. *Riding the Waves of Culture*. Burr Ridge Illinois: Irwin.

Vance, C. M., McClaine, S. R., Boje, D. M. & Stage, H. D. 1992. 'An Examination of the Transferability of Traditional Performance Appraisal Principles across Cultural Boundaries'. Reprinted in Davis, H. J. & Schulte, W. D. 1997. *National Culture and International Management in Asia*. Surrey UK: International Thompson Press: 497–510.

Wong-Mingji, D & Mir, A. H. 1997. 'How International is International Management? Provincialism, Parochialism, and the Problematic of Global Diversity'. In Prasad, P., Mills, A. J., Elmes. M. & Prasad, A. 1997. *Managing the Organisational Melting Pot*. Thousand Oaks CA: Sage: 340–66.

Yeh, R. & Lawrence, J. J. 1997. 'Individualism and Confucian Dynamism: A Note on Hofstede's Cultural Root to Economic Growth'. In Davis, H. J. & Schulte, W. D. *National Culture and International Management in East Asia*. Surrey UK: International Thompson Business Press.

Yuen, E. C. & Kee, H. T. 1993. 'Headquarters, Host-culture and Organisational Influences on HRM Policies and Practices'. Reprinted in Davis, H. J. & Schulte, W. D. 1997. *National Culture and International Management in East Asia*. Surrey UK: International Thompson Business Press.

Chapter 2

Australia

Helen De Cieri and Mara Olekalns

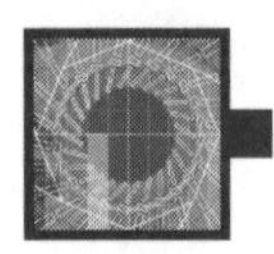

Introduction

As stated in chapter 1 of this book, there is no widely accepted definition of diversity. Diversity has been defined as referring to characteristics that differ between individuals, although there is a lack of consensus about the different characteristics that should be included. Diversity may refer to characteristics such as gender, age, language, ethnicity, cultural background sexual orientation, religious belief, marital status, family responsibility, educational level, work experience, socio-economic background, and geographic location.

The aim of this chapter is to examine the impact of various forms of diversity on workplaces in Australia. We discuss the major dimensions of diversity in Australian society and the workforce, outline the legal environment surrounding diversity management, and then analyse the business context for managing diversity in Australia.

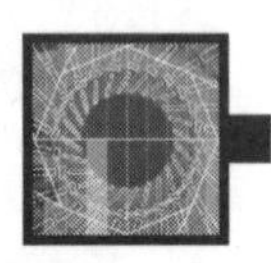

Forms of diversity in Australia

The Australian resident population is 18.7 million and the number of people employed in Australia has grown over the past 50 years from just over 3 million people to about 8.3 million people (Australian Bureau of Statistics 1999a). Diversity has become an increasingly important factor in Australian organisations as the workforce and general population have become more heterogeneous with respect to ethnicity, gender, education, age and other characteristics. Each form of diversity may present particular challenges for management and employees. The following sections provide an overview of the most significant forms of diversity in Australian workplaces.

Ethnic diversity in Australia

Ethnic diversity is a salient characteristic of the Australian population and workforce. Australia is one of the most culturally heterogeneous societies in the world, owing to several waves of migration from a broad range of cultural and geographic backgrounds (Wilkinson & Cheung 1999). The social, economic and political implications of this multiculturalism are significant for organisations and Australian society in general.

Indigenous Australians have one of the oldest cultures in the world, with a presence dating back at least 40 000 years. The European settlement of Australia that began in 1788 had a dramatic and largely negative impact on indigenous Australians, who were disadvantaged and marginalised by the social, economic and political policies of European colonists. These disadvantages remain evident in literacy rates, unemployment, health and housing problems (Graetz & McAllister 1994; Human Rights and Equal Opportunity Commission 1997).

Indigenous Australians currently represent approximately two per cent of the national population. Recent research has examined current practices and emerging opportunities for indigenous Australians in the workforce and noted that significant obstacles remain to be overcome. For example, the proportion of indigenous

Australians, male or female, who are self-employed is much lower than the national average (Schaper 1999).

National statistics indicate that certain groups of people, such as indigenous Australians, can experience special difficulties in gaining access to education or training opportunities. Indigenous Australians commonly have had lower levels of participation in post-compulsory education than the rest of the community. For example, in 1997 there was a lower proportion of indigenous workers with a post-school qualification (35 per cent) compared with the general population of workers (54 per cent). Indigenous workers, however, were more likely to intend to enrol for a post-school qualification in the three years following the 1997 survey of education and training (22 per cent) than the general population of workers (16 per cent). These results are partly explained by the younger age of indigenous workers, with younger workers being more likely than older workers to participate in study or training courses (Australian Bureau of Statistics 2000a).

Prior to the 1960s, the majority of migrants to Australia came from Europe, particularly the United Kingdom. Historically, multiculturalism in Australia was regarded as a governmental social policy problem. As Wilkinson and Cheung (1999: 106) explain:

> Attempts were made to reduce cultural heterogeneity by restricting immigration to white Europeans — the so-called White Australia policy. In general, emphasis was placed on the problems and costs involved in migrants adapting to Australian customs and practices and learning to speak English, if it was not their native language. Another type of problem was the tensions and conflicts between ethnic communities of historical origin being introduced into Australia . . .

There has, however, been increasing national awareness of the importance of Australia's Asian geographic positioning vis-à-vis European cultural heritage, with significant demographic change within Australia (Australian Bureau of Statistics 1994; Clark 1995; Tongzon 1995). In the past few decades, Australian social policy focus has shifted significantly to emphasise the benefits and opportunities to be gained in a multicultural society (Department of Immigration and Multicultural Affairs 1998).

In 1998–99, 25 per cent of people in the Australian workforce were born overseas. Approximately 46 per cent of these migrated from the United Kingdom, Ireland or North America. The workforce participation rate for people born overseas in countries where English is not the main language spoken was 54 per cent (Australian Bureau of Statistics 1999a). According to a report by the Australian Federal Race Discrimination Commissioner (1997), migrants in Australia have come from 160 countries, and 40 per cent of people in Australia are migrants or the children of migrants.

Approximately 58 per cent of the immigrant workforce is male. Of those employees born outside of Australia, approximately six per cent work as managers or administrators; another 32 per cent work as professionals or associate professionals; approximately 12 per cent are tradespeople; 28 per cent work in clerical, sales or service industries; 10 per cent work in production or transport; and 11 per cent work as labourers (Australian Bureau of Statistics 1997a).

In 1997, workers who were born outside Australia and whose first language was not English were just as likely to have a post-school qualification as all workers.

Overseas-born workers whose first language was not English participated in on-the-job or external training courses to a lesser extent (22 per cent and 14 per cent respectively) than the general population of workers (34 per cent and 21 per cent) (Australian Bureau of Statistics 2000b). (The numbers reported here recognise only first-generation immigrants. Given Australia's history of migration, it is evident that Australian workplaces also accommodate many second- and third-generation Australians whose values and beliefs are influenced by a mixed cultural heritage.)

Industry

In the early years of European settlement in Australia, between 1788 and 1850, Australia's economic development was led by the pastoral industry. In particular, growth in the wool industry enabled development of other sectors, such as the establishment of local manufacturing industries, to take advantage of emerging market opportunities. In the 1850s and 1860s, gold became Australia's major export earner, leading to rapid expansion of banking and commerce. Manufacturing industries continued to expand from the mid-nineteenth century, and by World War II the Australian manufacturing sector was sufficiently developed to respond to the demand for war materials and equipment. In the 1950s and 1960s, all Australian economic sectors experienced growth, until the oil crisis in 1973–74 brought worldwide recession. Employment growth between 1968 and 1979 was modest and restricted to service industries (Australian Bureau of Statistics 2000c).

The past two decades have seen a decline in the relative contribution to gross domestic product from manufacturing industries and a rise in the contribution from service industries, although manufacturing remains the most significant industry in terms of its contribution to gross domestic product (Australian Bureau of Statistics 2000c). The number of people employed in manufacturing has decreased markedly. The contrasting dramatic growth in service sector employment has culminated in more than 70 per cent of the Australian workforce being employed in various service industries (Walsh 1997).

A related factor important to the management of diversity is the type and hours of work being undertaken in Australian workplaces, with significant changes occurring in the nature of work itself, utilising new technologies, widespread multi-skilling, new forms of employment and varied hours of work. Recent Australian studies suggest evidence of a common pattern seen in other industrialised countries: employment is moving from the 'traditional' forms of full-time, permanent work towards a wide variety of working arrangements, including part-time work, temporary employment and contract employment (Van den Heuvel & Wooden 1997). Approximately 74 per cent of employed persons are in full-time work while 13 per cent of men in the workforce are in part-time employment and 44 per cent of women are employed part-time. For males, part-time work is most prevalent for younger men (aged between 15 and 24 years) and older men (aged 55 or older); for women, participation in part-time work occurs consistently across age groups (Australian Bureau of Statistics 1999b).

Gender diversity in the Australian workforce

An important form of diversity in the Australian workforce is related to gender representation. Over the past 50 years, female employment in Australia has increased from 0.8 million to 3.6 million, an increase of 350 per cent. In the last 20 years in particular, the proportion of women in the workforce has increased, as has the proportion of

women with family responsibilities who are in the workforce (Hartmann 1998). In the same period, male employment has virtually doubled (Australian Bureau of Statistics 1997b). The female participation rate in the Australian workforce was 54 per cent in 1998–99, compared with 73 per cent for males (Australian Bureau of Statistics 1999b).

Currently, women represent 23 per cent of managers and administrators in Australian workplaces (Australian Bureau of Statistics 1999b). Further, the higher the level of management, the lower the number of women found: women represent 35 per cent of junior managers in Australian private sector organisations, 25 per cent of middle management, 15 per cent of senior management and only eight per cent of executive management. Such proportions are found even in those industries dominated by women; for example, women represent 65 per cent of employees in the education industry but hold only 17 per cent of executive management positions (Australian Bureau of Statistics 1997b). Recent surveys show that only in large organisations (those employing more than 100 staff) have we seen substantial increases in the number of female managers. The more general trend shows that, over the past 10 years, the number of women in management has been relatively stable (Australian Bureau of Statistics 1997b).

Education levels in the Australian workforce

Education and training are also important considerations in diversity management. The term 'education' has traditionally been used in a broad sense to refer to long-term processes of obtaining knowledge, skills and abilities. Education is regarded as a lifelong process, typically developed during schooling and subsequent learning in formal institutional settings. In contrast, 'training' is a more specific type of learning, through which certain vocational skills are developed for practical application in the workplace (Kramar, McGraw & Schuler 1997).

The Australian Commonwealth Government plays a significant role in education and training policy, programs and funding. Total government expenditure on education and training in 1997–98 was $25 082 million, which represented 4.4 per cent of Australia's gross domestic product (Australian Bureau of Statistics 1999c). State and Territory governments in Australia have the major responsibility for education and training, including administration and substantial funding of primary and secondary schooling, and the administration and funding of technical and further education (TAFE).

In May 1998, 5.2 million people aged 15–64 (42 per cent of this age group) had completed a recognised post-school qualification. A further 6.5 million (53 per cent of this age group) had no recognised post-school qualification, and the remaining 0.7 million people (five per cent) were still school students. Women were more likely to have qualifications at the basic vocational, undergraduate-diploma, and postgraduate-diploma levels. Men were more likely to have qualifications at the skilled vocational and higher-degree levels (Australian Bureau of Statistics 1999d).

A national survey of education and training conducted in 1997 showed that 54 per cent of all wage and salary earners held a post-school qualification, while 28 per cent held a higher-education qualification, and a further 24 per cent held a skilled or basic vocational qualification (Australian Bureau of Statistics 2000b). Women were more likely than men to have a higher-education qualification (32 per cent compared with 24 per cent) and less likely to have a vocational qualification (19 per cent compared with 29 per cent). In the 12 months prior to this 1997 survey, 78 per cent of employed people aged 15–64 years undertook some form of training. More specifically, 70 per cent of employed people received on-the-job training and 21 per cent completed an external training program (Australian Bureau of Statistics 2000b).

In general, actual or intended involvement in study for an educational qualification or in work-related training differs little between men and women, but decreases with increasing age. In 1997, 94 per cent of workers aged 15–24 years had undertaken some study or training in the 12 months prior to the survey, compared with 73 per cent of those aged 45 years and over (Australian Bureau of Statistics 2000a).

Literacy

Literacy levels in the workforce have significant implications for productivity and organisational performance. Consistent with international practice, literacy in Australia is assessed on three scales (measuring prose, document and quantitative analysis skills). The resultant distribution is grouped into five levels, with Level 3 often regarded as the minimum level of competence required to cope with the demands of everyday life and work. Among Australians aged 15 to 65 years, 56 per cent have prose literacy of at least Level 3, compared with 75 per cent in Sweden and 54 per cent in the US. Similarly, 55 per cent of Australians aged 15 to 65 years have document literacy of at least Level 3, and 75 per cent have quantitative literacy of at least Level 3 (Australian Bureau of Statistics 1999e). In Australia, approximately 65 per cent of those with low literacy skills participate in the workforce, although this group has a greater chance of being unemployed than those with more literacy skills (Australian Bureau of Statistics 1999e).

Age differences in the Australian workforce

The ageing of the Australian workforce represents an increasingly significant aspect of diversity. A range of statistics shows the need for attention to issues of concern to older workers (defined by the Australian Bureau of Statistics (1999b) as 55 years and older), and the need for management strategies which have the flexibility to address the diverse needs of an ageing workforce. In 1998, 21 per cent of the Australian civilian population were in the 'older' category; this is projected to increase to 29 per cent by 2016 (Australian Bureau of Statistics 1999f). The workforce participation of older women has been increasing, and females now represent 34 per cent of the 'older' workforce (Australian Bureau of Statistics 1999b). Several factors may contribute to the increasing proportion of females in the 'older' workforce: the increase in service and information sectors, particularly in part-time employment, and changes in financial circumstances related to increased access for women to superannuation (Patrickson & Hartmann 1996).

As a proportion of employed persons aged 25 and over, older workers are most strongly represented in the occupational category 'managers and administrators' (representing 21 per cent of this category in August 1996). The proportions of older workers in all other major occupational categories are between eight and 14 per cent. Older workers are more likely to be self-employed than those in the 'prime age' group (those aged between 25 and 54 years). In August 1996, 28 per cent of older workers were self-employed, compared with 15 per cent of prime-aged workers (Australian Bureau of Statistics 1996).

In summary, these statistics reflect the broad diversity of the Australian workforce and population in general. In addition to the aspects of diversity reviewed above, several other forms of diversity have important implications for Australian workplaces.

These include religion, disability, work experience and sexual orientation. Each form of diversity may influence an individual's attitudes, values and behaviours at work. Such diversity creates an imperative for flexible and inclusive management (Dass & Parker 1999; Joplin & Daus 1997).

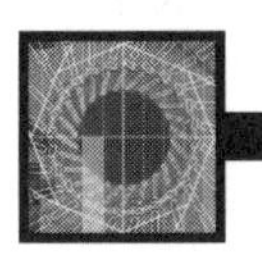

The legislative context for diversity in Australia

Legislation in Australia recognises a wide range of forms of diversity and prohibits discrimination in appointment, promotion and transfer of employees on the grounds of political affiliation, race, colour, ethnic origin, social origin, religion, sex, sexual preference, marital status, pregnancy, age, or physical or mental disability. Several Acts at federal and State/Territory levels operate to prevent discrimination in Australia (Kramar et al. 1997; Morris, Mortimer & Leece 1999). Employers in Australia must comply with Commonwealth legislation covering direct and indirect discrimination in employment. Further, Australian State and Territory governments have legislated to prescribe minimum conditions of employment, which apply notwithstanding any express provision in an employment contract. In 1999, industrial legislation in most jurisdictions (States, Territories and at the federal level) in Australia was amended to some extent, with alterations relating to workplace diversity issues either in progress or already implemented (Chapman 2000).

The relevant current Commonwealth legislation is outlined below.

- The *Racial Discrimination Act 1975* makes it unlawful to discriminate in employment on the grounds of race, colour, or national or ethnic origin.
- The *Sex Discrimination Act 1984* makes it unlawful to discriminate in employment on the grounds of a person's sex, marital status, pregnancy or potential pregnancy, or to sexually harass another person.
- The *Equal Opportunity for Women in the Workplace Act 1999* amends the *Affirmative Action (Equal Employment Opportunity for Women) Act 1986*, and is the result of the Government's response to recommendations made by the independent committee that conducted a regulatory review of the Act (Chapman 2000; Williams 1999).
- The *Human Rights and Equal Opportunity Commission Act 1986* provides for the rights of people with physical or mental disabilities and complaints of discrimination in employment on the grounds laid down in the International Labour Organisation (ILO) Convention 111. This Act defines discrimination to mean any distinction, exclusion or preference that has the effect of nullifying or impairing equality of opportunity or treatment in employment or occupation on the basis of race, colour, sex (including marital status), mental, intellectual or psychiatric disability, nationality, religion, political opinion, national extraction, social origin, age, medical record, criminal record, sexual preference or trade union activity.
- The *Disability Discrimination Act 1992* makes it unlawful for an employer to discriminate against a person on the grounds of the person's disability:
  - — in arrangements made for the purpose of determining who should be offered employment
  - — in determining who should be offered employment
  - — in the terms or conditions on which employment is offered.
- The *Occupational Health and Safety (Commonwealth Employment) Act 1991* places an obligation on all employers and employees to maintain a secure, healthy and

safe working environment. An employer has a duty of care to take practical precautions to prevent workplace harassment and to deal promptly and effectively with any complaint or harassment.

- The *Workplace Relations Act 1996*, in Section 170NB, prohibits discrimination on the basis of race, colour, sex, sexual preference, age, physical or mental disability, marital status, family responsibilities, pregnancy, religion, political opinion, national extraction or social origin. This Act prohibits discrimination on these grounds in the making of awards and agreements and in the termination of employment subject to some exceptions. Interestingly, the *Workplace Relations Legislation Amendment (Youth Employment) Act 1999* was enacted to exempt junior wage rates from provisions prohibiting age discrimination (Chapman 2000).
- The *Public Service Act 1999* prohibits discrimination among federal government employees. This Act replaces the *Public Service Act 1992* (Chapman 2000; Public Service and Merit Protection Commission 1998; 1999a).

Overall, the aim of this legislation, in combination with the legislation at State and Territory level, is to give legal support to the notion that all people in a society should have equal opportunities to enjoy the benefits of that society, including employment. While legislation places emphasis on the legal issues that surround diversity management, there are a number of other factors that affect diversity management. We suggest that an understanding of current issues and trends relevant to diversity management will be useful, in order to develop diversity management strategies that will provide numerous benefits to individuals and organisations.

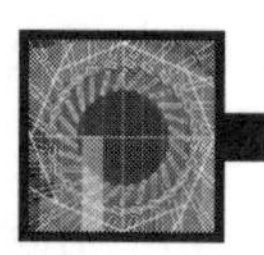

Conclusions

In this section, we examine some current issues and trends related to managing diversity in Australia, and identify strategies to promote effective diversity management in the future. In doing so, we review the diversity management literature and report on a series of interviews conducted with organisations operating in Australia.

Survey of diversity management in Australia

We interviewed human resource managers in a small number of organisations to determine the strategies that they use to manage diversity. We selected seven organisations with a reputation for leading practices in managing human resources. The organisations in our research are multinational companies and include manufacturing and services organisations in both the public and private sectors. Our seven respondents are senior human resource professionals in positions with responsibilities related to diversity management.

Our interview schedule was based on the approach reported by Joplin and Daus (1997). We asked the following questions:

1. What types of diversity do you have in your workforce?
2. Does your organisation have a formal, written strategy for managing diversity?
3. In your organisation, what are the primary business reasons for managing diversity?
4. In your organisation, are there challenging or pressing issues in managing a diverse workforce? If so, which do you find the most challenging?

5. What are the specific strategies your organisation has implemented to ease those challenges?
6. Does your organisation have specific plans for managing diversity that will be implemented in the near future?

To explore the prevalence of different forms of diversity in Australian workplaces, the first question asked was: *What types of diversity do you have in your workforce?* Our respondents identified many of the well-recognised forms of diversity existing in their workforce: ethnic background, educational level, part- and full-time employees, sex, age, religious background, marital status, physical abilities and parental status. A number of organisations also mentioned such issues as sexual orientation, and one organisation also identified trainees who were 'youth at risk', as well as people from low socio-economic backgrounds, the homeless, long-term unemployed and those with special needs.

Given this range of differences, it is inevitable that organisations face an enormous task in developing programs to meet the needs of their workforce. For example, whereas issues around parental status may lead organisations to consider the introduction of 'family friendly' policies, issues related to ethnic background and religion might require organisations to be more flexible in work arrangements in order to accommodate different religious holidays.

The business case for managing diversity

The business need for diversity management is arguably a response to factors such as changing workforce demographics, changing social values and globalisation of markets (Jackson & Ruderman 1995; Way 1999). Theoretical analyses of diversity suggest that there are several sound business reasons for introducing and managing diversity in the workforce (Lepak & Snell 1999; Nkomo & Cos 1996). The first of these relates to the *cost* of managing diversity poorly. When organisations fail to manage diversity, they experience increased turnover and absenteeism among minority groups. The price of recruiting and training new staff, estimated to be $75 000 per employee (Smith 1998), represents a significant cost for the organisation. In addition, organisations that do not manage diversity well may be in breach of legislation and will incur associated costs (Cox & Blake 1991; Robinson & Dechant 1997).

There are also indirect costs, such as the inability to recruit the best staff and to attract customers to the organisation. Organisations benefit from the ability to recruit staff from a large pool of potential employees. To the extent that organisations are recognised for their support of minority groups, they will attract applicants from those groups, consequently increasing the pool from which they are able to draw employees. Equally important, they are better able to retain staff and so also reduce turnover costs (Cox & Blake 1991; Robinson & Dechant 1997). A further benefit of a diverse workforce is that it gives the organisation greater *marketplace understanding*. This is especially important for multinational organisations: recruiting staff who reflect the cultures in which these organisations operate will increase market understanding. However, given the increasingly diverse population of most countries, this same benefit can be obtained by all organisations. Organisations that understand their market should increase market penetration. A diverse workforce will help organisations to understand the different needs and values of the cultural groups that make up their client base (Cox & Blake 1991; Robinson & Dechant 1997). Premier Foods provides one example of this strategy in action. In order to better market its products overseas and to increase cultural understanding, this Australian company recruits staff from overseas. These staff spend a number of years working in Australia before returning to their home country. Premier Foods believes that this improves their business capability in two ways: it helps them to market their product in the countries from which their staff are recruited and also improves management because, when these employees return to their home countries, they take with them a better understanding of the Australian side of the business (Tan 1999).

Finally, diversity improves both *decision making* and *creativity*. One of the reasons that group decisions are believed to be better than individual decisions is that, in any group, we find a greater range of skills and knowledge than we find in individuals. This heterogeneity means that individuals view problems from a wider range of perspectives, are able to generate more options for solving problems and so, in the long run, are able to find better solutions. Diversity provides one mechanism for introducing heterogeneity into a group and we would therefore expect to see diverse groups be more creative and effective in problem solving (Cox & Blake 1991; Robinson & Dechant 1997; Shaw & Barrett-Power 1998).

In a recent survey of 15 Fortune 100 companies, human resource executives identified several reasons for managing diversity. The top four were: to better use skills and abilities; to increase marketplace understanding; to increase the depth of understanding that organisational leaders have; and to improve creativity and problem solving (Robinson & Dechant 1997).

Based on this review of the extant literature, we posed the second question to our interviewees: *Does your organisation have a formal, written strategy for managing diversity?* Two of our seven respondents indicated that their organisations have a formal diversity policy. The remaining respondents indicated that they have a general framework of policies, programs and practices that encompass diversity principles. All of the organisations have policies to comply with State and federal legislation on matters such as equal opportunity employment. Other related policies include flexibility policies and policies focused on work-life balance concerns.

To further explore the organisational approaches to diversity, our third question was: *In your organisation, what are the primary business reasons for managing diversity?* Our respondents listed many of the reasons identified in the extant literature. In the Australian companies that we surveyed, the top three reasons in developing a business case for managing diversity were the ability to attract and retain good staff, the ability to be responsive to customers needs, and the ability to increase productivity. These respondents also cited increased activity, the ability to compete globally, the need to ensure workforce flexibility, and the desire to create an inclusive environment that was representative of society.

The broad challenges of managing diversity

Diversity management practices have been classified according to the degree to which they attempt to incorporate diverse values and attitudes into organisational culture and practice. In this framework, legislation that has focused on equal employment opportunity and affirmative action (Chapman 2000) can be seen as entry-level, compliance gaining strategies. Both are essentially assimilation approaches: those who are different from the traditional workforce are expected to conform to the values and behaviours of the dominant group. At the extreme, diversity-resistant organisations may choose to fight such legislation rather than to comply with it (Dass & Parker 1999).

Diversity management is more proactive than either equal employment opportunity or affirmative action concepts (Kramar et al. 1997). Diversity management differs from equal employment opportunity or affirmative action not only in addressing more characteristics but also in being management initiated rather than legislated. Organisations have the discretion to utilise a variety of human resource management strategies and practices in order to implement diversity management in varying degrees. For example, an organisation may focus on legitimating diversity through a range of activities, including diversity training for managers. By increasing awareness, managers are sensitised to the kinds of issues they will need to address when new employees join the workforce. Further, organisations may seek to ensure that minorities receive fair treatment in selection practices. However, indirect discrimination may still occur in subsequent career progression (Dass & Parker 1999) because the valuing of diversity is yet to be institutionalised. When organisations recognise that differences can add value to the workplace, they become more proactive in their diversity management practices. Responsibility for diversity management is moved in one direction, from managers to all employees, and in a second direction, from managers to the organisation (Dass & Parker 1999).

Whichever path organisations choose, they face a number of challenges to managing diversity effectively. Joplin and Daus (1997), in interviews with companies around the US, identified several common challenges. At the organisational level, members of majority groups may perceive that their power is being eroded, and may also perceive that poorly skilled individuals are being employed simply to meet equal employment opportunity or affirmative action targets.

Social justice and social responsibility are two imperatives that drive equal employment opportunity legislation and the management of diversity in organisations. However, these may present challenges for managers. For example, social and cultural expectations discourage many women from becoming engineers, and organisational practices often deny women engineers job opportunities, while a hostile work environment may force them to leave their jobs and the profession (De Cieri & Dowling 2000). Also, structural or systemic discrimination is the product of longstanding direct and indirect discrimination. It is the result of the interaction of decisions, actions, regulations, policies, practices and social attitudes which allow discrimination to become embedded within the system.

These problems may serve to reduce communication to reinforce existing stereotypes. This in turn may limit organisations' ability to harness the benefits of diversity. The importance of communication is recognised as essential to reaping the benefits of diversity effectively. At one extreme, problems such as the lack of basic literacy/language skills act to restrict the opportunity for employees to participate in the workforce (Australian Bureau of Statistics 1999e). At the other extreme, because both gender and culture (Gibson 1997; Tannen 1990) influence interaction goals, communication can be restricted and may result in more subtle misunderstandings. Whatever the reason, poor communication may lead minority group members to feel a lack of empathy, and this in turn may limit their willingness to participate in workplace processes. Accordingly, Joplin and Daus (1997) identify empathy, participation and the ability to incorporate diverse views as three challenges that managers face.

Recognising the issues identified in this literature, our fourth question was: *In your organisation, are there challenging or pressing issues in managing a diverse workforce? If so, which do you find the most challenging?* The organisations that we surveyed identified several challenges that they faced in managing diversity. For many organisations, the main challenge is to 'sell' diversity; that is, to build a business case for the management of diversity. Several mentioned that although employees understood the principles of diversity, these principles were not well implemented. For these organisations, the principal challenge is helping managers and other employees to recognise that they may not have sufficient skills for managing diversity and may not yet fully understand the needs of a diverse workforce.

This fits with a second theme in the challenges identified by the organisations that we interviewed. Organisations identified the need to recognise not only the wide range of issues that have to be considered, such as religious needs and childcare needs, but also the possibility that individuals' needs change depending on where they are in their career or life cycles. Several mentioned the need to maintain the balance between recognising the special needs of diverse groups in the workforce and not further singling them out and making them feel more different as a result of organisational programs. Finally, at least one organisation raised more structural issues — that is, the lack of diversity at senior levels and the need to develop programs that will effect culture change within the organisation.

How Australian companies manage diversity

The next issue identified as important is the need for organisations to develop effective diversity management strategies (Joplin & Daus 1997). Several Australian public and private sector organisations have been prominent in their development of diversity management strategies.

A comprehensive example of diversity management is evident in recent changes in the Australian Public Service (APS) (Public Service and Merit Protection Commission 1999b). The APS has recently replaced equal employment opportunity programs with workplace diversity programs. Although these new programs include all of the existing equal employment opportunity provisions of the Public Service Act, they focus more on the recognition that diversity can improve organisational effectiveness. Although each APS department is given responsibility for developing its own workplace diversity program, a system of self-evaluation and reporting creates accountability. The Public Service Commissioner assesses the effectiveness and outcomes of workplace diversity programs in each APS agency and the findings are reported annually (Public Service and Merit Protection Commission 1999a). Annual Workplace Diversity Awards are presented with the objective of recognising and promoting good employment practices with regard to workplace diversity. The 1999 Award was won by the Department of Family and Community Services for their initiatives to enhance the work environment for staff with disabilities. This included creation of a disability access coordinator position, establishment of a disability stakeholder group and inclusion of disability access principles in all corporate planning processes. Second prize was awarded to the Aboriginal and Torres Strait Islander Commission for the development and implementation of a six-month training program for indigenous employees, to provide them with the knowledge, skills and abilities to work and develop careers in the personnel section (Public Service and Merit Protection Commission 1999a).

Progress in diversity management is also evident in the private sector, evidenced by examples such as Qantas, Australia's international airline, which has used its multicultural workforce to achieve organisational objectives. The Qantas Flight Catering service has been very successful in securing catering contracts from other airlines by using their multicultural staff (based in Australia) to develop menus and

food preparation techniques to meet the culinary requirements of different cultural groups (Wilkinson & Cheung 1999).

Australia's multiculturalism has also encouraged foreign direct investment. For example, Wilkinson and Cheung (1999) report that American Express, Cathay Pacific Airlines and DEC all established operations in Sydney, partly owing to the readily available multilingual workforce and access to related multicultural services and expertise.

To supplement these examples identified in the extant literature, the fifth question posed to our interviewees was: *What are the specific strategies your organisation has implemented to ease those challenges?* The strategies reported for our survey organisations reflect and build upon those already identified.

First, recognising that managing diversity requires organisations to adapt to broader social and cultural changes, provision of diversity training and awareness campaigns was mentioned by several respondents. Specific elements include a section on diversity in the induction/orientation program for new employees, and workshops and individual consultations with managers to help them understand diversity management issues. The provision of more diverse training and development opportunities for employees is another strategy that was identified. Specific examples included financial support for high potential employees to focus on their own development, to be used for a wide variety of forms of learning.

Second, recognising that the legislative context proscribes certain behaviours and practices, specific strategies to prevent harassment were cited by two respondents, with promotion of 'zero tolerance' in terms of harassment, or the creation of 'diversity harassment advisors', being employees who are trained to handle difficult situations that occur in the workplace.

Third, recruitment and selection strategies were cited as important, with specific examples such as increasing the number of university graduates recruited to the organisation, or the establishment of a group of high-calibre, talented individuals within the organisation to accelerate career opportunities.

Fourth, linking diversity management to employee benefits provides an innovative approach — for example, via implementation of a benefits package which includes not only 'traditional' policies and procedures for matters such as maternity leave or study leave, but also provision of flexible work options, cheap movie tickets, access to free legal, counselling and insurance advice, and access to competitive prices on household purchases.

Fifth, information technology is increasingly useful in this, as well as many other management areas, as evidenced by the creation of diversity websites with information made available to all employees.

Sixth, monitoring and evaluation of the impact of diversity strategies is an important strategy; for example, one organisation conducts an annual staff survey that focuses on key issues of diversity. A second respondent reported that their organisation consistently reviews policies for areas such as flexible work options.

Finally, but by no means least important, senior management support and sponsorship for diversity strategies was cited by several of our respondents as a vital element for the success of diversity management strategies.

The future for diversity management

The need to manage diversity arises out of the changing demographics of the workforce as well as out of changing social values and the globalisation of economies and markets (Jackson & Ruderman 1995; Way 1999). Several writers have argued that effective management of diverse human resources will provide a key differentiator for successful organisations (Joplin & Daus 1997; Lepak & Snell 1999; Robinson & Dechant 1997). Wilkinson and Cheung (1999) show that issues of diversity extend beyond the workforce to the marketplace.

The final question included in our interviews was: *Does your organisation have specific plans for managing diversity that will be implemented in the near future?* All of our respondents saw diversity management as an area for increasing commitment and development. Their organisations are in varying stages of diagnosing the key diversity issues for their workforce, developing their approach to diversity issues and implementing specific diversity management objectives and action plans. Overall, the trend is towards broadening the scope of, and increasing investment in, diversity management strategies.

In summary, the emphasis and direction for diversity management in Australia appears to be, both within organisations and across organisational boundaries, building a culture that is not only tolerant of diversity but also encourages flexibility, inclusion and diversification.

References

Australian Bureau of Statistics. 1994. *Australian Social Trends, 1994*. Cat. no. 4102.0. Canberra Australia: Australian Government Publishing Service.

Australian Bureau of Statistics. 1996. *Labour Force Australia*. Cat. no. 6203.0, March. Canberra: Australian Government Publishing Service.

Australian Bureau of Statistics. 1997a. *Labour Force Australia*. Cat. no. 6203.0, March. Canberra: Australian Government Publishing Service.

Australian Bureau of Statistics. 1997b. *Year Book Australia 1997*. Cat. no. 1301.0. Canberra: Australian Government Publishing Service.

Australian Bureau of Statistics. 1999a. *Australian Demographic Statistics*. Cat. no. 3101.0. Canberra Australia: Australian Government Publishing Service.

Australian Bureau of Statistics. 1999b. *Labour Force Australia*. Cat. no. 6203.0, March. Canberra: Australian Government Publishing Service.

Australian Bureau of Statistics. 1999c. *Expenditure on Education, Australia*. Cat. no. 5510.0. Canberra Australia: Australian Government Publishing Service.

Australian Bureau of Statistics. 1999d. *Transition from Education to Work, Australia*. Cat. no. 6227.0. Canberra Australia: Australian Government Publishing Service.

Australian Bureau of Statistics. 1999e. *Year Book Australia 1997*. Cat. no. 1301.01. Canberra Australia: Australian Government Publishing Service.

Australian Bureau of Statistics. 1999f. *Labour Force Projections, Australia 1999–2016*. Cat. no. 6260.0. Canberra: Australian Government Publishing Service.

Australian Bureau of Statistics. 2000a. *Special Article — Educating and Training Australia's Workers*. Canberra: Australian Government Publishing Service.

Australian Bureau of Statistics. 2000b. *Australia Now — A Statistical Profile: Education and Training*. Canberra: Australian Government Publishing Service.

Australian Bureau of Statistics. 2000c. *Australia Now — A Statistical Profile: Industry Overview*. Canberra: Australian Government Publishing Service.

Chapman, A. 2000. 'Industrial Legislation in 1999'. *The Journal of Industrial Relations* 42(1): 29–40.

Clark, M. 1995. *A Short History of Australia*. Fourth Revised Edition. Ringwood Australia: Penguin.

Cox, T. H. & Blake, S. 1991. 'Managing Cultural Diversity: Implications for Organizational Competitiveness'. *Academy of Management Executive* 5(3): 45–56.

Dass, P. & Parker, B. 1999. 'Strategies for Managing Human Resource Diversity: From Resistance to Learning'. *Academy of Management Executive* 13(2): 68–80.

De Cieri, H. & Dowling, P. J. 2000. In press. 'Human Resource Management for Engineers'. In Samson, D. A. (Ed.). *Management for Engineers*. Third Edition. Melbourne Australia: Pearson.

Department of Immigration and Multicultural Affairs. 1998. *Australian Immigration: The Facts*. Canberra Australia: Australian Government Publishing Service.

Federal Race Discrimination Commissioner. 1997. *Face the Facts*. Canberra Australia: Australian Government Publishing Service.

Gibson, C. B. 1997. 'Do You Hear What I Hear? A Framework for Reconciling Intercultural Communication Difficulties Arising from Cognitive Styles and Cultural Values'. In Earley, P. C. & Erez, M. (Eds). *New Perspectives on International and Organizational Psychology*. San Francisco CA: Jossey-Bass.

Graetz, B. & McAllister, I. 1994. *Dimensions of Australian Society*. Second Edition. Melbourne Australia: Macmillan.

Hartmann, L. C. 1998. 'The Impact of Trends in Labour Force Participation in Australia'. In Patrickson, M. & Hartmann, L. (Eds). *Managing an Ageing Workforce*. Warriewood NSW: Woodslane.

Human Rights and Equal Opportunity Commission. 1997. *Bringing Them Home: Report of the National Inquiry into the Separation of Aboriginal and Torres Strait Islander Children from Their Families, Australia*. Sydney Australia: Human Rights and Equal Opportunity Commission.

Jackson, S. E. & Ruderman, M. N. 1995. *Diversity in Work Teams: Research Paradigms for a Changing Workplace*. Washington DC. American Psychological Association.

Joplin, J. R. W. & Daus, C. S. 1997. 'Challenges of Leading a Diverse Workforce'. *Academy of Management Executive* 11(3): 32–47.

Kramar, R., McGraw, P. & Schuler, R. S. 1997. *Human Resource Management in Australia*. Third Edition. South Melbourne Australia: Addison Wesley Longman.

Lepak, D. P. & Snell, S. 1999. 'The Human Resource Architecture: Towards a Theory of Human Capital Allocation and Development'. *Academy of Management Journal* 24(1): 31–48.

Morris, R., Mortimer, D. & Leece, P. (Eds). 1999. *Workplace Reform and Enterprise Bargaining: Issues, Trends and Cases*. Second Edition. Sydney: Harcourt Brace.

Nkomo, S. & Cox, T. H. 1996. 'Diverse Identities in Organizations'. In Clegg, S., Hardy, C. & Nord, W. (Eds). *Handbook of Organization Studies*. London: Sage: 338–56.

Patrickson, M. & Hartmann, L. 1996. 'Australian Gender Differences in Preferences for Early Retirement'. *International Employment Relations Review* 2(1): 1–19.

Public Service and Merit Protection Commission. 1998. *Workplace Diversity Practitioner's Handbook*. Canberra: Commonwealth of Australia.

Public Service and Merit Protection Commission. 1999a. *Workplace Diversity Report, 1998–99*. Canberra: Commonwealth of Australia.

Public Service and Merit Protection Commission. 1999b. *State of the Service 1998–99*. Canberra: Commonwealth of Australia.

Robinson, G. & Dechant, K. 1997. 'Building a Business Case for Diversity'. *Academy of Management Executive* 11(3): 21–31.

Schaper, M. 1999. 'Australia's Aboriginal Small Business Owners: Challenges for the Future'. *Journal of Small Business Management* 37(3): 88–93.

Shaw, J. B. & Barrett-Power, E. 1998. 'The Effects of Diversity on Small Work Group Processes and Performance'. *Human Relations* 51(10): 1307–1325.

Smith, D. 1998. 'The Business Case for Diversity'. *Monash Mt Eliza Business Review*, Nov: 72–81.

Tan, J. 1999. 'Making Cultural Diversity the Premier Solution'. *HRMonthly*, Aug: 8–9.

Tannen, D. 1990. *You Just Don't Understand. Women and Men in Conversation*. New York: Ballantine.

Tongzon, J. L. 1995. 'ASEAN–Australia Trade Relations: A Review of Recent Trends'. *Asian Economic Journal* 9(21): 169–75.

Van den Heuvel, A. & Wooden, M. 1997. 'Self-employed Contractors and Job Satisfaction'. *Journal of Small Business Management* 35(3): 11–20.

Walsh, J. 1997. 'Employment Systems in Transition? A Comparative Analysis of Britain and Australia'. *Work, Employment and Society* 11(1): 1–25.

Way, N. 1999. 'Workplaces of the World, Fragment'. *Business Review Weekly*. 12 December: 92.

Wilkinson, I. & Cheung, C. 1999. 'Multicultural Marketing in Australia: Synergy in Diversity'. *Journal of International Marketing* 7(3): 106–25.

Williams, D. 1999. *Sex Discrimination in the Workplace — Education and Awareness Protecting and Promoting Rights and Responsibilities*. Canberra Australia: Commonwealth of Australia.

Chapter 3

China

Beverley Kitching

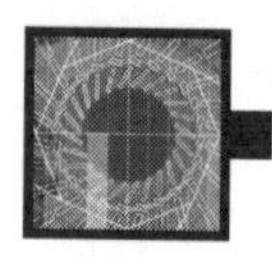

Introduction

Geographically, biologically and ethnically, China is one of the most diverse countries in the world, with the longest continuous culture and a written record extending back almost four thousand years. The management of Chinese society in traditional times — that is, before the 1911 revolution — involved several enduring characteristics. It was centrally organised, authoritarian, bureaucratic and patriarchal. Confucianism provided the guiding rules for everything from the behaviour of the individual to the governing of the state. This traditional period started after the establishment of the short-lived Qin dynasty more than 2200 years ago with the emperor at its head, and lasted until the toppling of the Qing dynasty in 1911 and the setting up of the first republic. The failure of this republic plunged China into a period of warlordism, civil war and invasion by Japan, until the end of World War II and the establishment by the Chinese Communist Party (CCP) of the People's Republic of China (PRC) in 1949. Official Communist Party policies espoused liberation and equality for all three groups considered in this chapter — women, people with disabilities and ethnic minorities — and sections of the first constitution enshrined minority rights.

However, women have numbered less than 50 per cent of the population in China for centuries and have suffered great discrimination in traditional Chinese culture. The disabled were also highly disadvantaged in traditional Chinese society. There are 55 officially recognised minority nationalities within the borders of the PRC. Many were in close contact with the Confucian state for over 1000 years but were still regarded as barbarians. In spite of official Party doctrine, between 1949 and the late 1970s Chinese government policies encouraged political and cultural conformity rather than diversity.

As China enters the global marketplace, managers within the state bureaucracy and in the developing private sector are faced with far more diversity within the workplace and among stakeholders and consumers than ever before. The 'open door' policy, coupled with tremendous change in communications technology, has resulted in strong external influences impacting upon China as it enters an international business environment which is itself undergoing enormous change. This is all the more difficult for China as a developing country which is emerging from a bureaucratic, state-controlled, planned system, with no market structure and a legal system in no way compatible with Western models. How then is China managing its diverse minority groups in such a dynamic and fast-changing environment?

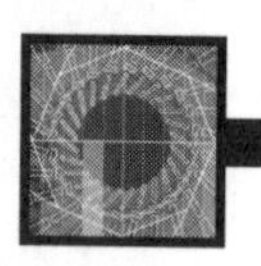

The legacy of the traditional system

Prior to 1911, the dominant philosophy in China was Confucianism, a doctrine which fostered traditionalism. The ideal of the Confucian scholar gentry (the upper class) was that of a traditional status, based on the assimilation of a traditional fixed body of literary culture. The intellectual climate, therefore, was not at all favourable to any form of experiment or innovation. Access to power came only through successfully negotiating a centrally controlled examination system based on a fixed body of knowledge. Ironically, in 1949, half a century of revolution merely replaced one accepted, overarching philosophy, Confucianism, with another, Marxism.

It was under the Han dynasty, which succeeded the Qin in 221 BC, that Confucianism was adopted as the intellectual underpinning of imperial rule, and a centrally-controlled examination system was put in place using the works of Confucius and Confucian scholars as its syllabus. This examination system became the only route to a position in the imperial bureaucracy until it was dismantled in 1906.

Successful entry to the bureaucratic elite gave a man and his family access to status, wealth and political power. Entry to this elite by the centrally-controlled examination system ensured that the subject matter of intellectual endeavour and the basis of bureaucratic management were both Confucian and conservative. The tools of intellectual expression and the keys to social power were artistic style and a cultivated knowledge of the approved classical texts. There was an intimate association between bureaucracy with the mastery of high culture, and the members of the elite owed their positions not to a professional technical specialisation but to knowledge of the humanities. This led to a situation in which manual labour, commerce and science were all despised.

Confucian philosophy was intimately bound up with social organisation. The rules of social behaviour were laid down with reference to the golden past. There was a correct way to manage relationships within the family and society. Following the Confucian 'rites', a man should aim to become a sage, in perfect harmony with himself and his surroundings. He should follow the rules for the five great relationships which would ensure harmony within his family, between his family and other families within his village, between that village and other villages and towns, and so on up to harmony between the state and the ruler. The perfect sage, of course, was the perfect ruler. Harmony within the social cosmos would ensure harmony between the human world and the natural world and between Earth and the supernatural world, heaven.

Women were subservient and undervalued in this social hierarchy and had no place in public life. A woman's place was within the house; she was the *neiren* or inside person. Traditional China was patriarchal, patrilocal and patrilineal. Authority rested with the oldest male of the senior generation, women married into their husband's extended family and lived in his family's household, which ideally would include five generations under one roof. Inheritance of property and descent came only through the male line.

The disabled were viewed as dishonouring the physical inheritance from their ancestors. It was a man's duty to maintain the body bequeathed to him in a healthy and undamaged condition and to produce physically and mentally sound sons. The woman was blamed if a mentally or physically disabled child was born. Even so, one ancient proverb claims that 'one lame son is worth a dozen golden daughters'. A woman's status within her husband's family depended on her ability to produce sons.

The disabled in traditional China were strongly discriminated against. In *The Book of Filial Piety*, Confucius is portrayed as teaching that even to cut one's hair or injure one's skin is to betray a sacred responsibility to preserve the body bequeathed by the ancestors. All the terms used to describe disabled people — *can fei*, *fei ji*, *can ji* — are strongly pejorative with connotations of being useless, spoiled and wasted. During the Yuan Dynasty (1271–1368) an imperial edict was issued which forbade crippled men from taking the imperial examinations and therefore barred them from the only route to power and status.

The management of business was modelled on family relationships, which were patriarchal, authoritarian and hierarchical. The terms by which people addressed one another were based on family relationships and these indicated position and status. Even today, the majority of Chinese businesses are family firms.

Women did work in family businesses, again mainly as *neiren*, with men controlling activities taking place in the public sphere. Wealthy women did sometimes own businesses but did not manage them.

Such a system produced a model of management and an understanding of law very different from the one which had developed in Europe and the Americas. Behavioural norms were internalised and focused on the good of the group, not the rights of the individual. Families were expected to control their members, and the local government official, the magistrate, was expected to keep the imperial peace. Serious political crimes could involve punishment of the whole family either by execution or banishment to remote border regions. Management aimed at harmony, unity and conformity — not diversity.

The extent to which Chinese society was open to external influences varied throughout the centuries. Chinese refer to their country as Zhongguo, literally the middle kingdom or the centre of civilisation. The predominant ethnic group (comprising 98 per cent of the population of the PRC today) was, and still is, the Han. In the worldview of the traditional Confucian state, Han culture was seen as civilised (*you wenming*), although to be regarded as a civilised person an individual had to be cultured (*you wenhua*) or educated. Non-Han people living within China's borders were viewed as barbarians (*yeman*). All those outside China's boundaries were called barbarians, and China was frequently under attack along its northern borders. Two dynasties were in fact non-Han conquerors — the Yuan (Mongols, 1206–1368) and the last dynasty, the Qing (1644–1911), who were Manchu. Mongols and Manchus (Man) are among the listed national minorities in the PRC today. At times China was open to foreign influences, as shown, for example, by its acceptance of Buddhism from India, but often it was extremely xenophobic. The most recent example of the latter was the Cultural Revolution/Gang of Four period from 1966 to 1976.

At present, the Chinese Government is pursuing an 'open door' policy and reforming its economic system into a socialist market system with Chinese characteristics. Recognition of the injustices perpetrated against women and the disabled and efforts to improve their status can be found in the reform movements of the late nineteenth century. Anti-footbinding societies were set up, schools for girls were established and education provisions were made for children with vision and hearing impairments. Women's liberation became part of the political platforms of first the Nationalists (KMT) and then the CCP, but with the instability of warlordism, civil war and invasion between 1911 and 1949, improvements were sporadic. Some educational facilities for the disabled were established, such as the Wuhan No. 2 School for the Deaf (opened in 1932), which was one of the earliest special schools (Ashman 1995: 56).

The liberation of women was a major focus of the Maoist period. In the 1950s, women's rights were enshrined in the constitution and in the marriage law and included the right to inherit property, choose their marriage partners, initiate divorce, retain guardianship of their children, work outside the home, earn equal pay and be active in politics.

There was much less focus on the disabled, although their needs were recognised. Before 1987 the only state-defined disability criteria of the PRC were those for Revolutionary Disabled Veterans drafted by the Ministry of the Interior in the early 1950s.

Factories and workshops were set up to provide employment for the disabled. The Shiwan Ceramic Arts Factory, set up in 1974 in Guangdong Province, has now become a major producer of ceramic tiles. It has changed its name to Eagle Brand Holdings Ltd, and was listed on the Singapore Stock Exchange in 1999 (Leung 1999: 12).

Special education was formally included in the education system of the PRC in 1951. The Decision with Regard to Reforming School Systems was promulgated, and it stipulated that special schools should be set up for deaf and blind people at all government levels and education was to be provided for those with physiological impairment (Xu 1994). There were, however, many problems including lack of financial support, few specialist teachers and shortages of equipment. The first school set up for people with an intellectual disability in Dalien in 1959 lasted only four years and no further attempt to provide education for the intellectually impaired was made until 1979 (Xu 1994).

During the 1930s and 1940s, the CCP sought the support of ethnic minority groups, some of whom, such as the Naxi of the Lijiang basin, adopted CCP policies with fervour, even to the extent of carrying out the land reform campaign of the 1950s twice (White 1997: 298–9). After liberation in 1949, autonomous minority administrative structures were set up. There are about 130 autonomous minority areas in the PRC at the level of the county, prefecture and region, and they comprise about 60 per cent of the land area. Since most of these areas are along China's borders, particularly the politically sensitive zones in the north and west, the extent of autonomy has been limited. This is because of fear of invasion from a number of the 12 countries bordering China to the north, west and south-west, such as parts of the former USSR, India and Vietnam, and the fact that these regions are very sparsely populated. What resulted was a government policy which encouraged the migration of Han Chinese into minority autonomous regions such as Xinjiang, Tibet, Inner Mongolia, Yunnan and Heilonjiang. In addition to security implications, the intention also appears to have been to acculturate and assimilate — 'Han-ify' — minority nationalities (Kormondy 1995: 164).

With the advent to power of the CCP in 1949 came other views of ethnic minorities in addition to the old Confucian doctrine. One such view originates with Marxist interpretations of Darwin, with Engels' version of Social Darwinism, and notions of unilinear social and political evolution. Minority nationalities are classified with respect to their stage of social evolution, which tended almost always to be presented as their degree of backwardness (*luohou*) in contrast to Han progress (*fazhan*). Seen as even more feudal (*fengjian*) than Han culture, this backwardness had to be overcome by the acquisition of 'technological and sociocultural features appropriate to the social evolutionary stage of socialism' (White 1997: 299).

A second 'discourse of hierarchy' (White 1997) in the PRC which impacted on the development of policies on ethnic minorities was Mao's interpretation of socialist modernity as it had been articulated in the Soviet Union from the works of Marx and Lenin. Modernity is equated with economic progress and is to be achieved through the power of science and technology. Ethnic minorities had to be modernised and therefore educated. After 1949 there was considerable emphasis on vocational-technical training in work-study middle schools (Fairchild 1992).

The theories of Lenin and Stalin, however, provided yet another discourse, which was that of authenticity under which minority nationality is legitimised. According to this view, linguistic and cultural practices are sanctioned, there is a place for tradition and authentic cultural practices (*zhenshi de*) and cultural diversity is tolerated (White 1997: 301). This view led to policies which gave preferential treatment to minorities —

for example, exemption from the one-child policy, preferential admission to higher-education institutions, exemption from land taxes and state payment of primary teachers in schools run by minorities (Kormondy 1995: 163). Such preferential treatment — especially exemption from the one-child policy — was the source of considerable resentment by Han Chinese.

One area in which ethnic minorities were seen to be particularly backward was in their religious beliefs and traditions, which were often castigated as feudal superstition. Resentment of attempts to suppress religion was particularly strong among Islamic groups in the north and north-west, and in Lamaist Tibet.

So how many of the traditional and Maoist influences are still at work in the China which is moving at such speed into the new millennium? What change has a century of revolution, war and Communist Party rule brought about in the social, political and economic life of the groups examined in this chapter? Are Chinese managers now managing for diversity rather than conformity? These issues will now be considered for the People's Republic of China.

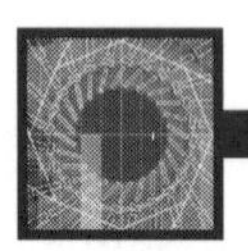

Gender issues in management and the workplace

Many questions can be raised about the position of women in organisations in China at the beginning of the twenty-first century. Have the Maoist period and the last two decades of reform given women greater opportunities to enhance their economic and social status? Are there women in managerial positions in private business and State Owned Enterprises (SOEs)? What proportion of new small businesses are owned by women and how does the situation in China compare with other countries? Are women involved in large businesses? Are women as strongly motivated as men to achieve managerial positions? Do men and women in China manage businesses differently? Do men and women have different personnel management styles? What are the career options for women? Are women subject to discrimination and harassment in the workplace? Does the 'glass ceiling' exist in China? Are the issues of concern for Chinese businesswomen similar to those of businesswomen elsewhere, or are their experiences determined more by specifically Chinese social and economic conditions?

The status of women

Under the terms of the 1982 Constitution of the People's Republic of China, women are guaranteed equal rights to men in all spheres of life since, as the Maoist slogan put it, 'women hold up half the sky'. Women have the right to work outside the home and are supposed to have equal pay to men for equal work. By law they are able to inherit land and property. They can initiate divorce and claim custody of their children. They can join the CCP and stand for political office, and they are supposed to have equal access to education. Ten years later in 1992, the Law Protecting Women's Rights and Interests was adopted, which was intended to ensure the protection of 'women's special rights and interests granted by law' (FBIS 1992: 17–20). As is so often the case, the gap between rhetoric and reality is quite large.

Compared with many other societies, Chinese women do have a high labour participation rate at 80 per cent, less than 20 percentage points behind men. The female/male wage ratio is 85.6 per cent, which is certainly not equal but, again comparatively speaking, is higher than in most other developing countries (Cheng 1998: 114–19).

There are about 400 million women in China aged 15 years and over, and of these, 300 million are economically active. Two-thirds of urban women and three-quarters of rural women engage in work outside the home. Forty-four per cent of employees are women, and they comprise the majority of agricultural workers. This is a great contrast to the traditional lack of participation of women in activities outside the home. There are, however, many impediments to full participation by women in Chinese society. They are under-represented politically (in 1993 they comprised only 21 per cent of deputies to the National People's Congress), under-represented in higher managerial positions, and over-represented in jobs requiring heavy labour, such as farming (Joint Economic Committee, Congress of the United States 1997: 373). Over the past two decades, fewer women have joined the CCP than during the Maoist period of 1949–76, particularly in rural areas, and fewer have been elected to office.

Divorce is still not common in China but the incidence has been increasing in recent decades as unemployment and economic hardship for women have increased. The majority of divorces are instigated by women. Many men refuse to pay child maintenance and it is difficult for a single mother to support her children on her own salary (*Family* 1991: 49; *Women of China* 1987: 42). Wife battering is cited as cause for divorce by many women. In 1992, the Institute of Women's Studies of China cited that 33 per cent of respondents in a survey reported abuse, and nine per cent reported that this occurred frequently. Another survey in Beijing in 1994 reported a 21.3 per cent rate of abuse.

Chinese statistics in 1990 showed that women accounted for 45 per cent of professional and technical personnel (up from 38 per cent in 1982); 11 per cent of all heads of authorities and government organisations, enterprises and institutions (up from 10 per cent in 1982); 26 per cent of office and clerical staff; 47 per cent of workers in commerce; 53 per cent of labourers in agriculture, forestry, animal husbandry and fisheries; and 36 per cent of workers in industrial production and transport. The 1990 population census showed that more women than men are shop assistants, workers on poultry farms, textile workers and tailors, and machine operators. More men than women are plasterers, truck drivers, purchasing agents, furniture carpenters, teachers in secondary schools, electricians and mining workers. The ratio is nearly equal for primary school teachers, accountants and auditors, vegetable growers and office staff (Hall 1997: 44). Secretary, interpreter, translator, businesswoman and tour guide are the top 'dream' jobs for Chinese women (Hall 1997: 52). Self-employment is also a dream for many Chinese women. There are 14 million self-employed people in rural areas engaging in commerce and service trades, and two-thirds of them are women (Hall 1997: 63). It is very difficult to try to work out how many women are purely self-employed and how many actually employ others. It is even difficult to estimate how many businesses are owned by women because often, when asked by a non-family member, they will say a firm belongs to their husband or is a family firm, even when they have provided the whole capital and are running it themselves. Traditional attitudes remain strong, particularly in rural areas.

Chinese women managers

It is only since the late 1980s that studies on issues related to women in management around the world have entered the Western management literature (see Adler & Israeli 1988, 1994). Investigations of women in management in China are very few. Hildebrandt and Liu (1988) surveyed 150 Chinese women managers and concluded

that, compared with other Asian women and with US women, they had little job mobility, worked longer hours, were less well educated, and their careers were strongly influenced by central government planning and a patriarchal tradition. A brief review of Chinese women's status in organisations and management was presented by Korabik (1994), and Chen and Yu (1997) addressed the question of motivation to manage. They found that the overall managerial motivation of Chinese women was as high as that of Chinese men. Far fewer women, however, are to be found in management positions in the PRC. Despite their qualifications, a high level of commitment to their careers, and a critical shortage of professionally trained people in China, female Chinese students are pessimistic about their prospects for career advancement (McKeen & Bu 1998: 171). Barriers cited included negative stereotypes, lack of mentors and role models, isolation and a lack of organisational policies. In a recent Chinese study, Yu and Zhu (2000) argued that female managers are less effective in time management than their male counterparts and work fewer hours. They reported that male managers spent more time than females 'presiding over and attending meetings, talking with subordinates, inspecting work, taking official trips, participating in official intercourse' (Yu & Zhu 2000: 35). Women spent less time leading, decision making, controlling and handling foreign affairs, less time at work and more time on domestic duties, which the authors concluded reflected traditional patriarchal values in which 'men are in charge of the outside world while women are in charge of the house' (Yu & Zhu 2000: 38).

Of the firms examined, in Yunnan province in south-western China, the smallest firm employed 10 people, the largest employed 2000 staff. Of the 2000, 35 per cent were female; however, women managers comprised only two per cent of the labour force and five per cent of the management staff, even though the CEO was a woman. Only two companies had more than 50 per cent women in their workforce — a hotel and a domestic goods retail outlet, both with 60 per cent. Female managers comprised 22 per cent of the retail firm's employees but only one per cent of the hotel employees (Kitching 1999).

The introduction of the 'socialist market system' in China has led to a variety of problems and opportunities for women in both urban and rural areas.

Women in private business

Private business is a fairly new area of opportunity for both women and men in the People's Republic of China. It was virtually non-existent until the reforms of the 1980s and it is only 10 years since an amendment to the Chinese constitution in 1988 legalised private business activities. From the beginning of that decade, private business activities were first tolerated and later encouraged because they created jobs and supplied much-needed goods and services (Li & Tang 1997: 17). Chinese entrepreneurs took up the new opportunities with great vigour and by the end of 1986 the Chinese media were reporting that there were 12 million licensed entrepreneurs, of whom eight million were women (*XINHUA* 1986).

As Lu and Tang (1997) have noted, however, some enterprises are more equal than others. State Owned Enterprises (SOEs) have priority in receiving raw materials at below-market prices and state bank loans at low interest rates (Lu & Tang 1997: 19). Foreign firms, both wholly owned and joint ventures, are better served by their regulatory frameworks and have more security of ownership of both capital and property. Private Chinese-owned firms have the least access to capital investment, are worst served by laws and regulations, and have much less access to and security for both capital and property.

Around the world it is estimated that firms owned by women account for between 25 per cent and 33 per cent of all businesses (National Foundation for Women Business Owners 1998: 2). In the United States, women-owned firms employ one out of every four company workers, and employment in women-owned firms with 100 or more employees has expanded six times faster than for all firms in the economy. In the US and Canada, growth of women-owned firms outpaces overall business growth by around 2:1. Similar findings are reported from Australasia and parts of Asia, with more women setting up new small businesses than men, and with a lower failure rate.

As was noted at the OECD Conference on Women Entrepreneurs in Small and Medium Enterprises held in Paris in April 1997, a situation where women are discriminated against in business has negative economic, social and political consequences for any country, and a lack of data on obstacles to women's entry or success in business makes policy formulation difficult (OECD 1998). If China was to follow a similar pattern to other societies during its development process, with respect to greater frequency of divorce, with a growth in single-parent families predominantly headed by women who are often living below the poverty line, the negative consequences could be severe. Concern for the welfare of women prompted the United Nations Development Plan (UNDP) to set up a program in China to provide funds for women to establish businesses and this seems to be meeting with some success.

From the early 1980s, Chinese women were undertaking entrepreneurial activities in astonishing numbers and with extraordinary success. By 1986, two-thirds of entrepreneurial licences countrywide had been taken out by women. In 1990, China Women's News announced that 4.6 million rural women were running businesses, which meant that a third of all rural businesses were owned and run by women. This means that within a decade, Chinese women in rural areas had reached the world average. The All China Women's Federation lists the Top Fifty Businesswomen annually and women regularly appear in the Top 100 CEO listings. Women have become millionaires. Yet one mainland Chinese feminist has dismissed business as 'merely a side road to development for women' (Li, cited in Gilmartin et al. 1994: 381).

Although most women enter business for the same entrepreneurial reasons as men, during the last two decades of the twentieth century women in a variety of countries, including the US and Australia, have expressed increasing frustration with their work environments. They cite the desire for greater challenge and the need for more flexibility in their work environment as reasons for moving to business ownership. The greatest reward of business ownership for women is in gaining control over their own working lives. Women report that their greatest challenge in business is to be taken seriously.

Women in urban business

Opportunities for women in the SOEs are declining. As Xiao-Zhou (1997–98: 24–8) points out, jobs in the urban areas are threatened by competition from rural factories set up under the new policies of economic liberalisation and by the government's response to market pressures on the SOEs with the emphasis on profitability. Women are not being recruited because they bear and rear children, care for the elderly and have to do the housework, all of which makes them less productive than men according to Chinese male managers. Also, the necessary welfare provisions such as maternity leave make the enterprise less profitable. Many women are forced to retire at 40–45 years of age, long before the average retirement age for men, and women are a primary target for state lay-offs because industries dominated by women such as textiles are the first to go. By 1993 women accounted for 60 per cent of the urban unemployed and the rate continued to increase through the nineties (Joint Economic Committee, Congress of the United States 1997: 374). The number of laid-off female workers may be as high as 10 million, and around 10 per cent are living in poverty. Even when not in abject poverty, those laid off report a sharp drop in living standards, increasing conflicts in the family, and being looked down upon by husbands and relatives. They also report feelings of disappointment, helplessness and loss of confidence (Wang Jinliang 1991: 6–15). Organisational change in the state sector is, therefore, disadvantaging women. One response to this is that more and more women are turning to jobs in the private sector.

In this sector, however, women are also encountering discrimination. Large private factories, both foreign owned and joint ventures, employ large numbers of women, but this female labour force consists almost exclusively of the young and unmarried and, frequently, of rural migrant workers. Management is almost exclusively male and there is considerable evidence of exploitation and harassment of women employees. Tang Can (1998: 64–71) reported that 36.8 per cent of respondents in a survey of female migrant workers claimed that they had been subjected to harassment. Only 14.8 per cent claimed never to have been subjected to it. Other problems include overwork, harmful working conditions, poor living conditions and no proper labour contracts. In 1991, 1993 and 1996 women died when locked doors prevented escape from fires in factories or dormitories (Tan Shen 1995: 332–42; *Oriental Daily* 1996: 1).

With greater economic freedom and more role models, it is likely that more and more women are going to start their own businesses, mostly on a small scale in enterprises which require little capital — for example, as street vendors or providing services such as tailoring and bicycle mending. Self-employment gives women of any age group and educational level the opportunity to control their own working lives and to have greater economic independence.

Women in rural business

In rural township or village enterprises, women are for the most part excluded from management, the few in such posts usually being politically well-connected through fathers or fathers-in-law. Judd (1994) showed that in rural villages in north China, women are still likely to be excluded from the critical economic activities of sales and procurement. This work requires travel and contact with buyers and suppliers elsewhere, which are activities thought more suitable for men. Traditional social custom, still very strong in rural areas, decrees that women should not travel long distances alone, have individual contact with unrelated men or go drinking. Also, each job is defined as a job for either a man or a woman of a certain age — men do heavy work, women do detailed work. Positions of authority are for older men, while female employees have little freedom or control over the production process. There is little sign of the kind of organisational change with respect to sexual equality of opportunity which is being experienced in developed, Western business cultures.

The area where rural women have found most opportunity is in the home-based, courtyard economy, and many women now take their produce to market and interact with numerous people there. Eighty to 90 per cent of meat, eggs and other fowl products are produced and marketed by women, so that during the 1980s farmers markets were dubbed 'streets of women'. Although this reflects significant employment opportunities for rural females, the female workforce is still smaller than the male workforce (Xiao-Zhou 1997/8: 25).

In some cases, women's work in the courtyard economy involves them in negotiating loans and arranging business deals as well as marketing. On the other hand, much of the work that women undertake, in activities such as weaving and handicraft production, is subcontracted, and women are not involved in the business side of the work (Jacka 1997: 153). Even where the work is not subcontracted, it is common for women not to be involved in business transactions with non-family members. Most females prefer the household economy because it is easier for them to cope with husbands or fathers than to conduct business with predominantly male local cadres or male managers of local enterprises.

Some rural women have been able to develop the potential of the courtyard economy to the full. They are running specialised households and private enterprises, such as growing grain, medicinal fungi, bonsai and flowers; raising cows, pigs and chickens; food processing; running hotels; running tailoring schools and grocery shops; machine-knitting jumpers; and sewing. Some have become private industrialists. A 1994 survey by the Zaoyang County Women's Federation in Hubei found that women had initiated 18 600 private enterprises. It is still very difficult, however, for rural women to gain access to or control over land and resources, as the patriarchal family system is still very strong.

Self-employment is difficult for women from the more patriarchal minority groups. The largest private enterprise in Xinjiang province was set up and run by an Uigur woman whose husband, a strong Muslim, had divorced her for making and selling children's clothes in the street when his income was insufficient to support his family (Hall 1997: 65–6).

Although business does provide opportunities for Chinese women, those opportunities, and whether women choose to take advantage of them, are constrained by their social and political environment.

Issues for women in business

The primary concerns of businesswomen throughout the world are similar. They comprise both day-to-day management issues, such as maintaining profits, finding good employees and managing cash flow, and external factors, such as government policy, the state of the economy, access to technology and access to capital.

Once women have become established in business in China, what do they identify as problems? Interviews by Kitching with women in Kunming, Yunnan province, in August 1998 produced the following list of problems for their businesses, which are grouped in order of frequency:

1. Lack of qualified staff
2. Lack of access to capital
3. Changes in government policy
Personnel management
4. Economic downturn
Too much competition
Low profits
Bad debts
Lack of opportunity to expand
5. Lack of opportunity to enter export markets
Lack of opportunity to enter import markets
Market price fluctuations
Communication problems between state and private business

Communication problems with foreign clients
Pirating of goods.

This list reflects the concerns identified by the National Foundation for Women Business Owners as being internationally the key concerns for women entrepreneurs, plus some problems more specific to China. The specific Chinese problems are: the lack of opportunity to enter export and import markets, communication problems between state and private business, and pirating of goods. Private Chinese business (in contrast to SOEs and foreign firms) is still discriminated against in China with respect to access to capital and security of investment, and women entrepreneurs face more difficulties than men.

The glass ceiling seems to be operating in China. Even in enterprises where 50 per cent of the employees are female, they are not equally represented at all levels. Women are clustered in the lower-paid, lower-status positions and only around 11 per cent of CEOs are women. In Kunming, only 10 per cent of the private firms are owned by women. Anecdotal evidence from cities such as Shanghai suggests that women travelling on business are subject to harassment, and as a result special female-only hotels are being set up to protect women travellers from unwelcome attention and even violence. Although government policy may declare equality between men and women, 'men have more power, de facto inequality still exists' (CASS Institute of Population Studies 1994).

Gender-based differences

Women and men differ in their management styles. Men tend to be more authoritarian, aggressive, like hierarchical structures, and be impatient of failure. Women are less hierarchical, may take more time over making decisions, seek more information, and are more likely to look for input from employees, other business owners and experts in special areas. Women place a higher value than men on relationships, responsiveness and reputation. Women tend to listen more, are more egalitarian and cooperative, will take account of employees' problems, and have better personal relations with colleagues and employees (National Foundation for Women Business Owners 1998).

Women interviewed in Kunming (Kitching 1998) were of the opinion that women think they are better at managing people than men, have good people skills, are good at personal relations, communicate better, are more sensitive, gentler and give their employees more opportunity to develop.

Men are thought to be more aggressive, do not want to discuss the personal problems of workers, order their employees to do things and shout at people when they do things the wrong way.

The businesswomen in Kunming also identified differences between the way men and women run a business. They claimed that men take a long-term view, see the bigger picture, are more aggressive, take more risks, waste money, don't pay attention to details, ignore things and fail more often. Women are more careful, pay more attention to detail, are better with money, more practical, more decisive, quicker at solving problems and succeed more often.

This fits with success and failure rates for small business in Australia and some other areas in Asia. Over the last ten years, more new small businesses have been set up by women than by men and they have a higher success rate.

One would expect to find these behavioural differences reflected in such areas as organisational structures, business strategies and decision-making styles. Very little work has been done in this area in China.

Career options for Chinese women

Differences are apparent between older and younger women. Of the businesswomen I interviewed in Yunnan, the younger women obviously have more choice of career, change jobs more frequently, expect to spend money on fashionable clothes, have mobile phones and have learned to drive, but compared with older women, they complain more of inequality, of being restricted and of discrimination because they are women. Those who are still employees or work with their husbands want to own their own businesses in the future. Working in large companies is seen as less desirable for women and as 'not such a good environment' (Kitching 1998). This parallels trends in the US and Australia where women working in business (even some who have made it to the top in large corporations) have pulled out and set up their own enterprises. The woman CEO of the largest company in my sample (the SOE), who got awards every year for being in the top 100 businesses in the province, commented that it was very difficult for women to reach that level, and still more difficult for a woman compared with a man to do her job at the senior management level.

Impact of the reintroduction of the market

Chan et al. (cited in Cheng 1998: 590) have called the post-Mao period 'an epoch of women's confusion', commenting that women have to compete with men in the market for employment, education and political participation. This is a painful experience for which the Maoist affirmative action policies did not prepare them. 'Forced' equality brought no real understanding of equal opportunity, and there is little indication that the problems preventing equal access for women are on the male-dominated political agenda in China today. In urban areas in particular, many women find the market hostile, seeing it as bringing insecurity, lack of social support, unfair competition and a threat to participation in the public sphere. For others, however, it represents choice, mobility, new opportunities for economic independence and increased status in the family and society.

Obviously the problems faced by many women in China are appalling — poverty, domestic violence, sexual harassment and discrimination in the workplace, and the triple burden of caring for the household, children and the aged while at the same time holding a full-time job or being unemployed. China is a developing country where the traditional and patriarchal culture is still very strong and women's opportunities are constrained by both those factors. Women's issues and problems have been marginalised in the period of market reform over the last two decades. Change takes time. In China today, although the pace of change is phenomenal, organisational change with respect to sexual equality of opportunity appears to be almost non-existent. Some Chinese women have found the road to economic success in ownership of, or employment in, private business, and thereby greater independence and influence in the family. The problems faced by women can be summed up in the following comments (Kitching 1998) from two women in Yunnan in 1998.

36-year-old minority-nationality millionaire business owner:

Society needs to value women more and give them better education. The social system suppresses women and says women must have men to support them. Ability is not enough, you need background and guanxi and men have better advantages here. Women are not recognised by society and cannot communicate with society, men can. There is a double standard. If women work closely with men their reputations suffer but the men's don't.

22-year-old employee of a Chinese/American joint venture firm:

Chinese men do not have the same responsibilities at home and think women are subordinate. It is not socially acceptable for a woman not to marry and have children. We need a proper legal system to be equal.

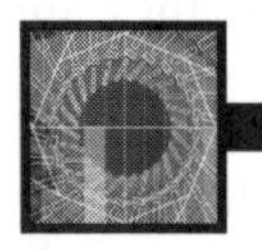

Issues for the disabled

Very little attention has been paid in Western literature to issues affecting the disabled in China. Within the PRC this area came to prominence only after the late Deng Xiaoping was rehabilitated and became China's paramount leader in the late 1970s. His son, Deng Pufang, had become a paraplegic during the Cultural Revolution when he leapt from a third-storey window to escape assault by Red Guards. During the 1980s and 1990s Deng Pufang championed the cause of the disabled. On his return from medical treatment in Canada, he set up the China Disabled Person's Welfare Fund, which grew significantly during the 1980s and eventually became the Disabled Persons' Federation.

In 1987, the first epidemiological survey of disabled people ever carried out in China was completed. The sample survey of 1.5 million people reported that 4.9 per cent had a disability, which, in conjunction with the results of the census of 1987, suggested a figure of 51.6 million disabled people in the PRC. This estimate had grown to around 60 million by 1999 (Kohrman 2000: 906). A breakdown into disability groups reported 7.55 million people with physical disabilities, 17.7 million with speech and hearing difficulties, 10.17 million with intellectual disabilities, 7.55 million blind persons and 1.94 million with multiple handicaps (Xiao Fei, cited in Ashman 1995: 48). Around eight million of those disabled are children (Ashman 1995: 48), and 66 per cent of those children are intellectually impaired (Sonnander & Claesson 1997: 180). As Sonnander and Claesson (1997) have pointed out, this means that China has more individuals with disabilities than any other country in the world.

During the reform and 'open door' policy decades of the 1980s and 1990s, there was considerable development in legislation and provision of services for people with an intellectual or physical disability.

Legislation

It is a provision of the current constitution of the PRC that the government must guarantee that 'the disabled enjoy the same civic rights as the able-bodied' (*Renmin Ribao* 2000). In 1982, the Chinese Government accepted the United Nations World Program of Action Concerning Disabled Persons and set up the China Organisational Committee of the United Nations Decade of Disabled Persons. In 1987, the PRC accepted the Convention Concerning Vocational Rehabilitation and Employment (Disabled Persons), which had been passed by the International Labor Conference in 1983.

In December 1990, the law of the People's Republic of China on the Protection of Disabled Persons was adopted by the Standing Committee of the National People's Congress. The formation of the law was said to be guided by the principles of 'equality', 'participation' and 'co-enjoyment'. Many important laws now have special provisions guaranteeing the rights and interests of the disabled in education, political participation, inheritance, marriage, and civil and criminal procedures. The Labor Law of the PRC and the Regulations for SOEs for Changes in Operating Mechanisms

include specific regulations guaranteeing the rights of the disabled to employment. Twenty-seven provinces, regions and municipalities have formulated local legislation setting a quota for disabled employees of at least 1.5 per cent in government-run organisations. According to a Government White Paper (*Renmin Ribao* 2000), 'Chinese laws prohibit discrimination, insult and injury against the handicapped or their ill-treatment and abandonment'.

Education

Since 1981, special classes for children with an intellectual disability have been promoted in regular schools. By 1986, there were 36 special schools and 55 classes. By 1992, there were 235 special schools and 1235 classes (Yang & Wang 1994; Xu 1994). The continuing problems of funding, and shortages of teachers and equipment, meant that by the mid-1990s only 0.5 per cent of intellectually impaired children were attending special schools, 61 per cent were attending regular schools, but 38.1 per cent were not attending school at all (Xu 1994). In its guidelines for the 1991–95 Five Year Plan for the Chinese Handicapped, the government set goals for the percentage of disabled children who should receive junior high school education at 60 per cent in developed areas and 30 per cent in moderately developed areas.

In January 2000, the Government White Paper reported progress. It claimed that some 2300 community rehabilitation centres, 750 disabled children's care centres and training classes, and 1300 work-rehabilitation centres for the mentally and intellectually disabled had been set up. Between 1997 and 2000 the number of special education schools had increased by 20 per cent per annum and special classes in regular schools had doubled. The number of children attending these classes and schools had increased by 30 per cent per annum and, in 1998 and 1999, some 4700 self-taught disabled persons had won college diplomas through special examinations. Twenty-eight vocational education centres had been established. Special education divisions were being established at universities, and teacher-training institutions for special secondary education were being set up in 27 provinces, regions and municipalities. Subsidies, fees exemption, scholarships and prizes had been instituted.

Employment

There is a system of government-supported welfare enterprises in which the disabled are employed. The number of such enterprises has increased from 1022 in 1979 to 42 000 by 1990, employing a total of 750 000 people (*Renmin Ribao* 2000). Government figures claim that 50.19 per cent of urban disabled people and 60.55 per cent of rural disabled people which is a total of some 13 million people, have employment. Disabled persons are also employed in regular government departments, SOEs and private business. Since instituting the disability tax credit system in 1984, the government has been increasingly urging disabled men and women to become independent business people as a means of reducing the state's welfare burden. By 1995, more than 500 000 'disabled entrepreneurs' were registered (Kohrman 2000: 906).

People with disabilities face some of the same problems faced by women in a rapidly changing economic system. The welfare factories are short of investment and impeded in efforts to compete in the new marketplace by outdated equipment. With the loss of jobs in the state sector, and because both state-owned and private business are emphasising profit, unemployment is increasing. Welfare facilities designed to accommodate those who are physically and mentally incapable of working, and have no legal providers or resources, are unable to meet the actual needs. The disabled are certainly to be found among the beggars, especially in poorer regions of the PRC.

Social attitudes

Over the past two decades, the government and the Disabled Persons' Federation have worked hard at creating a social environment in which the disabled are respected and helped. Many activities have been sponsored, such as the Young Pioneers 'Helping the Handicapped' Program, which has involved more than 30 million children over the last five years. There is a Humanitarian Publicity Week, a Day of the Disabled, and 19 May of each year is now the legal 'National Day for Helping the Handicapped'.

The question of 'access' is now being addressed to enable disabled to participate more easily in social activities. Standards for the Design of Urban Roads and Buildings for the Convenience of the Disabled have been developed and attempts are being made to implement them. Slopes and handrails are being built in shops, hotels, libraries, theatres, airports and other public places, but so far only in the more developed and richer cities such as Beijing, Shenzhen, Shanghai, Tianjin, Shenyang and Guangzhou.

In 1994, the Sixth Far East and South Pacific Games for the Disabled were held in Beijing with more than 30 000 volunteers involved. The PRC sent 87 athletes to the Paralympic Games in Sydney in October 2000.

As is the case with gender issues, there is a large gap between law and policy and the realities of life for many of the disabled. Much of the stigma against the disabled has survived the changes of the past century, particularly for men. This becomes apparent when comparing marriage rates of the disabled (*can ji*) with those of the general population which emerged in the 1987 sample survey of the disabled. In the general population only 0.7 per cent of women have never married, compared with 4.0 per cent of female *can ji*, whereas for men the rates are 7.0 per cent and 45 per cent respectively (Di 1989; Kohrman 2000: 890–91). The fact that men outnumber women in China is not sufficient explanation.

In his paper about *can ji* men, Kohrman (2000: 894) reports the comments of one elderly woman about disabled (*que*) men: 'men need to get out of the house and be fast on their feet. They [*que* men] just don't have what it takes to be a man, to go out and do what's expected of them. That's why they have such a hard time marrying.' Families of disabled persons try to prevent them marrying other *can ji*.

Disabled people employed in the regular workforce may face discrimination. One interpreter in a government institute I visited was lame and despised by fellow workers, especially those with a lower educational level. They made his life difficult in a variety of ways. In one incident the driver of the institute car deliberately drove off before the interpreter got in, forcing him to try to run to catch up. The driver laughed at his efforts to do so.

There are of course dedicated individuals trying to bring about change. One elderly female business-owner in Yunnan runs a factory making toys for disabled children. The profits from this enterprise she then uses to employ teachers to train mothers how to use these toys in helping to educate their children. She particularly tries to help rural families. She has visited Australia and has been very impressed with Australian equal opportunity legislation and with the provisions to ensure that the law is put into practice. She also admired the educational and care facilities in place to help the disabled and commented, 'we have a long way to go, it is not like that here' (Kitching 1998).

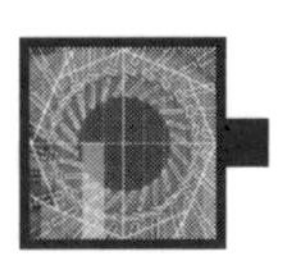

Issues for national minorities

There are currently 58 ethnic minority groups identified by the Chinese Government, 55 of which are officially designated as National Minorities. They are scattered throughout the PRC but are still most strongly concentrated in autonomous regions and provinces in the border regions of the north, such as Inner Mongolia, in the north-west, such as Xinjiang and Gansu, in the west, such as Tibet, Qinghai and Sichuan and in the south-west, such as Yunnan. Their origins and cultural traditions are very diverse, ranging from the nomadic herders of the northern plains (such as the Mongols), to hunter/gatherer groups in the tropical forests of Xishuangbanna (such as the Hani); from patriarchal Islamic groups (such as the Uighurs of Xinjiang), to the matriarchal Mosuo (labelled as Naxi by the PRC authorities) living on the Sichuan/Yunnan border. Their religious traditions are also extremely diverse and include Islam, Lamaism, Buddhism and animism. Many groups have been in contact with and influenced by Han culture for over a thousand years. Current government policy speaks of China as having been a united multinationality country since ancient times and describes the PRC as a united multinationality state founded jointly by the peoples of all nationalities (*Beijing Review* 1999: 16).

National minorities comprise nearly nine per cent of the population and have a higher growth rate than the Han Chinese because they are exempt from the one-child policy. A comparison between the 1982 census and the 1990 census showed a growth in the percentage from 6.7 to 8.7 per cent and some groups appeared to be growing in excess of four per cent per annum (Yusuf & Byrnes 1993: 3). An explanation for this 'explosion of ethnicity' (Gladney 1991) is that it would appear that people are now more ready to identify with their ethnic groups than they were in the past.

Legislation

Article four of the current constitution states that all nationalities are equal, and that discrimination against and oppression of any nationality is prohibited (*Beijing Review* 1999: 18). Minorities are guaranteed equal rights to vote and stand for election; freedom of religious belief; the right to education; the right to use and develop their own language; and freedom to preserve or reform their own folkways and customs, and to be assisted in economic development. This can provide a substantial challenge to government resources. For instance, 70 different languages with around 20 different scripts are in use. Only three minorities use Mandarin (SEDC 1988; Lin 1993).

The Electoral Law of the National People's Congress (NPC) guarantees that minority groups are represented by their own deputies. Of the 2979 deputies elected in 1998, 428 were from ethnic minorities, accounting for over 14 per cent of the total (*Beijing Review* 1999: 19). Among the vice-chairpersons of the Standing Committee of the NPC at present, 21 per cent are of ethnic minority origin and they comprise 9.6 per cent of vice-chairpersons of the National Committee of the Chinese People's Consultative Conference (CPPCC). On State Council, one leading member and two ministers are from ethnic minority groups.

China has joined international conventions such as the International Convention on the Elimination of All Forms of Racial Discrimination, the International Convention on the Suppression and Punishment of the Crime of Apartheid and the Convention on the Prevention and Punishment of the Crime of Genocide.

Education

In 1949, many of the minority languages had no written form. In the 1950s, national minority institutes were set up to study minority languages and cultures, and by the late 1990s ten ethnic groups were using the 13 languages provided with written versions. Around 100 newspapers and 73 journals are published in minority languages and more than 20 languages are used in radio broadcasts. By 1998, there were 36 publishing houses specialising in minority language publications in 23 languages.

Before 1949, there was only one university for minority students. In general, the literacy rate was very low. In areas such as Tibet and Ningxia 95 per cent of people were illiterate in 1949. The first tertiary institute in an autonomous area was set up in 1949 in Tibet. This was the School for Tibetan Issues, which later became the Northwest Nationalities University. The aim of the new minority institutions was to improve tertiary industry, help economic development, and train cadres and intellectuals needed in the autonomous areas. They were also intended to 'preserve and develop the characteristics of the nationalities in the context of international cultures' (Xie, cited in Kormondy 1995: 165).

Official figures report that, between 1952 and 1998, in National Minority Autonomous Areas there was substantial growth in education.

Table 3.1: ***Growth in education in national minority autonomous areas, 1952–1998***

Institution type	1952	1998
Tertiary institutions	11	94
Secondary schools	531	13 466
Primary schools	59 597	90 704

Source: Adapted from *Beijing Review* 1999: 16.

Since 1980, only one minority tertiary institution, the Central Institute for Nationalities in Beijing, has been designated as a 'key' institution. Some other 'key' universities, such as Xinjiang University, have considerable minority enrolment, but 75 per cent of 'key' institutions are in the southern and eastern coastal provinces and municipalities, with 22 in Beijing alone. This means that they are sited in the most developed and wealthy areas of China, which generally have fewer numbers of minority people. Since 1976, the 'key' universities have received higher funding, attracted the best teachers and provided them with better salaries, and enrolled the best students.

The question of language has had to be addressed. Most Chinese universities teach in Mandarin, which disadvantages ethnic minority students. In some areas, one-year bridging programs have been introduced to give students whose first language is not Mandarin the level of skill needed for a tertiary course. There are also special classes offered by universities to prepare minority students for entry to particular degree programs, such as chemistry. Entry to university is by national examination and special provisions for minority students include taking part of or sometimes the entire examination in their native language and adjusting the scores.

The major issues challenging the education system are, first, that most minority nationalities are in remote and rural areas, which have been well behind urban developments in education. Second, poor economic conditions have limited educational opportunities and development. The current goals are to 'train more talent and raise the standard of living' by introducing science and technology and improving the quality of education, described as 'the golden key' to economic development (Wei, cited in Kormondy 1995: 169).

Employment and finance

In 1949, there were very few industries in minority areas and modern infrastructure was largely non-existent. Agriculture was the primary economic activity, and in some areas this was of the 'slash and burn' type, with a few groups still not using iron tools. Over the past 20 years, the government has increased investment in minority areas in infrastructure construction of power stations, railways, roads and airports. In 1998, 62 per cent of the total increased financial investment by the state was used in central and western areas of the PRC. Since the 1950s, some 1400 industrial enterprises have been set up in the major minority areas (*Beijing Review* 1999: 25). Minority nationality people employed in SOEs face the same problems as women and the disabled as these enterprises are restructured to operate on a profit basis. There is now a preferential policy to direct more foreign investment to minority areas.

Since 1980, there has been a quota subsidy system in place for the five autonomous regions and the three provinces which have the highest number of minority people — Yunnan, Guizhou and Qinghai. In 1994, China began to reform its financial management system including its 'tax sharing scheme', which is the source of funding for the quota system. All the existing subsidies and special financial allocation policies for minority areas were retained and a transfer payment method worked out for what was seen as a transitional period. In 1998, the minority regions and provinces received 48 per cent of the total transfer payment sum.

Since 1963, China has had preferential policies towards ethnic trade and it guarantees the production of some 4000 items of 'ethnic articles' in daily use. A new package of preferential policies is included in the Ninth Five Year Plan (1996–2000), which involves funding the construction of an ethnic trade network and the technological upgrading of enterprises producing basic ethnic goods. The state-owned ethnic enterprises and the grass-roots supply and marketing cooperatives are exempt from value-added tax. State policy recognises that western China, where most minority people live, is 'relatively backward compared with the coastal areas in east China'. Improvement in living standards has been 'restricted by geographical conditions, a low social development level, poor production conditions and lack of scientific, technological and cultural knowledge' (*Beijing Review* 1999: 28). The word Han is not mentioned but some of the previous 'discourses' are still recognisable.

Private business

As has been the case with women and the disabled, ethnic minority people have identified the opportunities presented by the changing economic system and have become private entrepreneurs, particularly in the new tourism industry. In cities like Kunming, capital of Yunnan province, there are many ethnic minority restaurants which also offer entertainment by ethnic dancers and singers, and massage practitioners. Ethnic minority markets are found at many tourist sites, with stalls selling food, costumes, art and artifacts.

Some minority business people have become wealthy like the Uighur woman mentioned earlier. One Aini woman interviwed in Kunming (Kitching 1998) had become a millionaire with a wholesale firm selling fire alarms and sprinkler systems.

Social attitudes

Although many minority nationality people are very concerned to see their traditions, languages and cultural identities maintained, there are differences within and between groups about how and to what extent this should be done. One extreme is the case of Tibet, where a highly vocal expatriate community tries to influence global leaders to pressure the Chinese Government to allow Tibet to become an independent country. Within the Tibet Autonomous Region there are both supporters and opponents of this view. Some Tibetans have a vested interest in maintaining the status quo, including many of the Tibetans who make up 75 per cent of the cadres in the region. Many Han Chinese now live in Tibet, and during the 1990s this group increased in numbers substantially by taking advantage of business opportunities in the region. Many Tibetans live outside Tibet in Qinghai, southern Xinjiang and Sichuan province.

Separatist groups can also be found in Xinjiang and other areas along the northern border of China.

At the other end of the spectrum, there are individuals who see themselves as Chinese first, and then as members of an ethnic group. Many young people want to be 'modern' and up-to-date and they see greater opportunities in being competent in Mandarin and, for business, English rather than in a minority language. As one young Bai nationality academic said, 'I am Bai, my wife is Miao. Our children are Chinese' (Kitching 1998).

Many minority people are ambivalent about what it means to be a member of their ethnic group. In these debates there is often both a generation gap and a rural/urban dichotomy. Among the Naxi, White (1997: 302) noted that more prosperous villages looked down on poor villages and university-educated young people looked down on their peers who failed to get into tertiary institutions. City dwellers viewed rural villagers as 'relatively backward', less cultured and more conservative. This ambivalence about identity reflects both the contradictory policies pursued by the PRC Government and the various views or discourses which have informed the policy process. Undoubtedly there are also Han Chinese who still look down on ethnic minorities as 'barbarians' while resenting and envying their privileges.

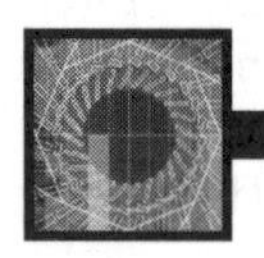

Conclusions

China is a multicultural, developing country which, over the past 20 years, has emerged from relative political and economic isolation into an international environment, undergoing the trauma of rapid technological and social change. The current situation for women, the disabled and ethnic minorities reflects a mixture of historical experience incorporating traditional value systems, political ideology and a variety of external influences. Change is constrained by economic conditions and the availability of resources. There are many problems and issues to be confronted in managing such a dynamic situation, although current policies suggest a much greater recognition of the need to 'manage for diversity' than was apparent 20 years ago. China is, however, still a one-party state whose government continues to stress unity and stability.

References

Adler, N. J. & Israeli, D. N. (Eds). 1988. *Women in Management Worldwide*. Armonk, NY: M. E. Sharpe.

Adler, N. J. & Israeli, D. N. (Eds). 1994. *Competitive Frontiers: Women Managers in a Global Economy.* Cambridge: Blackwell.

Ashman, A. F. 1995. 'The Education of Students with an Intellectual Disability in the People's Republic of China: Some Observations'. *European Journal of Special Needs Education* 10(1): 47–57.

Beijing Review. 1999. 'China's Policy on Minorities and Its Practice'. *Beijing Review,* October 18: 16–33.

Benewick, R. & Wingrove, P. 1995. *China in the 1990s*. Vancouver: UCP Press.

CASS Institute of Population Studies (Ed.). 1994. *Sampling Survey Data of Women's Status in Contemporary China*. International Academic Publishers.

Chen, Chao C. & Yu, K. C. 1997. 'Motivation to Manage. A Study of Women in Chinese State-owned Enterprises'. *Journal of Applied Behavioural Science* 33(2): 160–73.

Cheng, J. Y. S. (Ed.). 1998. *China in the Post-Deng Era*. Hong Kong: The Chinese University Press.

Di, Ya (Ed.). 1989. *1987 National Sample Survey of Disabled Persons*. Beijing: Office of the National Sample Survey of Disabled Persons.

Fairchild, J. K. 1992. *China. A New History.* Cambridge, MA: Belknap Press.

Family. 1991. 5: 49.

Foreign Broadcast Information Service. 1992. *Daily Report: People's Republic of China,* April 14: 17–20.

Gilmartin, C. K., Hershatter, G., Rofel, L. & White, T. 1994. *Engendering China. Women, Culture and the State*. Cambridge, Mass: Harvard University Press.

Gladney, D. C. 1991. *Muslim Chinese: Ethnic Nationalism in the People's Republic*. Cambridge: Harvard University Press.

Hall, C, 1997. *Daughters of the Dragon. Women's Lives in Contemporary China*. Scarlet Press.

Hildebrandt, H. W. & Liu, J. 1988. 'Chinese Women Managers: A Comparison with their US and Asian Counterparts'. *Human Resource Management* 27(3): 291–341.

Jacka, T. 1997. *Women's Work in Rural China: Change and Continuity in an Era of Reform*. Cambridge: Cambridge University Press.

Joint Economic Committee, Congress of the United States (Ed.). 1997. *China's Economic Future*. Armonk, NY: M. E. Sharpe.

Judd, E. R. 1994. *Gender and Power in Rural North China*. California: Stanford University Press.

Kitching, B. 1998. Unpublished interview data with women business owners and employees of both private and state-owned businesses in Kunming, Yunnan Province in South-western China.

Kitching, B. 1999. 'Gender-based Differences in Business Management in the People's Republic of China: A Pilot Study'. In *Organisations Looking Ahead: Challenges and Directions*. Proceedings of the conference held at Griffith University, Brisbane, November 1999.

Kohrman, M. 2000. 'Grooming *que zi*: Marriage Exclusion and Identity Formation Among Disabled Men in Contemporary China'. *American Ethnologist* 26(4): 890–909.

Korabik, K. 1994. 'Managerial Women in the People's Republic of China: The Long March Continues'. In Adler, N. J. & Israeli, D. N. (Eds). *Competitive Frontiers: Women Managers in a Global Economy.* Cambridge: Blackwell.

Kormondy, E. J. 1995. 'Observations on Minority Education, Cultural Preservation and Economic Development in China'. *Compare* 25 (21): 161–78.

Leung, J.1999. 'Spreading Its Wings'. *Asian Business*, February, pp. 12–13.

Lin, Y. 1993. 'Different Social and Cultural Types among the Chinese National Minorities: Their Transition to Socialism and Development Towards Modernisation'. In Kenichiro, H. (Ed.). *The State and Cultural Transformation*. Tokyo: United Nations University Press.

Lu, D. & Tang, Z. 1997. *State Intervention and Business in China*. Cheltenham: Edward Elgar.

McKeen, C. A. & Bu, N. 1998. 'Career and Life Expectations of Chinese Business Students: The Effects of Gender'. *Women in Management Review* 13(5): 171–83.

National Foundation for Women Business Owners. 1998. *Key Issues Affecting Women Business Owners in Argentina and Other Latin and Iber-American Countries*, April.

OECD. 1998. *Women Entrepreneurs in Developing Countries*. Paris: OECD.

Oriental Daily. 1996: 1

Renmin Ribao. 2000. 'Government White Paper on Guarantee of Human Rights for the Disabled'. Section 1X, 5 January.

SEDC (State Education Commission). 1988. *Education in China, 1978–1988*. Beijing: State Education Commission.

Sonnander, K. & Claesson, M. 1997. 'Classification, Prevalence, Prevention and Rehabilitation of Intellectual Disability: An Overview of Research in the People's Republic of China'. *Journal of Intellectual Disability Research* 41(2): 180–92.

Tan Shen. 'Zhongguo funu zhuangkuang' (Women's Situation in China) in Jiang Liu et al. (Eds). 1994–5. nian Zhongguo shehui xingshi fenxi yu yuce (Analysis and Prediction of the Social Situation in China 1994–5). Beijing: Zhongguo shehui kexue chubanshe, 332–42.

Tang C. 1998. 'Sexual Harassment: The Dual Status of and Discrimination against Female Migrant Workers in Urban Areas.' A speech delivered at the Asia University in Japan, *Social Sciences in China* 3: 64–71.

Thompson, G. (Ed.). 1998. *Economic Dynamism in the Asia Pacific*. London: Routledge.

Wang J. 1991. 'The Maimed 'Half-sky': The Employment Crisis of Women in China'. *Women, Education and Employment* 11(25): 6–15.

White, S. D. 1997. 'Fame and Sacrifice: The Gendered Construction of Naxi identities'. *Modern China* 23(3): 298–328.

Women of China. 1987. 5: 42.

Xiao-Zhou, K. 1997/8. 'Women Divided. The Blessing and the Curse of China's Changing Economy'. *Harvard International Review* XX(1): 24–8.

XINHUA. 1986. December 3.

Xu, Y. 1994. 'China'. In Winzer, H. & Mazurek, G. (Eds). *Comparative Study of Special Education*. Washington, DC: Genalland University, 163–78.

Yang, H. & Wang, H. 1994. 'Special Education in China'. *Journal of Special Education 28:* 93–105.

Yu, G. & Zhu, Y. 2000. 'Gender Differences of China's Managers in Time Management'. *Women in Management Review* 15(1): 33–43.

Yusuf, F. & Byrnes, M. 1993. 'Ethnic Mosaic of Modern China: An Analysis of Fertility and Mortality Data for Twelve Largest Ethnic Minorities'. Research Paper No. 374, Macquarie University School of Economic and Financial Studies, October.

Chapter 4

Hong Kong

Robin Kramar

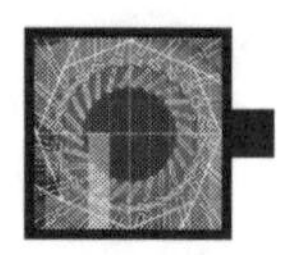

Introduction

In Hong Kong, legislation makes it mandatory to manage diversity along the dimensions of gender, disability and family status. This chapter examines this legislation and the impact it has had on management practices in Hong Kong. Although there are other dimensions of diversity, in the context of Hong Kong the dimension of gender has been given the most attention.

Definitions of diversity range from broad, expansive definitions that refer to differences between individuals, to much narrower definitions that focus on differences between particular groups in organisations. When diversity is defined in a broad way, it implies everyone is different and the concept reflects the notion of individualism that underpins much of our understanding of organisations. This broad view allows the identification of a variety of individual characteristics that could influence a person's experience at work, shape their perceptions of their environment and their method and style of communication (Loden & Rosener 1991: 21; Jackson, May & Witney 1995). This broad view of diversity has stimulated two main approaches to management actions.

The first approach is one where actions are taken that acknowledge and value differences among people in the workplace (Hermon 1996: 427; Jamieson & O'Mara 1991). These actions are designed to manage a collective, all-inclusive mixture of differences and similarities along a particular dimension such as parental status or race. They can include sensitivity training, advisory panels and initiatives that manage people with different characteristics along a certain dimension. The broad view has stimulated a second approach involving actions that create a culture that values and appreciates differences between individuals and groups and requires systematic change efforts (Bowens et al. 1993).

In contrast, when diversity is defined in a narrow way it refers only to people with particular personal characteristics, such as gender, race or ethnicity. This view of diversity focuses on issues that arise from discrimination based on these personal characteristics. Cross et al. (1994: xxii) indicate that diversity focuses on 'issues of racism, sexism, heterosexism, classism, ableism, and other forms of discrimination at the individual, identity group and system levels'. This narrow view of diversity focuses actions on removing discrimination from the workplace. It encourages the development of policies that provide for equal treatment of members of different groups by making concessions so that employees with certain personal or domestic arrangements can assimilate into the prevailing employment patterns.

The approach to diversity management in Hong Kong reflects a narrow view of diversity that focuses on removing discrimination against particular groups. This approach can be partly explained by Hong Kong's economic and social contexts. These are examined in the first part of the chapter, while the background and requirements of the discrimination ordinances are examined in the second part. The third part reviews briefly the effect of the ordinances on management practices, and the final part — outlining trends and conclusions — highlights some of the challenges associated with diversity management in Hong Kong.

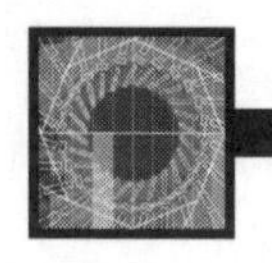

Context

Diversity is an integral part of Hong Kong economic and social life. Most people think of Hong Kong as an island. It is, but it is more than just one island — it is 236

islands and a piece of mainland, made up of Kowloon and the New Territories, bordering the south-eastern Chinese province of Guangdong. It is highly urbanised (notably on Hong Kong island and in Kowloon), but in other areas (such as the outlying islands) it is very sparsely populated. Hong Kong is now a Special Administrative Region (SAR) of the People's Republic of China. This means Hong Kong is part of China, but has its own laws and parliamentary body.

Although almost all of Hong Kong's population of approximately six and a half million people are ethnic Chinese (95 per cent) who display the persistence of Chinese traditions and value systems, Hong Kong has been strongly affected by Western influences, particularly British influences (Westwood, Ngo & Leung 1997: 47). The British systems of public administration were developed following the ceding of Hong Kong island to Britain in 1941 and the granting of a 99-year lease on the New Territories in 1898. The communist revolution in China in 1949 stimulated the transition of Hong Kong's trade-based economy to one based on manufacturing in which Western materialist, consumerist and individualistic values developed (Lau & Kuan 1988).

Despite the difficulty in estimating the nature of the beliefs, values and attitudes of the Hong Kong population, the Hong Kong social system exhibits a unique mixture of traditional Confucian and Taoist values and Western values (Westwood, Ngo & Leung 1997: 47). Westwood and Everett (1987: 187–202) found that although Hong Kong was a collectivist culture — with high power distance, weak uncertainty avoidance and a moderate degree of masculinity — individualistic attitudes and values were developing. The economic developments in Hong Kong also influenced the role and attitudes towards women, primarily because of the impact on the structure and function of labour markets and family (Westwood, Ngo & Leung 1997: 48–53).

The revolution in mainland China stimulated the migration of unorganised labour and a significant component of the capitalist class from Shanghai to Hong Kong. These refugees brought skills, capital and equipment and the stimulus for a fresh industrialising initiative (Haggard & Cheng 1987: 107). The growth in the manufacturing sector was accompanied by a rapid increase in the demand for labour that could not be met by the existing male labour force. As in other industrialising economies, women entered paid employment in increasing numbers. In Hong Kong the absolute number of women gainfully employed increased by 2.6 times between 1961 and 1981 and their participation rates increased from 36.8 per cent to 49.5 per cent (Westwood, Ngo & Leung 1997: 51). During the same period the modern nuclear family became more prevalent in Hong Kong, replacing the extended, patrilineal family (Yeung 1986: 235). Women married later and bore fewer children at a later age.

More recently, Hong Kong has developed from a manufacturing economy to the world's most service-oriented economy with high levels of foreign investment. In 1997 the service sector contributed 85.2 per cent of Hong Kong's gross domestic product (GDP) and employed 84 per cent of employees. Hong Kong's exports of services have grown strongly and they have exceeded domestic exports since 1994. In 1997 Hong Kong recorded a surplus of US$14.9 billion and in 1998 another surplus of US$11.4 billion (Department of Hong Kong Trade Development Council 1999). Although labour-intensive industries have shifted into South China, Hong Kong retains higher value-added functions such as procurement, product design, quality control, marketing and management. Hong Kong has become an information- and knowledge-based economy (Batson 1996: 39).

Foreign direct investment is strong in Hong Kong, particularly in the non-manufacturing sector. Foreign investment in manufacturing increased in 1997 by

5.5 per cent to US$6.5 billion. Japan (accounting for 41 per cent), the United States (21 per cent) and the Chinese mainland (6.8 per cent) were the most prominent investors in manufacturing in Hong Kong. Electronics received the largest share of investment in the manufacturing sector, amounting to 40 per cent of investment. Investment in high-tech industries is expected to grow as companies such as H & Q Asia Pacific, Motorola, Nortel, StarTV, Sybase, 3M and Vtech implement plans to invest in Hong Kong in the future.

The stock of foreign investment in the non-manufacturing sector was significantly greater than that in the manufacturing sector, amounting to US$87.4 billion at the end of 1997. The United Kingdom was the largest investor in this sector (accounting for 27 per cent). Banks and deposit-taking companies constituted the largest share of investment, accounting for one-third of investment in the non-manufacturing sector.

Hong Kong is the most important entrepot for the Chinese mainland with about 40 per cent of the mainland's foreign trade being handled in Hong Kong. It accounted for 11 per cent of the Chinese mainland's total trade in the first months of 1999. Hong Kong has been used as a regional base by multinational companies to manage their businesses in the Asia–Pacific, particularly the Chinese mainland. Countries with the largest number of regional offices in Hong Kong are the United States (479), Japan (456) and the United Kingdom (223). The International Chamber of Commerce established its base for Asian operations in Hong Kong in 1997 and the Bank of International Settlements (BIS) set up its Asia–Pacific regional office in 1998 (Department of Hong Kong Trade Development Council 1999).

The economy of Hong Kong has been undergoing major adjustment since the last quarter of 1997 in response to the regional financial crisis in Asia that commenced in 1997. The general economic conditions declined with a downturn in the stock-market, a decrease in property prices and an increase in unemployment. In 1998 real GDP fell by 5.1 per cent, private consumption contracted by 6.8 per cent and gross fixed capital formation declined by 6.1 per cent. The volume of retail sales declined in 1997–98 and the number of tourist arrivals declined by 16.7 per cent. However, the number of tourist arrivals grew by 13.4 per cent in the first quarter of 1999 (Department of Hong Kong Trade Development Council 1999).

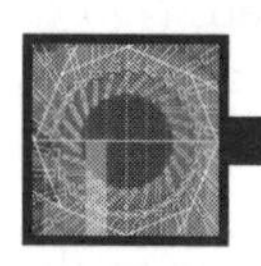

Labour force in Hong Kong

The labour force employed by Hong Kong firms is characterised by segregation along gender lines, increasing unemployment and the employment of significant numbers of people in mainland China. There are reports of a shortage of managerial skills.

Women represent a significant part of the labour force in Hong Kong. In mid-1999 they accounted for almost 40 per cent of the labour force (Census and Statistics Department 1999: 8). There is evidence of strong labour market segregation along industrial and occupational lines. Women are increasingly concentrated in service industries such as wholesale and retail trade, hotel and restaurant, community, social and personal services, and financial and business services. Although the dominance of manufacturing has declined, about 30 per cent of the female workforce is still engaged in this sector. In contrast, men are employed in a wider range of industries and dominate in the utilities, construction, transport, storage and communication sectors (Westwood, Ngo & Leung 1997: 67–71).

The changes in the distribution of the labour force across industries in Hong Kong are reflected in the distribution of men and women across occupations. Women are well represented in clerical, service and sales occupations and in the professional occupations of nursing and teaching. However, they are noticeably under-represented in administrative and managerial occupations (Westwood, Ngo & Leung 1997: 74–7). Cho (1987: 229) comments that sex segregation in the labour market is 'a reflection of the structure and mechanism of the labour market, and this in turn is a reflection of profit-making rationalism and of cultural tradition' — that is, the broader sexual division of labour in Hong Kong society.

Labour market conditions deteriorated during the 1997–99 period. The unemployment rate rose from 2.9 per cent during the December 1997–February 1998 period to 6.2 per cent for the January–March 1999 period. In June 1998 the government announced a number of initiatives designed to create more jobs, strengthen job-matching services and enhance further education and vocational training (Department of Hong Kong Trade Development Council 1999). The most significant rise in unemployment occurred in restaurants, wholesale/retail trades, manufacturing, import/export trade and business services, reflecting the weak performance of external trade and consumer spending. Although unemployment increased in finance, community, social and personal services, the rate was 'still at a low level' (www.info.gov.hk/hkecon).

About 97 300 Hong Kong residents are working in mainland China, predominantly in connection with manufacturing, commerce, restaurants and hotels and other business services. Hong Kong firms employ approximately five million people in China, mainly lowly skilled workers (Batson 1996: 38).

Ian Perkins from the Hong Kong General Chamber of Commerce claims that the skill level of the Hong Kong labour force is not keeping pace with the needs of the increasingly service-based economy. He states, 'There has been a huge influx of expatriates into Hong Kong because the demand is so great in the service sectors' (Batson 1996: 23). The lower level of English skills and understanding of Western business practices and a lack of analytical skills have resulted in a lack of home-grown managers in Hong Kong. This shortage is accentuated by Hong Kong firms preferring men over women in managerial/supervisory positions (de Leon & Ho 1994: 46–8). However, although local women are discriminated against, expatriate women managers appear to be given equal opportunity (Stening & Ngan 1997: 11–12).

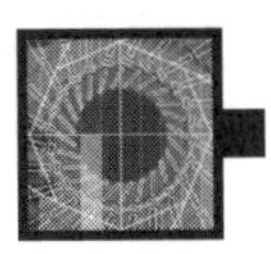

Anti-discrimination in Hong Kong: A narrow approach to diversity management

Background to anti-discrimination legislation in Hong Kong

The adoption of a narrow approach to diversity in Hong Kong reflects the actions of lobby groups and political and legal developments. The campaigns by women's groups for anti-discrimination legislation made little progress in Hong Kong until legal and political developments associated with the transfer of Hong Kong to China in 1997 influenced the government to abandon its opposition to the legislation. The Legislative Council became more democratic in 1991 when directly elected seats were introduced, and again in 1995 when all appointed seats were abolished. The increasing accountability of the legislators to the public stimulated their willingness to challenge established government policies, including a failure to address discrimination (Cheek-Milby 1995).

During the 1980s groups began campaigning in Hong Kong for the protection of the rights of women and disability groups through improved government services and policies (Tong 1997). Women's groups campaigned for the establishment of a Women's Commission and the adoption of the International Convention for the Elimination of All Forms of Discrimination Against Women (CEDAW). A coalition of 18 organisations formed the Campaign for a Women's Commission and for CEDAW in March 1992.

The government's response to this campaign was similar to that adopted in Australia during the early 1980s. Despite the government's earlier conclusion in 1991 that there was no discrimination against women, in 1993 it published a Green Paper (Hong Kong Government 1993) to consult the public on the question of equal opportunities for women and men. A study undertaken in 1994 revealed that discrimination against women was perceived to be common in public domains, particularly in employment. The popular impression that women were doing well in Hong Kong society was not supported by statistical analyses that demonstrated the existence of sexual inequality prevailing in educational attainment, pay differentials, occupational segregation, gender stereotypes and the division of domestic labour (Cheung 1997).

Women's groups envisaged the Women's Commission as a high-level office set up by the government with special responsibilities for representing the interests of women. The areas of concern for the Women's Commission were to include:

- the enactment of legislation protecting women from discrimination, including the adoption and the implementation of CEDAW
- sexual discrimination in the workplace
- social services, such as childcare, vocational training programs and health services
- women's images as projected by the media
- sexual violence such as rape, wife assault and sexual assault on children.

It was also anticipated that a complaints unit would be set up in the Commission to provide support and advice to women who seek advice or help (Campaign for a Women's Commission and for CEDAW March 1993, cited in Cheung 1997: 2–3).

The political transition of 1997 and the increased assertiveness of the Legislative Council enhanced the campaign for women's rights. The repeal of the legal prohibition of female inheritance of land in the New Territories in 1994 encouraged women to take on the broader issue of discrimination against women. The Hong Kong Women's Coalition for Beijing '95 (1997) drew up a plan of action for the government and fought for the introduction of legislation covering age and sex discrimination, equal pay for equal work, full pay for maternity leave, and the extension of CEDAW to Hong Kong (Cheung 1997: 4).

Two bills were proposed in 1994 by Anna Wu. A comprehensive Equal Opportunities Bill sought to prevent discrimination on the grounds of sex, marital status, pregnancy, family responsibility, disability, sexuality, age, race, and political and religious conviction. The Human Rights and Equal Opportunities Commission Bill proposed the establishment of a broad-based human rights commission with powers similar to those of the Human Rights and Equal Opportunities Commission (HREOC) in Australia. Although the Bill was defeated in the Legislative Council, it forced the government to introduce its own legislation against sex discrimination and disability discrimination and to actively consider the extension of CEDAW to Hong Kong (Cheung 1997: 4).

The government introduced two specific bills: the Sex Discrimination Ordinances (SDO) and Disability Discrimination Ordinances (DDO). Later in 1997 it enacted the Family Status Discrimination Ordinance (FSDO). A number of amendments were

made to these bills, and as a consequence, the provisions of the ordinances contained minor errors and inconsistencies. These errors and inconsistencies are now being dealt with by the EOC.

The ordinances have not entirely met the expectations of the activist groups. These groups were concerned about the number of exemptions included in the ordinances, the lack of legislation against age discrimination and the failure of the SDO to specifically address the needs of women. In addition, the government was responsible for the administration of and reporting on the implementation of CEDAW, and the EOC has responsibility for the development of women's policies and coordination of services (Cheung 1997: 5).

Discrimination legislation

Three pieces of legislation are designed to prevent discrimination in Hong Kong: the Sex Discrimination Ordinance (SDO), the Disability Discrimination Ordinance (DDO) and the Family Status Discrimination Ordinance (FSDO). The SDO enacted on 14 July 1995 and the DDO enacted on 3 August 1995 render unlawful acts that discriminate against persons on the grounds of gender, marital status, pregnancy or disability. Victimisation, sexual harassment and vilification of persons with a disability are also unlawful. The scope of the DDO is the same as the SDO; however, unlike the SDO, discrimination may also take place on the basis of the disability of an associate of an employee — that is, a spouse, a cohabitee, a relative, a carer, or a person in a business, sporting or recreational relationship (Lau 1996: 39). The SDO is based on the United Kingdom Sex Discrimination Act 1995 (Lau 1996: 38) and the anti-discrimination legislation in Australia (Cheung 1997: 1).

The ordinances stipulate it is illegal to discriminate either directly or indirectly. Direct discrimination refers to treating one person less favourably than another person in comparable circumstances because of a personal characteristic such as marital status, sex, or pregnancy. Indirect discrimination refers to applying the same treatment to men and women, people with different marital status and persons who are pregnant or not, but is in practice discriminatory in its effect. For instance, including a minimum height requirement could exclude a large proportion of women job applicants. This would constitute indirect discrimination unless there was justification for a minimum height requirement in the particular job. Sexual harassment refers to any unwelcome sexual behaviour in circumstances where a reasonable person would have anticipated that the harassed person would have been offended, humiliated or intimidated.

The ordinances, through codes of practice apply, to employment relationships in both the public and private sectors, the employment of contract workers, selection of partners in partnerships, membership in workers' or employers' organisations, the conferral of professional or trade authorisations or qualifications, employment-related training, the provision of services by employment agencies and the appointment of commission agents.

The ordinances apply to all employers, qualifying bodies, persons with the provision of vocational training, employment agencies, partnerships, trade unions, educational establishments, clubs and the government (Lau 1996: 38). These organisations are required to observe the ordinances unless employees do their work wholly or mainly outside Hong Kong. Small employers, those with fewer than 10 employees, were given three years' exemption. However, on 14 July 1998 and 3 August 1998, these employers came under the SDO and the DDO respectively.

Small employers, like all other employers, are required to observe the employment-related provisions of these ordinances. These provisions make it unlawful for a person to discriminate against another person in recruitment, training, promotion or dismissal. All employers, irrespective of size and structure, are also required to apply an equal opportunities policy incorporating a consistent set of selection criteria in recruitment, promotion, staff benefits termination and other policy areas.

Certain exceptions apply under the SDO. These include the situation in which being a man is a genuine occupational qualification for a job — that is, where the essential nature of the job calls for a man by reason of physiology or authenticity in dramatic performance or other entertainment, so that in either case the essential nature of the job would be materially different if carried out by a woman. Another exception would be where the job needs to be held by a man for decency or privacy. The exception also extends to the job being done inside the private home (Lau 1996: 39).

The Equal Opportunities Commission (EOC), established on 20 May 1996, is the statutory body established to implement these ordinances. The EOC seeks to create, with the support of the community, an environment in which there is no barrier to equal opportunities and no discrimination. The EOC seeks to achieve its purpose by:

- promoting equality of opportunity between men and women, between persons with or without a disability, and irrespective of family status
- eliminating discrimination on the ground of gender, disability or family status through legislative provisions, administrative measures and public education
- eliminating sexual harassment, and harassment and vilification of persons with a disability.

The ordinances empower the EOC to investigate complaints related to any act made unlawful by the ordinances and to issue enforcement notices. It is also empowered to issue codes of practice on employment. These codes of practice provide guidelines for employers on fair and unlawful practices in various aspects of employment related to SDO and DDO. These codes came into operation on 20 December 1996 and are particularly important in assisting employers to observe the provisions of the ordinances in Hong Kong where these discrimination ordinances are new areas of law. The codes deal in general terms with discrimination on the grounds specified in the ordinances. In applying the codes, employers may take into account consideration of the size and structure of their organisations. For instance, small organisations may require simplified procedures and, although they may not be able to carry out all of the codes' recommendations, they are required to ensure their practices comply with the three ordinances and the spirit of the codes. The codes may be used as guidance for employers as to what steps it is reasonable to take to prevent their employees from committing unlawful acts under the ordinances.

The EOC is also empowered to review the working of the ordinances and recommend the necessary amendments to achieve the effective functioning of the EOC. In addition to preventing and managing acts of discrimination, the EOC is empowered to change discriminatory attitudes through public education and publicity programs. The EOC became operational in September 1996.

The EOC has developed five main strategies to promote its vision. These strategies are:

- to secure compliance and reform through legislative means
- to promote education to raise awareness and achieve change
- to strengthen communication with community organisations to promote participation
- to build corporate partnerships to encourage practices and prevention
- to conduct research to guide our forward direction.

The EOC launched a funding program in 1996–97 designed to encourage community organisations to carry out inter-district or territory-wide activities in promoting equal opportunities. The program was offered again in 1997–98 and in a revised format in 1999–2000.

The EOC is empowered to investigate complaints filed by the public and it can require particular parties to attend conferences to resolve a case by conciliation. Where conciliation fails, the EOC can provide assistance in respect of proceedings before the district court. The EOC can also issue enforcement notices against anyone deemed to have committed any discriminatory act or sexual harassment. If a person continues to commit a discriminatory act or if, during the preceding five years, that person became subject to an enforcement notice or was found by the district court to have committed such a contravention, the EOC might apply to the district court for an injunction to restrain that person from committing further unlawful acts (Lau 1996: 39).

According to the SDO, an act regarded as either directly or indirectly discriminatory, or as sexual harassment or victimisation, may render the perpetrator and his or her employer liable. Employers are held liable for the actions of their employees in the course of their employment, whether or not these were performed with the employers' knowledge or approval. Similarly, an act carried out by a person as an agent for another may render both the agent and the principal liable.

Although failure to observe any of the recommendations in the codes of practice does not automatically make a person liable, if a person is accused of discrimination, sexual harassment or victimisation, failure to implement the recommendations outlined in the codes could be used as evidence in courts of law. This applies to employers, employees, agents and principals.

The remedies for the contravention of the discrimination ordinances include declaration, order for employment/re-employment/promotion, order for damages including compensation for injury to feelings or punitive damages, and/or an order to avoid contact which is inconsistent with discrimination, ordinances. There is no limit to the amount of damages to be awarded in the case of disability discrimination, and the limitation period is 24 months from when the act took place or when it was reported, whichever is the later. With regard to the SDO, the limitation period is the same; however, the remedies differ. The district court is empowered to order remedies which will be obtainable from the high court and there is a maximum limit of HK$150 000 (A$30 000) in case of an award of damages.

The ordinances place the burden of proof of harassment on the victim; however, lawyers point out that if the facts suggest there has been discrimination and an employer cannot rebut this evidence, then judgement is likely to go against the company (Forbes 1996: 22).

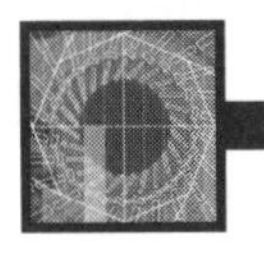

Impact of the ordinances

It was anticipated the ordinances would have a limited impact initially. Many in the business community are cynical about the ordinances, claiming they are 'Primarily symbolic, at worst a potential bureaucratic nuisance that could interfere with Hong Kong's mythic efficiency. Few think it will lead to a seismic shift in companies [sic] hiring policies or work practices' (Field 1996: 8). Ian McCormick, who is actively involved in the development of guidelines issued to members of the Hong Kong General Chamber of Commerce and the Employers' Federation, believes 'the impact will be

quite small at first, particularly for companies that have good human resources practices. Many of these companies will fall into line with the legislation. If you [sic] have policies and practices in place you won't have to do much' (Forbes 1996: 22). Lau, however, considers 'The Sex Discrimination Ordinance and the Disability Discrimination Ordinance represent a significant development in labour-related legislation in Hong Kong' (Lau 1996: 39). Hong Kong traditionally has practised a policy of positive non-intervention in human resource practices (Shaw, Kirkbride, Fisher & Tang 1995: 22–39), and the discrimination legislation represents a divergence from this tradition.

The number of enquiries and complaints received by the EOC indicates that the most frequent complaints relate to discrimination in employment. Most complaints for investigation and conciliation were in the employment field and on the grounds of disability. Between 20 September 1996 and 30 June 1999, 1265 complaints were received and 735 (58 per cent) were followed up or investigated (EOC 1999). More than 61 per cent of these complaints referred to disability discrimination, 36 per cent referred to sex discrimination and 3 per cent to family status discrimination. In circumstances where conciliation occurred in the employment area, more than two-thirds were successful in the area of sex discrimination, 43 per cent in the disability area and 60 per cent in the family status area (EOC 1999).

The EOC regularly monitors recruitment advertisements and works closely with publishers, advertisers and employment agencies to advise them of their legal responsibilities. The EOC believes self-regulation is the most effective way to eliminate discrimination in this area, and reports that as a consequence of their educational and publicity efforts, there has been a significant drop in the number of discriminatory advertisements in the print and media. The number fell from a high of 37 per cent in December 1996 to less than 1 per cent in the period 1 April 1997 to 31 March 1998 (EOC 1998a: 15).

The EOC is keenly aware of the need to generate awareness and public understanding of equal opportunities, discrimination issues and the ordinances, as well as its role and functions. The Baseline Surveys on equal opportunities on the basis of gender (EOC 1997a), on public attitudes towards people with disabilities (EOC 1998b) and on the employment situation of persons with a disability (EOC 1997b) were conducted to collect information on these issues.

The approach to diversity management in Hong Kong is consistent with the narrow view proposed by Cross et al. (1994). The legislation has focused on issues of sexism, disability and family status and is concerned primarily with removing discrimination from Hong Kong society and particularly the workplace. The EOC recognises that a broader view of diversity management is necessary. In order to promote this view it is targeting the younger generation through educational campaigns. They believe the younger generation 'will be the catalyst for change in shifting traditional and preconceived values. Promoting equal opportunities from childhood will cultivate new sets of values, based on respect for human dignity and empathy for those who are less privileged than they are' (EOC 1998a: 39–40).

In addition, having reviewed the complaints filed by individuals under the three ordinances, the EOC believes systemic discrimination exists in some of Hong Kong's established employment and educational practices. The EOC is now planning to tackle issues of systemic discrimination as well as dealing with individual complaints (EOC 1998a: 40). This concern with systemic discrimination reinforces a broader view of diversity.

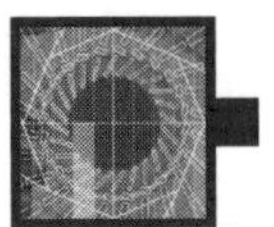

Conclusions

Attempts to manage diversity through the removal of discrimination by means of legislation face a number of challenges in Hong Kong. The model of human rights legislation on which this legislation is based is not consistent with the traditional Chinese way of thinking in which individuals do not have inalienable rights and in which confrontation should be avoided. The strong stereotypes, particularly gender stereotypes, evident in Hong Kong will also impede the removal of discrimination from the labour market. In addition, the legislation has limited coverage and the government relies on self-regulation to prevent discrimination on the grounds of personal characteristics such as age. A further challenge involves the pressures imposed by the urgent need for the Hong Kong economy to adjust to the financial crisis.

Concept of justice in the Hong Kong socio-cultural context

The anti-discrimination ordinances in Hong Kong are based on concepts of individual rights and Western models of human rights legislation. The concepts involved in these laws are unfamiliar to the Hong Kong public. According to Kuan (1992), 'in traditional Chinese thinking, law was the instrument of the ruler and was therefore primarily public law consisting of penal rules. The ruler used law as commands (or orders) backed by sanction (or threat of sanctions) to control and regulate the behaviour of his subjects ...' (Kuan 1992: 162). He further noted that 'legal philosophy in traditional China placed a strong emphasis on the penal aspects of law. This emphasis resulted in a belief in the efficacy of severe penalties to prevent crime or in the appropriateness of harsh punishment as retribution' (Kuan 1992: 165).

Similarly, views of justice in Hong Kong reflect the hierarchical social relationships between perpetrator and victim. Chiu (1991) found the fulfilment of role expectations to be a major criterion of justice judgement. There is a strong belief that individuals do not have inborn inalienable rights, but possess rights as a consequence of society rewarding the individual for good deeds. In addition, the traditional non-confrontational approach was widely adopted to cope with injustice.

The general public in Hong Kong is ignorant about legal matters and many find it difficult to understand the law and the legal system in Hong Kong. Opinions are often formed on impressions and hearsay when individuals have no distinct knowledge about specific aspects of the system (Lau & Kuan 1988, cited in Cheung 1997: 6).

> Thus, the SDO and DDO which provide for recourse for discrimination through civil proceedings in the court and complaint based conciliation by the EOC are totally foreign to the general public and concern groups alike.

Strong stereotypes, particularly gender stereotypes

Despite the participation of women in the economy, gender roles and identities are strong and lag behind the social realities. There is evidence that men and women in Hong Kong are expected to behave differently, with stereotypes for men being aggressive, ambitious, decisive and hardworking, while women are expected to be affectionate, considerate, and mindful of household chores and child minding (Lau & Wan 1987, cited in Cheung et al. 1997: 211). During the 1980s it was found male workers were preferred in certain industries such as transport, communications, public utilities and finance, while women were preferred in wholesale and retail trade,

and the hotel and restaurant industry. Similarly, men were preferred in managerial and supervisory occupations, while women were preferred in clerical occupations (Ho 1987, cited in Cheung et al. 1997: 221).

These gender stereotypes persisted into the 1990s in Hong Kong as revealed by the *Baseline Survey on Equal Opportunities on the Basis of Gender in Hong Kong* which was commissioned by the Equal Opportunities Commission in 1996. The survey was conducted by the Gender Research Programme and the Social Indicators Programme of the Hong Kong Institute of Asia–Pacific Studies, Chinese University of Hong Kong. The objectives of the survey were to:

- collect information about the public's perception of gender roles and stereotyping
- collect information on the public's perception and experience of equality or discrimination between men and women in the media, family, education, work and community participation
- establish baseline subjective indicators reflecting equal opportunities or discrimination on the basis of gender
- collect information about the public's knowledge of the establishment of the Equal Opportunities Commission.

A random sample of 2020 Hong Kong Chinese aged 16 or over was conducted and its socio-demographic characteristics coincided with the general population as reported in the 1996 census. More than 43 per cent were men, 51.5 per cent were women; about 66 per cent were married, 25.1 per cent never married, 8.9 per cent were either widowed, divorced or separated. Nearly one-third had a primary or no education, about one-half had a secondary education and one-eighth complete tertiary education. More than 14 per cent were classified as low income, earning less than HK$6000 a month, 53.3 per cent had a monthly income between HK$6000 and HK$14 000, and 32.5 per cent earned HK$15 000 or more a month.

The respondents were very gender stereotypic: each gender held more rigid norms for their own gender than the other gender. In general, respondents were more aware of male than female stereotypes in the media. Gender differences were also noted in respondents' level of awareness towards the presence of media gender stereotypes. More women than men were aware that the media portray women as dependent on men and the family as the best place for women. On the other hand, more men than women agree that the media often describe men as belonging to the workplace, protecting women and capable of making important decisions.

About half the respondents were dissatisfied with the media's reporting on sexual inequality, with only 27.3 per cent being satisfied. In general, respondents thought that both the print media and television tended to discriminate against women more than men, with the print media being more discriminatory. There were no gender differences in these perceptions. About 66 per cent of the respondents agreed that the government should legislate to curb discrimination against women in the media. Among the respondents of the survey, males had on average more than one extra year of education; however, for those aged 16–24 years, women had 0.85 years more education than men. Women still perceive a slight parental prejudice against education. Although an egalitarian attitude was adopted towards the distribution of housework, there was evidence of gender-biased attitudes regarding childcare responsibilities. A majority of respondents believe women do a better job looking after children. About 60 per cent of respondents still hold stereotypical views about their sons and their daughters.

All respondents were asked if inequality in the labour market existed. More than 60 per cent of the respondents perceive difficulties encountered by married women

in balancing work and family responsibilities, and more than 70 per cent perceived a gender gap in pay as common. Perceptions regarding the prevalence of women being dismissed because of pregnancy, sexual harassment at work and specification of sex in advertisements were widespread.

Therefore, a major factor that will impede the removal of discrimination from the labour market in Hong Kong is the traditional attitudes towards sex roles and the lower status generally accorded to women's roles. Cheung (1997: 8) states that 'agents of socialization via family models, school teachers and textbooks, and the mass media ... have been slow to incorporate the objective changes women have undergone in the socio-economic domains'.

Knowledge of the role of the EOC appears to be widespread. When the survey was conducted in 1996, more than a third of respondents claimed to know about the EOC and almost half of these respondents knew about the hotline service and the functions of the EOC. More than half of the respondents perceive sex discrimination as a common occurrence, with more women than men having this perception (EOC 1997a). Another survey was conducted in 1998, and although the results are not available, early indications 'show that awareness of the EOC has now increased to 85 per cent' (EOC 1998a: 17).

Similarly, it is widely believed in Hong Kong that people with disabilities are discriminated against in terms of employment opportunities, salary and promotion prospects. Surveys of more than 2000 Hong Kong residents in 1998 revealed 'employers are extremely or relatively unwilling to hire persons with a disability' (EOC 1999: 3). Ninety per cent of these respondents considered persons with disabilities had fewer or far fewer opportunities than persons without disabilities (EOC 1999: 19). Further almost 80 per cent of respondents believed people with disabilities are severely or somewhat discriminated against on the grounds of salary and promotion prospects (EOC 1999: 3).

Therefore, strongly held stereotypes still exist in Hong Kong. Although the strong patriarchal traditions of Chinese culture have been modified by urban lifestyles in Hong Kong, the family still remains the central focus of the society. The family also continues to be the primary reference group with which individuals identify, and the kinship network continues to function as an informal welfare system (Leon & Ho 1994: 43–5). This focus on the family influences perceptions of discrimination and the appropriate methods to manage differences in the workplace.

Limited grounds for discrimination

The management of diversity in Hong Kong is influenced by the nature of the ordinances. Hong Kong does not have any laws barring discrimination on the basis of race, age, religious beliefs or sexual orientation, but some members of the Legislative Council are trying to develop support to push through a private member's bill to cover these (Forbes 1996). The Hong Kong Government relies on self-regulation to remove these forms of discrimination.

Particular government departments are responsible for developing guidelines to prevent discrimination in employment on the basis of age, race and sexual orientation. These guidelines establish best practice, which employers and employment agencies are encouraged to follow on a voluntary basis to the best of their ability. For instance, the Education and Manpower [sic] Bureau has issued guidelines for employers on ways to eliminate age discrimination by using consistent selection criteria, adhering to equal pay for equal work, advertising without discrimination and using policies and criteria that prevent age discrimination in appraisal, promotion, training, dismissal, redundancy and grievance procedures (Education and Manpower Bureau 1998). However, in Hong Kong where the Confucian values demand respect for older family members, it is usual practice for families to care for their ageing relatives.

Discussions with a number of managers in Hong Kong indicate that many managers are unfamiliar with the Western notion of discrimination and diversity management. They see differentiating between persons of different nationalities and gender as part of the way business is done in Hong Kong. The population is predominantly Chinese, with managerial positions in multinationals being filled by expatriates or family members. For much of the postwar period the economy experienced a shortage of labour and women have been able to fill lower-level managerial positions in areas such as human resources (de Leon & Ho 1994). They are unfamiliar with the concepts of indirect and systemic discrimination and perceive differentiating between men and women as the way business is done.

Adjustment to the financial crisis

Since the onset of the Asian financial crisis in July 1997, the Hong Kong economy has been beset by a contraction of gross domestic product, private consumption expenditure, gross domestic fixed capital formation and in the global demand for commodities. The sluggish demand from neighbouring markets is also expected to lead to a drop in exports. The unemployment rate is expected to continue to rise across a range of occupations and groups, and wage levels will continue to decline (Leung & Lucas 1999: 34–6). Consequently, Hong Kong companies 'will have to get even meaner and more cost efficient' (Fung, cited in Leung & Lucas 1999: 41).

In these circumstances, it is unlikely organisations are going to give the issue of the removal of discrimination high priority. Instead, they will focus on corporate downsizing, resulting in more layoffs. They will also continue to introduce pay cuts.

Interviews with 20 human resource managers in Hong Kong during 1999 indicated they were particularly concerned with cutting costs and maintaining morale among staff. They considered the issue of discrimination in the workplace peripheral to the central business concerns that needed to be managed. During this period it was not possible to obtain information about employment practices that sought to build a culture that represented a broader view of diversity.

Summary

A narrow view to managing diversity has been adopted in Hong Kong. However, the enactment of ordinances that prohibit discrimination on the grounds of gender, disability and family status represent a significant step in an environment in which the government has traditionally taken a non-interventionist role in the employment area. The coverage of the legislation also represents an important step in an environment in which businesses are typically small and Chinese-owned.

However, the ability of the legislation to remove discrimination from the workplace is constrained by a number of social and economic factors. The Western concept of discrimination and its management through complaints does not fit easily with the Confucian values that underpin Hong Kong society. Similarly, the central role of the family shapes expectations and perceptions of appropriate social roles for men and women in Hong Kong. Despite this there is a widespread perception that women and men are discriminated against in employment in Hong Kong. Economic restructuring and the need to manage during a recession for the first time in many

years have taken precedence over managing diversity or removing discrimination from the workplace.

The mandating of certain standards of behaviour by the ordinances is a very important step in indicating to all employers in Hong Kong that discriminatory behaviour is unacceptable. The intention of the EOC to develop measures to remove systemic discrimination also indicates that additional steps could be taken in the future to change the expectations and perceptions of the younger generation in Hong Kong.

References

Batson, B. 1996. 'People, Politics and Profit'. *The China Business Review.* Washington, Nov.–Dec., 23.

Bowens, H., Merenivitch, J., Johnson, P. L., James, A. R. & McFadden-Bryant, D. J. 1993. 'Managing Cultural Diversity toward True Multiculturalism: Some Knowledge from the Black Perspective'. In Sims, R. R. & Dennehy, R. E. (Eds). *Diversity and Differences in Organisations.* Connecticut: Quorum Books.

Census & Statistics Department. 1999. *Hong Kong Monthly Digest of Statistics*, August.

Cheek-Milby, K. 1995. *A Legislature Comes of Age: Hong Kong's Search for Influence and Identity.* Oxford: Oxford University Press.

Cheung, F. M. (Ed.). 1997. *Engendering Hong Kong Society: A Gender Perspective of Women's Status.* Hong Kong: The Chinese University Press.

Cheung, F. M., Lai, L. L., Au, K.-C. & Ngai, S.-Y. S. N. 1997. 'Gender Role Identity, Stereotypes and Attitudes in Hong Kong'. In Cheung, F. M. (Ed.). *Engendering Hong Kong Society: A Gender Perspective of Women's Status.* Hong Kong: The Chinese University Press.

Cheung, F. M. 1997. 'Hong Kong's Anti-discrimination Legislation: Social Context, Philosophy and Challenges of Implementation'. Seminar on Equal Opportunities Law in International and Comparative Perspective, Hong Kong.

Chiu, C. Y. 1991. 'Role Expectation as the Principal Criterion Injustice Judgement among Hong Kong Chinese Students'. *Journal of Psychology* 125: 557–65.

Cho, H. 1987. 'Women's Participation and Their Status in the Economy'. In ESCAP, Social Development Division (Ed.). *Women's Economic Participation in Asia and the Pacific.* Bangkok: Economic and Social Commission for Asia and the Pacific, United Nations.

Cross, E., Kat, J. H., Miller, F. A. & Seashore, E. 1994. *The Promise of Diversity.* Burr Ridge, Ill: Urwin Professional Publishing.

de Leon, C. T. & Ho, S. 1994. 'The Third Identity of Modern Chinese Women: Women Managers in Hong Kong'. In Adler, N. J. & Izraeli, D. N. (Eds). *Competitive Frontiers: Women Managers in a Global Economy.* Cambridge, Mass: Blackwell Business.

Department of Hong Kong Trade Development Council. 1999. http://www.tdc.org.hk/main/economic.htm.

Education and Manpower Bureau. 1998. *Practical Guidelines for Employers on Eliminating Age Discrimination in Employment.* Hong Kong: Education and Manpower Bureau Government Secretariat.

Equal Opportunities Commission. 1997a. *A Baseline Survey of Equal Opportunities on the Basis of Gender in Hong Kong 1996–1997.* Hong Kong: EOC Research Report No. 1.

Equal Opportunities Commission. 1997b. *A Baseline Survey on Employment Situation of Persons with a Disability in Hong Kong 1997.* Hong Kong: EOC Research Report No. 3.

Equal Opportunities Commission. 1998a. *Equal Opportunities Commission Annual Report 1997/98.* Hong Kong: Equal Opportunities Commission.

Equal Opportunities Commission. 1998b. *A Baseline Survey on Public Attitudes Towards Persons with a Disability 1998*. Hong Kong: EOC Research Report No. 2.

Equal Opportunities Commission. 1999. *Statistics on Enquiries and Complaints*. Hong Kong: Equal Opportunities Commission.

Field, C. 1996. 'Some First Steps Are Taken in Hong Kong'. *Worldbusiness*. New York, September/October.

Forbes, A. 1996. 'Spotlight Turned on Discrimination and Secrets'. *Asian Business*, Hong Kong.

Frazee, V. 1997. 'Little Change Is Expected in Hong Kong'. *Workforce*, Costa Mee, July.

Gilbert, J. A., Stead, B. A. & Ivancevich, J. M. 1999. 'Diversity Management: A New Organisational Paradigm'. *Journal of Business Ethics*, August: 61–76.

Haggard, S. & Chen, T-J. 1987. 'State and Foreign Capital in the East Asian NICs'. In Deyo, F. C. (Ed.). *The Political Economy of the New Asian Industrialisation*. Ithaca, NY: Cornell University Press.

Hermon, M. V. 1996. 'Building a Shared Understanding and Commitment to Managing Diversity'. *Journal of Business Communication* 33(4): 427–42.

Hong Kong Government. 1993. *Green Paper on Equal Opportunities for Women and Men*. Hong Kong: Government Printer.

Hong Kong Women's Coalition for Beijing '95. 1997. 'Alternative Report on Women in Hong Kong'. In Cheung, F. M. (Ed.). *Engendering Hong Kong Society: A Gender Perspective on Women's Status*. Hong Kong: The Chinese University of Hong Kong.

Jackson, S. E, May, K. & Witney, K. 1995. 'Diversity in Decision Making Teams'. In Guo, R. A. & Salas, E. (Eds). *Team Decisonmaking Effectiveness in Organisations*. San Francisco: Jossey-Bass: 204–61.

Jamieson, D. & O'Mara, J. 1991. *Managing Workforce 2000*. San Francisco: Jossey-Bass.

Kuan, H. C. 1992. 'Legal Culture: The Challenge of Modernization'. In Lau, S. K., Lee, M. K., Wan, P. S. & Womg, S. L. (Eds). *Indicators of Social Development: Hong Kong 1990*. Hong Kong: Hong Kong Institute of Asia Pacific Studies, The Chinese University of Hong Kong.

Lau, V. 1996. 'Anti-discrimination Legislation in Hong Kong'. *International Commercial Litigation*, London, June.

Lau, S. K. & Kuan, H. C. 1988. *The Ethos of the Hong Kong Chinese*. Hong Kong: The Chinese University Press.

Leung, J. & Lucas, L 1999. 'Priced out of the Market'. *Asian Business*, Hong Kong, March: 34–41.

Loden, M. & Rosener, J. 1991. *Workforce America*. Homewood, Ill: Business One Urwin.

Petersen, C 1997. 'Anti-discrimination in Hong Kong: An Overview'. Seminar on Equal Opportunities Law in International and Comparative Perspective, Hong Kong.

Shaw, J. B., Kirkbride, P. S., Fisher, C. D. & Tang, S. F. Y. 1995. 'Human Resource Practices in Hong Kong and Singapore: The Impact of Political Forces and Imitation Processes', *Asia Pacific Journal of Human Resources* 33(1): 22–39.

Stening, B. & Ngan, E. F. 1997. 'Cultural Context of Human Resource Management in East Asia'. *Asia Pacific, Journal of Human Resources* 35(2): 3–15.

Tong, F. K. S. 1997. 'Implementing the Disability Discrimination Ordinance in Hong Kong: An Overview'. Seminar on Hong Kong Equal Opportunities Law in International and Comparative Perspective, Hong Kong.

Westwood, R. I. & Everett, J. E. 1987. 'Cultures Consequences: A Methodology for Comparative Management in South-East Asia?'. *Asia-Pacific Journal of Management* 4(3): 187–202.

Westwood, R. I., Ngo, H.-Y. & Leung, S.-M. 1997. 'The Politics of Opportunity: Gender and Work in Hong Kong, Part 1'. In Cheung, F. M. (Ed.). *Engendering Hong Kong Society*. Hong Kong: The Chinese University Press.

Yeung, D. W. T. 1986. 'The Changing Family System in Hong Kong'. In Kwan, A. Y. & Chan, D. (Eds). *Hong Kong Society: A Reader*. Hong Kong: Hong Kong Writers' and Publishers' Co-operative: 231–50.

Chapter 5

India

Lynne Bennington and Sugumar Mariappanadar

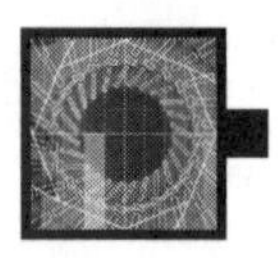

Introduction

The sources of diversity in employment are many and varied, but in India they relate primarily to gender, ethnicity, caste, religion and child labour. At the outset it is important to understand that the referent ideology of Hinduism sees that all men are born unequal with unequal capacities in order to perform functions of unequal importance (Dhesi 1998). Therefore, even though the state has a secular value system, the religious ideology is still deeply embedded. Tummala has captured one major aspect of the path India has been following with respect to the management of diversity in stating that India, 'in an effort to transform an essentially unequal and hierarchical society into a Sovereign Socialist Secular Democratic Republic has over the past 50 years embarked upon a serious measure of "reservations" to undo institutionalized social discrimination practiced over the millennia' (1999: 495).

Two events in particular during the past decade have made the issue of diversity management in India a topic of current interest. The first was the deregulation of foreign investment which occurred in 1991, allowing up to 100 per cent foreign equity in some deregulated industries (Ratnam 1998). This has made India an attractive country for investment owing to the availability of skilled labour, managerial personnel who are adaptable to Western-style practices, the use of English in business and government, and an established legal system based on British jurisprudence (Gopinath 1998). The second and ongoing issue is that International Labour Organisation (ILO) standards have assumed major importance in the global negotiations about trade, starting from the Uruguay Round to the recent Seattle talks, causing some concern to governments in developing countries, including India. Some of debate about labour standards relates to issues of human rights and diversity management.

In fact, a number of developing countries have chosen not to ratify the so-called core ILO standards relating to freedom of association, right to collective bargaining, the prohibition of forced labour, equality of treatment and non-discrimination in employment, and fixation of minimum wages (Mitra & Kaushal 1998). The concern has been that these labour standards would reduce their international competitiveness and cause them greater problems. Of the seven core labour conventions, India has ratified those concerning forced labour, equal remuneration and discrimination. India has focused on making its labour laws more flexible in order to attract greater foreign capital, but the concern has been whether this has been at the expense of labour standards (Mitra & Kaushal 1998). Heggade (1998) states that if the labour standards were introduced many employers would lose the apparent comparative advantage of hiring women and children and would therefore replace them with adult males thus causing unemployment among female and child workers.

World Trade Organisation pressures and the opening up of the Indian economy to foreign investment provide only part of the context for this discussion. However, the remainder of the picture is even more complex in that it is arguable that an unrivalled level of diversity exists in India (Frazee 1998). This makes workforce diversity in India a major challenge and opportunity for human resource management (Ratnam & Chandra 1996). Indian organisations have been categorised into Western industrialised firms; hybrid firms (which are family-dominated medium to large enterprises that often collaborate on joint ventures with Western firms) and indigenous firms (which consist of a large mass of small to medium enterprises, often as ancillaries to the former two categories of enterprises and usually proprietorial or family managed)

(Gopinath 1998). To understand the issue of diversity management in India, however, most of the discussion will focus on public sector organisations, which is where the government emphasis has occurred. The topic will also be broader than that normally discussed in respect of Western countries, however, owing to the issues of child labour and reservation of positions for particular classes of people.

Prior to examining some of these issues, the economic system, demography, culture, the caste system and literacy rates will be overviewed. An outline of the legal environment will precede a discussion of equal opportunity for women, sexual harassment, child labour and older workers. The final sections of the chapter will deal with legislative compliance, typical and best practices of companies, what multinational corporations (MNCs) should know, and our conclusions.

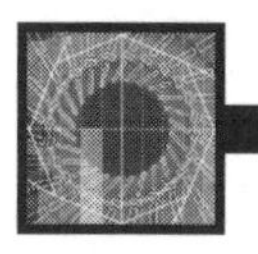

Context

Economic system

The economic system has been described as a 'mixed economy' as opposed to a planned or market economy (Mishra & Mohammed 1994). Although India has the largest middle class of any country in the world, per capita income remains at about US$400 per year, making India attractive for foreign investors. Labour in India is considerably cheaper than in Western developed countries, but is also cheaper than Korea and Mexico, with a production worker in India costing about US$1 per day (Anonymous 1998).

Of the 311 million in the labour force, nearly 27 million are in the organised sector, of which about 18 million are employed in the government sector (Jain & Ratnam 1994: 23). Only in a few states is private sector employment significant; for example, Maharashtra, West Bengal, Gujarat, Tamilnadu and Uttar Pradesh account for about 50 per cent of all private sector employment (Dasgupta 1994).

While the economy is largely agrarian, and substantial numbers also work in the informal sector, around 30 per cent of the adult labour force is engaged in industrial work (Lawler, Jain, Ratnam & Atmiyandana 1995). It is the traditional industries which account for about 54 per cent of employment while Khadi and Village Industries (those using traditional technology) account for about 12.5 per cent of employment (Singh, cited in Raghavan, Sharma & Sekhar 1994).

Demography

India is not only the seventh largest country in the world (Government of India 2000a) but is one of the most populous countries, with an estimated population in mid-1996 of 956 million (Bishop & McNamara 1998). Estimates vary because statistics from the 2001 census will not be processed for some time (Raman 1999). However, with its current growth rate, the population is likely to exceed that of China by the middle of the next century (Adlakha 1997).

Just over a quarter of the population lives in the urban areas (Government of India 2000a), and over one-third of the population is estimated to be below the poverty line (The World Bank 1997). However, somewhere between 200 and 300 million are thought to be middle class (Ghosh & Roy 1997). The average earnings of low castes, middle castes and Muslims are about 50 per cent of those of high castes (Dhesi 1998).

India is particularly complex from the perspective of size as well as its political, racial, ethnic, religious and other cultural differences. It is divided into 25 states and seven union territories (Government of India 2000a). The constitution now recognises 18 languages (Ratnam & Chandra 1996). Hindi is the official language but English is still used in official communications. There are also many other languages spoken — one way to conceive of the complexity is to note that there are over 2150 daily newspapers published in 92 different languages (Gopinath 1998). Eighty-two per cent of the population is Hindu, about 12 per cent Muslim, about two per cent Christian, nearly two per cent Sikh and nearly one per cent Buddhist (Bishop & McNamara 1998). About 72 per cent of the population is of Indo-Aryan ethnicity, about 25 per cent are Dravidian and Mongol; other ethnic compositions represent three per cent (Bishop & McNamara 1998).

Culture

There are a number of ways that the culture of India can be described. For example, it has been described as a high context culture (Frazee 1998). This means that feelings and thoughts are not explicitly expressed, requiring that one 'read between the lines' and interpret from an understanding of the context (Deresky 1997). A widely cited approach to culture is proposed in Hofstede's 1980 study in which he found India to be relatively high on power distance, low on uncertainty avoidance and slightly more masculine than feminine (Hofstede 1991). India was also found to be characterised strongly by collectivism on the individualism–collectivism continuum. There are certainly many companies in India which have endeavoured to capitalise on this by developing team-based organisational cultures; for example, Videocon International, Modi Xerox, Tisco, Philips India and Cadbury India empower teams and support teamwork (Bangera 1998). However, other researchers (Ali, Al-Shakhis & Nataraj 1991) have reported that Indian managers are highly individualistic and attribute a high priority to work over family; and that centralised decision making, together with bureaucratic and task-oriented styles, are predominant in Indian organisations.

Social system

One important characteristic of Indian society is the caste system, which has four main groups (the *brahmins* or priests, the *kshatriyas* or warriors, the *vaishyas* or traders, and the *sudras* or peasants and manual labourers) and thousands of sub-groups (Frazee 1998). Particularly relevant to our topic, however, is the notion of Scheduled Castes, which constitute around 15 per cent of the population, and Scheduled Tribes, which constitute around 7.5 per cent of the population (Tummala 1999). Then there is another 50 per cent of the population comprises socially and educationally backward classes, usually known as Other Backward Classes, whose definition is left open (Tummala 1999). Definition of the former two terms is not altogether clear and the identification of each is in the bailiwick of the local bureaucracy. Caste-based discrimination is assessed in terms of whether the caste or class in question:

> . . . can be served by clean Brahmans or not; can be serviced by barbers, water-carriers, tailors, etc. who service caste Hindus; pollutes a high-caste Hindu by contact or proximity; is one from whose hands a caste Hindu can take water; is debarred from using public amenities, such as roads, ferries, wells or schools; is debarred from the use of Hindu temples; will be treated as an equal by high-caste

> men of the same educational qualification in ordinary social intercourse; is merely depressed on account of its own ignorance, illiteracy or poverty and, but for that, would be subject to no social disability; is depressed on account of the occupation followed and whether, but for that occupation, it would be subject to no social disability (Jain & Ratnam 1994: 6–7).

Obtaining a certificate to establish that one is from a Scheduled Caste or Scheduled Tribe can be difficult, although some who do not belong, through the use of political pressure or other means, might be able to obtain a certificate (Jain & Ratnam 1994). In fact, Mitta (1994: 36) stated that 'the abuse of the caste-based reservations has been endemic'. Moreover, although there is a commitment to secularism, reservation is restricted to those who profess allegiance to Hinduism, Sikhism or Buddhism (Jain & Ratnam 1994).

Although women are in a minority in public service, no reservation based on sex has occurred, apart from in local bodies, even though the constitution provides the possibility for this to occur (Tummala 1999). A recent labour market survey, using a purpose-designed stratified sample of 993 households in the urban agglomeration of Lucknow district in Uttar Pradesh, found that low and backward caste women were significantly more likely to be in paid employment than high-caste women; caste was found to be independent with respect to men's participation rates (Kingdon 1998).

Literacy rates

Literacy rates have steadily improved; the adult literacy rate was estimated to be 52 per cent in 1995 (Adlakha 1997). However, India has one of the lowest female literacy rates in Asia; about 200 million Indian women are illiterate (Velkoff 1998). Literacy rates vary considerably between states; for example, Kerala has the highest female literacy rate of about 86 per cent whereas the two most populous states, Bihar and Uttar Pradesh, have literacy rates of less than 30 per cent. Similarly, the rates vary between the urban and rural areas. Literacy levels are correlated with low earning capacity. Only about three per cent of men and one per cent of women have a college education (Velkoff 1998). Although school attendance is free, the high poverty levels are thought to influence the literacy rate in that it is still costly for parents to transport children to school and to buy books and uniforms. Poor families in rural India are more likely to keep girls at home to care for younger children or to work in family businesses; and if a poor family has to choose between educating a son or a daughter, it is more likely that the son will be educated.

Education of males is likely to be seen as an investment because they will be responsible for caring for ageing parents whereas parents will not directly benefit from a daughter's education. It is possible that an educated daughter will also require a higher dowry because she may marry a comparably educated husband, although it has also been suggested that education may lower the dowry as it may be seen as an asset by the husband's family (Velkoff 1998).

Other factors thought to influence women's education include the shortage of female teachers and gender bias in the school curricula (Velkoff 1998), whereas Kingdon (1998) argues that parental discrimination against daughters and labour market discrimination are two of the most frequently cited reasons for the gender gap in education. (The government has recognised this problem and has initiated several programs to reduce the gender disparity in education, including a program aimed at fostering women's empowerment (Government of India 2000a).)

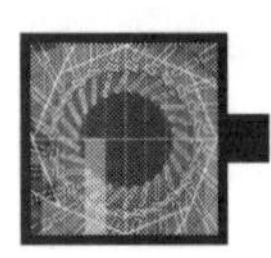

Legal environment

The Indian constitution holds a central position in Indian law and it is the preamble to the constitution that provides the legislative authority for equal opportunity legislation and programs. The constitution resolved to 'secure to all its citizens: JUSTICE, social, economic and political; LIBERTY of thought, expression, belief and worship; EQUALITY of status and of opportunity; and to promote among them all FRATERNITY assuring the dignity of the individual and the unity and integrity of the Nation' (http://www.uni-wuerzburg.de/law/in00000_.html). Part III of the constitution deals with 'fundamental rights' and includes articles pertaining to equality before the law (Article 14) and an anti-discrimination clause (Article 15) that states, 'The State shall not discriminate against any person on grounds only of religion, caste, sex, place of birth or any of them'. Similarly, this article prohibits discrimination by private persons with respect to the use of facilities, accommodation, wells, tanks, shops and restaurants, but employment is not included.

Article 16 provides not only for equality of opportunity in public employment but for affirmative action or 'protective discrimination' in that it allows for 'reservation' (i.e. the setting aside of a percentage of government jobs for disadvantaged Indian groups) in favour of the Scheduled Castes and Scheduled Tribes which are not adequately represented.

Something of a dilemma is created by the constitution because on the one hand affirmative action is allowed, while on the other hand the constitution recognises the principle of legal equality as a basic individual right (Faundez 1994). However, the issue has been considered by the Supreme Court of India in *Kerala v. N. M. Thomas,* which focused primarily on the 'untouchables'. This judgement held that the articles do allow the states to create job reservations for the benefit of the disadvantaged classes (Malkin 1990).

The constitution does not define the groups that may receive preference, neither does it provide standards by which such groups can be designated. Nonetheless, a summary of court decisions which may assist in interpreting what caste, sect and tribe membership actually mean may be found in Galanter (1989).

Article 24 provides for the prohibition of employment of children in factories, mines or any other form of hazardous employment unless they have reached 14 years of age.

The constitution also prohibits discrimination on the grounds of untouchability (Article 17) and forced labour (Article 323).

Part IV of the constitution contains 'Directive Principles of State Policy', which include provision for equal pay for equal work for both men and women; the principle that the health and strength of workers, and the tender age of children, not be abused; and the principle that citizens not be forced by economic necessity to carry out work unsuited to their age or strength (Article 39). Other articles in this section include the concept of a 'living wage' and maternity relief.

Part IVA contains the fundamental duties of every citizen and includes the duty to 'promote harmony and the spirit of common brotherhood amongst all the people of India transcending religious, linguistic and regional or sectional diversities; [and] to renounce practices derogatory to the dignity of women'. In fact, after centuries of oppression of women, the adoption of the constitution marked a watershed as far as women's status was concerned even though 'there is a great hiatus between the

constitutional precept and the prevailing practices' (Sarkar & Sivaramayya 1994: 4). Religious personal laws often prescribe diverse discriminatory norms and practices towards women which are in direct contradiction to the constitutional value of equality (Desai 1994).

There is no specific mention in the constitution of protection of the rights of the disabled, general age discrimination (other than in specific situations), carers (whether they be parents or those caring for older relatives), or those with alternative sexual orientations. But it is possible that they are still covered within the ambit of the more general provisions. For example, Article 46, which requires the state to 'promote with special care the educational and economic interests of the weaker sections of the people, and in particular the scheduled castes and the scheduled tribes and to protect them from social injustice and all forms of exploitation', can be seen to cover handicapped persons.

Age obviously is still considered to be important at the highest levels, because to become the President of India one must have 'completed the age of thirty-five years' (Article 58) as must the vice-president, and members of parliament must be not less than thirty years of age for seats in the Council of States and not less than twenty-five years of age for a seat in the House of the People (Article 84).

Some have argued that the labour legislation has provided excessive protection to labour in that it may have discouraged investment and consequently employment (Papola 1994). For example, Fallon (1987) found that there were over 127 statues at both central and state levels dealing with a whole range of labour issues, such as worker safety and welfare, industrial relations, contract labour and employment conditions in various industries. Although it was stated above that there are areas in which grounds of discrimination do not appear to be covered, there are other areas in which the government has legislated to assist workers in ways not evident in the Western world. For example, the *Factories Act 1948*, which covers any manufacturing activity with 10 or more workers (or 20 or more if there is no power used), requires that a creche be provided if 30 or more married women and widows work in the factory (Papola 1994), and night work for women is prohibited unless government permission is obtained from the Joint Commissioner of Labour (India Labour Law Survey 1997). While Ramaswamy (1997) has stated that this will never be granted between 10 p.m. and 5 a.m., Hazarika (1999) has indicated that some are keen to amend the Factories Act to allow women executives to do shift work. Further, Michigan (1999) states that consultation with women employees in the private sector had been initiated at the behest of the Confederation of Indian Industry to amend the Factories Act.

Other legislation that might be of interest includes:

- the *National Commission for Minorities Act 1992* (No. 19 of 1992), which establishes a commission for monitoring the situation of minorities and investigating alleged abuses of the rights of minorities
- the *Protection of Human Rights Act 1993* (No. 10 of 1994), which provides, among other things, for inquiries into complaints of human rights violations by public servants and reviewing safeguards provided by the constitution or other laws for protection of human rights
- the *Persons with Disabilities (Equal Opportunities, Protection of Rights and Full Participation) Act 1995* (No. 1 of 1996), which covers blindness, low vision, leprosy-cured, hearing impairment, locomotor disability, mental retardation and mental illness with a view to reviewing and coordinating organisations dealing

with these issues, developing national polices, taking steps to ensuring barrier-free environments for people so afflicted. Part of the brief under this legislation is to identify government posts which can be reserved for persons with a disability. The legislation also has interesting clauses that relate to the preferential allotment of land for persons with disabilities for certain purposes — such as the setting up of a business and the establishment of factories by entrepreneurs with disabilities (Section 43).

There are Human Rights Commissions in six states and Human Rights Courts in several other states. There has been a National Commission for Women since 1992. Other commissions to deal with relevant issues of diversity are the Backward Classes Commission; and the Scheduled Caste and Scheduled Tribes Commission.

Another interesting piece of legislation is the *Inter-State Migrant Workmen (Regulation of Employment and Conditions of Service) Act 1979,* which not only provides for the registration of establishments employing inter-state migrant workers but states that inter-state migrant workers should be paid a displacement allowance and that their wages should be equal to that of other workers. In other words, the legislation attempts to prevent discrimination among migrant workers within Indian states. Breman (1996), in his book on work in the informal sector, indicates that employers prefer imported labour as these people have little or no contact with the social milieu and do not therefore demonstrate a militant attitude, although he later says that this is somewhat of a mirage. Apparently, these workers will not hesitate to withdraw their labour if they consider the conditions unsatisfactory. For example, they might just simply desert in the middle of the night without finishing their work (Breman 1996).

Compliance with the legislation

As in all countries, the issue of evaluating the impact of the legislation and determining compliance applies in India. Not surprisingly, there is limited documented information available on this aspect. However, anecdotal evidence indicates that compliance levels are low. Certainly the Human Rights Committee Report (1997) expressed concern that the so-called backward classes and ethnic and national minorities continue to be subjected to severe social discrimination and to suffer disproportionately from many violations of their rights, including inter-caste violence, bonded labour and discrimination of all kinds.

Olsen (1998), too, has reviewed a range of research that does not paint a positive picture for women in India. For example, in the marine food processing area, there is evidence of 'repeated failure to pay minimum wages, use of piece-work and contracts to evade labour laws, and even the bonding of women to contractors by paying the workers' father a sum such as 2000 rupees before whisking the woman away to the women's hostel to do fish processing work' (Olsen 1998: 172).

Conditions obviously vary across industries but in the marine food processing area it has been found that women do the 'dirtiest, most tedious and repetitious work in wet conditions; unions are reported to be addressing issues of harassment of women in addition to other basic rights' (Olsen 1998). However, in non-unionised firms it is reported that none of the basic amenities are provided and women are limited to five-minute toilet breaks (Olsen 1998).

Another example cited by Olsen (1998) is that of an electronics and jewellery processing zone in Mumbai in which the vast majority of female workers are

employed on a casual or short-term basis whereas the male workers generally attain a permanent position with a regular salary and job security. Notwithstanding the presence of high-level Labour Administration officers within this area, the labour laws are reportedly not enforced. Even within the Labour Administration itself, evidence of glass (or stronger) ceilings has been found for women because they are assumed to have responsibilities preventing them from working overtime, handling violence or being transferred. Similarly, there is only limited evidence of attempts to enforce laws relating to women, such as the *Equal Remuneration Act (1976)* — relevant only to non-professional employees.

On the other hand, in the public sector, equal opportunity has led to an improvement in the status of urban, middle-class educated Indian women, as indicated by their numbers in senior positions (Ghosh & Roy 1997). Moreover, Ratnam and Chandra (1996: 90–1) state:

> Symbolically, women are employed 'everywhere' except in men's rooms. Women are becoming the kind of men they wanted to marry. Their own ambitions have been realized ... But in terms of the broad patterns of employment, traditional sexual division of labour is pervasive ... some employers have got over the 'males for sales' syndrome and allow not only young females but also housewives to pursue a career. However, women continue to face a number of hurdles.

A similar picture emerges with respect to the physically handicapped. Although the Indian Bureau of Public Enterprise and the Union Ministry of Home Affairs issued an executive order reserving one per cent of federal positions for each of the blind, the deaf and the orthopedically handicapped, Malkin (1990) states that because it is not a statutory requirement and because proper enforcement and monitoring does not exist, government agencies do not always adhere to this order. However, state-level job reservation policies have proven to be more effective (Malkin 1990).

There is a National Commission on Scheduled Castes (SCs) and Scheduled Tribes (STs) with the powers of a civil court that has the power to investigate all matters relating to the protections provided for these groups. But the affirmative action principles apply only to the public sector — that is, federal and state public services and public enterprises. Jain and Ratnam (1994) reported that the constitutional provisions on SCs and STs which officially only apply to the public sector are not known to be followed by any private sector enterprises, although in areas where there is a large proportion of SCs and STs some companies reportedly make efforts to recruit such people.

The law requires that any company employing more than 30 women must have a day-care centre run by the company on the premises. Many companies do not provide this benefit to women employees because they find it difficult to manage the centre owing to the stringent standards set by the *Factories Act 1948*. The other problem faced by management is that the employees visit the centre very often during the work day and this affects the productivity of the employees. Hence, many companies get around this by submitting statistics to the Joint Chief Labour Commissioner that their employees do not have children below the age of five. Moreover, companies may have all the facilities for a day-care centre but it may be used for other purposes.

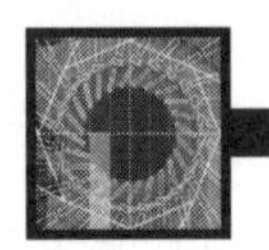

Equal opportunity for women

Women still occupy an inferior position in Indian society (Mayer 1999). This probably does not come as a surprise because, according to Tomasevski (1998), no country in the world has attained sexual equality. Nonetheless, Indian women remain under-represented in public life and in the higher levels of the public service, and are subjected to personal laws which are based on religious norms and which do not accord women equality (Human Rights Committee 1997).

At the process work level, having the right contacts, such as a relative who has a job in the same place, is perhaps the best predictor of both women and men obtaining work. So, even though there is an absence of formal barriers to employment, the stratification and segmentation of the labour force is reflected in the mechanism for obtaining work in which particularist sources of information — such as family, caste, community or personal contacts — dominate the formal processes (Deshpande & Deshpande 1994).

Different authors over the past decade have suggested different outcomes in terms of women's employment opportunities. For example, Ghosh and Roy (1997) observed that the percentage of women in the total labour force has been steadily declining since 1970 and technological change appears to have reduced the opportunities for women. Yet the fiftieth round of the National Sample Survey 1993–94 (NSS) (quinquennial survey) indicates that there is an increase in the percentage of women in the workplace from 18.5 per cent to 20.9 per cent and a consequent feminisation of the workforce in urban areas (Kundu 1997). It has also been pointed out that the number of women employed in the public sector is rising but their proportion is still low when compared to the total employment in the public sector (Hazarika 1999).

Three major trends have been noted in the population data according to Olsen (1998): the rate of growth of non-agricultural employment has been greater for men than for women; the growth has been mostly through casual or contract work; and the agricultural workforce has shrunk slightly, especially for men. The mechanisation of industrial work has tended to marginalise women (Breman 1999).

However, depending upon one's perspective, it could be argued that India is very progressive in many respects, including its acknowledgement of the need for legislation to provide for greater representation of women in public life. For example, legislation has been enacted which sets a minimum quota of 33 per cent for female membership of the village *panchayats* (Rai 1999). Panchayats are councils consisting of five or more members assembled to judge disputes and to determine group policy (Galanter & Baxi 1989). In December 1998, the Women's Reservation Bill was introduced to provide 33 per cent reservation for women in Lok Sabha (the lower house of the parliament) and State Assemblies, but that is yet to be passed in the Lok Sabha.

Ghosh and Roy (1997) also argue that the traditional prejudice against women in paid employment has slowly disappeared or is on its way to disappearing in the large urban areas. This is somewhat supported by a study of 162 male and female managers from private organisations (55 per cent), public organisations (24 per cent) and government-operated organisations (8 per cent) with average workforces of 15 000 employees, which found that both men and women thought that hiring

practices were based on merit (Gupta, Koshal & Koshal 1998). However, a number of other, perhaps more significant points are worth noting from this study:

- less than five per cent of the companies represented in the study had women in senior or middle level management
- both men and women believed that the possibility of pregnancy makes women less desirable recruits
- 72 per cent of women thought that promotions are based on gender rather than merit
- only 52 per cent of women indicated that their organisations were committed to using the talents of women and, even more important, only 20 per cent perceived that the business community was ready to accept women in key managerial roles
- most men were found to be uncomfortable with working with a female boss.

The creation and perpetuation of the segmented labour market (based on production — primary versus secondary, public versus private, and formal versus informal — or on wage levels) has been attributed to caste, religion, gender, location, labour laws and unions (Khandker 1992). The suggestion is that skill differentials among individuals cannot overcome the institutional barriers, whereas the segmented labour market perspective sees that good quality jobs are in short supply relative to demand and are thus rationed. Contacts and influence rather than market forces come into play, thus perpetuating the status quo.

Compensation

Pradhan (1994) found that on average a woman's salary is 81 per cent that of a man in the public sector, and 76 per cent that of a man in the private sector. Similarly, Kingdon (1998) found a significant earnings gap between men and women, of which about 45 per cent might be attributed to discrimination, although the author suggests that because women take more breaks than men from employment it is possible that there is a greater rate of human capital obsolescence among women than men. Overall, the sex differential in earnings may be explained only to a small extent by their less extensive education and more by the way the labour market rewards education for the two sexes (Kingdon 1998).

States like West Bengal, Uttar Pradesh, Punjab, Kerala, Haryana, Bihar and Orissa have very low per capita income for females compared with other states in farm employment. However, non-farm employment is higher in Punjab (66.9 per cent), Kerala (58.4 per cent) and West Bengal (45.9 per cent) respectively, which has increased women's economic status as compared to other states (Bharadwaj & Bharadwaj 1998).

The legislation which supposedly protects women's pay (Equal Remuneration Act) is applicable both to the public sector and to all of the organised and unorganised sectors, domestic and multinational companies and to all types of working arrangements. Yet the concept of work equality is so vague that payment of low wages to women can continue. Moreover, 'labour inspection machinery is weak, corrupt and small in size at the state and field levels' (Heggade 1998: 1038). Also, workers are unlikely to report breaches due to illiteracy and poverty and because 'the need for jobs far exceeds the need to practise gender justice' (Heggade 1998: 1038). The maximum penalty in respect of wage inequality is a Rs 10 000 fine and one month's imprisonment or both (Heggade 1998).

Maternity benefits

According to Breman (1999), the customary reason for hiring women (cheap labour) has lost some of its appeal owing to the fact that they have to be paid while on maternity leave. To be eligible for the maternity benefit under the *Employee State Insurance Act 1948* (ESI), the female employee should have been a member of the ESI scheme for a period of at least 13 weeks. Maternity leave consists of 12 weeks in total, of which not more than six weeks can precede the date of expected delivery; the required pay is 'fullpay' according to average daily wages stipulated by Minimum Wage Age or 10 rupees, whichever is higher. More recently this has been varied to four months' full pay maternity leave for women with up to two children, and the time can be taken before or after childbirth. Should the woman become ill as a result of her pregnancy she is entitled to a further month's leave with wages (Ramaswamy 1997). Nursing breaks are prescribed at the rate of two additional breaks of 15 minutes per day until the child is 15 months of age. Also, central and state governments have extended a week's leave with pay to all male employees at the time of childbirth in order to facilitate their domestic tasks at this time.

An employer must not dismiss a woman because she is pregnant, but even if an employer dismisses a pregnant employee, the employee is still entitled to all maternity benefits. There is also a medical bonus for pregnant women workers although, as the India Labour Law Survey (1997) indicates, nearly all labour laws relating to female workers are of paper value only; there is some question about the rate of implementation of these bonuses.

The *Maternity Benefit Act* 1961 is applicable to mines, factories, circus, industries, shops, plantations and other establishments employing 10 or more persons. The Employee State Insurance Act covers sickness, maternity and employment-related injuries and applies only to workers whose wages do not exceed Rs 3000 per month. The respective human resource managers need to make recommendations for the contract employees to get the benefits. But there are companies like Siemens Information Technologies, Bangalore, which have an explicit policy to grant maternity leave to all women employees in accordance with the provisions of the *Maternity Benefit Act 1961*.

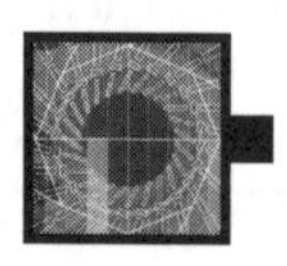

Sexual harassment

The fundamental rights of working women under Articles 14 and 25 of the constitution guarantee the right to equality, life and liberty. However, according to the Ninth Five Year Plan (Government of India 2000) violence against women in the workplace continues. The landmark court verdict to protect the position of working women against sexual harassment in India is entitled *Vishaka and Others v. State of Rajasthan* (Taneja 1997). The Supreme Court of India recognised that sexual harassment in the workplace is actually a violation of Article 19, which guarantees the right to practise any profession, trade or business and directs the rules and regulations of government and public sector companies relating to conduct and discipline.

Employers are now required to prohibit sexual harassment and provide for appropriate penalties against offenders. The court also directed private employees to take immediate steps to include prohibition of sexual harassment in the Standing Orders

under the *Industrial Employment (Standing Orders) Act 1946*. The employer is also obliged to initiate disciplinary proceedings as well as criminal action against any offender, and ensure that the harassed woman is not further victimised (Murthy 1997). Further, the judges suggested that a woman should head the Complaints Committee for sexual harassment. Based on the Supreme Court judgement mentioned above, the central government and most state governments have set up machinery at the firm, industry and office levels to protect women workers against harassment (Heggade 1998).

The government also issued a notification on 5 November 1999 stating that 'any behaviour whether directly or by implication involving physical contact and advances or a demand or request for sexual favours or sexually coloured remarks or showing pornography or any other unwelcome physical, verbal or non-verbal conduct of a sexual nature shall be construed as sexual harassment' (Government of India 2000b).

The Bombay (Mumbai) High Court in its first judgement on sexual harassment at the workplace applied the broad guidelines of the Supreme Court of India and required the employer, Saudi Arabian Airlines, to reinstate the aggrieved employee and pay compensation (Shah 1998).

Another issue related to sexuality is that of gay rights. This matter has not received a lot of attention from civil right groups in India. However, Indian culture and heritage have given sanction to all forms of sexual expression including homosexuality, yet the legal sanction that exists for homosexuality does not guarantee its social acceptance. Thus, in the prevailing anti-AIDS frenzy, homosexuals are particularly vulnerable to victimisation in the workplace (Balasubramanyan 1996).

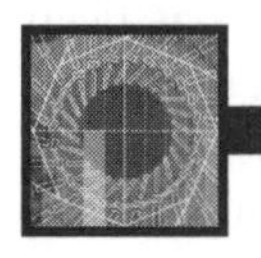

Child labour

India has the largest number of non-school-going child workers with estimates ranging from 17.4 to 44 million (Weiner 1995) to 114 million (Jain 1996) children under the age of 15 years working. However, because much child labour is illegal, there is a deliberate attempt to conceal it so the true figures are impossible to establish (Jain 1996). ILO Convention No. 138 states that the minimum age for employment should not be less than 15 years, so the *Child Labour (Prohibition and Regulation) Act 1986* does not meet this target (Subrahmanya 1987). The Child Labour Act focuses only on children working in hazardous industries, and it is so narrowly focused that it excludes 92 per cent of all children working in industries (Ganesan 1997).

But there are 14 major pieces of legislation that purportedly provide protection to children working in various occupations. These are the *Factories Act 1948*; *Mines Act 1952*; *Plantation Labour Act 1951*; *Merchant Shipping Act 1958*; *Motor Transport Workers Act 1961*; *Dock Workers' Regulation and Employment Act 1948*; *Children (Pledging of Labour) Act 1933*; *Employment of Children Act 1938*; *Apprentices Act 1961*; *Bidi and Cigar Works (Conditions of Employment) Act 1966*; *Contract Labour (Regulation and Abolition) Act 1970*; *Radiation Protection Rules 1971* — under the *Atomic Energy Act 1962*; Shops and Commercial Establishment Acts under different names in the various states; The *Juvenile Justice Act 1986* (Shah 1992).

The *Child Labour (Prohibition and Regulation) Act,* which came into force late in 1986 (but mirrored earlier legislation), simply lists processes in certain industries that children must not participate in if they are below 14 years of age. This Act does not apply to those children who work as part of a family business or those who work for state-funded or state-supported institutions.

Night work for children is also banned under the Factories Act, but according to Burra (1995) it continues, with children as young as seven years working night shifts. In fact Burra (1995) provides examples of labour laws being openly flouted with the connivance of the local bureaucracy. When employers know that factory inspections are to occur, the children are removed prior to the visit. Thus, child labour continues unabated (Shah 1992).

The Supreme Court of India judgement called for the abolition of child labour in occupations specified in the Child Labour Act, and the creation of a corpus fund for compulsory education of laid-off children. The court has directed that every employer be asked to pay compensation for every child employed in contravention of provisions of the 1986 Act, a sum of Rs20 000 (US$465), of which the state should pay Rs5000 (US$116) to each child if it failed to provide alternative employment to the adult member of the child's family. But the money should go the corpus welfare fund — the 'Child Labour Rehabilitation Fund' — the income from which would be used for the child's education and welfare (Rambabu 1996).

There are many arguments used to justify the employment of children, but essentially they provide very cheap labour; they are less status conscious; they are agile and quick, and less expensive to maintain; and they are easier to manage than adults because they do not question (Shah 1992). Sometimes they form a relatively small percentage of the workers in a particular industry; at other times, such as in carpet-weaving, they may form up to 75 per cent of the workforce (Burra 1995).

Gupta (1999) has posited that consumer activism in the Western world has been such that corporations benefiting from child labour will not survive, but goes on to say that these same activists are not concerned about what happens to the children when they are not allowed to work. Varandani (1994) says abolition of child labour is a distant dream because, without providing any additional source of income for the parents of working children, it would lead to starvation for some families.

Indian government policy announced in 1994 pledges to eliminate child labour for two million children in hazardous industries by the year 2000. The program involved an incentive for children to cease work and enter non-formal schooling for which they would receive a 100 rupees payment as well as a meal for attending school, but there was some question about the sincerity of the government given that it had not allocated anywhere near the funds required in its budget for this program (Human Rights Watch 1996).

The government has stipulated that registration with the Carpet Export Promotion Council is mandatory for all carpet exporters to ensure that they undertake to eradicate child labour, register their looms with the council for periodic inspections and contribute funds towards rehabilitation of child labourers, besides making a firm commitment not to involve children in the industry (Anonymous 1996).

However, Shobhana (1998: 5) states that most of the activities in which children are employed do not come under the Factories Act, even if they did, it would be difficult to contain employment of child labour owing to the 'sheer lack of popular will to prevent the oppression of the child workers in our society'.

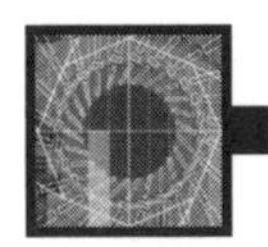

Older workers

Another element of diversity in organisations is that of older workers. In 1994, India ranked fourth in the world with a large population of older people, albeit a small proportion of its overall population. Given the growth in the older population along with industrialisation, urbanisation and changes in lifestyles and values of the young, including the decline in traditional family support systems, the elderly have become a large and vulnerable group (Gokhale, Pandit & Raj 1994). One labour market study found that paid work participation increases with age but at a decreasing rate, peaking at age 40 for women and at age 27 for men (Kingdon 1998).

However, a study covering five sites in India found that the majority of people above 60 were economically and physically active (even though they had been forced out of work at the statutory age of retirement), but that the majority of employers were not in favour of them because of their perceived slowness at work, unstable health or obsolescent skills (Gokhale, Pandit & Raj 1994). The exception to this was with respect to advisory positions in which experience, knowledge and connections were valued. One of the recommendations of this study was the setting up of 'grey skill banks', which if implemented could potentially be of great value to multinational corporations (MNCs).

The retirement age in the private sector starts at 55 years while the public sector retirement age commences at 58 years and in central government jobs it has recently been raised to 60 years. Some of the collective agreements now provide for a weighting of benefits for seniority of service (Ratnam & Chandra 1996), which may favour older workers, but this appears to be going against the trend to treat all employees on the basis of merit.

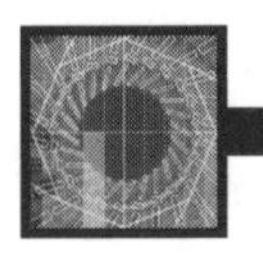

Multinational companies

Typical practices

It is difficult to generalise across multinational companies (MNCs) in India because of the diversity of their operations and the diversity of India itself, in addition to the fact that there is a 'virtual absence of empirical studies on employment practices in Indian firms that include reasonable sample sizes of MNCs' (Ratnam 1998: 579). However, it is known that the public sector has been a better provider of physical and social infrastructure than MNCs. In many cases MNCs, unable to manage the complexities of dealing with labour, have substituted people with technology (Ratnam 1998). This, of course, does not just apply to India, but when in many cases the cheap labour was one of the major attractions for entry into this market the irony is obvious.

In general, diversity is not considered to be an issue that concerns Indians; rather, it is seen as an American issue, and, even in US-based firms, the issue in India is not perceived to be a business one (Ratnam & Chandra 1996). Yet Ratnam and Chandra (1996) indicate that in an electronics company, after a three-stage program on diversity management which moved from awareness creation with top management to creating an inclusive climate to setting goals and targets, diversity management is now seen as critical to business success. These authors provide examples of hotel chains where, in semi-urban locations, divisions and dissent between different caste groups was a problem, as was disciplining employees from particular groups. This problem was tackled by employing, over some years, a more balanced workforce and finally staff being told that the hotel would not tolerate discrimination.

Furthermore, although affirmative action is applicable for SCs and STs in the public service and public enterprises, some private sector companies are known to make efforts to recruit these categories where they form a significant part of the population (Jain & Ratnam 1994).

Generally, though, nepotism and other forms of discrimination have characterised recruitment and selection practices in India. Some have argued that more impersonal selection criteria have begun to be used, but Breman (1999) has questioned whether that really means that achievement versus ascription-based qualities have been used. Recruitment through existing employees apparently continues at the lower levels, thus essentially maintaining the balance within the workforce.

Detailed case study analyses of eight organisations in India have found that, at the senior levels, recruitment practices rely on objective measures and formalised procedures to appoint the best people, but at lower levels all types of organisations (public, private and multinational) show a predisposition towards subjective criteria such as nepotism, personal and family connections, caste, community and regional affiliations (Jain 1991).

Many responsible large companies do not use child labour in their factory premises, but some turn a blind eye if small-scale suppliers use child labour, even though the Factories Act of 1948 prohibits using child labour. The second author's consulting work has revealed that few multinational companies insist that their suppliers not use child labour or conduct labour audits by making surprise visits to suppliers' factories.

As Vidyasagar, child labour consultant to UNICEF in Chennai, India, points out:

> ... what is needed are further amendments to the existing acts, especially the 1986 Act. For example, tiny (or household) industries, which are mainly family-based are exempt from this law, and it has been found that most of the child labour prevalent in the country is here. Therefore, many big units have found an easy way out, by decentralising their operations. In other words, they collect their output from the households, which employ their children, while at the same time, not breaking the law (cited in Rambabu 1996: 12).

In the second author's experience, in many family-run businesses the organisational culture has evolved from caste or ethnicity or religious beliefs. To strengthen the culture based on caste or ethnicity or religion, the management employs people from the same caste or ethnicity or religious beliefs of the family which owns the business. It is a normal practice in these organisations to have confidants in important positions and, more often than not, these are people from the same caste or ethnicity or religion as the business family. When these companies grow to become private limited or public limited companies they continue to retain the original culture to a large extent.

Another common practice in companies based on caste or ethnicity or religion is to provide holidays to employees for festivals unique to the particular religion or caste or ethnicity. For example, if the employees in an organisation are predominantly Brahmins then the organisation might provide a holiday for 'Avani Aveetam' (a festival for changing the sacred thread, which every Brahmin male wears across his chest).

Large companies have their own policies on recruitment and selection of women employees. While there are no legal obligations to hire women employees, many organisations consider this a social responsibility. There is a general perception among management that women are more efficient than their male counterparts. Balakrishnan (1999) conducted a study about the extent of employment of women in textile mills. The data was collected from 145 mill management personnel and 400 women workers. All the identified textile mills, which predominantly employed women, were located in Tamil Nadu. On a scale of ten job performance factors, including discipline and quality of work, female workers were found to be superior to their male counterparts except with respect to 'working relationship with co-workers'. Even in areas like output, quality of work and waste control, women were marginally superior to male workers.

Some employers may be concerned about hiring women owing to the requirement for travel or relocation. For example, the second author has experience with representatives of many software companies who are apprehensive about hiring women employees, not because they lack competence, but because they are hesitant to take up assignments which require them to relocate to another state or district where they have to work on-site at the client's premises. Women hesitate to relocate either because of their parents' cultural values or because it is not a normal practice in India for a woman to rent a house and live away from home.

Employers are also sceptical about employing unmarried women because the labour turnover is high compared with married women. In India most parents arrange marriages for their children and if a female employee marries someone from another part of India she will quit her job and relocate (Kundu & Gupta 1996).

In Vijaya Bank (one of the nationalised banks in India) there was an unwritten policy that women employees (clerical cadre) should be transferred only within the districts and, even if transfer outside the districts was required, it should be to stations where there were appropriate facilities for women and where spouses could also be accommodated (Bhatia 1999). The Karnataka High Court has upheld the validity of the transfer orders issued to 11 female employees of the Vijaya Bank, which were challenged on the ground that the said orders were *mala fides* and opposed to binding industrial settlements. The court also held that women, having secured employment on an equal footing with men, could not seek to secure implied protection on the ground that they belonged to the proverbial weaker section (Bhatia 1999).

Another factor which influences recruitment and selection policies is known as 'sons of the soil'. This requires that public sector companies and state government-owned corporations give first preference in employment to the natives of the state.

A further practice which affects recruitment occurs when large companies need to acquire land adjacent to state government-provided land for starting large industries. In these cases it is not uncommon for companies like Neyveli Lignite Corporation and Ennore Thermal Power Station, when commencing new manufacturing units in industrially backward areas, to provide employment to one adult per family that has sold their land to the company. In India this practice is not considered to be a coercive tactic used by the company to acquire land from private owners. This practice actually facilitates local community support.

Employers may also provide employment either to the employee's wife or to an adult child in the family if the employee dies while in employment and if the employee is the only breadwinner of the family. Further, some employers fill a certain percentage of vacant positions from the employees' kith and kin. Moreover, to promote good relations with the trade unions, it is not unusual for employers to adopt some 'unique' recruitment practices.

Notwithstanding that union membership is declining, as in much of the industrialised world, some of the more successful companies have adopted so-called 'softer HRM strategies to marginalise the influence of unions, [while] others are pursuing aggressive union exclusion policies' (Gani 1996: 54). Unionism varies in MNCs as does MNC recognition of unions. Some organisations have appointed staff on a commission basis to avoid unions, and others have induced staff not to be union members by offering pay deals — not unlike to some of the arrangements occurring in mining companies in Australia.

In the Export Processing Zones (EPZs) the Trade Unions Act and the Factories Act still apply (Ratnam 1998). Not unexpectedly, the actual protection of workers is poorly enforced, and a trade union study in an EPZ of Mumbai found that employers avoid providing benefits (such as maternity and redundancy) by employing through contractors (Ratnam 1998). Opposing goals exist. For example, the Indian Government wishes to project an image of labour legislation being implemented in EPZs so that it is seen as a suitable trading partner, but Indian private sector investors are quite content with the diversity in the legal framework and MNCs would prefer a framework with greater certainty (Ratnam 1998).

Best practices

Mehra (1999) reports that gender relations in corporate India are healthier than in other sectors of employment and points to policies that assist both men and women employees achieve a better balance between work and home. For example, pregnant or nursing employees at Hewlett Packard in India can work from home or attend the office for half-days, on alternate days or every alternate week. IIS Infotech Ltd in Noida (Mumbai) runs a creche within the business premises for employees' children; children are also picked up from school or the bus stop and brought to the creche (Mehra 1999). The advertisements of one five-star hotel chain in India typically state that it takes special care of women employees, provides creche, nursery and other day-care facilities for the children of employees, allows periodic breaks during the day to let mothers take care of infants, has separate rest rooms for women, and provides escort facilities for women who enter or leave the office after dusk and before dawn (Ratnam & Chandra 1996).

Some employers have begun to open up positions formerly the preserve of men to women; for example, USV Ltd advertised for housewives with a degree in biological sciences in the age group 30–40 years (Ratnam & Chandra 1996).

Some organisations such as NIIT (National Institute of Information Technology) offer half-day jobs and special allowances for new parents to take an auto-rickshaw to check on their baby during the lunch hour (Ratnam & Chandra 1996). Along the same lines, Ratnam and Chandra (1996) indicate that a few Indian companies have begun to provide parental leave in addition to statutory maternity leave, and a number of non-governmental and international organisations have commenced programs on sexual harassment.

Bhargava and Herr (1996) have made suggestions as to how organisations might best use female managers. For example, they suggest that after marriage a female employee who is under new pressure would be eased considerably if she were allowed to commence work one hour later than normal. Then, once the woman has children, the company can either provide a good quality creche or allow the

employee to work from home or work half-days. They further suggest that female managers' roles be redefined to that of consultants — so they are kept on a 'flexible leash' (Bhargava & Herr 1996: 156). As pointed out, though, these policies would require that work performance be measured in terms of productivity and not just hours in the office. This also means that there would be no reason why the policies could not be applicable to men.

What should the MNC know and do?

The management of MNCs operating in India should customise their policies and practices according to the local cultural values and beliefs (Ratnam & Chandra 1996). Management of multinational companies operating in India may be expected to be difficult owing to the myriad of rules and regulations controlling foreign investment (As-Saber, Dowling & Liesch 1999), the entrenched bureaucracy, the undeveloped infrastructure, hierarchical relationships, autocratic management styles and nepotism at all levels (Deresky 1997). Then, once the business is set up, the next major challenge is probably the management of diversity. This of course will raise questions about equity and equality. Reservations and perceived preferential treatment have led to divisiveness as many have striven for classifications of backwardness. Innovative organisations respond to diversity issues as major organisational issues but they tend towards a 'gentle rain over time' approach (Ratnam & Chandra 1996: 102).

The International Labour Organisation's tripartite Declaration of Principles concerning MNCs and social policy expects that MNCs will not only respect the laws and sovereign rights of the countries that they are operating in, but will also respect international standards of human rights. This means, among other important things, that MNCs are supposed to eliminate discrimination and promote equal opportunity in employment. It has also been suggested that MNCs observe lower standards with respect to unions than domestic firms in similar industries. Therefore, there would appear to be some scope for re-examination of MNC practices in India.

Based on their empirical study on women managers, Gupta, Koshal and Koshal (1998) have suggested that gender is an important issue in corporate India and that greater exposure of women to top management, job rotation, career and leadership development programs, mentoring programs, active recruitment of women at senior levels, surveying of women's views, and good childcare facilities at work would assist. It is quite likely that similar recommendations would come from studies on any other area of difference.

One possible advantage is that India provides an additional capital subsidy for new industrial units (small, medium or large firms) that employ more than 30 per cent of females in their workforce. The subsidy includes an additional capital subsidy of five per cent on investment in fixed assets subject to a ceiling of Rs500 000 (SIDBI 1999). However, some industries — for example, food processing, garment, leather goods, hosiery and matchbox — are not eligible for this scheme (SIDBI 1999).

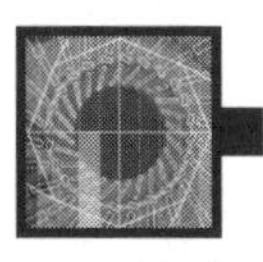

Conclusions

Structural adjustments in the Indian economy, including an unprecedented number of mergers and acquisitions, have added a new source of diversity for Indian organisations (Ratnam & Chandra 1996). Demographic changes in India, as elsewhere in the world, are also leading to customer diversity, suggesting that there might be good business reasons, beyond simply upholding basic human rights, for not only allowing for diversity in workforces but actively encouraging and managing diversity (Mohanty 1999). But diversity management in India is an incredibly complex issue. Affirmative action policies such as those pursued by the Indian Government have led to some problems due to the extension of reservations from initial recruitment to include promotions. The effort to extend the reservation system has resulted in fewer opportunities for the forward castes, but these extensions are perceived to be based on political expediency rather than on any satisfactory rationale. The policy of reservations was not meant to be an ongoing one, yet it is continually being extended at regular 10-year intervals. There is also the suggestion that people are clamouring for inclusion in the backward class list, and the process has led to more demands from the backward classes and an even more polarised society (Tummala 1999).

What is needed, according to Heggade (1998), is care to define the material contact and level of labour standards which will not displace women from the workforce, attitudinal changes at the cultural and family level, involvement of trade unions in protecting the interests of women and a job evaluation system which assists in accurate determinations of equal pay for equal work.

Multinational companies should be aware that because the affirmative action policy does not apply to the private sector, there may be resistance from unions to the privatisation of government enterprises. For example, Jain and Ratnam (1994) indicated that there had been some efforts to stall privatisation initiatives in railway catering and cleaning where SC and ST employees outnumbered the employees belonging to 'forward castes'. However, the government proceeded with the privatisation.

Employees do not wish to lose their basic benefits, so private organisations may need to develop policies to accommodate diversity issues when considering buying government enterprises. In fact, given that interest groups have raised demands for an extension of the reservation system to the private sector, this may be a moot point.

Increasingly, social auditing in corporate enterprises is occurring, but to date there has been no suggestion that equal opportunity or diversity management should be one of the objectives. However, Batra (1996) recommends, among other things, that the corporate social audit should include such issues as working conditions, opportunities for economically backward classes, fair and reasonable remuneration, employment adequacy and promotional opportunities. Moreover, it is suggested that the government should impose compulsory social audits on companies.

It may be expected from the Ninth Five Year Plan that ongoing attention will be directed at diversity issues, with increasing senior appointments such as the Commissioner for Women's Rights, gender sensitisation programs, more extensive legislation and better enforcement of existing legislation, and emphasis on non-government organisations further participating in monitoring in this area. We predict that the private sector will come under increasing scrutiny in this area even though the emphasis to date has been on the public sector. But the trends suggest that the government might not enforce the extension of the reservation system to private industry because of the emphasis on attracting foreign investment.

References

Adlakha, A. 1997. *Population Trends: India*. Bureau of the Census, US Department of Commerce.

Ali, A., Al-Shakhis, M. & Nataraj, S. 1991. 'Work Centrality and Individualism: A Cross-national Perspective'. *International Journal of Manpower* 12(1): 30–38.

Anonymous. 1996. 'Child Labour in Carpet Making: Concern over US Move on Investigators'. *Business Line,* 20 September: 9.

Anonymous. 1998. 'Reservation for SC/ST in Promotion: Bank Unions Contest Judges' Order'. *Business Line,* 13 March: 2.

As-Saber, S. N., Dowling, P. J. & Liesch, P. W. 1999. 'Managing the Host-country Legal Environment: A Study of Australian–Indian Joint Ventures in India'. Paper presented at ANZAM '99, Hobart Tasmania, December.

Balakrishnan, M. S. 1999. 'Mills Turning "Women-intensive" '. *Business Line*, 12 March: 5.

Balasubramanyan, V. 1996. 'Gay Rights in India'. *Economic and Political Weekly* 31(5): 257–8.

Bangera, B. T. 1998. 'Programme on Team Spirit in Work Culture'. *Business Line*, 24 February: 12.

Batra, G. S. 1996. 'Dynamics of Social Auditing in Corporate Enterprises: A Study of the Indian Corporate Sector'. *Managerial Auditing Journal* 11(2): 36–45.

Bharadwaj, J. L. & Bharadwaj, S. 1998. 'Gender Related Development Index for Major States of India: An Economic Analysis'. *Indian Journal of Economics* 79: 9–19.

Bhargava, S. & Herr, H. 1996. 'How to Manage Gender Bias'. *Business Today* 7(21): 154–7.

Bhatia, S. 1999. 'Women Bank Staff Lose Transfer Plea'. *Business Line,* 20 September: 9.

Bishop, B. & McNamara, D. 1998. *The Asia–Australia Survey 1997–98*. South Melbourne: MacMillan Education.

Breman, J. 1996. *Footloose Labour: Working in India's Informal Economy.* Cambridge: Cambridge University Press.

Breman, J. 1999. 'Industrial Labour in Post-colonial India'. *International Review of Social History* 44(27): 249–300.

Burra, N. 1995. *Born to Work: Child Labour in India.* Delhi: Oxford University Press.

Dasgupta, A. K. 1994. 'Emerging Pressures on the Labour Market: Process of Adjustment and Signals'. In Sarkar, L. & Sivaramayya, B. (Eds). *Women and Law: Contemporary Problems.* New Delhi: Vikas Publishing House, pp. 296–330.

Deresky, H. 1997. *International Management: Managing Across Borders and Cultures*. Second Edition. Reading: Addison-Wesley.

Desai, A. R. 1994. 'Gender Role in the Constitution'. In Sarkar, L. & Sivaramayya, B. *Women and Law: Contemporary Problems*. New Delhi: Vikas Publishing House, New Delhi, pp. 41–9.

Deshpande, L. K. & Deshpande, S. 1994. 'Segmentation and Structural Adjustment'. In Raghavan, K., Sharma, H. & Sekhar, L. (Eds). *Impact of New Economic Policy on Manpower and Employment in India*. New Delhi: Agricole Publishing Academy, pp. 222–243.

Dhesi, A. S. 1998. 'Caste, Class Synergies and Discrimination in India'. *International Journal of Social Economics* 25(6/7/8): 1030–48.

Fallon, P. R. 1987. *The Effects of Labor Regulation upon Industrial Employment in India*. Report No. DRD287, Development Research Department, World Bank.

Faundez. J. 1994. *Affirmative Action: International Perspectives*. Geneva: International Labour Organisation.

Frazee, V. 1998. 'Working with Indians'. *Workforce* 3(4): 10–11.

Galanter, M. 1989. *Law and Society in Modern India*. Delhi: Oxford University Press.

Galanter, M. & Baxi, U. 1989. 'Panchayat Justice: An Indian Experiment in Legal Access in Galanter, M. (Ed.). *Law and Society in Modern India*. Delhi: Oxford University Press, pp. 54–91.

Ganesan, A. 1997. 'Interview with Christian Aid Researcher'. *Human Rights Watch*, April.

Gani, A. 1996. 'Who Joins the Unions and Why? Evidence from India'. *International Journal of Manpower* 17(6/7): 54–65.

Ghosh, R. N. & Roy, K. C. 1997. 'The Changing Status of Women in India: Impact of Urbanization and Development'. *International Journal of Social Economics* 24(7/8/9): 902–17.

Gokhale, S. D., Pandit, N. & Raj, R. 1994. *Economic Potential of the Elderly and Local Level Policy Development on Consequences of Ageing in India*. New York: United Nations.

Gopalan, S. & Stahl, A. 1998. 'Application of American Management Theories and Practices to the Indian Business Environment: Understanding the Impact of National Culture', *American Business Review* 16(2): 30–40.

Gopinath, C. 1998. 'Alternative Approaches to Indigenous Management in India'. *Management International Review* 38(3): 257–75.

Government of India. 2000. *Ninth Five Year Plan: 1997–2002 Volumes I and II*. http://www.nic.in/ninthplan.html

Government of India. 2000a. *India 2000: A Reference Annual*, Research, Reference and Training Division, Publications Division, Ministry of Information and Broadcasting.

Government of India. 2000b. *100 Days of the New Government (October 13–January 20, 2000): Policies Programmes & Initiatives*. Press Information Bureau. http://pib.nic.in/archive/100daysgovt/eng100days20.html

Gupta, A., Koshal, M. & Koshal, R. K. 1998. 'Women Managers in India: Challenges and Opportunities'. *Equal Opportunities International* 17(8): 14–26.

Gupta, D. 1999. 'Out of Sight, Out of Mind'. *Business India,* 26 July–8 August: 111.

Hazarika, A 1999. 'Public Sector Undertakings Keen on Permitting Shift Duty for Women'. *Business Line*, 12 February: 2.

Heggade, O. D. 1998. 'International Labour Standards and India — The Case of Women Labour'. *The Indian Journal of Economics* 41(4): 1035–43.

Hofstede, G. 1980. *Culture's Consequences: International Differences in Work-related Values*. California: Sage Publications.

Hofstede, G. 1991. *Cultures and Organizations: Software of the Mind*. London: McGraw-Hill.

Human Rights Committee. 1997. *Treaties and Reports to Treaty Bodies*. Geneva: ILO.

Human Rights Watch. 1996. *The Small Hands of Slavery — Bonded Child Labor in India*. New York: Human Rights Watch.

India Labour Law Survey. 1997. *Asia Women Workers Newsletter*, January.

Jain, H. C. 1991. 'Is There a Coherent Human Resource Management System in India'. *International Journal of Public Sector Management* 4(3): 18–30.

Jain, M. 1996. 'Child Labour: A Growing Phenomenon in India'. In Raghavan, K. & Sekhar, L. (Eds). *Poverty and Employment*. New Delhi: New Age International Publishers.

Jain, H. C. & Ratnam, C. S. V. 1994. 'Affirmative Action in Employment for the Scheduled Castes and the Scheduled Tribes in India'. *International Journal of Manpower* 15(7): 6–25.

Khandker, S. R. 1992. *Earnings, Occupational Choice, and Mobility in Segmented Labor Markets of India*. Washington: World Bank Discussion Papers, no. 154.

Kingdon, G. G. 1998. 'Does the Labour Market Explain Lower Female Schooling in India?'. *The Journal of Development Studies* 35(1): 39–65.

Kundu, A. 1997. 'Trends and Structure of Employment in the 1990s — Implication for Urban Growth'. *Economic and Political Weekly* 32(22): 1399–1405.

Kundu, A. & Gupta, S. 1996. 'Migration Urbanisation and Regional Inequality'. *Economic and Political Weekly* 31(52): 53.

Lawler, J. J., Jain, H. C., Ratnam, C. S. V. & Atmiyandana, V. 1995. 'Human Resource Management in Developing Economies: A Comparison of India and Thailand'. *The International Journal of Human Resource Management* 6(2): 319–46.

Malkin, S. A. 1990. 'Employment Legislation: A Vehicle for Promoting Equality of the Handicapped in India and in the United States'. *Comparative Labor Law Journal* 11(3): 352–71.

Mayer, P. 1999. 'India's Falling Sex Ratios'. *Population and Development Review* 25(2): 323–5.

Mehra, P. 1999. *An Executive Guide: Work Culture*. The Hindu Business Line on Indiaserver. com, 20 November.

Michigan, A. 1999. 'Public Sector Undertakings Keen on Permitting Shift Duty for Women'. *Business Line*, 12 February: 2.

Mishra, R. K. & Mohammed, A. L. S. 1994. 'Privatisation in India: A Case for the Joint Venture'. *International Journal of Public Sector Management* 7(1): 67–76.

Mitta, M. 1994. 'Racketeering in Quota'. *India Today*, 15 November: 36–8.

Mitra, P. P. & Kaushal, A. 1998. 'International Labour Standards in India: Some Key Issues'. *The Indian Journal of Labour Economics* 41(4): 1013–9.

Mohanty, R. P. 1999. 'Value Innovation Perspective in Indian Organizations'. *Participation and Empowerment: An International Journal* 7(4): 88–103.

Murthy, L. 1997. 'Sexual Harassment: Who Will Slay the Dragon?'. *Business Line*, 15 September: 17.

Olsen, W. 1998. 'Extended Review: Women at Work in India'. *Work, Employment & Society* 12(1): 169–74.

Papola, T. S. 1994. 'Employment Growth and Social Protection of Labour in India'. *Indian Journal of Industrial Relations* 30(2): 117–43

Pradhan, N. B. 1994. 'The Male–Female Wage and Employment Differentials of Educated Manpower in India'. *Journal of Scientific & Industrial Research* 53, March: 248–52.

Raghavan, K., Sharma, H. & Sekhar, L. 1994. *Impact of New Economic Policy on Manpower and Employment in India*. New Delhi: Agricole Publishing Academy.

Rai, S. M. 1999. 'Developing Explanations for Difference(s): Gender and Village-level Democracy in India and China'. *New Political Economy* 4(2): 233–49.

Raman, S. 1999. 'Daunting Demographics: Examining India's Census'. *Harvard International Review* 21(2): 74–7.

Ramaswamy, G. 1997. *Women and Law*. Hyderabad: UNICEF and Women Development & Child Welfare, Government of Andhra Pradesh.

Rambabu, G. 1996. 'Supreme Court Ruling Must Be Backed by Political Will'. *Business Line*, 13 December: 12.

Ratnam, C. S. V. 1998. 'Multinational Companies in India'. *The International Journal of Human Resource Management* 9(4): 567–89.

Ratnam, C. S. V. & Chandra, V. 1996. 'Sources of Diversity and the Challenge Before Human Resource Management', *International Journal of Manpower* 17(4/5): 76–108.

Sarkar, L. & Sivaramayya, B. 1994. *Women and Law: Contemporary Problems*. New Delhi: Vikas Publishing House.

Shah, N. A. 1992. *Child Labour in India*. New Delhi: Anmol Publications.

Shah, S. 1998. 'Midnight Call & Three Memos'. *The Week*, 13 December http:www.the-week.com/98dec13/life2.html

Shobhana, M. V. 1998. 'History of Legislation on Child Labour in Colonial India', *Social Action* 48(1): 1–6.

Small Industries Development Bank of India. 1999. Information brochure on *How to Start Business*. India: SIDB.

Subrahmanya, R. K. A. 1987. 'Can the Child Labour Act of 1986 Effectively Control Child Labour?. In Gupta, M. & Voll, K. (Eds). *Young Hands at Work — Child Labour in India*. Delhi: Atma Ram & Sons.

Taneja, R. 1997. 'Sexual Harassment of Working Women'. *International Legal Practitioner* 22(4): 136–8.

The World Bank. 1997. *India: Achievement and Challenges in Reducing Poverty*. Washington, DC.

Tomasevski, K. 1998. 'Rights of Women: From Prohibition to Elimination of Discrimination'. *International Social Science Journal* 50(4): 545–58.

Tummala, K. K. 1999. 'Policy of Preference: Lessons from India, the United States, and South Africa'. *Public Administration Review* 59(6): 495–508.

Varandani, G. 1994. *Child Labour and Women Workers*. New Delhi: Ashish Publishing House.

Velkoff, V. A. 1998. *Women's Education in India*. Bureau of the Census, US Department of Commerce.

Weiner, M. 1995. Foreword in Burra, N. *Born to Work: Child Labour in India*. Delhi: Oxford University Press.

Chapter 6

Indonesia

Lynne Bennington

Introduction

Issues of diversity have been paramount in Indonesian society over the past few years. In fact, this period has been described as presenting one of the biggest political, social and economic challenges Indonesia has faced for 30 years (Brown 2000). The latest problems began with the economic crisis in August 1997. The result has been dire consequences for the country including social unrest, involving riots and the killing and raping of ethnic Chinese citizens; food scarcity; a reduction in the number of children receiving education; insolvency of a large number of companies; and dependence on foreign aid for basic survival (Levinson 1998). There has also been an exodus of people and capital from the country and two changes of president, so the world's attention has been focused on Indonesia.

Until recent times, though, Indonesia, the fourth most populous country in the world (Manning 1998), has been one of the least known internationally (Bresnan 1993). Much of what has been written about the country is not in English — it is either in Dutch (owing to the Dutch colonisation and influence from the early 1800s until 1950), or in Bahasa Indonesia. What is known, however, from both the author's field research and the literature, is that Indonesia is a country with enormous diversity and human resource management challenges. Labour and human rights issues, in addition to human capital issues, are at the forefront of Western thinking about Indonesia. The Indonesian Government, on the other hand, has made it very clear that, despite international criticism of its labour and human rights violations, Indonesia will not simply toe the Western line. Indonesia, like some other developing countries, maintains that human rights need to be considered in the context of the culture of the country, and any attempt to import standards is viewed as an illegitimate interference in its affairs (Woodward 1996).

Indonesia is now possibly more divided along religious, ethnic, economic, social and political lines than ever before. However, there are attempts to change this situation. Indonesia has been a signatory for some time to four core International Labour Organisation (ILO) conventions: ILO Convention No. 87, on freedom of association and protection of the right to organise (through Presidential Decree No. 83/1998); Convention No. 98, concerning the right to organise and bargain collectively (through Law No. 18/1956); Convention No. 29, on forced labour (through Indische Staatblad No. 261/1933); and Convention No. 100, concerning equal remuneration for men and women workers for work of equal time (through Law No. 80/1957). In recent times many other conventions have been ratified — for example, Convention No. 105 concerning the abolition of forced labour, Convention No. 111 on discrimination in employment and Convention No. 138 on the minimum working age (*The Jakarta Post* 1999a); and there have been many changes to the military, indicating the possibility of structural changes. Another example is that of a political party, Partai Reformasi Tioghoa Indonesia, which has been established to improve relations between ethnic Chinese and Pribumis, and to transfer business skills to Pribumis. There are also some rare examples of non-discriminatory employment policies: for example, the Indonesian Astra Group not only has a female chief executive officer who is Pribumi but also has a blend of Pribumi, and Chinese Indonesian top and middle management (Habir & Larasati 1999).

In general, though, aspirations for equal opportunity may seem futile when the issues are not simply about pay differentials or retirement age but about people being abducted and interrogated, if not killed, over diversity issues (Gall 1998). These issues provide compelling reasons for those planning to invest in the country to understand the circumstances on the ground in Indonesia. Currently, the situation is changing at a very fast rate, so every effort needs to be made to obtain up-to-date information prior to making decisions in this business environment.

To provide a context for discussion, the demography of Indonesia will be outlined first in this chapter. Then issues of organisational behaviour will be examined, followed by the legal and industrial relations context, general employment conditions, and specific areas of diversity (forced and child labour; women; ethnic, religious and language diversity; people with disabilities; indigenous people; the military; and older workers). The chapter will conclude with some examples of diversity policy and practice.

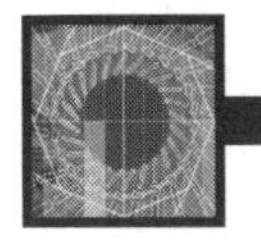

Demography

The Republic of Indonesia (referred to hereafter as Indonesia) comprises over 13 000 islands and a land area of about two million square kilometres (Tambunan 1995); the main language of the 202 million people (Harsono 1999) is Bahasa Indonesia, although there are 250 other regional languages and dialects (Bishop & McNamara 1997). Approximately 70 per cent of Indonesians live in rural areas (Levinson 1998). There are at least 200 ethnic groups (*Straits Times* 1997) although only four are considered to be significant: Javanese (45 per cent), Sundanese (14 per cent), Madurese (7.5 per cent), and Coastal Malays (7.5 per cent) (Levinson 1998). Ethnic Chinese represent less than five per cent of the population yet control 60 to 80 per cent of Indonesia's economic activity (*Straits Times* 1997). Muslims constitute 87 per cent of Indonesians, Protestants are represented by six per cent, Roman Catholics by three per cent, Hindus by two per cent and one per cent by Buddhists (Levinson 1998).

Indonesia's Human Rights Stipulation of the People's Consultative Assembly No. XVII/MPR/1998 sets out a Human Rights Charter that proclaims the right to life, personal development, justice, freedom of association and employment, and provides for protection from discrimination, yet Foster (1998) states that the world of Indonesians is structured in clear castes relating to privilege. The number of people living below the poverty line had soared to 95.8 million (or about 48 per cent of the total population) by the end of 1998 (Harsono 1999). After years of seven per cent annual growth, a severe economic contraction of about 15 per cent has occurred (Liong 1999). Even prior to the contraction there were estimates of over a third of the Indonesian labour force being either underemployed or unemployed (Hadiz 1997).

Different pictures exist, though, with *The Jakarta Post* (1998b) stating that over 50 per cent of the 90 million workforce is underemployed and Manning (1999) arguing that unemployment has never been high compared with other developing countries. The official figures can swing quite markedly almost overnight — for example, from five million unemployed to 23 million unemployed. *The Jakarta Post* (1999d) suggests that this is due to a game played by administrators in terms of how they define unemployment. For example, the current Minister for Manpower bases his definition on the number of people seeking jobs, whereas a previous administration defined someone as employed if he or she had worked even one hour in the previous week.

Although the definition of unemployment might be debatable, Manning (1999) states that nearly 70 per cent of unemployment in towns and cities occurs in young senior high school and tertiary graduates. The rates of unemployment in these groups were between 15 and 30 per cent in 1996, and the rates were higher among females than males (Manning & Junankar 1998). Youth unemployment, partly explained by Manning and Junankar (1998) as being due to selective job search behaviour, was also high before the economic crisis of 1997. Female graduates take longer to find work than male graduates; the differences have been explained by the fact that more women eventually work in the civil service and this process takes longer owing to the lengthy application and recruitment procedures (Report A 1997).

Small enterprises account for about two-thirds of all employment (van Diermen 1997). The labour force may be divided into the following categories: agriculture 41 per cent; trade, restaurant and hotel 19.8 per cent; manufacturing 14 per cent; construction 4.8 per cent; transport and communications 4.75 per cent; and other 15.65 per cent (CIA 1999). Most of the 'employed' do not figure in the story of human resource management (HRM) and diversity management, though, since nearly 70 per cent work in the informal sector (Firdausy 1995).

In the formal sector, the proportion of women has increased markedly; for example, between 1980 and 1990 the participation rate increased from 32.7 per cent to 39.2 per cent (Triaswati 1996). Unfortunately, though, there has been a feminisation of the workforce low-skilled, labour-intensive industries which may be related to employer views that women 'are more easily repressed and that women are by nature more docile and controllable' (Hadiz 1997: 112).

Women dominate the workforce in industries such as tobacco, textiles, and food and beverages, and there is a preference for employing them due to their perceived dexterity, patience, unassertiveness and deference to authority (White 1990). Triaswati (1996), in referring to an unpublished World Bank report, points out that women always receive lower wages than men for certain basic skills, business skills and technical skills but that income disparity between men and women diminishes significantly with greater educational achievement.

Although some women have attained senior positions in both the public and private sectors, in the civil service women represent 37.4 per cent of employees but only 5.5 per cent are in positions of authority (Bureau of Democracy, Human Rights and Labor 1999). The gender gap in 1990 in the various categories of employment in Indonesia indicated that men were 540 per cent more likely to hold management positions, 74 per cent more likely to hold professional positions, 205 per cent more likely to hold clerical positions, 60 per cent more likely to hold sales positions, and 40 per cent more likely to hold service positions (Cheng 1999). It is perhaps not surprising, therefore, that there has been a State Minister for Women's Empowerment since 1983 (Tjiptoherijanto 2000a).

Notwithstanding this, the Indonesian Government claims that Indonesian women have attained equality as evidenced by their participation in the military, although the actual roles they perform should be carefully examined before accepting this assertion (Sunindyo 1998).

Triaswati (1996) states that the women workers in Indonesia typically follow the Asian rule that requires women to have full responsibility in managing the family so they, in turn, hire low-skilled women from rural areas for childcare, cooking and cleaning duties. My observation, while conducting research in Indonesia, was that it was not uncommon for the domestic staff to 'live-in' and to send most of their

earnings back to their villages where their children were cared for by extended family members.

The educational level of the population is not particularly high. Compulsory education has been raised from six to nine years, but the law, passed in 1994, has not been implemented fully because of inadequate school facilities and the lack of family financial resources to support children to stay in school. Official and unofficial fees for public education, including payments for registration, books, meals, transport and uniforms, have become prohibitively high for many families (May 1999). Every year at least a million children drop out of school mainly because of the costs and the need for children to supplement family income, but this drop-out rate increased dramatically with the economic crisis (Bureau of Democracy, Human Rights and Labor 1999).

At the same time, children's advocates and labour analysts agree that the number of working children has increased significantly owing to the economic crisis which continues to affect the country. According to recent government statistics, eight per cent of all children between the ages of 10 and 14 work; of these, half go to school and also work, and half work exclusively (Bureau of Democracy, Human Rights and Labor 1999). Unofficial estimates of working children are higher.

According to the Ministry of Social Affairs, 20 000 street children lived in Jakarta in 1997 but NGOs report that the number may have increased by more than 60 per cent as a result of the economic crisis (Bureau of Democracy, Human Rights and Labor 1999); and the increase was obviously not confined to Jakarta. The street children perform a variety of tasks such as selling newspapers and other small items, shining shoes, and helping to park or watch cars. According to so-called credible sources, there are several thousand children working in hazardous conditions on fishing platforms off the east coast of north Sumatra (Bangun & Sprague 1999). Many thousands also work in factories and fields (Bureau of Democracy, Human Rights and Labor 1999).

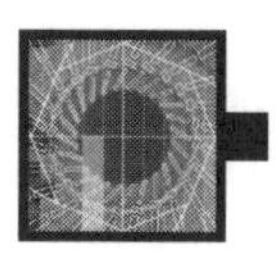

Organisational behaviour

The profile of organisational behaviour is quite different from that of Western countries, and from many other Asian countries. Hofstede (cited in Stening & Ngan 1997) places Indonesians very high in power distance and collectivism, and quite high in 'femininity' and in 'uncertainty avoidance', although other researchers have detected a narrowing of the differences between Indonesian and American managers when compared with Hofstede's earlier findings (Heuer, Cummings & Hutabarat 1999).

According to Foster (1998), many of the Indonesians' characteristic behaviours have arisen from their religious beliefs — for example, never touching people on the tops of their heads, which they consider the holiest part of the body. Other behaviours that should be observed by foreigners include:

- a 'soft' handshake
- a slight bow or dipping of the head as a sign of respect when being introduced to someone
- no direct eye contact with superiors
- greeting others according to their titles or positions, for example — 'Mr Engineer'
- use of the word 'we' rather than 'I', since this is considered less confrontational (Foster 1998).

It has been said of Indonesian management that it is 'traditional, patrimonial and hierarchically oriented, and international practices like empowerment, participation and incentive orientation' are irrelevant or, at best, in need of adjustment to, and secondary to, Indonesian indigenous characteristics (Habir & Larasati 1999: 548).

Some interesting examples of multicultural clashes are described by Elashmawi (1998), who reports on communication issues between American, Japanese and Indonesian team members in an Indonesian telecommunications joint venture. He suggests that the Indonesians are concerned with group harmony, cooperation, seniority and relationships, whereas the Americans, in contrast, are concerned about openness, self-reliance, risk taking and profit. Elashmawi (1998) discusses some of the very practical 'mistakes' that can be made in joint ventures in Indonesia, such as expecting people to arrive on time, and expecting only invitees to attend meetings whereas others may also attend. In the course of the meeting, Indonesians will expect that the senior person be asked to comment before others; side discussions, considered the height of rudeness in some Western countries, will be commonplace; food should be served with tea; frequent breaks in meetings will be anticipated; and breaks for prayers may be expected.

Hutchings (1996) in comparing Singapore, Malaysia and Indonesia, comments that Indonesia is the least open of these countries to foreign workplace practices. In citing Vatikiotis, it is pointed out that MNCs activities will be monitored through the authority exercised by the military and police (Hutchings 1996). Lasserre and Schutte's (1995) research also indicated that foreign managers experience difficulties with access to, and the reliability of, information. This research also indicated that local staff inclined to low levels of loyalty and high 'job hopping' behaviours, and employers tended to be paternalistic.

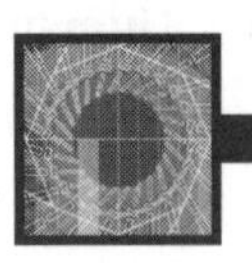

Legal and industrial relations context

The law in Indonesia arises from numerous sources, is extremely complicated and somewhat vague, and much discretion is left to government authorities. The system has been described as 'either primitive or ... entirely coopted by the military–business elite or both', and the law essentially supports the political culture of the time (Lindsey 1999: 11).

Many 'safeguards' are provided in Indonesia's legal code, but 'in many important respects that protection is not available in practice ... The legal system [is] unresponsive, corrupt, politicised and ineffective, [and] offers little recourse to the individual in righting perceived wrongs' (Schwarz 1994: 245). At the same time, Indonesia has sought to tightly control the labour force in order to maximise the attractiveness of Indonesia to foreign investors (Islam 1989).

There are three types of employment regulated by the Employment Law: fixed period employment, which requires a written contract in Bahasa Indonesia; indefinite period or 'permanent' employment, for which a written contract is not mandatory; and traditional employment in the informal sector, which is essentially unregulated (Surowidjojo 1999). A three-month probationary period applies to permanent appointments and once this period has expired the termination of a person's employment is almost impossible; government approval is needed (Surowidjojo 1999).

Before discussing the general conditions of employment in the next section, the industrial relations framework will be summarised. The labour relations system in

Indonesia is based on the national ideology of Pancasila, the rhetoric of which has been developed to suggest that industrial relations should be conducted in the context of partnership and production; partnership and profit; and partnership and responsibility towards: God the Almighty, nation and state, the community, fellow employees and family, and the employee (Fehring 1999). Hadiz (1997) suggests that industrial relations are reflected in the role of the benevolent father to both capital and labour, with no acceptance of the right of workers to strike as this would contravene the family-based principles which govern Pancasila. One of the more disturbing features of the recent history of industrial relations is that those who have protested about the prohibition of labour unions and demanded better conditions of employment have been sentenced to jail, have disappeared or have been killed (Woodward 1996).

Three months' imprisonment or a fine of up to 100 000 rupiah are commonly prescribed penalties for non-compliance with labour legislation, although the new labour Bill provides for fines of 50 million rupiah and a maximum sentence of six months in jail (*The Jakarta Post* 1997b). Yet there have still been calls for employers to treat workers better. For example, the Governor of Jakarta, in quoting the findings of a joint city administration and University of Indonesia study, indicated that there are six factors that can lead to disputes between employers and employees: the minimum wage, workers' demands for pay increases, overtime fees, doing overtime, incompatible worker–employer relationships, and lack of freedom to pursue career or education (*The Jakarta Post* 1997e).

One of the major features of the culture in Indonesian organisations is the *keluarga besar* concept, which means that staff are seen as part of 'one big family which shares common purposes, and friendly and familiar relationships' (Rohdewohld 1995: 115). This is exemplified in the public sector by the compulsory membership of Dharma Wanita, the organisation of civil servants' wives. Another illustration is the practice of either paying married workers more than unmarried workers or providing extra allowances for those with a spouse and children (for example, a larger allocation of rice per month).

Although independent trade unions are now legally sanctioned in practice they have not been tolerated. For many years there has been foreign pressure on Indonesia to recognise worker rights and independent trade unions, and since the demise of President Soeharto there has been a decision to permit independent trade unions, but it is too early to predict the consequences (Fehring 1999).

Private sector workers are now free by law to form worker organisations without prior authorisation, and unions may draw up their own constitutions and rules and elect their representatives. In 1998 the government ratified ILO Convention 87 on freedom of association and issued a new regulation on the registration of workers' organisations (*The Jakarta Post* 1998a). The new regulation eliminates numerical and other requirements that were previously a barrier to union registration. It provides for registration of unions at the factory, district, provincial and national level, and allows unions to form federations and confederations. The regulation prohibits unions based on political orientation, religion, gender or ethnic groups.

Under the Law on Manpower Affairs enacted in October 1997, workers may form unions on the basis of 'democratic consultation' with other workers in the same company and may join with other unions to form sectoral and intersectoral federations. The law was scheduled to take effect on 1 October 1998, but Parliament amended it to postpone implementation until 1 October 2000 to allow time for revision, consultation with concerned groups and preparation of implementing regulations (Surowidjojo 1999).

The Indonesian Prosperity Trade Union (SBSI) claims that companies are continuing to fire SBSI members because of their affiliation with the union or because they sought to organise SBSI units within their factories; and the SBSI has indicated difficulties in registering some of its workplace units (Bureau of Democracy, Human Rights and Labor 1999).

Civil servants must belong to KORPRI, a non-union association. State enterprise employees, defined to include those working in enterprises in which the state has a five per cent holding or greater, are usually required to join KORPRI, but a small number of state enterprises have SPSI (Federation of All-Indonesian Trade Unions) units.

Prior to 1995 police approval for all meetings of five or more people was required and, although the government stated that this regulation would be relaxed, in practice, it continues to apply to union meetings. While Pancasila principles call for labour–management differences to be settled by consensus, private sector strikes are frequent, even though the law still requires intensive mediation and prior notice (not approval) before a strike can occur. In practice, dispute settlement procedures are rarely followed, and formal notice of the intent to strike is rarely given because Department of Manpower procedures are slow and have little credibility with workers (Bureau of Democracy, Human Rights and Labor 1999).

New revisions to the law allow workers to go on strike without fear of losing their wages (*The Jakarta Post* 1997b), provided that at least 72 hours' notice is given to the government and the employer, but street rallies are banned — strikes must be confined to the factories or workplaces where the disputes occur. Other revisions include the requirement for trade unions to register themselves and the names of all of their members with the Ministry of Manpower. An editorial in *The Jakarta Post* (1997c) expressed the opinion that the new legislation still fails to guarantee workers' most basic rights but provides some assurance to investors that their operations will not be continually disrupted by strikes.

Charges of anti-union discrimination are adjudicated by regional and national labour dispute resolution committees, and their decisions can be appealed to the State Administrative Court. An interesting decision was made by this body in September 1997, when the State Administrative Court reversed a ruling that ordered the Hong Kong Bank to reinstate 166 union members who went on strike, despite government regulations making it illegal to fire workers solely for striking or for other union activity (Bureau of Democracy, Human Rights and Labor 1999).

Decisions such as this have led many union members, believing that the system is biased in favour of employers, to go directly to the National Human Rights Commission, Parliament, and NGOs (Bureau of Democracy, Human Rights and Labor 1999).

There are reports that the police and the military continue to be involved in labour matters, although their involvement is now less visible. One exception to this was when army troops, who were pelted with rocks and other missiles, fired rubber bullets on striking workers at a steel plant near Jakarta — 23 workers, as well as three soldiers, were injured (Bureau of Democracy, Human Rights and Labor 1999). However, the most common form of military involvement in labour issues reflects collusion between police and military personnel and employers, and usually 'takes

the form of intimidation of workers by security personnel in civilian dress' (Bureau of Democracy, Human Rights and Labor 1999: 11).

The constitution does not explicitly forbid discrimination based on gender, race, disability, language or social status. However, it stipulates equal rights and obligations for all citizens, both native and naturalised. The 1993 Guidelines of State Policy (legal statutes) explicitly states that women have the same rights, obligations and opportunities as men. However, guidelines from 1978, 1983, 1988 and 1993 also state that women's participation in the development process must not conflict with their role in improving family welfare and the education of the younger generation. Marriage law dictates that the man is the head of the family. Marriage law for Muslims, based on Islamic law, allows men to have up to four wives if the husband can provide equally for each of his wives. Civil servants who wish to marry a second woman also must have permission from their supervisors. Cabinet officials and military personnel customarily have been forbidden to have second wives.

Some interesting laws exist that may cause concern particularly to foreigners living in Indonesia. The 1958 Citizenship Law states that children's citizenship is based on the citizenship of the father only (Bureau of Democracy, Human Rights and Labor 1999). Children of citizen mothers and foreign fathers are considered foreigners and need visas to remain in the country until the age of 18, when they can apply for citizenship (Bureau of Democracy, Human Rights and Labor 1999: 11). Such children must attend international schools and are prohibited from attending Indonesian schools. The children of foreign women married to citizens are deemed to be citizens and are not allowed to attend international schools in Indonesia. These women usually are taxed as the foreign head of household, but they do not have property, business or inheritance rights. The need for change in these areas has been acknowledged, but change is slow to occur.

Labour law applies in export processing zones (EPZs) as in the rest of the country, although nongovernmental observers believe that in practice enforcement of laws in EPZs is weaker.

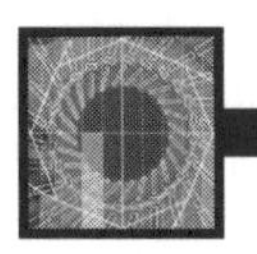

General conditions of employment

It is important to understand the general conditions of employment in Indonesia before examining specific legal and diversity factors. The conditions of employment are highly regulated (Surowidjojo 1999) and quite onerous in many respects for employers. However, it could be argued that the balance is certainly in favour of the employers because employees are often required to work very long hours for little pay (White 1990).

As already stated, the informal sector is larger than the formal sector so most workers are not covered by employment regulations. Employers do not register these people. Moreover, many employers only pay workers' social security contribution fees (which cover old age, death, disability, permanent disability, occupational accidents and diseases contracted in the workplace) with respect to permanent workers and not to those employed on a contract basis (*The Jakarta Post* 1997f). Notwithstanding the sheer size and importance of the informal sector, the discussion here necessarily will focus on the formal sector.

A minimum wage is set but differs depending upon the region, although the discussion in Indonesia is now turning more to an appropriate wage rather than a minimum wage. For Jakarta, the minimum wage in May 1999 was set at Rp150 000 per month (or approximately US$8.82). Manning argues that 'minimum wages have been set conservatively and are still substantially lower . . . than the official estimates of minimum physical needs even for a single worker' (1993: 72). Hadiz (1997) states that in the early 1990s state officials admitted that the minimum wage covered only 60 per cent of a worker's minimum physical needs; it is now believed to provide for about 95 per cent of the minimum physical requirement of people (*The Jakarta Post* 1997h). In comparison with other Asian countries such as Thailand, the Philippines, South Korea, Taiwan, Hong Kong and Singapore, the average wages are significantly lower (Tjiptoherijanto 1998).

Despite this, many employers do not pay the government-decreed minimum wage rates. Although changes began to occur in 1994, there is still provision for employers to seek compliance deferral for up to 12 months, thus providing an escape from paying the minimum wage in some cases. Many businesspeople have complained that their businesses cannot afford increases in the minimum wage because of the very high prevalence of so-called 'invisible costs' of doing business, which range from graft to money made available to ensure cooperation from the military. The 'fees' paid by employers to various government agencies are seen as normal practice in bureaucrat–business relationships (Lesmanaa 1999; *The Jakarta Post* 2000b). These 'fees' facilitate procurement of licences and protect the employers from 'harassment' by workers. It is this collusion between employers, bureaucrats and security officials that is seen as responsible for peaceful conditions at production facilities, but also as responsible for workers being paid only 60 per cent of their wage entitlement while the remaining 40 per cent goes to numerous government officials (Lesmanaa 1999). However, estimates of these invisible costs range widely from two to in excess of 30 per cent of total operating costs (Hadiz 1997)

The other minimum employment conditions include: paid annual vacation leave of not less that two weeks per year; 12 paid public holidays per year; seven hours per day or 40 hours' work per week with one hour of rest for each four hours of work; incremental overtime rates; sick leave up to 12 months, not all fully paid; accident compensation, which covers all medical costs, including death benefits, social insurance (the employer must contribute five per cent of the employee's salary, the employee contributes one per cent and the government contributes two per cent); severance pay; service pay based on organisational performance; and wage protection with interest to be paid on unpaid wages. Protection is also granted specifically to those who suffer from illness, in that they cannot have their services terminated if they are absent for less than 12 months. Sick leave payments consist of 100 per cent of salary for the first three months, 75 per cent of salary for the second three months, 50 per cent of salary for the third three months and 25 per cent of salary for the final three months (Geringer, Frayne & IPMI 1993).

The Ministry of Manpower continues publicly to urge employers to comply with the law. However, government enforcement and supervision of labour standards is generally weak. Breaches of labour laws have been explained as a consequence of the shortage of labour inspectors, lack of effective sanctions, unwieldy procedures for conflict resolution and possibly unrealistic standards for Indonesia's level of development (Manning 1993).

In the civil service, conditions of employment are somewhat different, complex and opaque. Apart from the usual rights, civil servants participate in health and pension insurance schemes, and, at least until recently, had lifetime security of employment. Sometimes, though, the income of a civil servant does not reach the minimum standard set by the government and is not sufficient to cover the cost of living (Rohdewohld 1995), so salary supplements exist in the form of various standardised allowances such as rice and family allowances, special allowances when working in remote areas, housing or a housing allowance, medical care, and either transport to and from work, or a petrol allowance. When working on specific 'aided' projects, extra payments, which can be very substantial, are also paid; for example, one civil servant interviewed received a house, a voucher for 150 litres of petrol per month, rice for himself, his wife and child, and project honoraria (Bennington 2000).

Some argue that there are fewer employment regulations in Indonesia than elsewhere and that compliance is not a problem, while others state that compliance is a problem and/or that there is greater regulation than elsewhere but virtually no enforcement. The real problem is that very few people actually know the extent of the regulations owing to 'the lack of public access to legal information' (Rohdewohld 1995). The last English translation of the legislation was published in 1992.

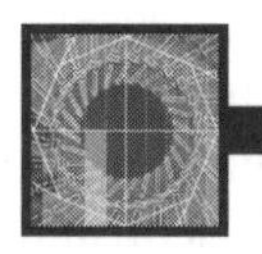

Special diversity factors

Forced labour and child labour

The government prohibits forced and bonded labour by children but does not always enforce this effectively. About two million children work at least four hours a day, although this number is believed to have risen further as a result of the economic crisis (Bureau of Democracy, Human Rights and Labor 1999). Children often work long hours, receive low pay, have little information about their rights and are far from their families.

Employers are allowed to hire children but they must give them access to education, socialisation and 'mental and spiritual' guidance, and they must not work them for more than four hours a day (*The Jakarta Post* 1997g).

In March 1997, the government and the ILO signed a memorandum of understanding on child labour which commits Indonesia to 'promote conditions to enable the government to protect working children and progressively prohibit, restrict and regulate child labor with a view to its ultimate elimination' (Bureau of Democracy, Human Rights and Labor 1999). A statement of intent was also signed and witnessed by President Habibie and the ILO director in Jakarta committing the government to ratify the ILO convention on minimum working age no later than June 1999, yet in February 2000 a newspaper report indicated that the Minister of Manpower had suggested that Indonesia ratifying ILO Convention No. 182 on Elimination and Immediate Action for Elimination of Worst Forms of Child Labour (*The Jakarta Post* 2000a), so some of these changes do not occur with great haste. Although the ILO has sponsored training of labour inspectors on child labour matters, enforcement remains lax.

The government acknowledges that some children have to work for socio-economic reasons, so in 1987 a regulation was issued on 'Protection of Children Forced to Work which legalises the employment of children under the age of 14 who must work to contribute to the income of their families' (Bureau of Democracy, Human Rights and Labor 1999). It requires parental consent, prohibits dangerous or difficult work, limits work to four hours daily and requires employers to report the number of children working under its provisions. It does not set a minimum age for children in this category but states that adolescents (aged 15 to 17) cannot work during certain hours of the night, below ground, in mines or in jobs that would have an adverse effect on morality, such as in entertainment facilities (Bureau of Democracy, Human Rights and Labor 1999). There are no known prosecutions of employers for violation of the child employment legislation.

One recent report describes the conditions of 10- to 17-year-old children who live and work on isolated fishing platforms with little or no amenities, no beds, perched metres above the waves, 15 to 50 kilometres off the coast, working for up to 20 hours a day for somewhere between $7.50 and $12 per month for a minimum of three months at a time (Bangun & Sprague 1999). It is suggested that there may be several thousand children working under these conditions. Most are recruited from farming communities, and once they arrive at the work site, miles offshore, they are held as virtual prisoners and are not permitted to leave for at least three months and until a replacement worker can be found. There are reports of physical, verbal and sexual abuse of the children. In November 1997, the Department of Manpower issued a circular letter having the force of law which prohibits the hiring of persons under the age of 14 on fishing platforms (Bureau of Democracy, Human Rights and Labor 1999).

There are still reports of bonded labour: for example, in East Kalimantan a logging company reportedly has trapped Dayak labourers in a cycle of debt and turned them into bonded labourers (Bureau of Democracy, Human Rights and Labor 1999). Also, there were reports in 1997 that the military forced villagers to perform uncompensated labour in Irian Jaya, but the military denied such reports (Bureau of Democracy, Human Rights and Labor 1999).

Women

Although the constitution states that women are equal to and have the same rights, obligations and opportunities as men, in practice, women face some legal discrimination (Bureau of Democracy, Human Rights and Labor 1999). As already stated, female workers in manufacturing generally receive lower wages then men, and many jobs are gender stereotyped. For example, a study of the tourism industry in Bali, a Hindu community in a Muslim state, found that men have many more opportunities than women for employment primarily because some occupations are regarded as more appropriate for men (Cukier, Norris & Wall 1996). The roles of bellboy, gardener, security guard and driver were perceived to be more appropriate for men owing to strength requirements and the possible need to work at night; occupations such as cook, front office clerk, table waiting and guest relations jobs were seen as more appropriate for women.

In addition to receiving lower wages, when women are employed in factories they are often hired as day labourers instead of as full-time permanent employees, so that companies avoid providing benefits, such as maternity leave. Often women are not given the extra benefits and salary that are their due when they are the head of household, and in some cases they do not receive employment benefits for their husband and children, such as medical insurance and income tax deductions.

Some special provisions exist for women, though, in that they are entitled to three months' paid maternity leave, two days' paid menstruation leave per month, and they

are protected from dismissal due to marriage, pregnancy or confinement. Other protections include special conditions with respect to working at night (e.g. the employer is obliged to make a written request to the local office of the Department of Manpower which sets out the kind of business and character of the job and the reasons why they want to employ women at night). The employer is required to give full protection in relation to safety, health and 'sexuality' by ensuring that the female worker is not pregnant and is at least 18 years old; and the employer must provide transportation, and good nutritious meals and drinks. Women are also 'prohibited to work in mining and any jobs that are dangerous for their health, safety and honour' (Triaswati 1996: 20).

In spite of the laws that provide women with maternity leave, the government has acknowledged that pregnant women often are dismissed or replaced while on leave; and some companies even require that women sign statements that they do not intend to become pregnant (Bureau of Democracy, Human Rights and Labor 1999). *The Jakarta Post* (1997a) reports that one Social Legal Aid Information Centre (Sisbikum) recorded an 80 per cent increase in legal cases for women in the two years until 1997, with half of the complaints related to pregnancy, about a quarter related to marriage to co-workers, and about seven per cent related to employers refusing to allow time for breastfeeding at work. Some job advertisements require that female applicants be single (*The Jakarta Post* 1997a).

Although the Employment Law mandates two days of menstrual leave per month for women, this leave is not allowed in all cases, and some women in management positions would not openly take such leave but might instead report that they were working at home (Bennington 2000). This issue remains sensitive. For example, workers in Jakarta marched 10 kilometres in protest, demanding their right to maternity leave, menstruation leave and annual leave as well as increases in their daily meal and shift allowances (*The Jakarta Post* 1999b).

Some companies insist that young unmarried female workers reside in company-provided dormitories in which there are strict controls on their behaviour even outside of working hours (Hadiz 1997). Questions about whether this is protective or oppressive might be debated.

Hill (1996) found, on a union study tour of Indonesia, that women suffer from a range of illnesses due to repetitive and hazardous work conditions. He also found that sexual exploitation of women was common. For example, he reports that women are 'induced to exchange sex for the opportunity of further overtime. And those who, as a consequence, become pregnant are often disowned by the supervisor responsible and sacked' (Hill 1996: 29). Even though only a small percentage of harassment incidents are reported, when they reach court, women generally lose their cases (Triaswati 1996).

Notwithstanding the protective legislation for women in some areas, the regulations are reported to be commonly neglected (Grijns & van Velzen 1993). Employers can avoid hiring women if they so choose; and, in fact, one female HR manager suggested that many managers now have to think about whether they are prepared to hire women given that the same productivity is 'unlikely' to result owing to the special conditions, such as menstruation leave, which apply to them.

It is possible that the situation for women will improve, if the symbolic action of signing the protocol of the United Nations Convention for the Elimination of All Forms of Discrimination Against Women (UN–CEDAW) in March this year has any effect (*The Jakarta Post* 2000c).

Ethnic, religious and language diversity

Although the government officially promotes racial and ethnic tolerance, the ethnic Chinese, who constitute approximately three per cent of the population and are major players in the economy, have been denied the right to run businesses in rural Indonesia (Bureau of Democracy, Human Rights and Labor 1999). Regulations also prohibit the operation of Chinese schools, exclusive Chinese cultural groups or trade associations, and public display of Chinese characters, although they are still found on products. The government has its own Chinese-language daily newspaper, but otherwise legislation bans Chinese-language material. An exception to this apparent intolerance is the government-sanctioned Chinese-language instruction for employees in the tourism industry, and the distribution of locally printed Chinese-language tourist brochures, programs and similar material to Chinese-speaking tourists.

Chinese language instruction generally is prohibited, although the University of Indonesia offers Chinese language courses. State universities have informal quotas that limit the number of ethnic Chinese students. Also, the law forbids the celebration of the Chinese New Year in temples or public places, but enforcement is limited (Bureau of Democracy, Human Rights and Labor 1999). There has been some concern that Chinese-language publications will exacerbate racial tensions.

The government has systematically discriminated against the Chinese by placing a special symbol on their identity cases so that they can readily be distinguished from other Indonesians (Ching 1998). Moreover, the Chinese have been restricted from joining the civil service, the armed forces and the police force, and from entering university.

Different religious beliefs are accommodated in the workplace, although, since over 85 per cent of the population is Muslim (Bishop & McNamara 1997), the focus is on providing for their religious needs. For example, although a prayer room is not compulsory, many employers will provide a suitable venue, and employees are provided with time — not more than ten minutes five times a day — for the purpose of praying, and extra time on Friday. However, one area of concern is that typically there are religious differences between the majority of factory workers and their supervisors and employers, the former being Muslim and the latter foreign or Chinese and non-Muslim (Hadiz 1997). A Korean employer, interviewed by Hadiz (1997), reported that employers in Indonesia sometimes complain about the time lost when workers observe the Muslim requirement of daily prayers at the set times (two out of five of which take place during normal work hours). Furthermore, a common worker demand during strike action is for the provision of adequate places for worship within the workplace. Nevertheless, public holidays recognise days of religious importance to those of many different faiths.

One interesting case arising out of religious diversity is the strike by women workers at the Tanashin Indonesia factory who demanded money instead of the packaged snacks offered by management during Ramadan — a period in which Muslims cannot eat during the day (Anonymous 1997). The Japanese owners of the factory initially refused, suggesting that the workers should take the snacks home rather than receive money in lieu. The striking workers eventually won on this issue.

The Sabbath for Muslims is Friday, so many businesses actually slow down or even close on Thursday evening, but may open again on Saturday or Sunday.

People with disabilities

According to United Nations, there are 10 million disabled persons in Indonesia, although the Ministry of Social Affairs estimates that three per cent of the population, or six million persons, are disabled (Bureau of Democracy, Human Rights and Labor 1999). However, there are no precise statistics. Families often hide their disabled family members to avoid social stigma or embarrassment. The disabled face considerable discrimination in employment, although some factories have made special efforts to hire disabled workers. Nevertheless, many disabled citizens beg for a living.

The current laws protecting the disabled include Law No. 4/1997 and Presidential Decree No. 83/1999, but they are reported to be somewhat ineffective because they really only 'appeal' to companies to recruit people with disabilities (*The Jakarta Post* 1999c). Also, implementation regulations have not been issued, so the impact of the law remains unclear. The law seeks to provide access to education, employment and other assistance for the disabled. It requires companies that employ over 100 persons to give one per cent of their jobs to the disabled. The law mandates accessibility for the disabled to public facilities. However, virtually no buildings or public transportation have been designed with such accessibility in mind.

Indigenous people

All Indonesians except ethnic Chinese are considered indigenous by the government. Nonetheless, it does specifically recognise both the existence of several isolated communities in which about 1.5 million live, and their right to participate fully in political and social life (Bureau of Democracy, Human Rights and Labor 1999).

Currently, there are concerns that the government's plans to resettle people from densely populated areas to sparsely populated areas outside Java will threaten indigenous cultures and create social problems because, in some areas, relations between transmigrants and indigenous people are hostile (Bureau of Democracy, Human Rights and Labor 1999). Tjiptoherijanto (2000b) has advised that recent incidents in West Kalimantan involving a clash between Dayaks, an indigenous people, and Maduranese, incoming people from Madura, illustrates that 'unity in diversity' is still merely a slogan. An increase in the frequency of clashes between indigenous people and transmigrants has been attributed to resentment over the facilities given to the transmigrants (Tjiptoherijanto 2000b).

The military

The role of the military is also worth noting in this context, given the obvious power that members of the military have in Indonesian politics. The armed forces follow the principle of *dwifungsi*, which means that the military plays the dual role of a national army and an active political and economic force in the governing of the country (Levinson 1998). Their power appears to extend even further. Even though, in some countries, there is concern about discrimination against those with military backgrounds, the military owns many businesses and current members of the military and retired members are on the boards of private and state-owned companies (Levinson 1998).

Older workers

Age discrimination legislation does not exist in Indonesia. Advertisements in Indonesian newspapers and on the Internet commonly refer to age, sex and the need to

provide a photograph. Although ethnicity is not generally specified, it has been argued by interviewees that for certain positions there is a preference for Chinese (e.g. finance and marketing). The publicly stated (or politically correct) position is that ethnic and religious differences are not of concern in the workplace. However, Habir (1995) reported that ethnic differences remain sensitive (and events since this time would certainly support this view).

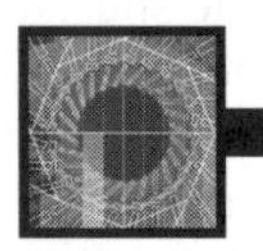

Conclusions

Diversity policy and practice

Hutchings' (1996) comparative study of equal employment opportunity practices in Australia, Singapore, Malaysia and Indonesia found that equal opportunity was not particularly important for either Japanese or Australian companies operating in Indonesia. Moreover, Hutchings has suggested that even among local Indonesians there is not a great deal of interest; for example, she says there is an 'underlying dynamic between class, ethnic and gender relations', meaning that women of privileged ethnicity or class see no value in focusing on the interests of women from other groups (Hutchings 1996: 66).

Certainly, the large multinational firms have been subject to considerable criticism about their management of workers in third world countries, yet Hadiz (1997) argues that there is little evidence that they treat their workers any worse than other firms. The point perhaps needs to be made here that, in some cases, this is hardly the best benchmark to be used. However, Hancock (1997), an Australian researcher, found that women in a rural Nike factory (which is a Taiwanese joint venture) are considerably worse off than those who work in other factories — the local community refer to the women from Nike as walking ghosts who work in Satan's factory' (*mereke pergi dan pulang seperti hantu dari pabrik Setan*). He also reports that when the factory next to Nike was also given a Nike contract the impact on the workers was both sudden and negative (Hancock 1997). In respect of the subsistence level wages paid to workers in Indonesia, Beeson and Hadiz (1998) quote the chief executive officer of Nike as saying that there are still thousands of Indonesians lining up for jobs at their factory gates.

Interestingly, although Hancock (1997) found that the majority of export-oriented factories studied (not including the Nike operation) adhered to national laws with respect to wages and working conditions, only one of the 20 factories actually paid the women all of their wages, benefits and leave requirements. Yet most of those interviewed by Hancock were content with their employment conditions. Many factories were found to provide two prayer times per day, and one extra prayer session if overtime was worked. Hancock (1997) also interviewed an ex-supervisor from the Nike factory who stated that he had left his job because it insulted his culture and his religion, especially in terms of the disrespect shown to women. This type of situation is seen to be the result of the powerlessness of local leaders to challenge the power of combined Taiwanese, Chinese Indonesian and American capital when international capital is required to create employment (Hancock 1997).

Multinational companies operating in Indonesia are perceived to be able to take advantage of workers, particularly female workers. Women are not seen as long-term

employees so little or no money is spent on their training. Hutchings (1996) says that although MNCs may have been respecting local customs and conforming to local practices, it has been to their advantage. Although in some countries (e.g. India) companies might provide childcare facilities, it has been argued that childcare provisions and flexible hours are unheard of in Indonesia because it would not be culturally acceptable for parents not to take care of their own responsibilities, so such provisions would not be used even if provided (Hutchings 1996).

There are restrictions on the recruitment of expatriate workers, yet this issue remains sensitive because of the number of applications for extensions of work permits and the publicity their numbers have attracted over recent years. The maximum number ever approved is one expatriate for every 10 local persons employed (King 1993). Expatriates have increasingly come from India and the Philippines to fill middle management ranks, although the majority of registered expatriates are from the US (Hugo 1993). According to *The Jakarta Post* (1997d), there are about 70 000 expatriates working in Indonesia earning a total of US$3 billion. The differences in salaries between local workers and expatriates is a sore point, as indicated by the government decree requiring expatriates to pay US$100 per month during the period of their contracts to finance vocational training programs for local workers (*The Jakarta Post* 1997d). By regulation, foreign workers are permitted to work only in roles that cannot be filled by Indonesians (Tjiptoherijanto 1998). There is also a regulation to ensure the 'Indonesianisation' of positions held by expatriates.

In terms of other practices by foreign companies or foreign joint-venture organisations operating in Indonesia, the following examples have been provided by senior expatriate managers on the understanding that the names of their companies not be disclosed.

FIRM A, a well-established consulting firm operating in Indonesia for over 20 years with mostly Muslim staff (apart from an Australian expatriate manager), comprising a mix of Javanese and non-Javanese, has indicated that:

- most staff observe their daily prayers and the male staff attend the nearest mosque on Fridays
- religious holidays as decreed by the government are provided
- staff are allowed to take their annual leave during Idul-Fitri (celebrated for two to three days after the fasting month of Ramadan, which is when Muslims abstain from food, drink and other sensual pleasures from dawn until sunset)
- during the fasting months, there is an attempt to accommodate religious activities by providing an early start and finish so that fasting breaks can be attended with families
- maternity leave is provided for three months
- menstrual leave is not provided, but if requested it would be considered on an individual basis (with six women working in the office, the manager has pointed out that the menstrual leave would result in a loss of 144 working days per year, which, in a multi-tasking work environment, would cause a real problem).

Although this consulting firm is an 'equal opportunity' employer, the manager pointed out that they take a different approach at their site office. For example, in their Bali office the manager and community facilitators need to be Balinese for political (positive discrimination) reasons and for financial reasons related to relocation costs.

FIRM B is a large multinational mining organisation operating in a joint venture in Indonesia. It has a small team of about 30 expatriates (mostly Australians) and a local staff of well over 2000. Most of its workforce are under 40 years of age, 70 per cent attended senior high school and 5.3 per cent are female. Approximately 80 per cent of the workforce are married. The mining operation was established in a sparsely populated area, so most of the staff have migrated from distant population centres, many from other provinces.

Management clearly sees that the success of B's operation rests significantly on its continuing ability to successfully manage diversity across varying cultures and ethnic groups. Areas where HR management policy reflects the Indonesian mining environment include:

- *Observance of religious customs*: B does not discriminate on the basis of religious beliefs, and the characteristics of its workforce do not differ markedly from those indicated by national statistics — about 70 per cent are Muslim and most of the rest are Christian. B manages shift change timing to facilitate attendance at main Muslim prayer times, and on the weekly Muslim holy day (Friday) normal production cycles are disrupted with most Muslim production workers/operators taking an extended break from work at midday to go to a prayer location set up in one of the work areas. The attitude of Christians to this 'time off' work has required careful management although, to date, the tolerance and respect that the Muslim and Christian workforce have shown to each other has averted any problems. Conflict can be prevented by sensible management at first-line supervisor level, as was highlighted by the case of a Christian operator who sought some flexibility from his supervisor at Christmas time to attend a religious ceremony with his family. The request was poorly handled, resulting in a group of Christian operators requesting 'equal prayer time' to their Muslims co-workers. Management did believe that these operators actually wanted or expected to be given such time off, but the example illustrates the underlying sensitivities. There are five non-production days per annum at B which balance both Muslim and Christian main holidays and occasions and on which all coal production ceases for 24 hours.
- R*acial, ethnic or religious tensions*: The nature and history of development of the operation at B leaves the community generally free (or perhaps 'sheltered') from much of the ethnic and religious violence reported in other regions of Indonesia and which affects attendance at work in some large mining operations. Originally, there was only a relatively small local population in the region of B's operations, so, as a result, the current township of around 50 000 people (mainly immigrants from other parts of the province and from other provinces) has arguably developed with B's creed of 'honesty, fairness, dignity and trust as the basis of all actions'. Any tensions will directly affect the livelihood of the whole of township. Tolerance is evident. Both Muslim and Christian clerics attend important public events to provide a type of 'ecumenical' input — for example, during Independence Day celebrations. Another example of B promoting tolerance was seen some months before the 1999 Indonesian general elections when there were predictions of widespread law and order problems. A formal ceremony was held in the township involving B's senior management and community and religious leaders at which all parties took and signed pledges that there would be no problems or tensions in the local community, especially during the period of the general elections. B's community development

programs are carefully balanced to take account of the potential for creating tensions, whether the support be towards the construction of a mosque or a church, or a primary school servicing an area in which one ethnic group predominates.

- *Managing for success across cultures*: This is the name given to a two-day workshop that must be attended by every expatriate employee when they start at B. Family members are also welcome to attend. Also invited are Indonesian employees from across the archipelago who come from diverse Indonesian cultures. The aim of the workshop is to help employees maintain interdependent and collaborative working relationships that span cultural borders. The purpose is to help employees and business people to work in multicultural environments; to recognise and be aware of their own cultural orientation; to understand and respect that others with whom they work may have cultural orientations which have developed very differently; and to expand their ability to recognise and reconcile differences that could interfere with successful leadership, team development, mergers and alliances, and negotiations.
- *Language training*: According to B's management, an important aspect of managing diversity is developing a bilingual capability in the workforce. The undertaking to attain a basic level of competency with the Indonesian language (Bahasa Indonesia) is a prerequisite of expatriate employment at B. It requires a resource commitment by the company and B has a full-time language training section that teaches Bahasa Indonesia to expatriate employees (and their families, if desired), as well as English as a second language to Indonesian employees. The company encourages employees to reach the highest level they believe they are capable of in each language, and where appropriate it will send selected employees off-site to specialist language training schools if they reach the maximum level of fluency possible through B's training.
- *Drugs and alcohol in the workplace*: Although some Australian organisations might have voluminous policy documents, covering legal issues, testing specifications, counselling programs and industrial relations procedures in respect to drugs and alcohol in the workplace, this is not the case here. B's two-page policy document takes a reactive approach if abuse is suspected or if there is a workplace accident. There is no random testing in B's workplace as this would offend Muslim sensitivities and convey an impression that B believes there is a social problem in existence, when, in fact, there is not. The Indonesian Government legislation is strict and very clear on this issue; however, anyone found to be under the influence of drugs or alcohol in the workplace is liable to immediate dismissal. This disciplinary approach is in contrast to the counselling and medical treatment approach which is generally mandatory in Australia.
- *Code of conduct for expatriates*: B expects that the behaviour of expatriate employees and their families will be beyond reproach and culturally sensitive. Behaviour that might be regarded as not extraordinary and worth only censure in their home country could warrant immediate termination of a contract at B, followed by repatriation. De facto relationships are not generally accepted in Indonesian society and expatriate employees are not able to obtain temporary residency visas for their families to live there unless a copy of their marriage certificate from their home country is produced. Furthermore, B does not recognise de facto relationships for the purposes of providing the wide range of benefits available to married Indonesian employees.

- *Special types of leave*: B does adhere to regulations in respect of maternity and menstrual leave. B also provides for one and a half months' leave with pay for a legally married employee who has a miscarriage. B provides a Muslim employee of three years' standing with a one-off period of 40 days' special leave with pay to go on an official Haj pilgrimage. To maintain a balanced approach to all religions, employees of other religions may be considered for similar pilgrimages, though few have ever requested it.
- *Employment policies*: B hires employees based on merit and it favours no particular ethnic group with the following exception. Affirmative action local employment policy is a typical feature of any large mine operating in a location such as B's. Under Western standards this could be seen as discriminatory, but the situation is not very different from, say, a mining operation in a remote area of Australia that gives priority of employment (or training and development) to local Aboriginal/land-owning people, if there are any.
- *Land ownership issues*: The nature of land ownership in most South Pacific and South-east Asian nations makes sound local employment policy critical. The company has no illusions that unless it gets the policy balance right and maintains it that way, it will face significant problems, which could eventually threaten the viability of the operation. A complicating factor at B is that the original 'local' population was so small it was a minority in the local community while many others purported to be 'true' locals. B has established a Local Employment Committee (LEC), chaired by a local Kutai leader, to assist with management of this issue. The committee advises B in regard to priorities when B and its major contractors are selecting local people for employment. The people must have the required qualifications and experience to do the job. B must work closely with all local community leaders and groups as issues arise about priorities for employment. The priorities are:

  Priority 1 — People who the LEC agrees are local Sangatta Kutai.

  Priority 2 — People born in the local area regardless of their parents' origin.

  Priority 3 — People who went to school locally from six years of age.

The management of firm B admits that it does not have all the answers but says that it is part of an ongoing learning process.

FIRM C, a foreign-controlled joint venture involved in food manufacturing, operating with two Australian staff and about 500 local employees, has indicated that Indonesian law is used as a minimum standard for employee relations but the personnel policies of its Australian parent are also used as a guide for policy, albeit they are modified for local conditions. The company observes all declared religious holidays and allows employees to take annual leave for special religious or ethnic events. It also provides a defined retirement benefit for staff. One of C's expatriate managers summarised the situation by stating, 'Indonesia is ethnically, culturally and religiously a very diverse nation which despite recent well-publicised difficulties is proud of it tolerance. C has found the same basic factors which lead to success in Australia also work in Indonesia — honesty, fairness and respect for the variety of cultures, religions and ethnic groups.'

Challenges

The challenges are many and varied. The system is particularly complex in respect to the many cultures, the plethora of labour regulations, the chaotic legal system, and

the volatile ethnic and religious tensions, all pointing to the need for incredible management sophistication. One person interviewed stated that some companies have difficulties in doing business in Indonesia because they have declined to partner firms operating 'unethically' with respect to a range of business practices, including human resource management practices. This indicates that the potential consequences for firms can be severe, so the management of employment issues, including diversity issues, will remain complex and international managers will do well to seek the best available local advice before formulating their policies. Companies that are surviving in this environment need to demonstrate a great deal of sensitivity not only to follow the indeterminate Indonesian laws but to show a level of leadership that protects and enhances the interests of both employees and the communities in which they operate.

The philosophy of unity in diversity launched after Indonesia's independence is facing a lot of challenges. However, it is believed that with K. H. Abdurachman Wahid, a Muslim Ulama, and Megawati Soekarno Putri, a democratist-daughter of former President Soekarno, there is a new hope for the society (Tjoptoherijanto 2000b). Recent incidents in several areas reflect that freedom from fear, freedom from uniformity and freedom to express views have a certain social cost; and the situation within the military, the crime rate and violation of social laws reflect the distance to be travelled to fulfil the promise behind the slogan (Tjoptoherijanto 2000b).

References

Anonymous. 1997. 'A Strike from the Shop Floor'. *Hecate* 23(1): 135–7.

Bangun, T. & Sprague, J. 1999. 'Caught in the Net'. *Asiaweek* 25(30): 40–2.

Beeson, M. & Hadiz, V. 1998. 'Labor and the Politics of Structural Adjustment in Australia and Indonesia'. *Journal of Contemporary Asia* 28(3): 291–309.

Bennington, L. 2000. 'Issues for HRM in Indonesia'. Paper submitted to Seventh Conference on International Human Resource Management, Durban, South Africa.

Bishop, B. & McNamara, D. 1997. *The Asia–Australia Survey 1997–98*. South Melbourne: Macmillan Education Australia.

Bresnan, J. 1993. *Managing Indonesia*. New York: Columbia University Press.

Brown, C. 2000. 'Sukarno to Suharto'. In Mackerras, C. (Ed.). *Eastern Asia: An Introductory History*. Frenchs Forest, NSW: Longman: 273–88.

Bureau of Democracy, Human Rights, and Labor. 1999. *Indonesia Country Report: Practices for 1998*. The US Department of State, February. Available at http://www. usis.usemb.se/human/human1998/indonesi.html.

Cheng, L. 1999. 'Globalization and Women's Paid Labour in Asia'. *International Social Science Journal* 51(2): 217–28.

Ching, F. 1998. 'Building a Better Indonesia'. *Far Eastern Economic Review*, September 3: 31.

CIA. 1999. *The World Factbook*. Available at http://www.odci.gov/cia/publications/factbook/id.html.

Cukier, J., Norris, J. & Wall, G. 1996. 'The Involvement of Women in the Tourism Industry of Bali, Indonesia'. *Journal of Development Studies* 33(2): 248–71.

Elashmawi, F. 1998. 'Overcoming Multicultural Clashes in Global Joint Ventures'. *European Business Review* 98(4): 211–16.

Fehring, I. 1999. 'Unionism and Workers' Rights in Indonesia'. In Lindsay, T. (Ed.). *Indonesia: Law and Society*. Leichhardt: The Federation Press: 367–80.

Firdausy, C. M. 1995. 'Role of the Informal Service Sector to Alleviate Poverty in Indonesia'. *The Indonesian Quarterly* 23(3): 278–87.

Foster, D. 1998. 'Waiting and Winning in Indonesia'. *Global Workforce*, September: 28–9.

Gall, G. 1998. 'The Development of the Indonesian Labour Movement'. *The International Journal of Human Resource Management* 9(2): 359–76.

Geringer, J. M. & Frayne, C. A. & IPMI. 1993. *Caterpillar Inc. In Indonesia (A.)*. Jakarta: Institute Pengembangan Manajemen Indonesia.

Grijns, M. & van Velzen, A. 1993. 'Working Women: Differentiation and Marginalisation'. In Manning, C. & Hardjono, J. (Eds). *Indonesia Assessment 1993*. Political and Social Change Monograph 20. Canberra: ANU.

Habir, A. D. 1995. 'The Emerging Indonesian Managerial Elite'. *AustAsian Paper No. 2*. Research Institute for Asia and the Pacific, University of Sydney.

Habir, A. D. & Larasati, A. B. 1999. 'Human Resource Management as Competitive Advantage in the New Millenium: An Indonesian Perspective'. *International Journal of Manpower* 20(8): 548–62.

Hadiz, V. R. 1997. *Workers and the State in New Order Indonesia*. London: Routledge.

Hancock, P. 1997. 'The Walking Ghosts of West Java'. *Inside Indonesia*, 51, July–September.

Harsono, A. 1999. 'The Markets: A Fickle Friend'. *UNESCO Courier* 23(2).

Hess, M. 1995. 'Economic Development and Human Resource Management: A Challenge for Indonesian Managers'. *The Indonesian Quarterly* 23(2): 149–58.

Heuer, M., Cummings, J. L. & Hutabarat, W. 1999. 'Cultural Stability or Change Among Managers in Indonesia'. *Journal of International Business Studies* 30(3): 599–610.

Hill, G. 1996. 'Indonesia: Workers Right to Join a Union'. *Australian Nursing Journal* 3(7): 28–9.

Hugo, G. 1993. 'International Labour Migration'. In Manning, C. & Hardjono, J. (Eds). *Indonesia Assessment 1993*. Political and Social Change Monograph 20. Canberra: ANU: 108–23.

Hutchings, K. 1996. 'Workplace Practices of Japanese and Australian Multinational Corporations Operating in Singapore, Malaysia and Indonesia'. *Human Resource Management Journal* 6(2): 58–71.

Islam, I. 1989. 'Management and Industrial Relations in ASEAN'. *Labour and Industry* 2(2): 282.

King, H. R. 1993. 'Indonesia'. *IFLRev Special Supplement*, February: 19–24.

Lasserre, P. & Schutte, H. 1995. *Strategies for Asia Pacific*. South Melbourne: Macmillan Business.

Lesmanaa, T. 1999. 'Workers Need to Better Their Bargaining Power'. The Jakarta Post.com, 9 December.

Levinson, J. 1998. 'Living Dangerously: Indonesia and the Reality of the Global Economic System'. *Journal of International Law and Practice* 7(3): 425–64.

Lindsey, T. 1999. 'From Rule of Law to Law of the Rulers — to Reformation?'. In Lindsey, T. (Ed.). *Indonesia: Law and Society*. Leichhardt: The Federation Press: 11–20.

Liong, L. S. 1999. 'The Chinese Minority in Indonesia'. Paper presented at the conference 'The Asian Crisis — A Chance for Democracy and Human Rights?'. Berlin, 26–28 March.

Manning, C. 1993. 'Examining Both Sides of the Ledger: Economic Growth and Labour Welfare'. In Manning, C. & Hardjono, J. (Eds). *Indonesia Assessment 1993*. Political and Social Change Monograph 20. Canberra: ANU.

Manning, C. 1998. *Indonesian Labour in Transition*. Cambridge: University of Cambridge.

Manning, C. 1999. 'Poverty Decline and Labour Market Change in Indonesia'. *The Indonesian Quarterly* 27(2): 122–45.

Manning, C. & Junankar, P. N. 1998. 'Choosy Youth or Unwanted Youth? A Survey of Unemployment'. *Bulletin of Indonesian Economic Studies* 34(1): 55–93.

May, M. 1999. 'Nine Years' Schooling for All? Children, Work and Schooling in Eastern Indonesia'. *Development Bulletin* 48: 9–12.

Report A. 1997. A report provided by a government official on the understanding that the report would not be named.

Rohdewohld, R. 1995. *Public Administration in Indonesia*. Melbourne: Montech.

Schwarz, A. 1994. *A Nation in Waiting: Indonesia in the 1990s*. St Leonards: Allen and Unwin.

Stening, B. W. & Ngan, E. F. 1997. 'The Cultural Context of Human Resource Management in East Asia'. *Asia Pacific Journal of Human Resources* 35(2): 3–15.

Straits Times. 1997 'Ban Ethnic Chinese from Some Industries in Indonesia'. 25 October.

Sunindyo, S. 1998. 'When the Earth Is Female and the Nation Is Mother: Gender, the Armed Forces and Nationalism in Indonesia'. *Feminist Review*, Spring, 58: 1–21.

Surowidjojo, A. T. 1999. 'Employment Law in Asia: Indonesia'. *Asia Business Law Review* 25: 24–39.

Tambunan, T. 1995. 'Poverty and Human Resource Development in Indonesia: A Brief Survey'. *The Indonesian Quarterly* 23(2): 159–74.

The Jakarta Post. 1997a. 'Women Workers Still Face Challenges in Indonesia'. 23 February. The Jakarta Post.com

The Jakarta Post. 1997b. 'House Passes Labor Bill'. 12 September. The Jakarta Post.com

The Jakarta Post. 1997c. 'A New Labor Law'. 13 September. The Jakarta Post.com

The Jakarta Post. 1997d. 'Soeharto asks Latief to Socialize New Labor Law'. 13 September. The Jakarta Post.com

The Jakarta Post. 1997e. 'Employers Told to Treat Workers Better'. 18 September. The Jakarta Post.com

The Jakarta Post. 1997f. 'A Worker Killed Every Other Day'. 16 October. The Jakarta Post.com

The Jakarta Post. 1997g. 'Nothing Wrong With Child Labor, says Official'. 30 October. The Jakarta Post.com

The Jakarta Post. 1997h. 'Military Involvement seen Hurting Labor Protection'. 11 December. The Jakarta Post.com

The Jakarta Post. 1998a. 'President Habibie Signs ILO Convention on Unions'. 6 June. The Jakarta Post.com

The Jakarta Post. 1998b. 'Workers' Freedom'. 12 June. The Jakarta Post.com

The Jakarta Post. 1999a. 'Human Rights Court Could Be Formed'. 24 April. The Jakarta Post.com

The Jakarta Post. 1999b. 'Protesting Workers Make 10 km March'. 10 June. The Jakarta Post.com

The Jakarta Post. 1999c. 'Government Studies Required Hiring of Disabled'. 3 September. The Jakarta Post.com

The Jakarta Post. 1999d. 'Bomer Breaks Ground on Indonesia's Labor Front'. 12 December. The Jakarta Post.com

The Jakarta Post. 2000a. 'Government Submits Two Labor Bills to House'. 15 February. The Jakarta Post.com

The Jakarta Post. 2000b. 'Corruption Keeps Money from Wage Earners: Official'. 3 February. The Jakarta Post.com

The Jakarta Post. 2000c. 'RI Signs UN Protocol on Women's Rights'. 1 March. The Jakarta Post.com

Tjiptoherijanto, P. 1998. 'Social and Economic Consequences of International Labour Migration: Indonesian Case'. *The Indonesian Quarterly* 26(3): 28–95.

Tjiptoherijanto, P. 2000a. Personal communication, 9 March.

Tjiptoherijanto, P. 2000b. Personal communication, 23 March.

Triaswati, N. 1996. 'Women and Children Labour Force in Indonesia'. *The Indonesian Quarterly* 14(1): 19–30.

van Diermen, P. 1997. 'Labor Remuneration in Jakarta's Small Enterprises: Exploitative or Equitable?'. *World Development* 25(12): 212–41.

White, M. C. 1990. 'Improving the Welfare of Women Factory Workers: Lessons from Indonesia'. *International Labour Review* 129(1): 12–33.

Woodward, K. H. 1996. 'Neo-colonialism, Labor Rights, and the "Growth Triangle" of Indonesia, Malaysia, and Singapore: Who Will Protect the "Hinterland" and Indonesia's Workers?'. *Dickinson Journal of International Law* 15(1): 171–99.

Chapter 7

Japan

Jean Renshaw

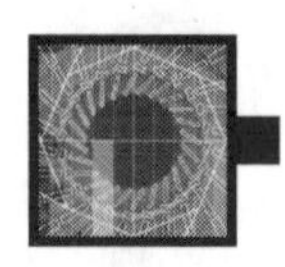

Introduction

An examination of how diversity is managed in Japan involves consideration of history, culture, politics, demographics, as well as management issues. This chapter will initially consider the ideology of homogeneity in Japan, followed by a history of minority groups and the factors that have allowed them to be invisible. Each minority group will be discussed briefly and the largest minority, women, will be considered in greater depth, based on the author's research on Japanese women managers (Renshaw 1999). Then the laws against discrimination will be considered, followed by a discussion of forms of change and resistance that are occurring in Japan, and the challenges for Japanese management now and in the future.

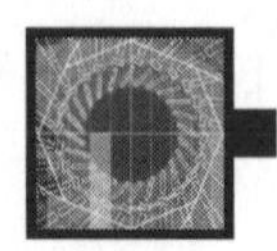

Ideology of homogeneity

One foundation of Japanese society has been a strong belief in the uniqueness of the culture and the homogeneity of the Japanese people, a belief that Japanese organisations share (Hicks 1997; Reischauer 1977).

> Japan proclaims itself a homogeneous society of a unique and distinctive character. To the world at large, it is widely perceived as such. The Japanese establishment regards homogeneity as an essential element in its national ethos and power structure and [homogeneity] is credited as the key to Japan's outstanding success (Hicks 1997).

The ideology of homogeneity means that minorities are not recognised and leaves little room for considerations about managing diversity. Diversity is an alien concept. The Japanese language has no word for ethnicity, as opposed to race or nationality, so a foreign or *katakana* word is used. While official statistics reveal the numbers of resident foreigners in Japan (see table 7.2), gender is the only point of difference recognised in labour force and employment statistics. The number and percentage of women in the labour force are contained in employment data, but statistics are not provided for any other group.

A belief in homogeneity separates people who might look and act the same into those who belong and are termed insiders or 'real Japanese', and those who are different and do not belong, who are called outsiders. As an island nation, Japan has been able to maintain this belief effectively.

In ancient times, the earliest people who populated the islands intermarried with succeeding waves of invaders and the conquered peoples from successful excursions to other countries. In 1600, after centuries of feudal and tribal warfare over territory and power, one of the lords, Tokugawa, was victorious. He was then able to unite the country, bring peace to the warring tribes and seal the national boundaries to other countries in order to develop a national identity. This isolation was maintained for 250 years until the arrival in 1853 of the 'black ships', commanded by the American Admiral Perry, who forced an opening to the world and precipitated Japan's rapid modernisation. The extended period of isolation was an important factor in fostering a culture of shared values and conformity to group identity and norms. Existing minority cultures were moulded to fit the national ideals.

This history helps to explain why the Japanese act as though diversity on their islands does not exist. Concerns about racial and sexual discrimination have until recently been kept at a safe distance from corporate culture. The strong prevailing belief in a homogeneous culture held both within and outside Japan allows organisations to maintain the image of a homogenous workforce. Managing as if the workforce were homogeneous simplifies management and allows those who don't fit to be pressured to fit or, if they do not, to leave. The emphasis on homogeneity and harmony has been a factor in the rapid growth of production and the economy both in the years of war preparation and the subsequent reconstruction.

However, those who don't fit are a problem conceptually and practically. Problems like *sekahara*, or sexual harassment, and legal actions by women and minorities against discrimination, combined with critiques by international organisations, are forcing some issues of diversity to the forefront. Effectively, the management of diversity requires a recognition that diversity exists and an examination of the implications of differences.

To provide a context for the discussion of minorities, some general parameters for Japan are given in table 7.1.

Table 7.1: ***Measures of modern Japan***

Population	126 486 000
Size	145 882 square miles including Northern Territories
Real Gross Domestic Product	$5390.59 billion
Per Capita GDP	$24 070
Unemployment Rate	4.1%

Source: Derived from *Japan Almanac 1999,* Tokyo: Asahi Shimbun Publishing Company.

Japan's total land area is approximately 1.5 times that of Great Britain. Japan is one of the most densely populated countries in the world, with 44 per cent of its population concentrated in the three major cities of Tokyo, Osaka and Nagoya. Its gross domestic product is second only to the United States and its per capita gross domestic product ranks number four in the world, behind only Canada, Norway and the United States. The official unemployment rate is also among the lowest in the world, but unofficial estimates place this as high as 11 per cent if one includes long-term and discouraged unemployed in the current recessive climate.

Because of the emphasis on harmony and homogeneity, distinctions between insiders and outsiders are very important. A continuum of insider–outsider in Japanese social and economic life might be drawn as follows.

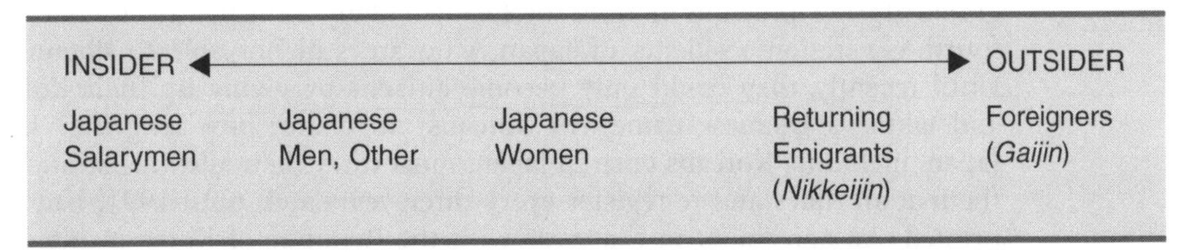

Figure 7.1: ***Insider and Outsider***

In a speech to the Self-Defense Forces on 9 April 2000, the governor of Tokyo, Ishihara, was an articulate spokesperson for the insider–outsider attitude, warning that the soldiers should be prepared for riots by *sangokujin*, in the event of a major earthquake. The word, *sangokujin*, is a derogatory term that was used in the 1930s and 1940s to refer to people from the former Japanese colonies of Korea and Taiwan, and it is still particularly hurtful to Korean and Chinese minorities today. It also summons memories of the aftermath of the great 1920s earthquake when Koreans, who were thought to be responsible, were killed. Ishihara went on to say later that there was no need to apologise since he was referring only to illegal immigrants, not long-term Korean residents. This did little to reassure minorities, and serves to illustrate the pervasiveness of fear of minorities and the ambiguity about their role in Japanese society.

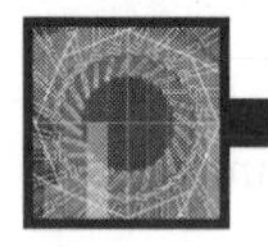

Minorities in Japan

Minorities or outsiders can be categorised as non-Japanese outsiders and Japanese outsiders.

Non-Japanese minorities

Non-Japanese minorities 'look different' from Japanese and are therefore more readily distinguishable than Japanese minorities.

The number of legally resident foreigners in Japan, according to the Ministry of Justice, is 1.5 million (Management and Coordination Agency 1995–2000). The total population of Japan is 126 486 000, making officially recognised foreign residents slightly more than one per cent of the population (Asahi Shimbum 1999). The Japanese labour force numbers some 67 930 000, with legal foreign workers comprising approximately 0.5 per cent of that workforce (Asahi Shimbun 1999). Statistics from other sources closer to the minorities produce quite different figures, with Hicks (1987) estimating six per cent legal foreign workers as a low figure.

Official and semi-official data list 750 000 Korean permanent residents, and at least 400 000 Japanese Brazilians and Peruvians. The largest groups listed in official population statistics are Koreans, Chinese, Filipinos, Brazilians, Peruvians and Americans (see table 7.2). The contradiction between official statistics and data from other sources can be seen as an indicator of the assumptions made about minorities and homogeneity (Wehrfritz & Hideko 2000: 12–17).

Koreans comprise the largest group in the official data. Even so, this does not include naturalised Koreans or Koreans passing as Japanese. The Han Society claims the total Korean population is over one million (Buraku Liberation and Human Rights Research Institute 1998). The majority of resident Koreans were brought as slave labour to Japan during the Japanese occupations of Korea (1910–45) or immigrated during previous periods of history. Many Koreans are second-, third- and fourth-generation residents of Japan, who are still not able to obtain citizenship. Until recently, they could only become citizens by giving up their Korean identity and taking a Japanese name. All Koreans, no matter how long they have lived in Japan, including Koreans born in Japan, must carry their alien registration cards with them at all times and re-register every three years and, until 1991, had to be fingerprinted. An agreement in that year with the Republic of Korea resulted in uniform permanent residence for all resident aliens and the end of fingerprinting. The legality of the fingerprinting requirement was finally tested and successfully resisted by a Korean woman on her exit from the country in 1998.

Table 7.2: ***Non-Japanese outsiders — registered foreign residents in Japan, 1970–98***

Year	Korea N. & S.	China	Philip-pines	US	Brazil	Peru	Other*	Total
1970	614 202	51 481	932	19 045	891	134	21 773	708 458
1975	647 156	48 728	3 035	21 976	1 418	308	29 221	751 842
1980	664 536	52 896	5 547	22 401	1 492	348	35 590	782 810
1985	683 313	74 924	12 261	29 044	1 955	480	48 635	850 612
1990	687 940	150 339	49 092	38 364	56 429	10 279	82 874	1 075 317
1995	666 376	222 991	74 297	43 198	176 440	36 269	142 800	1 362 371
1996	657 159	234 264	84 509	44 168	201 795	37 099	156 142	1 415 136
1997	645 373	252 164	93 265	43 690	233 254	40 394	174 567	1 482 707
1998	638 828	272 230	105 308	42 774	222 217	41 317	189 442	1 512 116

Source: Derived from *Nihon tokei nenkan* (Japan Statistical Yearbook), Government of Japan.
*Thailand, Vietnam, Indonesia, India, Iran, United Kingdom and others

The prejudice against Koreans by Japanese carries over to other countries in which Japanese multinational companies operate. In a recent tragic story, a Korean man married a Japanese woman while both were students in Australia. They went to the United States hoping for a better chance of a free life. He went to work for a Japanese company in the US but was fired after a company therapist revealed some of his problems to the company. He committed suicide at age 39, leaving a young wife and two young children. After his death, his diary was shown to document long-term harassment about his Korean identity from his Japanese co-workers, who questioned why a nice Japanese woman would marry him when she could have done better.

Most Chinese date their arrival in Japan from the period of the Japanese occupation of Manchuko between the 1930s and 1945. A second wave of Chinese immigrants came during the upheavals in China and the Japanese bubble economy years. Irrespective of the length of their residency, they also must carry alien papers and renew their registration every three years.

Illegal foreign workers, according to estimates by the Ministry of Justice (Wehrfritz & Hideko 2000), reached a peak of 64 341 in 1993, and in 1998 were estimated at 40 535. Popular opinion and the media would give a higher estimate. As in most industrialised countries, there is a visible illegal foreign workforce doing the jobs that locals are unwilling to do. The large number of Iranian men in Ueno Park on Sundays has become bothersome to the Japanese people who use the park, and a thorn in the side of the local government. Philippine and Thai women have been brought to Japan to work in the entertainment and household service industries. The majority of these women are included in the statistics on illegal foreign workers and are not considered a legitimate part of the Japanese labour force.

Japanese minorities

Japanese minorities, whose appearance often cannot be distinguished from local Japanese, include *burakumin* (ethnically and racially Japanese, but at the bottom of the caste system), Okinawans, Ainu and *nikkeijin* (returning emigrants).

Nikkeijin is a special category of re-immigrants to Japan from countries such as Brazil, Peru and Bolivia. Most of them emigrated from Japan during the great depression of the 1930s. Additionally, a small number of Japanese children were left behind in China during the Japanese army's hurried, forced exodus at the end of World War II, and small numbers have been returning to Japan during the boom years. For some, their difference is not noticed and they are able to 'pass' as natives, virtually fit into the mainstream population and so become semi-insiders. But Japanese managers who detect them do not consider these groups insiders. Those in this category, who wish to maintain their cultural or ethnic identity, usually separate. The elderly and the disabled are also considered as outsiders making up the invisible minorities in Japan. One might contrast Japan with Singapore, a nation with high population density and conformity to shared values, but based on ethnic diversity.

Official statistics do not categorise Japanese ethnic minorities. Data are available from organisations that have formed to research and mobilise minority populations that experience discrimination. One such organisation is the International Movement Against All Forms of Discrimination and Racism (IMADR), which is a non-governmental human rights organisation devoted to promoting the rights of people subject to racism and discrimination. It was formed by the Buraku Liberation League and other *burakumin* and international human rights groups in 1988 (Buraku Liberation and Human Rights Research Institute 1998). *Burakumin* are ethnically and racially Japanese. *Buraku* is a Japanese word referring to village or hamlet and *min* refers to people. The feudal caste system of the seventeenth century had four classes — warrior, farmer, artisan and merchant. The outcasts from this system are the antecendents of the present *Buraku* people. These outcasts were outside the caste system, called *eta,* and were seen as extreme filth and *hinin* or non-human, probably because of their trades. They disposed of the dead, tended graves, guarded tombs, swept the streets, collected garbage, and worked as butchers, tanners and leather craftsmen. The Shinto belief in pollution associated with the dead and the Buddhist prohibition against the killing of animals probably contributed to their status as outcastes (Kodansha Publishing Company 1998).

Although the caste system was abolished in 1871 by the Meiji Government's Emancipation Edict, no enforcement mechanisms were established and many *burakumin* suffered and still suffer flagrant discrimination in employment and marriage. While the household register, or *koseki*, from which *burakumin* ancestry could be ascertained, is no longer legally available to the public without the permission of the family being investigated, employers and prospective in-laws still check clandestine versions to ascertain whether prospective employees or marriage partners are of this 'lower class'. A 1993 government survey estimated 1.2 million *Buraku* people in 4442 *Dowa* districts or *Buraku* communities nationwide, but the Buraku Liberation Movement estimates 6000 *Buraku* communities with over three million *burakumin*.

Ainu people are generally considered the indigenous people of Japan. *Mishihara*, or 'hairy people', was the term used to refer to the pre-modern people of northern Japan assumed to be the ancestors of the Ainu, a proto-Caucasoid group from the Neolithic era who migrated to Japan in prehistoric times. Abundant hair, often tinged with red, broad noses and relatively flat faces are the distinguishing characteristics of

modern Ainu. Their number has shrunk to below 20 000, with intermarriage leaving few pure Ainu. Most Ainu live in Hokkaido, the Sakhalin islands and northern territories. Few are known in Honshu, having either intermarried or emigrated further north as the Japanese moved north. One Ainu is now in parliament, which is a milestone for the Ainu people.

Okinawans are another minority who experienced discrimination historically, and still do today. The Ryuku Kingdom, which predated modern Okinawa, was once a powerful nation which provided a major trade route to China. It was first invaded by the Shimazu, rulers of the Satsuma domain in Kyushu, in the early seventeenth century, and it remained a Japanese territory until after World War II. Okinawans were under United States occupation from 1945 until 1972, when the United States returned the islands to Japanese sovereignty. Although Okinawans are now a part of Japan, their history as an independent kingdom of people ethnically and racially different from the Japanese has ensured that they continue to face discrimination in employment and society. The income of Okinawans is considerably lower than that of mainland Japanese, although it has increased with the prosperity of Japan and the subsidies provided by the Japanese Government. The Japanese Government has relegated the major part of the United States military forces stationed in Japan, under the Status of Forces agreement, to Okinawa, where it is a continuing irritant.

Persons of mixed ancestry also face social and legal discrimination and prejudice. Until relatively recently, because Japan's legal system is based on *jus sanguinis*, citizenship by blood, not *jus soli,* citizenship by birthplace, only those with Japanese fathers were automatically citizens. Children of Japanese mothers and foreign fathers were not citizens of Japan until the Ministry of Justice decreed in 1985 that a child shall be a Japanese national 'when the father or the mother is a Japanese national' (Kodansha Publishing Company, 1998).

A rapidly growing minority is the population who are over 65 years of age. Company policy and practice has been for men to retire at 60 and women at 55, with the company often arranging a good job in a subsidiary or smaller company for their valued male salarymen. In the years of recession and downsizing, those over 50 were hit the hardest. Having devoted their lives to a company, they assumed they would have lifetime employment and a healthy pension. When they were downsized, the suicide rate in this group was alarming, with tales of men dressing for work and then sitting in the park during work hours for a whole year rather than tell their families they had been retrenched.

The traditional recruitment and hiring process involves employing college students on graduation for a lifetime of employment. Discrimination against hiring the elderly, except at the very top management levels, is very strong. Since Japanese life expectancy is the longest in the world, at 84 years for women and 77 years for men, Japan has one of the largest populations over 65 in the world (Asahi Shimbun 2000). Nineteen hundred and ninety-eight was the second straight year in which more people were in the 65 and over age group in Japan than in the 0–4 age group. Combined with a decreasing birth rate, down to 1.38 per cent in 1999, the demographics are a national concern. Despite labour shortages, those over 65 still face prejudice and discrimination. Older women are hardest hit — even though they may have 30 years of life after the retirement age, they often have difficulty finding jobs and are forced into much lower positions.

People with disabilities also face discrimination in terms of employment and their social status. According to official estimates, there were 2.9 million physically disabled and two million intellectually disabled people in Japan in 1998. Efforts to eliminate discrimination against people with disabilities led to the Promotion of the Employment of the Handicapped Law (*Shintai Shogaisha Koyo Sokushin Ho*) in 1960. The law set standards for the employment of those with a disability — 1.7 per cent of the workforce for government and 1.3 per cent of the workforce for private industry (Kodansha Publishing Company 1998: 195). However, there is no penalty for not meeting the standard and the law has not been enforced. The infrastructure to support the employment of a disabled or ageing population is not available. Such basics as wheelchair ramps and elevators in public buildings are very sparse in Japan and the low status of those with a disability is an ongoing problem.

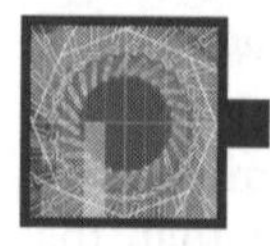

Women — the largest Japanese minority/majority

Japanese women are not a minority, but they are viewed generally as outsiders in the workplace. They are certainly insiders in Japanese society, expected to fulfil the well-defined and honoured gender role of 'good wife, wise mother'. Yet they are also essential to the labour force. Working women are both insiders and outsiders, and therefore completely puzzling to many managers and men in general. Traditionally, they have served as a buffer to cushion companies against the negative impacts of economic cycles, performing essential tasks when the economy is growing, and becoming expendable when they are no longer needed. Japanese women workers have tended to be more acceptable than immigrant workers because they are of the same culture and thought to be more adaptable and manageable. However, women's unquestioning acceptance of this role can no longer be guaranteed.

As table 7.3 shows, women comprise 51 per cent of the total Japanese population. They are the largest group of people facing discrimination in employment. They also form the largest minority in the workforce, comprising 41 per cent of the total labour force (20 per cent is considered a critical mass in sociological terms (McCorduck & Ramsey 1996)).

It is hard to pretend women don't exist because of their numbers. But one of the reasons they, along with other minorities, have not made a greater impact on the culture is that they are confined to lower societal levels and, as many women told me, 'male attitudes conspire to keep it that way'. Women are expected to conform to rigid gender role stereotypes both at home and in the office — that is, where the male is dominant and the female serves. However, women are no longer behaving as they once did.

The number of Japanese women in management has increased to 10 per cent of all managers. They are successfully managing small and large businesses and female and male employees. Increasingly, they are starting their own businesses when thwarted by traditional corporate culture. Women are the only minority in management listed in labour force management statistics. Women managers are represented in almost all industries (see table 7.4). Although the official statistics do not list women managers in agriculture, mining and utilities, I interviewed women managers in each of these fields. Perhaps the number was statistically insignificant, or this is a new phenomenon. However, Japanese women have been called the most flagrantly underutilised resource of Japan. While their work is essential to the economy, women are not rewarded equally or acknowledged fully. Table 7.5 compares the salaries of male and female managers, and women tell me the statistics are more generous to women than the actuality.

Table 7.3: ***Women in Japan***

	Number	Percentages
Total Women	64 568 000	51.0
Women in the Workforce	27 670 000	40.8
Managers	293 700	10.2
Employed Married Women	0.5	56.9 Including divorced and widowed 66.5
Women in the Diet	68	9.1
Community Services	20.0	19.9

Source: Derived from *Nihon tokei nenkan* (Japan Statistical Yearbook), Tokyo: Government of Japan.

Table 7.4: ***Female and male managers in Japan, ranked by industry percentage***

Women				Men	
Industry and rank	Percentage of managers	Number of managers	Percentage of total workers	Industry and rank	Percentage of managers
Wholesale/Retail (Rank 1)	12	70 000	50.0	Agriculture (Rank 1)	100
Construction (Rank 2)	8	30 000	16.3	Mining (Rank 1)	100
Finance (Rank 2)	8	30 000	44.9	Utilities (Rank 1)	100
Social Services (Rank 2)	8	30 000	48.3	Production (Rank 2)	94
Production (Rank 3)	6	40 000	38.8	Transport (Rank 2)	94
Transport (Rank 3)	6	10 000	16.1	Construction (Rank 3)	92
Agriculture	0	0	46.2	Finance (Rank 3)	92
Mining	0	0	16.7	Social Services (Rank 3)	92
Utilities	0	0	15.1	Wholesale/Retail (Rank 4)	88
Overall average	8	210 000	40.7	**Overall average**	92

Source: Derived from: *Yearbook of Labour Statistics*, Geneva, Switzerland.

Table 7.5: ***Japanese managers: average earnings by gender and number of employees***

	Number of employees and average earnings	
	100 or less	**1000 or more**
	Yen	Yen
Male		
Monthly	320 400	344 900
Annual	3 844 800	4 138 800
Bonuses	1 158 400	1 381 300
Total male annual	5 003 200	5 520 100
Female		
Monthly	211 100	230 600
Annual	2 533 200	2 767 200
Bonuses	722 700	876 800
Total female annual	3 255 900	3 644 000
Ratio female/male earnings	65.0%	66.0%

Source: Adapted from *Policy Planning and Research* and Japanese Ministry of Labour Employment Statistics, Tokyo, Japan.

As illustrated in figure 7.1, women are closest to insiders by birth, ethnicity and socialisation. However, they are still outsiders in terms of leadership and decision-making positions in companies and government. The progress of women can be used the ways in which Japan deals with difference. The history and treatment of women is the most conspicuous example of the impact of a labour force minority on management practices and laws.

Laws against discrimination

The basic law of the land governing treatment of all citizens is contained in the constitution of 1947, drafted by the occupation administration after Japan was defeated in World War II. This constitution gave Japanese women rights for which they had been fighting for a long time. These included the vote, equal access to education, and the right to enter state universities, to inherit property and to choose their own marriage partners. As was the case with the United States Constitution, after which the Japanese Constitution was modelled, the changes did not happen immediately, except for the vote and educational opportunities, but it provided the model and legal basis for changes to be made. In the first election after the inauguration of the constitution, more women were elected to the Diet (Parliament) than have ever been elected since.

Because the constitution is the basic legal document for enforcing equity, several articles are quoted here in full.

- Article 1: 'The conditions necessary for being a Japanese national shall be determined by law.' While this seems a logical statement, it has been used to prevent certain categories of people from becoming citizens and has come under criticism from United Nations human rights groups.
- Article 13: 'All of the people shall be respected as individuals. Their rights to life, liberty and the pursuit of happiness shall, to the extent that it does not interfere with the public welfare, be the supreme consideration in legislation and in other governmental affairs.'
- Article 14:
  '1. All of the people are equal under the law and there shall be no discrimination in political, economic or social relations because of **race, creed, sex, social status or family origin** [emphasis added].
  '2. Peers and peerage shall not be recognised.
  '3. No privilege shall accompany any award of honour, decoration or distinction, nor shall any such award be valid beyond the lifetime of the individual who now holds or hereafter may receive it.'

The statement, 'All of the people are equal under the law and there shall be no discrimination' is interpreted through Japanese eyes. For instance, when signs on bathhouses saying 'Japanese only' came under international scrutiny in the year 2000, the signs were changed to read 'Members Only', thereby accomplishing the same purpose.

Laws against discrimination:

- Article 24: 'No employer shall discriminate against or for any worker by reason of nationality, creed or social status in wages, working hours, or other working conditions.'
- Article 25: 'Marriage shall be based only on the mutual consent of both sexes and it shall be maintained through mutual cooperation with the equal rights of husband and wife as a basis.'
- Article 26: 'All people shall have the right to receive an equal education correspondent to their ability as provided by law. Compulsory education for boys and girls shall be free.'
- Article 27: 'All people shall have the right and the obligation to work.'

Constitutional articles related to employment, occupation and freedom of movement:

- Article 22: 'Every person shall have freedom to choose and change his residence and to choose his occupation to the extent that it does not interfere with the public welfare.'

The courts' interpretation of the civil code and the Labor Standards Act prohibits sex discrimination in wages and requires protective measures for women in other areas. 'The fundamental principle of equality requires that unreasonable discrimination be prohibited and any collective bargaining agreement, employment regulation or employment contract that is unreasonably discriminatory is null and void.'

For women and minorities seeking equity, these statutes which directly prohibit certain forms of discrimination unfortunately have been interpreted to prohibit only *unreasonable* discrimination. Employers have learned to justify many instances of discrimination as reasonable, even the necessity to travel. The highly suspect relegation of women to purely domestic roles is explained and justified as 'traditional' and the employer has usually been the one to define reasonableness.

Laws which specifically focus on women are the major source of additional legislation opposing discrimination and supporting equal treatment. The Labor Standards

Act, Article 4, states that 'The employer shall not discriminate women against men concerning wages by reason of the worker being a woman'.

The original Equal Employment Opportunity Law was passed in 1986 in response to internal demands and external pressure, combined with Japan's desire to become an accepted member of the international community and to join the United Nations. It was amended in 1997, effective in April 1999, after pressure and a great deal of work by Japanese women's groups. While it is still criticised as having no effective enforcement, the amendments have strengthened the law. The requirement for a complaint to be made with the mutual consent of employee and employer has been changed, and the language of the law was changed from 'encouraged to comply' to 'required to comply' and the names of employers found guilty of discrimination to be made public. These changes were seen as minimal by most women, but welcomed as a way forward.

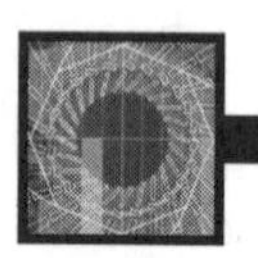

Forms of change and resistance to discrimination

Given the present status of laws, traditions and practices which create barriers to women's entry into leadership and management, progress is impressive.

The 1995 Beijing International Women's Conference was an important milestone for Japanese women. Although Japan had the largest visiting delegation at the conference, with 6000 women attending, the delegation had a male leader, which embarrassed some of the women. Nevertheless, Japanese attendees formed alliances, learned about international opinion and actions for women's equity, and brought the networks and the skills home to Japan. One striking example of the importance of networking and learning from others may be found in the delegation of Okinawan women who, on their return from the conference, learned about a crime committed during their absence by a US soldier stationed in Okinawa, and mobilised to work together to ensure that the crime was neither hidden nor forgotten. They gathered data to support their concerns about crime on their island, brought it to international attention and continue to work today to eliminate violence against women. From Okinawa, they have enlisted international women's networks and peace groups that continue to fight crimes against women and work to change the large American military presence in Okinawa.

Table 7.6: ***International measures of human development***

Index	Japan's rank
Human Development	4
Gender-related Development	8
Gender Empowerment	38

Source: Derived from *Human Development Report 1999*, New York: Oxford University Press.

The human development indices (table 7.6) serve to measure not only a nation's economy but also its quality of life and treatment of women and men. Japan's highly successful economy and standards of health and education place it in the top five nations of the world. This contrasts with its eighth ranking for gender-related development. When women's roles in leadership, policy, decision making and capital (gender empowerment) are considered, Japan falls to thirty-eighth. The publication of the data serves as a motivator to many women to speak out and bring public attention to the status of women.

Recent events in Japan indicate that the face of Japan is changing. Responding to the Prime Minister's report on Japan's goals in the twenty-first century, an editorial in the *Nikkei Weekly,* Japan's premier business publisher, was headlined, 'Resistance to Change No Longer an Option'. The Prime Minister's report said, 'We share a sense of urgency, an anxiety that Japan might go into decline if things stay unchanged' (Report of the Prime Minister's Commission on Japan's Goals for the Twenty-first Century 2000). Women and minorities are an essential part of that change. They are speaking out and sometimes being heard on the subject of inequities in employment, leadership, decision making and wages. They are using networking to join together to actively pursue opportunities. WIN WIN (Women in New World International Network), an organisation of women leaders patterned after Emily's List in America, raises money for female political candidates and supported two successful women in the 2000 election.

The Prime Minister's office created an Office for Gender Equity that sponsors workshops, publications and education for a better society with 'active and joint participation of women and men at home and work' (Prime Minister's Office 2000). Each year the office sponsors a contest for a poster to represent the goals of gender equity. The 1999 poster showed a well-known male performer holding his son, for whom he had taken childcare leave. The legend stated that a real parent shares in the care of his children. Such a seemingly innocuous poster created tremendous controversy, which spread even to the floor of the Diet, where one of the members asserted angrily, 'Men have more important things to do', an indication of the resistance to change and the work still to be done.

More minorities, particularly Koreans and Chinese, have started their own companies. *Softbank*, a successful information technology company, is an example of such a business founded by a Korean entrepreneur, Masayoshi Son, who kept his Korean name and later negotiated to buy the Nippon Credit Bank. Although people like Son are eroding stereotypes about Koreans, treatment of Koreans in Japan still leaves much to be desired.

Korean activist groups include *Mintohren* (Young Koreans Against Ethnic Discrimination in Japan), *Mindan* and *Seine*. Recent events in North and South Korea lend an added sense of urgency to Koreans wanting to fully participate in Japanese society. *Burakumin* groups have used denunciation and active demonstrations to achieve recognition and funding for community development and education. The Ainu have become more politically active and are working for recognition and education.

Japanese South Americans, who were initially recruited and welcomed with open arms as Japanese, later found themselves shunned and discouraged, because they were considered to be not really 'Japanese' but outsiders, not conforming to Japanese norms. Now many young Japanese locals seek out the music, dance and outgoing nature of the Japanese Brazilians whom they admire and emulate.

All the groups, and especially women, have been using networking strategies very successfully. Several books have been published recently listing hundreds of different kinds of networks available for women (Tamura 1996; Saito 1995). They have enlisted the support of fathers and husbands and sometimes sons to make people more aware of gender issues. Corporate culture remains one of the last bastions of the samurai culture in which men find refuge. Women have succeeded within the system, by 'working harder, learning more and competently leading and speaking up more' (Renshaw 1999). Shidzue Kato was an early proponent of women's rights who introduced the ideas of Margaret Sanger and birth control to Japan and was elected to Parliament in the first postwar election. On her one hundredth birthday, her advice to Japanese women (gleaned from years of civil and human rights activities) was, 'Japanese women are now among the best educated and the richest in the world, but we need to push ourselves forward more, to elbow our way into more decision-making jobs ... Men's attitudes will not change unbludgeoned.'

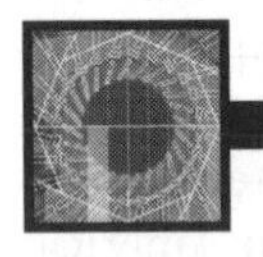

Conclusions

One view of diversity is that it is to be controlled and contained; another is that it is to be expanded and used for innovation and creativity. Until fairly recently the view in Japan has been exclusively the former. Recent events have brought the second into consciousness, at least verbally. Reform and creativity are key concepts encouraged by corporate management and government. Inherent in creativity and innovation are new and diverse perspectives. Japan's challenge, along with the rest of the world, is how to successfully incorporate diversity while maintaining a comfortable degree of tradition.

It is important for a foreign or *gaijin* manager working in Japan to understand the ambivalent attitudes towards diversity in Japan as well as the degree of successful integration in their own country. Expatriate managers may adapt to the culture and also take advantage of the changing scene. While foreign employees and managers are clearly outsiders, they can also be accepted and given an opportunity to use their difference and creativity. The role and status that the individual, male or female, carries is extremely important in Japan and is key to being accepted as a manager. The business card, or *meishi*, is the first statement of who one is and helps the Japanese to assess one's status. I was told to put all my credentials on my *meishi* — president, PhD, professor, Fulbright senior research scholar — and this would help to establish my credibility and allow me access to places I needed to enter. That proved to be true and, along with the prestigious Japanese sponsors I was fortunate to have, allowed me to engage with top management. Setting the stage, establishing credibility and adequately supporting a foreign manager or employee is an important part of the integration process. Being introduced by and vouched for by a Japanese with prestige is also helpful.

On the other hand, foreign companies and managers are able to hire extremely competent women and minorities who, generally, have not been employed by traditional Japanese companies. In the instances when they have been employed, they have not been given equal opportunity or salary. In employing Japanese women and minorities, foreign managers may serve as role models for Japanese managers reluctant to espouse or practise diversity.

Japan's goals for the twenty-first century, proclaimed in the millennium project, identified the major areas of concern as information and telecommunications, the ageing population and the environment. Japan's priorities for the millennium are

creativity, security, the rebirth of the economy, peace and globalisation (Report of the Prime Minister's Commission on Japan's Goals for the Twenty-first Century 2000).

Women and other minorities are important contributors to each of these goals. It will require the cooperation of all elements of Japanese society to use their contribution effectively. Women need to speak out, assert themselves and come out from behind the protective screen of invisibility. If men recognise the advantages that are possible when they share the work at home and in the office, they are more likely to be supportive. Overworked salarymen may welcome the opportunity to alleviate the extreme pressures of their corporate lives with this shared vision. Productivity and quality of life can increase with the inclusion of women and minorities. Broadening the range of perspectives, and sharing in the care and nurture of home, families and children, may enrich men's lives.

Successful corporations know that people are their most important resource and that the best people are needed to succeed in a global world. The exclusion of minorities and women also excludes some of the best candidates. Closed systems are not only closed to a specific category of people, but are often closed to new ideas, creativity and innovation. This statement in no way implies that women and minorities are superior to men in Japan, only that their absence can be read as one symptom of a closed system. The hard work of changing practices and attitudes to include women and minorities to invigorate the economy and bring new, innovative options still lies ahead.

References

Asahi Shimbun. 1999. *Japan Almanac 1999*. Tokyo: Asahi Shimbun Publishing Company.

Buraku Liberation and Human Rights Research Institute. 1998. *The Han World — Korean Residents in Japan*. 5 November.

Chung, E. A. 2000. *Exercising Citizenship: Korean Voluntary Associations in Japanese Civil Society*. Cardiff, CA: Japan Policy Research Institute, July.

Fukuoka, Y. & Tsujiyama, Y. 1992. 'Mintohren: Young Koreans Against Ethnic Discrimination in Japan, *The Bulletin of Chiba College of Health Science* 10(2).

Hicks, G. 1997. *Japan's Hidden Apartheid: The Korean Minority and the Japanese*. Aldershot: Ashgate Publishing Limited.

International Labour Office. 1996a. *Yearbook of Labour Statistics*. Geneva, Switzerland.

International Labour Office. 1996b. *Policy Planning and Research*. Geneva, Switzerland.

Japan Institute of Labor. 1998. *Japanese Working Life Profile 1996–97*. Labor Statistics, Japan Institute of Labor.

Japanese Ministry of Labour Employment Statistics. 1996. Tokyo, Japan.

Kodansha Publishing Company. 1998. 'Minority Rights'. *Kodansha Encyclopedia of Japan*. Tokyo: Kodansha Publishing Company.

Management and Coordination Agency. 1995–2000. *Nihon tokei nenkan* (Japan Statistical Yearbook). Tokyo: Government of Japan.

McCorduck, P. & Ramsey, N. 1996. *The Futures of Women: Scenarios for the Twenty-first Century*. Reading MA: Addison Wesley.

Prime Minister's Office. 2000. *Women in Japan Today*. Tokyo: Office for Gender Equality, January.

Rabson, S. 1999. 'Life on the Mainland: As Portrayed in Modern Okinawan Literature'. In Chalmers, J. (Ed.). *Okinawa: Cold War Island*. Cardiff, CA: Japan Policy Research Institute.

Reischauer, E. O. 1977. *The Japanese*. Cambridge Mass: Harvard University Press.

Renshaw, J. R. 1999. *Kimono in the Boardroom: The Invisible Evolution of Japanese Women Managers*. Oxford: Oxford University Press.

Report of the Prime Minister's Commission on Japan's Goals in the Twenty-first Century 2000. *The Frontier Within: Individual Empowerment and Better Governance in the New Millennium*. Tokyo.

Saito, K. 1995. *Mohito Ganbari, Working Women: One More Effort*. Tokyo: NTT.

Shidzue, K. 1996. *The Economist*. 1 June.

Tamura, M. 1996. *Josei Kigyokatachi, Women Entrepreneurs New Power to Transform Business Society.* Tokyo: Nihon Keizai.

United Nations Human Development Programme (UNDP) 1999. *Human Development Report 1999*. New York: Oxford University Press.

United Nations 1998. 'Problems of Foreigners and Minorities'. Ch. 2. *Alternative Report to the Fourth Periodic Report of Japan on the International Covenant on Civil and Political Rights*. Nichibenren.

Upham, F. K. 1987. *Law and Social Change in Postwar Japan*. Cambridge, Mass: Harvard University Press.

Wehrfritz, G. & Hideko T. 2000. 'A New Open Door Policy?'. *Newsweek*. 5 June: 12–17.

Weiner, M. (Ed.). 1997. *Japan's Minorities: The Illusion of Homogeneity.* London, New York: Routledge.

Chapter 8

Malaysia

John Burgess and Siva Muthaly

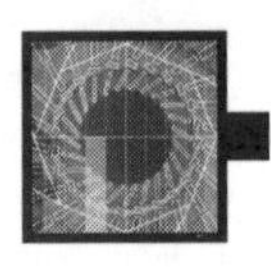

Introduction

Modern Malaysia is descended from British colonial administration, independent sultanate states, trading colonies and immigrant workers. Malaysia is geographically and ethnically diverse, it is an economy of high growth and rapid transformation, and it retains an effective one party political system that exercises strict control over the media and trade unions and has minimum tolerance for political opposition. At the core of Malaysia is diversity in ethnicity and religion. The three major ethnic groups are Malays, Indians and Chinese. The major religions are Islam, Hinduism, Buddhism and Christianity. The New Economic Policy (NEP) of 1971 incorporated diversity and affirmative action into the development program of the country.

This chapter is organised as follows. An overview of Malaysia, including its history and geography will follow. The discussion will then consider economic and labour market developments within Malaysia. Labour legislation is then outlined and following this the labour rights and legislative aspects of workforce diversity are examined. The analysis then turns to a discussion of how diversity is managed in practice within the workforce. Finally, the discussion reflects on the progress and the challenges facing Malaysia with respect to managing workforce diversity. Although the institutional and legal arrangements are not conducive to openness and participation, the imperatives of economic progress and transformation to an advanced economy will place pressure on workplace managers to be more responsive to the aspirations and needs of an increasingly skilled and sophisticated workforce. The expectation is that diversity management will become an important challenge for enterprises that wish to upgrade workforce skills, reduce labour turnover and retain productive workers.

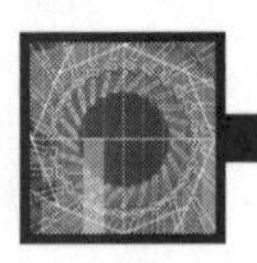

Geography and history of Malaysia

Malaysia has a land area of 329 758 square kilometres with a total population of 23.26 million in 2000. The South China Sea geographically separates peninsular Malaysia from East Malaysia. There are 11 states in peninsular Malaysia and two states located on the island of Borneo. The country fronts Thailand in the north on the Asian mainland and is linked to Singapore in the south by a 1056-metre causeway. Sabah and Sarawak in East Malaysia border the territory of the Republic of Indonesia. Peninsular Malaysia is strategically located in South-east Asia, occupying an area close to the shortest sea route between India and China and almost equidistant between both countries. The country also lies across the main air and sea routes between Australia and Europe. In terms of both trade and diplomacy Malaysia can be said to be at the centre of one of the most dynamic regions in the global economy.

Over 80 per cent of the population lives on the Peninsula and the remainder in East Malaysia. As with many other growing economies Malaysia is becoming increasingly urbanised as a result of the population drift away from plantation and agricultural sectors towards urban centres with manufacturing and service sector jobs. Over 60 per cent of the population reside in urban areas. The ethnic distribution of the population is approximately Malay 60 per cent, Chinese 30 per cent and Indian 10 per cent (Islam & Chowdhury 1998: 224). Since independence the Malay share of

the population has increased while the Chinese and Indian shares have declined (Jomo 1995). Malaysia also has a relatively high population growth, since 1988 the population has increased by nearly 40 per cent and as a consequence it has a relatively young population distribution. Table 8.1 contrasts the population distribution of Malaysia with that of Japan which has an ageing population profile.

Table 8.1: ***Population age distribution: Malaysia and Japan, 1998***

Age	Malaysia %	Japan %
0–14	34.00	15.11
15–19	11.04	6.21
20–29	17.99	15.03
30–39	14.91	12.87
40–49	10.72	14.48
50–59	6.28	14.02
60–69	3.73	11.52
70+	2.16	10.71

Source: Adapted from International Labour Office, (1998), *Yearbook of Labour Statistics*, Geneva.

Peninsular Malaysia was settled by traders and colonial powers as a result of its strategic location and its natural resources, in particular rubber, timber, tin and rice. Colonial administrators and influences include the Dutch, the Portuguese and predominantly the British. During the nineteenth and early twentieth century there was a steady flow of immigration from India and China, supported by colonial trading companies and administrations, to service the trade, mining and commodity sectors (Jomo 1995: 190). The country was occupied by the Japanese during World War II and endured internal insurrection in the immediate post-war period as the Communist Party opposed the reintroduction of British colonial rule. This period was associated with strict government control and strong laws associated with the ongoing state of emergency. The post World War II Federation of Malaya was an amalgam of British colonies, sultanates and protectorates.

In 1957 Malaya was granted independence from British rule and in 1963 the Federation of Malaysia was established to include Sabah, Sarawak and Singapore. Subsequently, in 1965 Singapore became an independent republic after it was expelled from the Federation. In 1969 there were race riots in Kuala Lumpur where ethnic Malays targeted the businesses of ethnic Chinese. In 1971, the New Economic Policy (NEP) proclaimed growth and sharing as the twin virtues for Malaysia (Woodiwiss 1998: 190).

Within the constitution, ethnic Malays do enjoy special privileges under section 153 including rights to public sector jobs, business licences, share ownership in new companies, and access to education scholarships. This was part of the post-independence settlement to incorporate ethnic Malays more into the growing economy and to ease some of the ethnic tensions associated with the dominance of commerce by ethnic Chinese.

The New Development Policy (NDP) proclaimed in 1990 targets developed country status for Malaysia by 2020. This policy implied annual growth rates of over seven per cent per annum and a significant transformation of the economy away from resources and plantation sectors towards manufacturing and services (Mahbob 1997: 7). The government was keen to encourage foreign investment, especially in electronics, and to encourage the expansion in education and training across the population. This stage of development would be marked by a move towards high tech sectors, a growing capital intensity of production and an increasing integration into the global economy (Woodiwiss 1998: 195).

Managing ethnic diversity has been one of the key political issues confronting Malaysia since its independence. To date diversity management has been achieved through a combination of strong and stable government, centralised intervention across the economy, a constitutional program of affirmative action for ethnic Malays, a program of rapid economic transformation and high growth rates and rising average material living standards. Nevertheless, there is the perception that despite these developments, each ethnic group has retained its own distinct cultural and ethnic identity (Islam & Chowdhury 1998: 224).

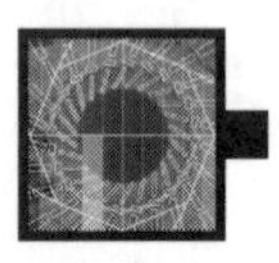

Economic and labour market developments

Economic growth and transformation

The experience of Malaysia since the NEP has been one of ongoing growth and diversification within the context of a national economic development program. Economic growth averaged over eight per cent per annum between 1988 and 1996 while over the decade to 1995 real per capita income increased from US$2050 to US$3389 (Mahbob 1997: 1). Over the decade to 1995 the manufacturing share of output increased from 0.18 to 0.31 while agriculture's share fell from 0.21 to 0.14 for the same period (Mahbob 1997: 2).

Policy has aimed at strategic targets such as investment in particular industries, training and education, and attracting large international corporations and their managerial expertise. As a result, the economy has thrived on the back of sustained and high rates of economic growth, a diversification of the economy, improving average living standards and low rates of unemployment. Malaysia has also benefited from the high growth rates realised within the region by neighbours (until 1997) including Singapore, Thailand and Indonesia. The Asian 'tiger' status accorded to the region and to Malaysia was also important in attracting foreign investment.

In terms of the standard macroeconomic indicators, the Malaysian economy has, with few exceptions, progressed significantly since independence. Table 8.2 demonstrates that a high growth rate, a low inflation rate and low unemployment rates have been the norm and the envy of many OECD countries. For example, Australia's unemployment rate has averaged nine per cent throughout the 1990s and GDP growth has rarely exceeded 4.5 per cent.

The exceptions to the high growth experience were the mid 1980s collapse of commodity prices and the Asian currency crisis of 1997. Although both events can be regarded as an aberration to the secular record of sustained growth and improvements in living standards, they did highlight the fact that global integration also has its downside and its risks.

Table 8.2: *Malaysia: GDP growth, inflation and unemployment, 1986–98*

Year	GDP growth %	Inflation %	Unemployment %
1986	1.2	0.7	8.5
1988	8.9	2.5	7.2
1989	9.2	2.8	6.3
1990	9.7	3.1	5.1
1991	8.7	4.4	4.3
1992	7.8	4.7	3.7
1993	8.3	3.6	3.0
1994	8.5	3.7	2.9
1995	9.4	3.4	2.8
1996	8.6	3.5	2.6
1997	7.7	2.7	2.6
1998	–6.7	5.3	3.9

Sources: Adapted from Mahbob (1997: 2); and International Monetary Fund (1999).

Table 8.3: *Sectoral Shares of GDP for Malaysia, 1985–98*

Year	Manufacture	Agriculture	Construction	Services	Other
1985	19.7	20.8	4.8	43.5	11.2
1994	31.7	14.5	4.2	44.5	5.1
1998	34.4	12.3	3.9	42.2	7.0

Sources: Adapted from Mahbob (1997: 2); and International Monetary Fund (1999).

As to be expected with a high growth economy there has been a major transformation in the structure of the economy (see table 8.3). The importance of raw materials, plantation and extractive industries has gradually diminished. In turn, this has reduced the economy's vulnerability to commodity price volatility and to the secular decline in the terms of trade associated with commodity export dependence. New jobs are located in manufacturing, especially electronics, and in services, such as finance and tourism. The migration of labour from agricultural-based rural areas to urban areas has lifted productivity growth and contributed to the relative material advancement of the ethnic Malays who previously dominated small agricultural holdings. Immigrant workers are utilised to offset skill shortages in construction, plantation and professional service employment.

However, Malaysia continues to play an important role in the world market for the export of certain primary products. It is still an important source of rubber, although no longer the largest single supplier, however, it produces over half of the world's palm oil. Thus, within the primary commodity category, earnings are predominantly from palm oil, timber, oil and gas (MPI 1999). Manufacturing accounts for close to 60 per cent to 70 per cent of gross export earnings (Economist Intelligence Unit 1999). Electronic goods formed the fastest growing and the single most important category in the post 1990s, and Malaysia occupied a strong international position in some parts of this sector (World Bank 1999). The Malaysian Government has directed its attention to increasing the domestic content of exports, by means of introducing a campaign to add higher value to imports to counteract the depreciation of the ringgit.

The financial crisis, triggered in mid-1997 by heavy selling of the ringgit and shares, degenerated into a full-blown recession in 1998 as investors became increasingly concerned about the emergence of weakness in the economy and their investments (MITI 1999; Sherman 1999). Prime Minister Mahatir was quick to condemn foreign speculators and currency traders for the 1997 collapse of the ringgit and instituted a regime of currency and exchange regulations. While there were immediate real effects of the crisis such as a decline in output and increasing unemployment (see table 8.2), the impact on Malaysia was relatively short, sharp and of less intensity as elsewhere, for example, Thailand. While there was a banking crisis within Malaysia related to the exposure of many banks to bad debts, the Malaysian economy was able to come through the financial shock. Unlike its neighbours, the government was running a fiscal surplus, domestic savings rates were high and the government instituted an offsetting and expansionary fiscal and monetary program (IMF 1999). In addition the central bank addressed the issue of non-performing loans that was threatening the integrity of the national banking system through a process of restructuring and amalgamation within the sector.

The labour market

Just as production has become increasingly diversified by industry, so too has the workforce. The past two decades have witnessed strong labour force growth and an industrial transformation in the workforce composition. The labour force and employment have been growing at rates well in excess of four per cent per annum and unemployment rates have remained relatively low throughout the 1990s (see tables 8.2 and 8.4). Table 8.5 indicates the strong shift away from traditional agricultural employment towards manufacturing and services employment.

Table 8.4: ***The Malaysian labour force, 1988–98***

Year	Population (millions)	Labour force (millions)	Employment (millions)	Labour force participation rate %	Unemployment rate %
1988	16.194	6.654	6.175	58.2	7.2
1990	17.763	7.044	6.685	59.6	5.1
1995	20.689	7.846	7.618	64.9	2.8
1998	22.180	8.881	8.538	64.3	3.9

Sources: Adapted from IMF (1999); International Labour Office (1991).

Table 8.5: ***Workforce sectoral composition (% shares), 1985–98***

Sectors	1985	1990	1998
Agriculture	30.3	24.5	18.8
Mining	0.8	0.5	0.3
Manufacturing	15.0	19.9	22.2
Electricity	0.5	0.7	0.6
Construction	7.4	6.3	8.7
Trade, hotels, cafes	17.6	18.2	18.8
Transport	4.3	4.5	4.9
Finance, banks	3.9	3.8	4.9
Community Services	20.0	19.9	20.8

Source: Adapted from International Labour Office, (1998), *Yearbook of Labour Statistics*, Geneva.

Table 8.6: ***Occupational distribution of workforce for major ethnic groups, Malaysia, 1998***

	Profes-sional	Admin	Clerical	Sales	Services	Agricul-ture	Produc-tion
Malay	11.7	3.6	10.5	7.7	12.4	20.2	34.0
Chinese	8.2	10.2	4.4	21.4	6.8	8.1	40.9
Indian	10.1	4.5	9.3	9.1	12.1	9.3	45.5

Source: Adapted from Department of Statistics (1998), *Labour Force Survey Report*, Malaysia.

At the same time, the ethnic composition of the workforce (table 8.6) is also changing. At the time of independence Malays dominated small agricultural holdings, the Chinese dominated mining and commerce and the Indians dominated plantation sectors. Overall there was an ethnic division of labour based on colonial labour use policies (Jomo 1995). The colonial division of labour assigned particular ethnic groups to given occupations or industries. This in turn contributed to the exclusion from the growth dividend of ethnic Malays who were segregated into small rural holdings and low productivity agriculture. However, since NEP the Malay share of the workforce is increasing on average and it is increasing across all sectors. The official labour force data demonstrate that the overall occupational structure of the Indian and Chinese workforces has changed only moderately, while there has been a dramatic transformation in the ethnic Malay workforce from the early 1970s away from agriculture towards manufacturing and services (Jomo 1995: 197). The share of women in the workforce is also increasing and they are becoming less segregated by sector. The share of women in the workforce increased steadily since the 1950s through to the early 1980s across all ethnic groups (Jomo 1995: 199). Since the mid-1980s the female workforce share has been around one-third of the workforce (International Labour Office). Males dominate employment in the mining, electricity, construction and transport sectors. The female employment share is relatively high in manufacturing (40 per cent), trade and hospitality (40 per cent), finance and banks (42 per cent) and community and social services (41 per cent).

It should also be mentioned that immigrant workers play an important part in filling labour shortages within the economy (Rasiah 1995: 78). There has been large-scale use of immigrant labour in agriculture, construction, manufacturing and services. This labour enters Malaysia legally and illegally from Thailand, Indonesia, India, the Philippines and Bangladesh. It is estimated that there are between 500 000 and 1.5 million immigrant workers, mainly illegal, within Malaysia (Jomo 1995: 207). While there is a registration system for immigrant labour, the incentives to avoid compliance, employment laws and pay below legally minimum wages is considerable (*The Economist* 1997a). After the 1997 currency crisis and the subsequent fall in employment, the government instituted a crackdown on illegal immigrant workers and deported tens of thousands back to their country of origin (*The Economist* 1997a).

The imperative of economic growth, together with the affirmative action program for ethnic Malays, has opened up more opportunities for participation by women and ethnic Malays. The colonial ethnic and gender division of labour is being eroded through high growth and the industrial restructuring of the workforce. Like its colonial predecessors the government has sanctioned the legal and illegal use of immigrant labour to overcome labour shortages and to control wages growth (*The Economist* 1997a).

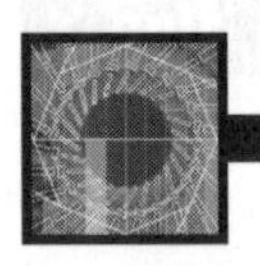

General employment legislation

The major areas of employment legislation are the *Employment Act 1955*, the *Trade Union Act 1959*, the *Industrial Relations Act 1967* and the *Employees Social Security Act 1969* (Aminuddin 1996: 9). Various aspects of the legislation will be outlined and discussed in this and the following section.

The *Employment Act 1955* is the main legislation on labour matters in Malaysia. It establishes rights and obligations of both employer and employee. The legislation is comprehensive in its coverage, and some of the key aspects in this Act are as follows:

- normal working hours — not exceeding eight hours or 48 hours in one week
- paid holiday — at least 10 gazetted public holidays in one calendar year
- paid maternity leave — 60 days
- paid annual leave for employees (less than two years of service) — eight days
- paid annual leave for employees (two or more but less than five years of service) — 12 days
- paid annual leave for employees (over five years of service) — 16 days
- payment for overtime work (normal working days) — one and a half times the hourly rate of pay
- payment for overtime work (rest days) — two times the hourly rate of pay
- payment for overtime work (public holidays) — three times the hourly rate of pay.

The *Employees' Social Security Act 1969* administers social security schemes for workers earning wages not exceeding RM2000 (A$1000) per month (Loh 1998).

This Act ensures that the employer contributes 1.25 per cent of the employee's wage under the Employment Injury Insurance Scheme.

In addition, the *Employees' Provident Fund Act 1991* (Act 452) states that a minimum contribution is 12 per cent of the employee's monthly wages by the employer and 11 per cent of the employee's monthly wages by the employee. Whereas for foreign workers earning less than RM2500 (A$1250) per month, the employer contributes RM5.00 or A$2.50 per month and the employee pays 11 per cent of the monthly wage. Other key Acts and Regulations include the *EPF Rules and Regulations 1991*, *Occupational Safety and Health Act 1994*, *Control of Industrial Major Accident Hazards Regulations 1996* and *Safety and Health Officer Order and Regulation 1997* (NCCIM 1999).

Utilisation of foreign skills may not be cost-effective as the employment of expatriates earning more than RM2500 (A$1250) per month are highly taxed with no levy (NCCIM 1999). In addition, the processing fee for an employment pass is RM200 (A$100) per year for an expatriate in a management/professional/technical post and RM300 (US$150) per year for an expatriate in a key or permanent post. This of course only applies to the use of legal immigrant labour.

Foreign workers have to abide by the general estimates of monthly salaries of executives and non-executives provided in table 8.7; however, the ranges may vary according to location and industrial sector (MIDA 1999; NCCIM 1999). For example, salary rates would be higher in Selangor, Federal Territory, Perak and Penang (major states in West Malaysia) compared to Sabah (state in East Malaysia) due to the standards of living. Apart from basic salary, most companies also provide fringe benefits (annual leave based on position level and length of service, medical treatment, personal accident insurance, free or subsidised transport, annual and discretionary bonus, salary increment, retirement benefits, loans and enhanced contributions to the Employees Provident Fund) (MIDA 1999; NCCIM 1999).

These employment regulations would affect the mode of entry via the following:

- entry via wholly owned subsidiaries may involve importing skills and, based on the employment acts, this would not be cost effective as the Malaysian Government is currently encouraging foreign companies to hire local skills
- joint ventures and strategic alliances with a strong local company would be the best mode of entry as this would ensure cost-effective strategies and easier comprehension of local culture
- when employing local staff, foreign companies must abide by a number of employment rules and regulations to ensure smoother operations.

Overall, the general employment legislation is comprehensive in its coverage and very prescriptive. However, there are three areas of concern with respect to employment legislation. First, enforcement or compliance, which is not widespread given the estimated large numbers of illegal immigrant workers (*The Economist* 1997a). Second, the very strict regulations imposed over collective organisation and trade unions. Third, the absence of specific legislation addressing workforce diversity. The following sections turn to these last two concerns.

Regulation of industrial relations and trade unions

There is a high degree of state regulation and control imposed over trade unions and the industrial relations system (Peetz & Todd 2000: 171). Under the state of emergency decreed by the British colonial administration in 1948 there were very strict regulations imposed on trade union organisation and activity. Communist

Table 8.7: ***Salary estimates of executives and non-executives (per month) in Malaysia, 1998***

Position	Min (RM)	Max (RM)	Min (US$)	Max (US$)
General Manager	7615	14509	2004	3818
Financial Controller	6357	14046	1673	3696
Human Resource Manager	4959	9251	9251	2434
Factory Manager	4876	9768	1283	2571
Marketing Manager	4668	8648	1228	2276
Branch Manager	4292	7516	1129	1978
Production Manager	4086	7452	1075	1961
Chief Accountant	4083	7149	1074	1881
Purchasing Manager	4045	7277	1064	1915
Quality Control Manager	3812	7545	1003	1986
Administration Manager	3560	6500	937	1711
Training Manager	3294	6073	867	1598
System Analyst	2502	4409	658	1160
Electronic/Electrical Engineer	2425	4664	638	1127
Mechanical Engineer	2253	4739	593	1247
Chemist	2208	4377	581	1152
Executive Secretary/Personal Assistant	1987	1987	523	960
Company Secretary	1967	1967	518	1456
Marketing Executive	1925	1925	507	1111
Programmer	1437	1437	378	752

Source: Adapted from NCCIM (1999a),1 *Investor's Guide to Malaysia*, Kuala Lumpur: National Chamber of Commerce and Industry, Malaysia.

associated trade unions were deregistered (often associated with ethnic Chinese workers) while responsible trade union activity was supported (Jomo 1995: 204; Woodiwiss 1998: 209). This central regulation and distrust of trade unions continued post-independence. Indeed, industrial relations policy is an arm of economic policy, largely based on suppressing labour unrest and opposition, providing a stable labour environment for investment, and enshrining managerial prerogatives in the workplace.

In general while there are many trade unions, over 500, many are small and local. In total there are over 700 000 trade union members, but they represent less than

10 per cent of the workforce (Peetz & Todd 2000: 172). Over the past decade the number of trade union members has increased by more than 100 000, but this is only a small proportion of total workforce growth (Yong 1996: 197). In terms of the ethnic composition of trade unions there has been a dramatic shift since independence when Indians accounted for over 60 per cent of trade union members. This was the consequence of the large employment share in the plantation sector and the prevailing colonial division of labour among the ethnic groups. However, as the economy restructured and ethnic Malays increased their share of the workforce and their share across industries, they increased their share of trade unions from around 20 per cent at independence to over 60 per cent by the early 1990s (Jomo 1995: 210). Similarly, as female labour force participation rates and employment shares have increased, so has the female trade union share. At independence the female trade union share was around 25 per cent, by the early 1990s this had reached 30 per cent (Jomo 1995: 211).

Since independence the ethnic composition of trade union membership has shifted in line with the growing population and employment share of Malays. At the time of independence the ethnic trade union composition was approximately 60 per cent Indian and 20 per cent each for Malays and Chinese. By the late 1980s the ethnic shares were 60 per cent Malay, 25 per cent Indian and 15 per cent Chinese (Jomo 1995: 210).

Trade union registration, structure and size are subject to a range of regulations enshrined under the *Trade Union Act 1959* and the *Industrial Relations Act 1971* (Yong 1996: 198). Union leaders cannot belong to political parties, unions may not operate across industries and since the early 1980s the government has expressed a preference for and encouraged enterprise or in-house unions. This is meant to encourage company loyalty, increase work effort and stifle independent trade union activity (Jomo 1995: 195; Peetz & Todd 2000: 172). Under the Employment Act, pioneering firms were given a start-up exemption from trade union presence (Rasiah 1995: 77). In general, there are long delays and difficulties associated with obtaining official government recognition and registration of a trade union. In 1992, of the 116 claims for trade union recognition lodged, 45 were recognised, 13 were rejected or withdrawn and 58 were still awaiting decision in 1996 (Yong 1996: 200).

Trade unions are not permitted to operate within the electronics industry, largely on the insistence of the US-based foreign investors (Jomo 1995: 188; Peetz & Todd 2000: 172). There are strict controls over strike activity and various types of strikes (e.g. political, sympathy) are illegal. There are three peak labour organisations: the Malaysian Trade Union Congress, the Congress of Unions in the Public Sector and the Malaysian Labour Organisation. This final body was formed in 1989 and is seen as an attempt by the government to stifle trade union opposition and to make labour more compliant to the interests of the government (Peetz & Todd 2000).

It is not surprising to find that within such a labour regime strike activity is relatively minimal. Most industrial action has been confined to the manufacturing and agricultural processing sectors (Jomo 1995: 218). Over the 1990s the number of strikes has averaged around 15 per year with the number of employees involved being between one and 5000 in total (International Labour Office).

Overall unions operate within a strict regulatory framework as set by the Director General of Trade Unions (Peetz & Todd 2000: 172), with the balance of bargaining power clearly tilted towards employers. Despite this, trade unions remain resilient and, as with the workforce, their composition is changing to reflect the increasing participation of women and ethnic Malays across the economy.

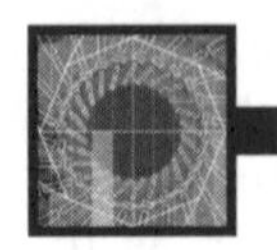

Rights, equality and legislation promoting equality

The Malaysian constitution provides the usual guarantees associated with civil society such as protection of life and private property, and freedom of expression and religion. However, these rights are circumscribed by other sections of the constitution and other legislation. The *Internal Security Act 1960* allows for sanctioned detention without trial and widespread government controls over association and expression. The constitution also allows parliament to pass laws that can override any of the civil guarantees and human rights (Woodiwiss 1998: 203–5).

Malaysia is a signatory to only 11 clauses of the International Labour Organisation (ILO) labour rights conventions. This is compared to Singapore's and the Philippines' ratification of 21 clauses, but is on par with Thailand's ratification of 11 clauses (Aminuddin 1996: 7). As a result of the strict regulations of trade union activity and organisation, Malaysia has, in the past, been accused of contravening some of the fundamental labour rights, including freedom of association and the right to collectively bargain (Jayasingham 1997: 78)

The rights to organise, bargain and engage in collective action are also subject to state regulation. Child labour as such is not illegal, however, there is regulation of the type of work and hours of work for child labour under the *Children and Young Person's Employment Act 1967* (Aminuddin 1999: 22).

There is no EEO, sexual harassment or anti-discrimination legislation in Malaysia (Aminuddin 1999: 92), though the Employment Act does exclude women from employment in underground mines and does limit their working hours (Rasiah 1995: 77). EEO is largely a matter for management to develop at the workplace as part of company HR policy (Yong 1996: 226). As mentioned there is a form of affirmative action for ethnic Malays enshrined in the constitution however, this does not reach to private sector employment. The Employment Act does enshrine basic employment conditions including holiday leave and maternity leave. The Human Resources Development Act 1992 provides for a one per cent levy on employees' wages to fund approved training programs (Jayasingham 1997: 101). Foreign workers are subject to special licensing requirement under the Employment Act however, it is argued that the majority of immigrant workers in the plantation, construction and land development sectors are illegal workers (Jomo 1995: 207).

Overall, in comparison with OECD countries labour rights are very limited and special employment legislation promoting workforce equity is non-existent. The government heavily regulates trade unions and is keen to demonstrate an industrial relations system marked by an absence of strikes and conflict, and one that is conducive to facilitating the conditions favourable for attracting foreign investment. Industrial relations policy is largely an adjunct to economic policy and the targets associated with the NDP (Peetz & Todd 2000: 171). While the balance is very much tilted towards the rights of employers and managers, the imperatives of high rates of economic growth and labour skill shortages will force both employers and the government to address issues such as workplace training, employee participation and the facilitation of basic labour rights.

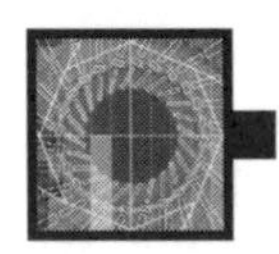

Conclusions

The imperatives for managing workforce diversity in Malaysia

Malaysia has one of the most ethnically and religiously diverse workforces in Asia. While this outcome reflects the country's rich historical heritage it means that at a political level, participation and multiculturalism have become an imperative and a hallmark of the nation's development. Malays have been given direct state assistance in their quest to share in the benefits of economic progress. There has also been a growing workforce representation by women.

More effectively managing human resources, raising labour productivity and increasing the depth and spread of workforce skills occupies a central position within the government's modernisation program (Todd 1999: 4). Indeed, the imperatives of a high-growth economy have placed pressure on the capacity of Malaysia to provide the necessary range and quality of labour skills to facilitate this growth (Rasiah 1995: 78). Attracting foreign investors to Malaysia is not only important in accessing capital, it is also important in providing skills and expertise, together with training, in technical and managerial occupations (Todd 1999: 5). For its part, the government has recognised the importance of training and skill acquisition for its globally competitive ambitions, and to this end the *Human Resource Development Act 1992* provides employers with the funds for skill acquisition within company workforces. It has also provided for generous tax deductions for multinational companies who invest in training (Rasiah 1995: 76).

Malaysia is keen to upgrade the skills of its workforce, improve the quality of its managers and promote itself as a modern, high-tech and highly educated country. Indeed, it is attempting to become the IT and education hub of Asia through the development of the multimedia corridor to the south of Kuala Lumpur (*The Economist* 1997b).

The challenge for Malaysia is that the low wage and low cost route associated with large-scale use of illegal immigrant labour and the suppression of collectivism will not overcome the problems of skill shortages. Already, high skill labour is attracted to Singapore and Australia where wage rates are relatively higher than those offered in Malaysia. Employers will have to confront the necessity of attracting workers, retaining workers and upgrading the skills of workers. This will mean that there will be a greater reliance on HR policies that offer career paths and enterprise training, which link wages and employment conditions to skill acquisition and seniority and provide a safe working environment. The pressures will build up within enterprises which will no longer be able to rely on labour controls and migrants to keep wage costs down and remain competitive. As Malaysia becomes wealthier, workers will expect a share of the growth dividend. In turn, Malaysia's neighbours such as Thailand and Indonesia will be able to provide lower nominal wage cost advantages to foreign investors.

In short, there is a need for an alternative to the cost minimisation model in Malaysian enterprises. The government has recognised this through additional funding for education and training, and through the support of best practice methods to promote training and improve skills across sectors (Todd 1999: 16). The government, as the largest employer in the country (Yong 1996: 202), can lead the way by adopting model employer practices.

In the absence of legislative requirements and limited workforce collectivisation it will be up to the private sector to institute HR policies that do recognise and nurture diversity in the workplace. HR policies can be used to promote equal opportunity, equity and non-harassment within the workplace as a means of increasing employee attachment to the enterprise and improving workplace efficiency. As Malaysia seeks to replicate Western, especially US, management systems, it will by necessity be forced to embrace policies that do encompass the management and development of workforce diversity (Warner 1996: 7). In particular, as organisational culture moves away from very centralised and authoritarian control and very bureaucratic structures towards the flatter management structures of US organisations, such developments will become more plausible and possible.

Challenges

Malaysia remains an economy of rapid growth and transformation. It is also a very ethnically diverse culture. The post-independence development of Malaysia has been characterised by a one-party government and an ongoing circumvention of civil and labour rights (Woodiwiss 1998: 185). Trade unions are strictly regulated and parliament and civil servants can easily circumvent labour rights.

As Malaysia further develops and modernises its economy, its competitive advantage will depend upon a high productivity and an adaptive skill base. Low wage sectors will be less able to compete in the global market. This is already recognised through ambitious plans to develop Malaysia as the high-tech hub of Asia (*The Economist* 1997b). In this context there is scope for believing that private companies will develop internal policies and HR programs such as best practice programs and benchmarking that are based on ability, skill acquisition and employee retention. However, this will require a change in management culture and an emphasis within organisations on participation, inclusion and skill-based competitive advantage (Warner 1998). In this context it is not unreasonable to believe that there will be an important competitive imperative for effectively managing workforce diversity.

References

Aminuddin, M. 1996. *Malaysian Employment Law and Industrial Relations*. Kuala Lumpur: McGraw-Hill.

Aminuddin, M. 1999. *An A-Z for Malaysian Employment Law*. Kuala Lumpur: McGraw-Hill.

Department of Statistics. 1998. *Labour Force Survey Report*. Malaysia.

Economist Intelligence Unit. 1999. *Country Report: Malaysia*. London: Economist Intelligence Unit.

International Labour Office. Various years. *Yearbook of Labour Statistics*. Geneva.

International Monetary Fund. 1999. *Malaysia: Recent Economic Developments*. IMF Staff Country Report 99/85. Washington, DC.

Islam, I. & Chowdhury, A. 1998. *Asia Pacific Economies: A Survey*. London: Routledge.

Jayasankaran, S. 1999. 'Road to Recovery'. *Far Eastern Economic Review* 26(96).

Jayasingam, P. 1997. 'Employment Law: Rights and Liabilities'. In Cheang, L. *The Business Guide to Malaysia*. Singapore: Butterworth-Heinemann, 77–102.

Jomo, K. 1995. 'Capital, the State and Labour in Malaysia'. In Schor, J. & You, J. (Eds). *Capital, the State and Labour: A Global Perspective*. Cheltenham: Edward Elgar, 195–237.

Loh, S. C. 1998. *The Business Guide to Malaysia*. Singapore: Butterworth-Heinemann Asia.

Mahbob, S. 1997. 'The Malaysian Economy: Current Position and Trends'. In Cheang, L. *The Business Guide to Malaysia*. Singapore: Butterworth-Heinemann, 1–9.

MIDA. 1999. *Malaysian Policies, Incentives and Facilities*. Kuala Lumpur: Malaysian Industrial Development Authority.

MITI. 1999. *Business Opportunities in Malaysia After the Economic Crisis*. Kuala Lumpur: Ministry of International Trade and Industry.

MPI. 1999. *Ministry Introduction*. Kuala Lumpur: Ministry of Primary Industries.

NCCIM. 1999a. *Investor's Guide to Malaysia*. Kuala Lumpur: National Chamber of Commerce and Industry Malaysia.

NCCIM. 1999b. *Taxation*. Kuala Lumpur: National Chamber of Commerce and Industry Malaysia.

Peetz, D. & Todd, P. 2000. 'Otherwise You're on Your Own: Unions and Bargaining in Malaysian Banking'. In Burgess, J. & Strachan, G. (Eds). *Research on Work, Employment and Industrial Relations 2000*. Proceedings of the Fourteenth Conference of the Association of Industrial Relations Academics of Australia and New Zealand, Newcastle. 4: 171–80.

Rasiah, R. 1995. 'Labour and Industrialisation in Malaysia'. *Journal of Contemporary Asia* 25(1): 73–92.

Sherman, M. 1999. 'New Dawn for Asia'. *Reaction* 19(2): 24–6.

The Economist. 1997a. 'Sent Packing: Malaysia'. 8 February, p. 40.

The Economist. 1997b. 'Multimedia Super Corridor'. 1 March, p. 67.

Todd, P. 1999. 'The Impact of Foreign Multinational Corporations upon Malaysian Employment Relations: A Study of Six Australian Companies Manufacturing in Malaysia'. *International Journal of Employment Studies* 7(2): 1–24.

Warner, M. 1998. 'Culture, Human Resources and Organisations in Asia: Seeking a Model with Chinese Characteristics'. *International Journal of Employment Studies* 6(2): 1–18.

Woodiwiss, A. 1998. *Globalization, Human Rights and Labour Law in Pacific Asia*. Cambridge: Cambridge University Press.

World Bank. 1999. *Country Brief: Malaysia*. New York: World Bank.

Yong, A. 1996. *Malaysian Human Resource Management*. Kualar Lumpur: Malaysian Institute of Management.

Chapter 9

New Zealand

Janice Burns and Trudie McNaughton

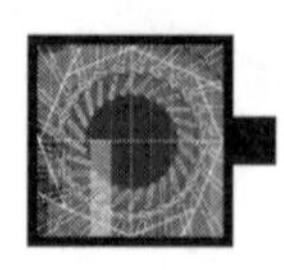

Introduction

Aotearoa New Zealand has a bicultural and multi-ethnic population of 3.6 million people. Originally populated by the Maori, the country was colonised by the British in the mid-nineteenth century and diverse peoples have immigrated since then, in particular people from the Asia–Pacific region. The most recent population census showed that the population consisted of approximately 77 per cent European/Pakeha (non-Maori New Zealanders of European descent), 14.5 per cent Maori, 5.6 per cent Pacific peoples and 3 per cent from other ethnic groups (Statistics New Zealand 1996). Almost 51 per cent of the population are female, it is estimated that up to 10 per cent of the population are lesbian or gay, and 22 per cent of the population have some form of self-described disability.

Projections by Statistics New Zealand about the composition of the future labour market indicate that New Zealand will experience increasing ethnic diversity, particularly in terms of Maori and Pacific peoples of working age (Statistics New Zealand 1999a). Like many other economies, New Zealand also has an ageing labour force. Currently 28 per cent of the labour force is 45 years or older. In 10 years, 43 per cent of the labour force will be in this age bracket (Statistics New Zealand 1999a).

These demographic issues have increased the imperative for the development of diversity attitudes and skills among New Zealand employers.

Any discussion of the valuing of diversity within the New Zealand labour market needs to be prefaced by a description of three factors that define the context within which this takes place.

First, the relationship between the Maori and the colonising British was formalised in 1840 by an agreement between Maori *iwi* (tribes) and the British Crown — the Treaty of Waitangi. The Treaty specified the rights and obligations of these two parties. While there is historical and contemporary dispute over the extent to which the Crown honoured its promises to the Maori, the existence of the Treaty acknowledges the rights of the Maori as *tangata whenua* (the indigenous people of the land). Settlements of grievances in relation to the illegal or immoral confiscation or appropriation of Maori land and assets have been a strong feature of the past 15 years. There would be few New Zealanders who are not aware of the Treaty and the discussion of its implications in contemporary New Zealand's social, legal, economic and cultural life.

In order to recognise the Maori as the indigenous people of Aotearoa New Zealand, diversity initiatives need to ensure they are not relegated to one of several target groups. Their unique status as *tangata whenua* should be reflected in the approach taken across the board in terms of appropriate consultation, processes, implementation and monitoring of initiatives.

The second condition to create an impact on the development of diversity initiatives in New Zealand are the dramatic changes to New Zealand's economic and industrial life since the mid-1980s. For much of the twentieth century, the New Zealand economy relied heavily on primary industries, in particular agriculture, and its primary trading partner was Britain. The radical restructuring of New Zealand's economy and labour relations in the 1980s and 1990s dramatically affected employment patterns, labour market practices and its trading relationship with the rest of the world. New Zealand is often held up as a model for labour and trade liberalisation, but the resultant labour market deregulation and ideology of minimal intervention by

government into business have posed particular challenges for the acceptance and implementation of EEO or diversity programs within organisations. Such policies are seen by some of those who have not recognised the business benefits of diversity as interventionist and antithetical to the prevailing orthodoxy.

The third key contextual factor is that since 1996 New Zealanders select their parliamentary representatives on the basis of a proportional representation electoral system (replacing the first past the post system). Two elections have been conducted on this basis and in both cases neither of the major political parties, Labour (centre left) and National (centre right) had a majority sufficient to govern without the support of formal alliances with smaller parties. Trade-offs on some policy issues are necessary under these conditions, and smaller parties can influence policy direction in a significant manner. The 1999 election result led to a change in government, with the Labour Party now governing in an alliance with a smaller and more left-wing party, the Alliance. This alliance may affect policy outcomes in areas such as the labour market and employment conditions.

This chapter examines diversity and the New Zealand labour market. It describes the history of diversity and equal employment opportunities (EEO) — two terms that are used interchangeably in New Zealand. It then examines the current labour market, including changes occurring in the talent pool available to that market and the barriers that exist to the fulfilment of that promise. Then follows a discussion of what is happening in New Zealand workplaces and the role of employers in recruiting and in valuing diversity. Finally, some conclusions are drawn about the trends apparent, and where these may be leading New Zealand in this new millennium.

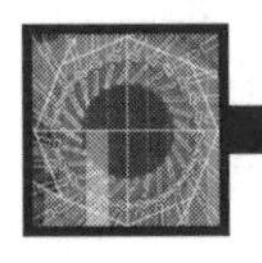

History of EEO/diversity policy and practice

Anti-discrimination focus: Initial approaches towards EEO

Equal employment opportunities started to become acceptable to New Zealand policymakers during the 1970s and 1980s. The initial focus was on eliminating discrimination against defined groups, and these groups were seen as the sole beneficiaries of such moves.

In the 1970s once it became clear that the *Equal Pay Act 1972* (designed to close the gender pay gap) was of limited effectiveness, feminists identified the need for equal employment opportunities. The initial anti-discrimination focus was apparent, for example, in the New Zealand Working Women's Charter of 1973, which demanded the elimination of discrimination on the basis of sex, race, marital or parental status, sexuality or age (New Zealand Council of Trade Unions National Women's Committee 1994).

The 1979 United Nations Convention on the Elimination of All Forms of Discrimination Against Women was signed by New Zealand in 1980 and ratified in 1984. Article 11 of the Convention contained guidelines on the elimination of the barriers preventing women's participation at all levels of occupations and across the range of jobs.

The *Race Relations Act 1971* outlawed discrimination on the grounds of race, colour and ethnic or national origins. The *Human Rights Commission Act 1971* was passed prohibiting discrimination on the grounds of sex, marital status, religious or ethical belief. The *Human Rights Act 1993* brought the provisions of these two Acts

together and expanded the grounds for discrimination to include sexual orientation, disability, age, family status, employment status and political opinion.

The *Labour Relations Act 1987* contained a section on discrimination which covered colour, race and ethnicity or national origin, sex, marital status, religious or ethical belief and trade union involvement. These requirements were carried over into the *Employment Contracts Act 1991*. The Employment Contracts Act is due to be repealed and replaced with the *Employment Relations Act 2000*, which is likely to retain these provisions.

Complaints of discrimination can either be made using the Human Rights Act or the Employment Contracts Act. Both avenues can result in financial compensation for the complainant.

Affirmative action focus: EEO in the public sector

The anti-discrimination focus evolved into one based on affirmative action. This term has a usage in New Zealand different from that in the United States, and does not refer to positive discrimination. Instead it means providing opportunities to assist particular groups of people to fully participate in employment, which may mean providing different but equivalent opportunities.

The 1980s also saw a shift to a greater understanding that EEO would benefit not just women, the Maori and other target groups, but would provide business benefits to employers.

The first official document on EEO was the government employing authorities' statement on EEO in 1984 (State Services Commission 1984). This signed agreement recognised the need for government employers to take a leading role in the development of EEO (State Services Commission 1985). The EEO Unit of the State Services Commission (a central government agency which until 1988 employed all departmental chief executive officers and public servants) was established in 1986 and began producing resources to assist organisations to develop and implement EEO policies.

By the mid-1980s the debate was less about whether EEO was a good strategy, but how to deliver it. This debate centred on whether employers would voluntarily practise EEO because they recognised the benefits of doing so, or whether legislation was necessary because these benefits were not recognised by employers. For example, in 1985 the New Zealand Employers' Federation said it 'wholeheartedly supports the principle of equal opportunity in employment, education and training. It regards the elimination of discrimination as an essential step forward in social progress', and further that 'it is in the best interests of firms to help all their employees develop their full potential in employment, regardless of sex or ethnic grouping' (New Zealand Employers' Federation 1985).

The first legislation derived from an affirmative action rather than discrimination based model of EEO was the *State Sector Act 1988*. Section 56 of the Act sets out the requirement for the chief executive of a public service department to be a 'good employer'. The Act also required these chief executives to develop, ensure compliance with and report on an EEO program each year that was:

> ... aimed at the identification and elimination of policies, procedures and other institutional barriers that tend to cause or perpetuate inequality in respect of the employment of any persons or groups of persons.

This Act covered core public sector agencies. Other Crown agencies are covered by good employer requirements in other pieces of legislation, although not all have specific obligations to comply with the development and monitoring of EEO programs.

This Act dramatically changed employment relationships within the public service. Individual chief executives were now the employers of their own staff and were accountable through performance agreements with their Minister of the Crown for the delivery of agreed outcomes, including good employer provisions.

The public service has in most cases been in advance of human rights and EEO legislation, particularly in the recognition of the employment rights of groups covered under the newer grounds of the *Human Rights Act 1993*, such as disability, age, sexual orientation and family status (State Services Commission 1995). This is true not just for the core public sector but for other government funded agencies. For example, the University of Auckland's EEO policy statement in 1990 was wider than the anti-discrimination measures of the *Human Rights Commission Act 1977*, and its EEO Plan for 1991–93 included sections on part-time staff and staff with family responsibilities (The University of Auckland 1991).

The previous government continued to state its commitment to EEO, as an employer and exemplar to other employers. For example, 'the government is committed to the practice and promotion of EEO in all employment sectors as a strategy which supports its strategic plan for the future', 'the government provides leadership to other employers by promoting and modelling EEO policies and practices' and 'the principles and practice of EEO remain a core public service value, contributing to its integrity and to its high performance' (State Services Commission 1997). This commitment is likely to continue under the new government.

EEO in the private sector

EEO remained voluntary in the private sector until the *Employment Equity Act 1990*, which was repealed within months of its enactment by the incoming National (centre right) government. The new government replaced the equity legislation with the EEO Trust in November 1991. Governed by a board of trustees comprising public and private sector senior managers, its membership is drawn from the public, private and voluntary sectors. The EEO Trust has as its mission statement:

> The purpose of the Equal Employment Opportunities Trust is to promote to New Zealand employers the implementation of EEO principles and EEO best practice in the workplace as a means of improving their effectiveness, efficiency and competitiveness through the successful management of diversity.

However, although the EEO Trust was established to replace legislation directed at private sector employers and has this as its primary focus, it sees all employers to a greater or lesser degree as part of its audience for services, including access to its database and published resources. The EEO Trust is a not-for-profit, membership-based, and independent organisation. Membership is voluntary and open to any organisation that wishes to join. Members pay an annual donation based on the number of employees. As at June 1999, 329 organisations were members of the EEO Trust.

In 1997 the EEO Trust's EEO Employers Group was formed. These organisations are a sub-group of the EEO Trust members who make a specific commitment to quality employment practices in EEO/diversity. They are entitled to use the EEO Employers Group logo to identify their organisation as committed to EEO practices and the achievement of success through diversity. In August 2000, there were 290 members.

Another important development in the work of the EEO Trust has been the annual *EEO Trust Diversity Index* which examines New Zealand trends in leadership and decision making, as well as benchmarking workplace profile and practice by means of an annual diversity survey of employers. Much of this chapter draws on information from the *Diversity Index* (EEO Trust 1999) and its associated survey. An expectation is widespread that the new Labour Alliance Government will introduce legislation on issues such as paid parental leave, EEO requirements for private sector employers and possibly pay equity.

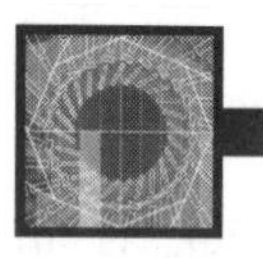

The New Zealand labour market

As in many countries, the New Zealand labour market continues to be characterised by disparities between different groups of participants. These disparities can be characterised in three ways:

- differences in qualifications and training
- differences in labour market participation
- differences in income and earnings.

Qualifications and training

Historically, many groups experienced some kinds of disadvantage or barriers to participation in educational opportunities. The barriers were of many kinds — some structural, some attitudinal and some financial.

Information from the 1996 Census shows that women and men from Maori and Pacific Islands ethnic groups are still more likely to have no formal qualifications.

Table 9.1: ***Percentage of the population with no formal qualifications, 1996***

	Males %	Females %
European/Pakeha	27	27
Maori	48	46
Pacific peoples	48	44
Total	**31**	**30**

Source: Derived from *1996 Census of Population and Dwellings.* Statistics New Zealand.

On a more optimistic note, recent education statistics suggest that women and members of non-European ethnic groups, especially the Maori, are starting to gain better representation in tertiary institutions (Ministry of Education 1999).

Table 9.2: ***Percentage of tertiary enrolments by gender and ethnicity, 1998***

	Percentage of national degree/diploma students	Percentage of postgraduate university students
All women	58.0	52.4
Maori women	6.4	3.8
Maori men	3.6	2.7
Pacific Islands women	1.8	1.1
Pacific Islands men	1.3	0.9
Asian women	5.3	4.5
Asian men	5.1	6.7

Source: Derived from *Education Statistics to the Year End 1998*, Wellington: Ministry of Education.

Apart from Asians enrolled in postgraduate courses, women represent a slightly higher proportion of all 1998 tertiary enrolments.

Te Puni Kokiri (the Ministry of Maori Development) has also expressed cautious optimism. In a 1999 report it said that, while Maori participation in all levels of education and the achievement of formal qualifications has increased dramatically over the past five years, there still remains a substantial gap between Maori and non-Maori in terms of most economic indicators. However, the report noted that:

> ... the increased education participation levels should bode well for improved Maori employment and incomes in the medium term, as qualified school leavers and graduates enter the labour market or start their own businesses (Te Puni Kokiri 1999).

Similar increases over recent years are also observable in the participation of women and non-European ethnic groups in industry training. This means the supply of skilled labour to the market is diversifying in New Zealand. Poorer labour market outcomes for women, non-European and other groups will become harder to sustain on the basis of difference in educational attainment, talent or skills.

Labour market participation

As in most countries, the participation of women in the labour market has increased over time. Currently 57.3 per cent of all working age women are in the labour market, compared with 73.5 per cent of men. However, not all New Zealand women and men participate equally. Differences by ethnicity are marked, as the tables below show.

Over the past 10 years the proportion of both men and women in full-time work has declined. Women make up a much higher proportion of the part-time workforce, although the rate of growth for men working part-time is higher than that for women. The available information does not differentiate between permanent part-time work and casual part-time work, which is a serious limitation as the deregulation of the labour market increased significantly the incidence of casual and often insecure employment. Anecdotal evidence suggests that the employment experience

Table 9.3: ***Labour market participation rate by ethnic group for males, 1989/1994/1999***

Average for year ended March	Pakeha/European %	Maori %	Pacific peoples %
1989	75.4	74.2	79.0
1994	74.0	70.6	71.3
1999	74.9	71.0	70.1

Source: Derived from *Household Labour Force Survey*. Statistics New Zealand.

Table 9.4: ***Labour market participation rate by ethnic group for females, 1989/1994/1999***

Average for year ended March	Pakeha/European %	Maori %	Pacific peoples %
1989	53.7	48.5	51.6
1994	55.0	49.7	51.0
1999	58.7	53.0	54.0

Source: Derived from *Household Labour Force Survey*. Statistics New Zealand.

of casual work is quite different in terms of stability of income and employment conditions from those in permanent part-time work. The national Household Labour Force Survey suggests that one-fifth of women in part-time work want to work more hours, compared with 10 per cent of men.

Results from the first National Childcare Survey suggest some relationship between employment and childcare (Department of Labour and National Advisory Committee on the Employment of Women 1999). Key findings of relevance to this paper are that:

- there is a relationship between labour force status, household composition, age of children and the amount and type of early childhood education and care
- both mothers' and fathers' employment is affected by their childcare responsibilities — lack of access to quality affordable early childhood education and care constitutes a barrier to their participation in paid work — especially for sole parents and those on lower incomes
- mothers are more likely than fathers to have taken time off work to care for sick children, to have looked after them during the school holidays and to report that access to early childhood education and care arrangements had impacted on their ability to participate in work (paid and unpaid) or in study/training
- while access to early childhood education and care affected employment participation for similar proportions of Maori and European parents, the way in which this participation was affected differed. Of those Maori parents whose employment was affected, 74 per cent were prevented from looking for a job compared with 57 per cent of European parents
- nine per cent of parents found access to early childhood education and care affected their participation in study and training.

Occupational segregation by sex remains a feature of the New Zealand workforce. Women's participation in the labour market is generally in a narrower range of occupations than men's. For example, women are heavily represented in four occupational groups: clerical, service and sales, professional, and technical and professional, with just under half of all employed women working in the first two occupations (Statistics New Zealand 1996). Relatively few are employed in the trades, where women account for only 6.1 per cent of workers. Women are about one-third as likely as men to be employed as plant and machine operators and assemblers (Statistics New Zealand and Ministry of Women's Affairs 1998).

Maori women tend to be concentrated in different occupations from non-Maori women. In 1996 the most common occupation for Maori women was service and sales, with one in four employed in this group.

This is reinforced by similar gender stratification in graduate employment. A report by the Vice-Chancellors' Committee on the destination of graduates showed that while a quarter of female respondents graduated in social and behavioural sciences, and another quarter in commerce and business, a third of the men graduated in commerce and business with the rest spread through all other fields (New Zealand Vice-Chancellors' Committee 1998).

Why are there different patterns of participation? Differences in qualification levels are likely to be one contributor to patterns of labour market participation in New Zealand. However, Maori and Pacific peoples' lower participation rates can also be attributed to the structural changes that took place in the New Zealand labour market in the early 1980s. These resulted in the decline of industries and occupations which had formerly been more likely to employ Maori and Pacific peoples.

Yet ethnicity may also appear to be a factor determining success in gaining employment. The Vice-Chancellors' Committee report on graduate destinations highlights differences in the proportions of recent graduates who are employed and unemployed by ethnicity.

Table 9.5: ***Percentage of each ethnic group with Bachelors or Bachelors with Honours who are unemployed, 1997***

Group	%
European/Pakeha	22.0
Maori	22.0
Pacific peoples	27.8
Indian	33.9
Asian (Chinese and other Asians)	38.2

Source: Derived from *University Graduate Destinations Report for the Year Ended 31 December 1997*, Wellington: NZVCC.

On current evidence, it would be foolish conclude that simply giving people equivalent qualifications will secure their equal access to employment.

A recent survey conducted by the EEO Trust on the *Employment Experiences of Sri Lankan Migrants to New Zealand* (1999) supports these findings. Sri Lankans are the ethnic group with the highest level of tertiary qualifications in New Zealand. Key findings of that survey show that despite very high levels of tertiary qualifications, professional experience and fluency in English, more than half have taken up positions lower than those previously held in their own country, and 40 per cent have faced discrimination. They found New Zealand employers preferred New Zealanders even when the immigrant applicant was better qualified. Those Sri Lankans without employment are caught in a vicious cycle: the most frequently mentioned barrier to getting a job was not having work experience in New Zealand, yet because of the discrimination from employers and recruitment consultants they are unable to get that experience.

Similar discrimination practices face older workers. While all projections signal an ageing of the labour market, current research suggests that in the recent past older workers have been reducing their participation in the labour market. In particular, the research indicates a change in the labour force participation rate of workers over 45 years of age.

> There is good evidence mounting that we are in the midst of a historic shift in the nature and spread of work. The first — and irreversible — effect is the disappearance of work after about age 45 for large fractions of both men and women. We're already deeply into this change, which is happening so fast and so contrary to expectations of values or wishes that few yet recognise it or are willing to confront its implications (Thompson 1999: 3).

Based on an analysis of the labour force participation rates of both men and women from 1951 to 1996 the same report suggests that:

> New Zealand women still have relatively low rates of paid employment by international standards, and it has been widely assumed that their employment levels would go on growing towards those of other developed countries. Further, it has been widely assumed that the widening experiences of paid employment which women have had in their 30s and 40s would carry on to their 50s and 60s — that is, that women were fast approaching the 'classic' male lifetime employment pattern. Among other things, many projections of government income have been built upon such assumptions of marked future growth in female employment — and so of taxpaying and of personal savings for retirement. But these things seem not to be happening: women, like men, are moving out of employment, most noticeably after about age 45. Significant earnings in mid-life have already disappeared for large portions of men and women, and look likely to be a minority phenomena within a very few years (Thompson 1999: 3).

The report identifies the explanations for this as being due to:

- technological change
- restructuring and globalisation of labour
- attitudes towards older workers
- affluence of some workers
- occupational pensions (for mainly men)
- lifestyle choice.

These reasons are a mixture of those chosen by the individual and those over which the individual has little control. The data are confirmed by preliminary results of the EEO Trust's recent survey of recruitment professionals which shows that older

workers are the group reported to experience most discrimination during the process of obtaining employment.

Many factors influence labour market participation. New Zealand employers not only will need to meet the challenges of the changing demographics of the talent pool, but also will have to examine their current and future employment practices to take advantage of these changes.

Differences in income and earnings

In New Zealand the gap between men's and women's earnings persists. For the year ending February 1999, women still earned only 83.6 per cent of men's average ordinary time hourly earnings and 78.2 per cent of men's ordinary weekly earnings — the same as they had the previous year. Average ordinary time weekly earnings increased by 3.5 per cent for both men and women in that period to NZ$732.38 and NZ$572.50 respectively (Statistics New Zealand 1999b). The distribution of personal income by quintiles showed 65 per cent of people in the bottom quintile were female. Males made up 74 per cent of the top income quintile (Statistics New Zealand 1999b).

The earnings gap between men and women is a concern to more than the individual women affected, for the following reasons:

- a growing number of families depend on women's incomes. In 1996, 19 per cent of non-Maori women with dependent children were sole parents, as were 43 per cent of Maori women with dependent children
- the New Zealand population is ageing; on average women live longer than men and will need to provide for their retirement for a longer period. The ability to save will be influenced by the level of their pay while in employment and the number of people the pay has to support
- if women believe and see that they will be paid less than men even when they have equivalent qualifications, they may be less motivated to invest (time and money) in obtaining further education. This will ultimately have an impact on the level of skilled people available in the labour market
- insufficient income can affect a citizen's ability to participate fully in society. The Women's Access to Justice Project highlighted low pay as a factor that prevents women being able to access their legal rights (Morris 1999)

There has always been debate about the reasons for the earnings gap. It is clear that women tend to be concentrated in low-paying sectors of the economy and have a lower market participation rate. However, often the debate about the reasons for the earnings gap between men and women degenerates into a claim that women 'choose' lower paid employment, perhaps as a trade-off for more flexible hours to meet the needs of their families. There has been no research in New Zealand to test that assumption. Orthodox economists argue that the gap is simply due to differences in human capital between men and women, and that the remedy lies in increasing women's access to education and training, and for women to make different choices about their participation in the workforce. Other commentators have judged that between 20 and 30 per cent of the earnings gap can be attributed to discrimination against women.

Data from the Vice-Chancellors' Committee's survey found that 'average salaries for New Zealand Bachelor and Bachelor with Honours respondents in full-time employment in New Zealand are higher for males than females in all fields. Salary outcomes for the Bachelor/Bachelor with Honours group are important as they reflect,

in the main, first-degree graduates entering the workforce on a full-time basis for the first time' (New Zealand Vice-Chancellors' Committee 1998: 40). In all but two of the 10 fields of study for Masters/Doctorate programs the average salary for males was higher than for females. The New Zealand 1998 Income Survey compares male and female income when qualifications are equivalent, and found that male income at all levels of qualifications was higher than that of women (Statistics New Zealand 1998).

It is possible that indirect discrimination may contribute to lower levels of pay (Ministry of Women's Affairs 1999a). For example, the particular skills associated with jobs in which women are employed may not be valued as highly as those skills typically associated with jobs in which men are employed. Rewards may be more available for more senior jobs that are likely to be dominated by men. New Zealand research supports international literature findings that homecare work is predominantly carried out by women, is low paid, and requires skills which are not formally recognised and not valued or recompensed. As such, homecare work almost certainly contributes to the gender pay gap (Ministry of Women's Affairs 1999b). The findings of this study suggest that further work on the value given to 'women's' skills and 'women's' work relative to that given to 'men's' work needs further investigation.

Statistics New Zealand data show the emergence of an earnings gap between men and women early in their working lives, and supports other similar research from the United Kingdom (Women's Unit 1999).

Income differentials exist between other groups as well. Disability statistics show that 'A total of 2700 females aged between 15–44 years with a disability are currently taking tertiary studies compared to 1900 males. On current trends only about one-third of these graduates will find jobs' (NZCCS 1999).

And as well as being less likely to be in paid employment, Maori and Pacific peoples receive on average less income from paid employment than European/Pakeha. While from 1987 to 1998 the average nominal income of Maori households rose 64 per cent (from NZ$26 000 to NZ$43 000), comparable and sometimes larger increases by non-Maori resulted in a continuing disparity between the economic status of the two populations (Statistics New Zealand 1998).

Over the years both men and women in the New Zealand public service have increased their representation in the higher earning brackets, although men do so at a greater rate. However, as table 9.6 shows, the lowest paid public servants are still much more likely to be women and the highest paid to be men.

Table 9.6: ***Composition of top and bottom salary band (per cent) by gender, 1998***

	<$30 000 pa	$80 000+ pa
Women	73.3	27.6
Men	26.4	72.4

Source: Derived from *EEO progress in the Public Service as at June 1998,* Wellington: State Services Commission.

Maori, Pacific and Asian peoples have also increased their representation in the NZ$60 000 and over salary group but remain clustered in the lower salary grades. For people with disability there has been a decrease in representation in the NZ$60 000 and over salary band in the last couple of years.

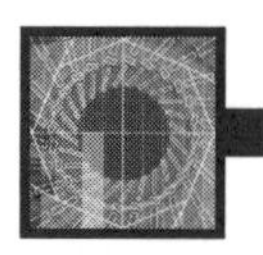

What is happening in New Zealand workplaces?

The annual EEO Trust Diversity Survey is designed to gather information about the implementation of EEO/diversity within New Zealand organisations. It is the only information source of its kind in New Zealand. The survey seeks information on a number of key indicators of EEO/diversity progress within organisations. These indicators are those most likely to have been adopted as a part of good human resource practice in those New Zealand workplaces which are either covered by legislation (public sector) or have recognised the business benefits of diversity/EEO and voluntarily taken steps to maximise access to the increasingly diversified talent pool (private sector). These include having:

- an EEO policy and documented implementation plan
- responsibility for EEO/diversity in managers' contracts
- anti-harassment initiatives
- work and family initiatives
- representation in top levels of management

A summary of the 1999 data is presented below.

EEO/diversity policies and plans

Experience of implementing EEO/diversity within both the private and public sectors in New Zealand has confirmed that EEO does not 'just happen'. It needs a planned and systematic approach to its development and implementation. As with other aspects of organisational life, this generally means having a planning process and some goals for achievement.

The diversity survey showed that while over three-quarters of the organisations surveyed in 1999 had a policy endorsing EEO, just over a quarter have both a policy and a plan for implementation. The public sector is much more likely to have both a plan and a policy, reflecting the legislative imperative on this sector.

Responsibility for EEO/diversity in managers' contracts

For EEO/diversity programs to succeed in organisations there needs to be active leadership and support from managers. As a signal that an organisation takes the benefits of EEO/diversity seriously, it needs to ensure that managers see this as a legitimate and active part of their role. Using either the employment or performance contract agreement can be an effective mechanism. Less than one-fifth of the organisations surveyed were placing any formal contractual expectations on their managers for EEO/diversity and this was a slight reduction from the previous year's results.

Anti-harassment initiatives

The Human Rights Commission received 300 complaints of discrimination in the year to June 1999. Of these complaints, 58 per cent were in the area of employment. Twenty-four per cent of the complaints were on the grounds of sexual harassment and of these, 90 per cent were in the area of employment (New Zealand Human Rights Commission 1999).

In 22 sexual harassment cases heard by the Complaints Review Tribunal from 1992 to 1999, damages awarded for humiliation and loss of dignity (separate from costs such as loss of wages) ranged from NZ$800 to NZ$25 000, with the most frequently

awarded costs being between NZ$7000 and NZ$8000. However, the judge in a 1998 High Court case suggested the Tribunal would need to look carefully at the level of financial compensation being awarded because it was lower than that being granted overseas (*PC v Laursen,* High Court 1998).

In one case, the Court of Appeal ruled that a partner in a company was vicariously liable for sexual harassment committed by another partner of the firm (*Proceedings Commissioner v Hayton*, Complaints Review Tribunal). *The Employment Contract* commented that 'Although this case was decided in relation to partners acting in partnership it is equally applicable to the managers and supervisors appointed by an employer. Managers are authorised by employers to deal with staff on behalf of the employer. They act as the employer's agent in this respect. If a manager sexually harasses a subordinate employee, then following the reasoning in this case, the employer will be liable for these acts' (Victoria Link Limited 1999: 5).

A survey of lesbian and bisexual women's experience of discrimination showed that 22 per cent of these women reported they had been harassed at work (Rankine 1997).

As a summary, results from the 1999 EEO Trust Diversity Survey showed that anti-sexual harassment policies seem to be well established across all the respondent organisations and there has been some increase in the proportion of employers taking anti-harassment action. As with the results from the previous surveys, the lowest level of activity in the harassment area is in the training of managers and staff. While the proportion of organisations providing training for managers had declined from the previous year (to 28 per cent of respondents), a more optimistic note is that there was an increase in those providing training for staff. The proportion of EEO Employers Group members providing training to managers had declined by two per cent. Public service respondents are almost twice as likely to train managers and staff than are private sector employers.

New Zealand employers still appear to be slow to take preventative action (particularly in training managers) in an area that can pose significant risk to their budget and their reputation.

Work and family initiatives

In 1986, 21 per cent of mothers with a child under one were in paid work. By 1996, this had risen to 31 per cent. Of all New Zealand families with a child under five, 35.8 per cent have both parents in paid work.

There is a high chance that many employees (and managers) will have responsibility for dependents (children, older parents or other family members with a disability) at some stage of their working life. Workplaces that are sensitive to the need to balance these commitments are becoming the employers of choice.

The EEO Trust Diversity Survey 1999 showed that 41 per cent of respondents included work and family provisions in their employment contracts. This indicates that for these employers, responding to work and family issues is becoming a mainstream issue. However, when it came to detailing specific work and family provisions (such as eldercare, school holiday programs or after school care), the level of activity remains fairly low.

The National Childcare Survey also had findings relevant to New Zealand employers:

- sixty-eight per cent of parents with at least one child under 14 years of age are in the paid workforce

- unpaid care by family members (other than the child's parents) was the most common form of childcare used
- fifteen per cent of parents said that access to childcare was a barrier to their participation
- almost half (46 per cent) of children had childcare arranged for them in the last school holidays, most of them being cared for by a family member (other than their parent) on an unpaid basis. Fifteen per cent of children aged five to 13 years attended a school holiday program
- changes to childcare were wanted for 20 per cent of all children under 14 years of age — the strongest demand for change is in the provision of before and after school care programs (Department of Labour and National Advisory Committee on the Employment of Women 1999).

Paid parental leave

While the *Parental Leave and Employment Protection Act 1987* provides employees with unpaid parental leave, New Zealanders have no statutory right to paid parental leave. (Twelve months' unpaid parental leave with the right to return to the same or an equivalent job is available under the legislation to employees who have been with the same employer for at least six months and work 10 hours or more a week.)

In spite of the lack of legislative pressure, some New Zealand organisations have made the link between provisions such as paid parental leave and the retention of valued staff. One-third of the EEO Trust Diversity Survey respondents have some form of paid parental leave. In a 1999 survey by Simpson Grierson, 13 per cent of respondents provided paid parental leave and 34 per cent approved of some form of statutory requirement for such a provision (Simpson Grierson Employment Law Group 1999). The current Labour Alliance Government has made a commitment to some form of paid parental leave, although details such as length of time and eligibility have not yet been determined.

Representation at the top of organisations

New Zealand research on women and other groups in influential positions within New Zealand organisations shows a mixed picture. The representation of women and Maori is certainly increasing, but the levels are low compared to their representation in the labour market as a whole.

The 1999 EEO Trust Diversity Survey provides information on the percentage of women in the top three tiers of management within respondent organisations. Similar information is available from the New Zealand Public Service and the Australian Affirmative Action Agency.

While women represent 45 per cent of the New Zealand labour market (as at June 1999) they are between 25–29 per cent of top management. Maori made up almost 5 per cent of the top three tiers of management.

In 1999, there were 39 public service CEOs. Six of these were women in permanent positions and one was acting in the position.

Another 1999 poll reports that women comprise just 7.36 per cent of total management directorships in New Zealand (Fintel 1999). The research publishers say, 'In a workplace environment where competition is more intense that ever, this represents an alarming statistic in the drive for gender equality. Women managing directors preside over smaller businesses when measured by sales and they also manage fewer staff. As a society and as a business community we need to decide

Table 9.7: ***Percentage of women in top three tiers of management, June 1999***

	EEO Trust Diversity Survey 1999 (1998 figure in brackets)	New Zealand Public Service 1999 (1998 in brackets)	Affirmative Action Agency (Australia) 1997 (1996 in brackets)
Women in total top three tiers of management	27.3% (24.6%)	29% (29.0%)	25.2% (23.6%)

Sources: *EEO progress in the Public Service as at June 1999*, State Services Commission, and Affirmative Action Agency, Sydney, Australia.

whether this lack of female input is hampering the success of New Zealand businesses and the local economy.'

The Institute of Directors (representing 2200 directors) collects data on the gender profile of their membership. Between 1997–99, the proportion of women has increased by five per cent and women are now 15 per cent of directors (information provided to the authors). A poll by PriceWaterhouseCoopers showed female directors are more common in smaller organisations (less than $5 million turnover).

The representation of females is strongest in the public sector. Women accounted for 35 per cent of government appointments in 1998 compared with 25 per cent in 1993. The May 1999 survey showed (1998 results in brackets):

- 4.5 per cent (3.4 per cent) of non-executive chairpersons are women
- 10 per cent (7.7 per cent) of non-executive directors are women
- 7.6 per cent (4.5 per cent) of executive directors are women

Between 1997 and 1999 female chairpersons or directors of New Zealand Crown company boards rose from 19 to 30 per cent. Of the 93 women directors, 12 per cent are Maori women (Ministry of Women's Affairs 1998a). The increase is the result of government pressure to increase diversity on these boards, as outlined in this statement:

> As part of New Zealand's response to the Beijing Platform for Action, the Ministry of Women's Affairs is working with other government agencies to enhance women's role in decision-making through a government commitment to gender balance on all government appointed committees, boards and other relevant official bodies. The Ministry of Women's Affairs is aiming at 50 per cent of women on statutory boards by the year 2000 (Ministry of Women's Affairs 1998b: 24).

Yet what happens when women do achieve senior positions within organisations? The Sheffield Consulting Group annually publishes a newsletter examining whether gender impacts on the remuneration packages for senior executives in New Zealand. For the sixth year in a row they concluded that the answer is 'yes'. Executive women in 1999 received 76.5 per cent of male executives' total packages. Male executives were more likely to have received a pay increase — 22.5 per cent compared with 13.3 per cent of women. The survey found that even in a female dominated executive profession such as human resources, male executives on average earned NZ$10 000 a year more than women in that role (Sheffield Newsletter 1998).

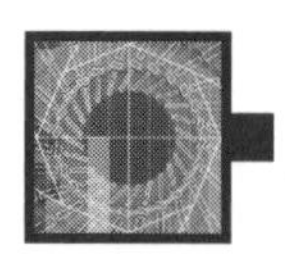

Conclusions

The worst excesses of discrimination have been eliminated through anti-discrimination law (the *Human Rights Act 1993*) and the personal grievance procedures of the *Employment Contracts Act 1991*.

Affirmative action policies are integrated throughout the public service as part of 'good employer' requirements of the *State Sector Act 1998*. Core agencies report against these policies and are monitored for compliance.

In the private sector, those employers who have voluntarily responded to the EEO Trust's promotion of the business benefits of EEO are increasing gradually. For these employers there have been two key motivators. The first relates to the changing social and economic patterns of women's and men's employment and family responsibilities, which means increasingly most employees have some out of work responsibilities that have an impact on their working lives. As employers have increasingly recognised that supporting their staff to balance their dual work and life commitments brings increased productivity and loyalty, as well as reduced absenteeism and lower turnover, they have responded by developing a range of work and family initiatives. These have been encouraged and promoted by the EEO Trust's annual Work and Life Awards, which have showcased leaders in this field to much media and public interest.

The other key motivators have been the changing market place — including increasing globalisation demanding skills from employees in dealing with customers from diverse markets, particularly throughout Asia — and the demand for knowledge-based workers — who need to come from a diverse range of backgrounds in order to bring to workplaces the breadth of thinking and experience required in today's market place.

With the worst aspects of discrimination outlawed and no longer considered socially acceptable, the focus is increasingly not on anti-discrimination measures but more on actively valuing diversity, and the many benefits this brings employers. These are increasingly recognised by many employers as creating an enhanced ability to recruit talent, improved customer service and access to wider markets, greater problem-solving and creative thinking ability on teams, better public perception of the company, improved productivity and staff morale and reduced staff turnover and absenteeism as staff feel more valued.

Valuing diversity is a challenge for managers in New Zealand organisations as they respond to demographic changes, changes in the composition of the available talent pool and increasing empirical links between diversity and business success. Simply keeping within the current anti-discrimination legislation and expressing a wish to be a 'fair' employer will not be sufficient. Most organisations are, however, not taking the necessary creative steps and in not doing so may risk losing talent to national and international competitors. The businesses that become this millennium's movers and shakers will be those that pro-actively and creatively respond to the changing economic and social conditions of future New Zealand.

References

Department of Labour and National Advisory Committee on the Employment of Women. 1999. *Childcare, Families and Work: The New Zealand Childcare Survey 1998: A Survey of Early Childhood Education and Care Arrangements for Children*. Wellington.

EEO Trust. 1992. *Annual Report Inauguration (November 1991 – 30 June 1992)*. Auckland.

EEO Trust. 1999. *EEO Trust Diversity Index 1999*. Auckland. (Available from the EEO Trust, PO Box 12 929, Penrose, Auckland, for NZ$30.)

EEO Trust. 1999. *Employment Experiences of Sri Lankan Migrants in New Zealand*. Auckland.

Fintel. 1999. *National Business Review* — Dun & Bradstreet Market Poll, reported 1 July 1999.

Ministry of Education. 1999. *Education Statistics to the Year End 1998*. Wellington.

Ministry of Women's Affairs. 1998a. *Status of Women in New Zealand: CEDAW Report*. Wellington.

Ministry of Women's Affairs. 1998b. *New Zealand Report on the Status of Women. APEC Women Leaders' Network, Kuala Lumpur*. Wellington.

Ministry of Women's Affairs. 1999a. *Performance Pay Systems and Equity*. Wellington.

Ministry of Women's Affairs. 1999b. *Homecare Workers: A Case Study of a Female Occupation*. Wellington.

Morris, Joanne. 1999. *Women's Access to Legal Services*. Wellington: Law Commission.

New Zealand Council of Trade Unions' National Women's Committee. 1994. *Family, Work & Unions*. Wellington.

New Zealand Employers' Federation. 1985. *Positive Action Manual: Implementing EEO in the Workplace*. Wellington.

New Zealand Human Rights Commission. 1999. Auckland.

New Zealand Vice-Chancellors' Committee. 1998. *University Graduate Destinations Report for the Year Ended 31 December 1997*. Wellington.

NZCCS. 1999. Media release drawing on the *Statistics New Zealand 1996 Household Disability Survey and the 1997 Disability Survey of Residential Facilities*.

Rankine, Jenny. 1997. *The Great Late Lesbian and Bisexual Women's Discrimination Survey*. Auckland.

Sheffield Newsletter. 1998. *Executive Benefits — The Hidden Pay Gap*. Auckland: Sheffield Consulting Group.

Simpson Grierson Employment Law Group. 1999. *The Holidays Act*. Auckland: Simpson Grierson.

State Services Commission. 1984. *Statement of Government Employing Authorities on Equal Employment Opportunities*. Wellington.

State Services Commission. 1995. *Equal Employment Opportunities Progress in the Public Service as at June 1995*. Wellington.

State Services Commission. 1997. *EEO Policy to 2010 Future Directions in the New Zealand Public Service*. Wellington.

State Services Commission. 1998. *Report on EEO Progress in the Public Service as at June 1998*. Wellington.

State Services Commission. 1999. *Report on EEO Progress in the Public Service as at June 1999*, Wellington.

Statistics New Zealand. 1989. *Household Labour Force Survey 1989*. Wellington.

Statistics New Zealand. 1994. *Household Labour Force Survey 1994*. Wellington.

Statistics New Zealand. 1996. *1996 Census of Population and Dwellings*. Wellington.

Statistics New Zealand. 1998. *Income Survey 1998*. Wellington.

Statistics New Zealand. 1999. *Household Labour Force Survey 1999*. Wellington.

Statistics New Zealand. 1999a. *Demographic Trends*. Wellington.

Statistics New Zealand. 1999b. *Quarterly Employment Survey February 1999*. Wellington.

Statistics New Zealand and Ministry of Women's Affairs. 1998. *New Zealand Now — Women*. Wellington.

Te Puni Kokiri. 1999. *Maori in the New Zealand Economy*. Wellington.

The University of Auckland. 1991. *Equal Employment Opportunities Plan 1991–93*. Auckland.

Thompson, Professor David. 1999. 'Our Ageing Workforce — Benefit or Burden?'. University of Auckland Winter Lecture Series.

Victoria Link Limited. 1999. *The Employment Contract*. 29:7.

Women's Unit. 1999. *Women's Individual Income 1996/1997*. United Kingdom: Government Statistical Service.

Chapter 10

The Philippines

Mari Kondo

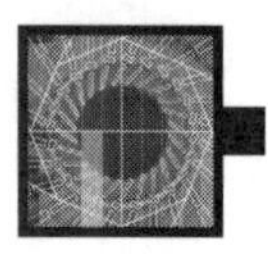

Introduction

One of the largest archipelagos in the world, the Philippines is located at the centre of what were early trade routes between China, India, Indonesia, other South-east Asian countries and the American continents, and thus it has become home to people from many different origins, religions and languages. Two countries, the United States of America and Spain, with different governing and management systems, colonised the country. With such a history, there are many factors that affect diversity in the workplace in the Philippines.

This chapter will cover a background to the people of the Philippines, followed by a brief discussion of the influence of regionalism on management practices. Then gender issues are discussed, which is the central theme of this chapter. The Philippines is unique in Asia because of the relatively high social status of women compared to other South-east Asian countries. By closely looking at the complexity of Philippine society — its history, colonisation, religion, ethnicity, migration, urbanisation, legal tradition and civil society — one can understand the issues that women face. Following the section on gender, overseas workers, child labour and workers with disabilities are discussed. These three areas also serve to deepen the understanding of the complexity that the Philippines faces in relation to gender issues.

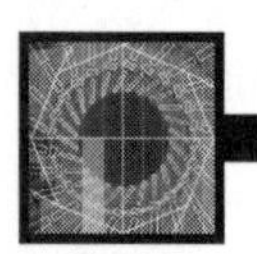

The people

The Philippines is made up of more than 7000 islands, of which there are three key island groups. These are Luzon in the north, Visayas in the centre, and Mindanao in the south. The present Filipinos are divided into groupings according to language and religion. Insularity and regionalism help account for the continued use of 80 different native languages comprising 111 linguistic groups.

The population of the Philippines was 69 million according to the census taken in 1995. According to the National Statistics Office (NSO), 'the overall population density is 230 persons per square kilometer' (NSO 2000). The population of the Philippines has continued to increase in recent years, which in part can be attributed to Catholicism. The crude birthrate per thousand population is high (27 per cent) while the crude mortality rate is low (six per cent) (NSO 2000).

Population growth is one of the causes for the mass migration of unskilled labour from the smaller and less farmable central islands to crowded urban areas such as Manila in the north, and to the Muslim territories in the south. Both migrations have had an impact on diversity management in the Philippine workplace. The inflow of unskilled labour, including women, to the urban areas has created a large pool of informal sector workers, and led to the casual use of cheap labour by many labour-intensive industries. These issues are discussed in detail in this chapter.

The indigenous people of the Philippines are the Aetas or Belugas who most likely came from mainland Asia across land bridges during the last Ice Age. The people we know today as Filipinos are of Malay descent and originally came from the south-eastern Asian mainland, from the islands we now refer to as Indonesia, and from Borneo.

The Malays, with their brown skin, medium height and straight black hair, are the ancestors of 95.5 per cent of the present Philippine population (comprising Christian Malays 91.5 per cent, and Muslim Malays four per cent). Their way of life

has persisted to a large extent despite the late infusion of other cultures. The remaining four and a half per cent of the population comprises Chinese (1.5 per cent) and others (three per cent).

The main religions of the Philippines are Catholicism, Islam and Protestantism. Eighty-three per cent of the population is Catholic. Prominent among the minority groups are the Moro Muslims on Mindanao and neighbouring islands. They were influenced by the Spanish colonists but were never completely subdued. Even today they are still independence oriented and actively pursue the establishment of an autonomous Muslim region.

Filipinos of Spanish and Malay heritage are referred to as *mestizos* and those of Chinese and Malay heritage are referred to as *mestisong intsik*. Many of their forebears were landowners who comprised the well-educated ruling group of society. It is often said that around 200 families control the majority of the wealth of the Philippines. Most of these families are *mestizos* and *mestisong intsik*. The population of Indians in the Philippines is small compared to other South-east Asian countries and therefore this group has a limited influence on the economic, political and social life.

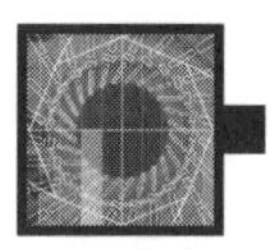

Regionalism

Officially, corporate and business practices in both the private and public sectors in the Philippines are based on the American merit system. However, in reality personal relationships are considered to be extremely important and, in particular, people from the same region are drawn to each other. This regional loyalty is very strong in the workplace and it influences to varying degrees almost every aspect of human resource management. This regional influence is strongly linked to language, ethnicity and religious beliefs.

In some urban organisations, regionalism often dictates the hiring and promotion of employees. For example, if an applicant comes from the same province or town as the person doing the hiring, the applicant will have a greater chance of being appointed to the position as long as they can meet the qualification requirements of the job. Because of this, the applicant often looks for some connection before he or she applies for a position.

Workers who come from the same provinces tend to stay together and support each other in the workplace. Sometimes they deepen their relationship through the *kompadre* system, which in the Catholic religion involves people becoming godfather or godmother to others at weddings, baptisms and confirmations. In Philippine society it is considered an honour to be asked to become a godfather or godmother and this results in stronger ties between people, similar to that of the extended family. The extensive use of *kompadre* system to build social ties is considered to be one of the important characteristics of Filipino society.

Also, the patron–client relationship is considered essential for success within organisations. If an employee is seen as a client of a patron who occupies a senior position, other employees will be very careful about competing with this client. It is understood that the client will be given a series of important jobs so that he or she can move up the corporate ladder quickly, without seeming to contradict the official system of meritocracy. However, the workings of the patron–client relationship can vary as regionalism plays an important role. Here, a client frequently uses the *kompadre* system in order to cement and mutually confirm their patron–client relationship.

The connections made through such informal ties can be the source of office politics, and lead to ethical concerns. In order to protect fellow employees from the same region, others are not inclined to report mistakes and abnormalities, such as kickbacks, in the workplace. Thus, human resource managers in the Philippines take extra care to balance the employment of new employees from certain regions. By avoiding a concentration of employees from the one region, and having several competing regional groups in the organisation, human resource managers can assume that the rival relationships of different regional groups will function as a monitoring device for employee behaviour.

Within Philippine organisations the hierarchical gap is significant. Most Philippine corporations are family businesses and, although there are more professionals who have been appointed in recent years, the key executive positions are reserved for family members. The class gap in the society is wide, as is the gap between ordinary workers and professional salaried workers.

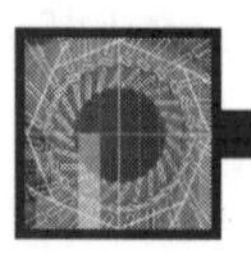

Gender issues in the workplace

Status of women in Philippine society

Women enjoy a relatively high status in Philippine society generally, compared to most of their counterparts in other Asian countries. This is reflected in the Gender-related Development Index (GDI) and Gender Empowerment Measure (GEM), both of which were introduced as part of the Human Development Report on United Nations Development Program (UNDP) in 1995. These are composite measures that reflect gender inequalities in human development.

The GDI captures achievements in basic human development adjusted for gender inequality. The closer a country's GDI is to its Human Development Index (HDI), the less gender disparity there is in that country. According to the latest UNDP report, the Philippines is in sixty-fifth place, which is well above most Asian countries. The GEM captures gender inequality in key areas of economic and political participation and decision making and it focuses on women's opportunities. The Philippines' GEM ranks only after Japan and The People's Republic of China in the Asian economies (UNDP Office 1999).

The relatively high status of women in the society and the workplace comes from the combined efforts of the government and strong non-government organisation (NGO) activities. This can be attributed to the pre-Hispanic tradition of seeing women as vital partners in the community. This egalitarian view was somewhat undermined by the male-dominated heritage of Spain (and the United States), but it still remains a part of the Philippine heritage.

The Spanish Catholic missionaries imposed Roman Catholicism on the people as a way of governing the colonised islands. The Spanish also introduced their notion of womanhood, which viewed a woman's position in society as being derived from her role as mother and wife and from her relationship to men. This Hispanic ideology of women was widespread among the upper class of Philippine society; however, it did not reach women of lower socio-economic status who kept working to support the day-to-day life of their families. It is reported that, even at the time of Spanish colonisation, women enjoyed a high degree of autonomy and economic importance. In marriage, property was held jointly by both spouses and women retained control

of their bride-wealth. Further, divorce did not interfere with a woman's livelihood, status or kin support system (Illo 1997: 4).

The United States introduced a more liberal ideology to the Philippines. The public school education system, a method of governing Filipinos used by the Americans, gave males and females an equal chance to be educated. Women won the right to vote in 1937 and joined the labour force as factory workers, clerks, sales staff and teachers. However, although women have participated in strikes and other political action in relation to workers' rights, today the area of politics, including the leadership of trade unions and peasant movements, is still dominated by men (Illo 1997: 4–5).

Today, a woman in the Philippines typically is employed, but is still expected to be the dutiful, loving wife and mother at home, making her domestic duties her priority. In this predominantly Catholic society contraception is disapproved of and divorce is not recognised. Because women in the Philippines value their reproductive role highly, most married working women have a number of children (Illo 1997: 4).

Ethnicity and gender issues

There are significant differences between the various ethnic groups of the Philippines in regard to gender issues faced by women. The diversity of the population and underlying gender systems have been identified as two of the complex issues that women face today. These differences are not only between the dominant Christians and minority Muslims, there are also issues that affect non-Christian and non-Muslim women (Illo 1997: 37).

Women's views about the Muslim community are seen from two quite different perspectives. Christian women are sometimes condescending towards their Muslim sisters. These attitudes are often based on media images of hooded Muslim women and generalisations about the status of women in Islamic society. Muslim women, on the other hand, do not see their position as inferior, nor do they acknowledge a sexist bias in their custom and practices. They express pity for Catholic women because they do not enjoy the privilege of divorcing their husbands (Jiminez-David 2000a).

Some Muslim women work in the formal sector and, in most cases, these women belong to the upper class of Muslim society and are used to liberal ideas. Many of them, however, see the contradiction and acknowledge the difficulty of being a Muslim woman who professes the Islamic faith but is living in a Catholic country. Furthermore, they are educated in a Western educational system, which indoctrinates ideas contrary to the Muslim culture (*Philippine Daily Inquirer*, 20 May 2000).

Most Muslim women find that their culture tends to restrict their education and their participation in the formal workforce. Literacy levels are low in Muslim communities, compared with much higher levels of education in Christian areas. About 50 per cent of Muslim children drop out of school before they reach sixth grade. Adult female literacy levels are dramatically lower than those of male adults because Muslim parents give preferential treatment to boys and their daughters are subject to stricter rules. On Mindanao, schools have to accommodate the separate gender space requirements of Muslims if parents are going to send their daughters to school. Yet, Muslim women from poor families must work for their survival regardless of their traditional role at home. Due to their poor educational levels, most Muslim women do not participate in the formal work sector and, because of their economic status, they are being pushed into the informal sector (Illo 1997: 12).

Women and work

Class and dual responsibilities of women

The total labour force of the Philippines numbered 48.9 million in April 2000. The labour force participation rate was 65.1 per cent, and women workers comprised almost 40 per cent of the labour force (NSO 2000). According to the National Statistics Office, the annual growth rate of females in employment increased by 4.4 per cent during the period 1989–92. In 1995, it increased by 7.2 per cent compared to men (4.2 per cent).

Men reportedly head about 88 per cent of Philippine households. In this context, power and authority rest with them and they are accustomed mostly to having a greater say in financial matters. While men enjoy their authority and power, most people see women in the traditional role of wives and mothers (UCWS/UNICEF 1996) and thus a woman's area of authority is considered to be in child-rearing and household budgeting (Illo 1997: 13). Today, many women work to help their husbands support the family. However, when they leave the office and return home, women are still expected to take on the responsibilities of home and childcare. Though women's dual responsibilities are prevalent regardless of their class, notable differences still exist.

Women in the higher socio-economic bracket are often well-educated and exposed to liberalising ideas, and therefore they do not necessarily want to conform to the traditional role of women in Philippine society. For them, a respectable job outside their home serves as a status symbol and, because they are unable to manage both home responsibilities and work, they often hire domestic helpers from the large pool of unskilled women workers from the provinces who come to the cities. Some of these professional women actually do not know how to cook or sew. As in many developing countries, professional women are able to devote all their energies to their jobs because of the existence of women who are at the other end of the social strata. Further, since these women tend to occupy leading positions, the need for flexible arrangements in the workplace has not been articulated for other working women.

Middle-class women in urban areas are forced to work to pay for their children's education and to support their expensive urban lifestyle. However, husbands generally are willing to help their wives with domestic labour (cooking and cleaning) and childcare, much more so than their South-east Asian counterparts. Many such husbands have proudly told me that they often cook for their families on Sundays. However, women still carry the more fundamental and regular responsibilities of domestic work. In addition, they are expected to contribute their share financially, thus, many of them are involved in informal money-making activities, such as selling goods in their workplace.

Informal money-making activities

It is a common practice for middle-class women, such as secretaries working in offices, to engage in selling goods to other office workers. In many Metro Manila offices, employees conduct these sales openly. Office-based selling of goods is more prevalent among female employees than male employees because sales work is considered to be a feminine job. Officially, Philippine companies do not approve of employees' vending activities in the office, however, in reality it is very difficult to stop the practice. This is because informal selling by women is considered a way for them to augment the family income. Because of the regular flow of wages or salaries that the employees receive, offices are considered as very good venues for selling. In many cases, sales are done on an instalment (or lay-by) basis, because of the low risk and low transaction costs.

One executive of a multinational company in Manila reported that secretaries sell almost anything and commented, 'One of the filing cabinets in their desks is often full

of their merchandise'. Products include fruits in season, peanuts, cakes, shoes, dresses, suits, jewellery, and the like. Who sells what product is known by everyone in the office, and sometimes, even managers place orders. For example, one female jewellery seller reported that her boss asked her one morning to buy a gold chain that day because it was his wife's birthday. During lunchtime, the office worker went to a store in Chinatown where she is a *suki* (a good customer to whom suppliers often extend their credit lines) to buy the gold chain. Even if she returned late from lunch she would not be castigated. Everybody seems to be involved in some form of informal income generation activities.

Generally the products that the employees sell reflect the hierarchy within an office, or at least the differences in their income. The junior secretary may sell peanuts while the secretary of the president may sell jewellery. Also, there is an unwritten agreement that no two workers will sell the same product. In other words, co-workers cannot become competitors in office selling. The key to the success of this informal business is good sourcing. Usually, salespeople get their merchandise from special sources. For example, a suit seller's source may be a relative who works at a factory that specialises in tailoring suits for export and can manage to bring out some samples or seconds. A gold jewellery seller may have a relative who works in the Middle East who is able to smuggle gold jewellery from Bahrain, or they may have established a good relationship with a reliable store in Chinatown. Often goods come from the underground economy. Because of special sourcing, fewer overheads, and lower risks and transaction costs, prices of products sold in the office are usually cheaper than equivalent merchandise sold in stores.

Another reason for the success of these sales is the access to good customers, that is, their co-employees. The sellers are likely to have information on the credit-worthiness of customers and can be assured that instalment payments will be made every payday. For this reason, it is more advantageous for these sellers to work in bigger offices where they have access to a larger number of regular employees.

Gender job stereotyping

In general, women in the Philippines are among the most literate in Asia and their literacy level is the same as that of men (Illo 1997: xi). Also, more females than males undertake secondary and tertiary education. This is because boys can survive doing male-specific work without the need for tertiary education, while girls need to have secondary or tertiary education to access a range of employment options, from domestic work through to higher-paid salaried positions. Although females are better educated, they tend to choose courses that are regarded as female-oriented. These include teacher training, nursing, and business administration which, in the Philippines, is a course for bank tellers, clerks and secretaries (Illo 1997: xi–xii; 12–13).

Reflecting their high educational level, more and more women are finding their way into professional and technical positions. In 1995, women professionals totalled about 0.9 million (or 10 per cent of all employed women) while men hardly reached 0.5 million (or 3 per cent of all employed men). However, women still tend to be at the lower end of the employment spectrum, both the professional and non-professional levels.

The 'feminine' courses women undertake reflect the type of work available to Filipino women. These jobs, such as teaching or nursing, are an extension of women's domestic role and they are generally undervalued in Philippine society. The manufacturing sector in the Philippines only employs 10 per cent of the workforce and, without proper industrialisation, the country has developed a predominantly service-based industry, consisting of finance, real estate, business, community, social, and personal services, which employ 20.8 per cent of the workforce. The balance of the workforce is in agriculture, fishery, and forestry (41.7 per cent), wholesale and retail trades (14.8 per cent), transport, storage, and communications (six per cent), construction (5.7 per cent), mining and quarrying (0.4 per cent) and electricity, gas, and water (0.4 per cent) (see table 10.1). The transformation from an agrarian to a service economy without industrialisation has bolstered the feminisation of the labour market. More and more women are being tapped for the 'social skills' requirements of the service sectors. For example, in sales work alone, 68.9 per cent of the workers are women. However, these women stay at the lower end of the job spectrum (Illo 1997: 24–8).

Table 10.1: ***Employed workers, by occupation and sex, 1996***

Industry/Occupation	1996		
	Male (%)	Female (%)	Total (%)
Agriculture, fishery, and forestry	48.4	30.3	41.7
Mining and quarrying	0.6	0.1	0.4
Manufacturing	8.9	12.0	10.0
Electricity, gas, and water	0.6	0.1	0.4
Construction	9.0	0.2	5.7
Wholesale and retail trade	8.2	26.1	14.8
Transport, storage, and communication	9.1	0.8	6.0
Financing, real estate, and business services	2.4	2.6	2.5
Community, social, and personal services	12.7	27.8	18.3
Total employed workers ('000)	**17 308**	**9505**	**27 442**

Source: Derived from census data from the Bureau of Labor and Employment Statistics (BLES).

It is the norm for promotion and training to be given to male workers because there is a belief that men are more available to take on greater responsibilities and that they will stay longer in employment. Some women take the option of leaving employment after marriage, and others might refuse training because of requirements attached to promotion. For this reason advertisements for job openings for women usually have a 'preferably single' clause attached to them. Where promotion and training are open to both men and women equally, marriage and pregnancy tend to cut short the career advancement of women. Married female workers bear the brunt of discriminatory practices, such as little or no maternity benefits and leave. Some companies disallow employment of both a husband and wife in order to avoid nepotism and, if faced with this situation, the woman employee normally resigns.

As a result of discriminatory practices, relatively fewer women than men (1.5 per cent and 1.8 per cent respectively in 1995) occupy the top positions in administrative, executive, and managerial positions (Illo 1997). Among those who attain executive appointments, women still occupy the lower level positions.

Gender job stereotyping is prevalent in managerial positions. For example, an administrative job is considered to be 'feminine', while engineering is felt strongly to be 'masculine'. In the same way, senior positions are considered to be for men. The following research data show the stereotyping in several private and public organisations in the Philippines.

In March 2000, Patricia Denise Lopez, Horacio Borromeo Jr. and Maria Carmela Maravillas-Salim of the Asian Institute of Management (AIM) conducted a survey on gender-related issues in the workplace, and the results were presented in a public lecture, 'Sexuality in the Workplace'. The survey had 195 respondents who were alumni of the AIM. The respondents consisted of 126 (64.6 per cent) male and 69 (35.4 per cent) female professional managers who came from different industries: manufacturing (20 per cent), wholesale/retail (eight per cent), transportation and communication (10 per cent), financial services (31 per cent), professional services (17 per cent), and other industries (14 per cent).

The respondents were asked whether they thought a male or a female applicant would be likely to be hired for an administrative position. Fifty per cent of the Philippine managers responded 'either' and a further 40 per cent responded 'a woman'. According to the survey, both male and female respondents thought that a woman would be more likely to be hired for an administrative position.

Then the respondents were asked who they thought would be hired for an engineering position. Eighty per cent of the respondents answered 'a man', while 20 per cent of the respondents answered 'either'. None of the respondents thought that a woman applicant would be likely to be hired for the position.

The survey also asked respondents who they thought would be promoted to top management positions. Sixty per cent of the respondents stated male employees, almost 40 per cent thought either a man or a woman, and one per cent thought a woman would be likely to be promoted.

A good example of women being located in middle level positions is apparent in the national government service where, in 1995, women made up about 59 per cent of all workers. They worked as regular employees in the career service, and women constituted 74 per cent of all first-level career executive service positions. Though many of them occupied second-level positions (professional, technical, and scientific positions including teachers), only 27 per cent of women in the national government service were in the top positions, according to the Bureau of Labor and Employment Statistics (Illo 1997: 24).

Women in the informal sector

Relative to the very few upper class women and small number of middle class women workers, there are masses of poor women working in the Philippines. Most of these women are forced to work for their survival and the survival of their families. Women's contributions have been an important source of income to many poor urban households, comprising 25–35 per cent of the total family earnings. Most of these women are pushed into informal sector activities and, if they live in urban areas, they contribute to the pool of unskilled labour. Women are often exploited by being subcontracted to work on production tasks in their homes; thus reducing overhead costs for factories. These subcontracting operations often violate labour standards, and workers are not able to cover themselves under the social security system, simply because they do not earn enough money to enrol themselves. These home-based labourers, predominantly women and children, are underpaid, and almost all are completely outside the legal labour protection system (Illo 1997: 25–26).

During the Aquino administration, the *Kalakalan 20 1989* (Republic Act 6810) and the *Magna Carta for Small Businesses 1990* (Republic Act 6977) were set up to aid small businesses in the Philippines. These laws grant micro, cottage and small- and medium-sized enterprises (MCSME) access to the formal credit market. However, many of the poor women's micro enterprises are perceived to be too small to be included in such programs.

There are two main reasons why more of the Philippines' population, especially women, are being pushed into the informal sector: the slow growth of formal sector (regular) employment opportunities, and the rapid and substantial inflow of labour from the provinces to the urban workforce. Filipino managers and company owners have been pressured to increase flexibility in their employment strategies because of economic stabilisation and restructuring programs, which led to the deregulation of the economy. Thus, they tend to use subcontractors and short-term casual workers rather than hire employees for regular positions (Illo 1997: 25–6). As a result, the growth of formal sector employment opportunities for women is further decreased and the wages of women further reduced.

Legislation for elimination of discrimination against women

The Philippines is a model country in terms of its legislation, including the elimination of gender discrimination. The Philippines has ratified several International Labour Organisation (ILO) conventions and United Nations declarations related to the elimination of discrimination against women. These conventions are: ILO Convention No. 100, on equal remuneration for men and women workers for work of equal value (May 1953); Convention No. 111, on discrimination in respect of employment and occupation (May 1960); Convention No. 122, on employment policy (December 1974); and the Sixtieth Session of ILO Conference 1975, the declaration of equality of opportunity and treatment for women workers. The Philippine Government also signed the United Nations Convention on the Elimination of All Forms of Discrimination Against Women (CEDAW 1996) and has committed to the Nairobi Forward Looking Strategies and the Beijing Platform for Action for the Universal Declaration of Human Rights. In terms of its commitment to international conventions and declarations, the Philippines has put its greatest efforts into the elimination of discrimination against women (Illo 1997: 39–40).

In regard to national laws, the principle of gender equality is affirmed in legislation. The 1987 Constitution, which was declared by the first woman president, Corazon Aquino, and is currently observed, recognises the equality of women and men before the law. Strong lobbying of women in NGOs, based on this Constitution, has resulted in various laws and regulations being enacted. A woman's right to own property, to be employed and to apply for credit without her husband's consent, was enacted by the *New Family Code 1987*. The majority of working women are based in the agriculture sector, and the *Comprehensive Agrarian Reform Law 1988* guarantees equal right of ownership of land. In 1992, the state recognised the role of women in nation building by adopting the *Women in Development and Nation Building Act* (Republic Act 7192) (Illo 1997: 40).

The Philippines has several landmark national laws that cover issues of discrimination towards women in the workplace. One is the Republic Act 6725, which prohibits discrimination against women in regard to employment, promotion and training opportunities. Article 135 of the *Labor Code of the Philippines (May 1974)* amended by Republic Act 6725 states that it is discriminatory to pay women less than men in regard to wage, salary or other forms of remuneration and fringe

benefits, and to favour a male employee over a female employee with respect to promotion, training opportunities, study and scholarship grants based solely on their gender. Article 136, on the other hand, covers employment and marriage. This article prohibits an employer from making it a condition of hiring or continuing to employ a woman that she does not marry. An employer cannot request a woman employee to leave her job because of her married status.

According to the *Labor Code of the Philippines (1974)*, organisations which allow discrimination against women are penalised. In addition, the aggrieved party has the right to file a separate and distinct claim for damages and financial compensation. If the institution is found guilty of impeding employees from filing a claim for damages, it will be fined between P1000 and P10 000. Employers who discriminate against women can be imprisoned for three months to three years or both fined and imprisoned at the discretion of the court, as stated in Articles 288 and 289 of the *Labor Code of the Philippines* (Foz 1999: 27).

The Philippines has ratified international treaties to protect women workers. The Philippine Government signed the Night Work (Women) Convention 1919, which covers the employment of women during the night. (The term night signifies a period of at least 11 consecutive hours, including the hours of 10 o'clock in the evening and six o'clock in the morning.) The convention generally prohibits women, regardless of age, from being employed during the night in any public or private industrial establishment unless other members of the same family are also employed (ILO 1999).

The government also ratified the Maternity Protection Convention 1919, which covers the employment of women before and after childbirth. This convention prohibits women from working two weeks before and four weeks after the delivery or miscarriage of a child and upholds a woman's right to take leave from work. It is unlawful for an employer to dismiss a pregnant employee on account of her situation or while she is on maternity leave. It is also unlawful to dismiss a pregnant employee or to refuse her re-employment on the basis that she might get pregnant again. The Maternity Protection Convention also allows a woman to be absent from her work and be paid sufficient benefits for herself and her child (ILO 1999). According to the *Social Security Act 1997* (Republic Act 8282), a female employee who is covered by the social security system and has paid at least three monthly contributions in the 12 months period immediately preceding the semester of her childbirth or miscarriage, shall be paid a daily maternity benefit equivalent to 100 per cent of her average daily salary credit for 60 days or 78 days in case of caesarean delivery.

Today, even though the legal framework to protect women workers is considered sufficient, the actual implementation and monitoring of legislation is weak due to yet-to-be-developed public governance systems.

Sexual harassment

According to the International Labour Organisation, sexual harassment includes unwelcome sexually oriented behaviour such as physical contact and advances; sexually coloured remarks; the showing of pornography and other sexually explicit material; and sexual demands made by word or by actions (Aeberhard-Hodges 1996: 500).

In 1995, the Philippines enacted a specific law, the *Anti-Sexual Harassment Act* (No. 7877), which declares sexual harassment unlawful generally, and also in the employment, education or training environment (Aeberhard-Hodges 1996: 501). The law declares that 'the state shall value the dignity of every individual, enhance the development of its human resources, guarantee full respect for human rights, and

uphold the dignity of workers, employees, applicants for employment, students or those undergoing training, instruction or education'. The law made it the duty of the employer or the head of the work-related educational or training environment or institution to develop policies and procedures for dealing with sexual harassment in the workplace, in consultation with employees, trainees or students, through their designated representatives (Foz 1999: 589–90).

There is a penalty for people who are convicted of violating the Act. They will be imprisoned for a period ranging from one to six months, or fined between P10 000 and P20 000, or both fined and imprisoned at the discretion of the court (Foz 1999: 591).

However, despite the existence of the law, there is a need to create more awareness regarding the Act and its implementation among the Philippine establishment, officials, law enforcement agencies, and the judiciary (Jiminez-David 2000a). For example, there are only a few companies with an existing Committee on Decorum and Investigation, which aims to increase understanding among employees and others of sexual harassment, prevent such incidents, and conduct investigations of alleged cases of sexual harassment. This lack of action and awareness stems from the fact that the law does not provide any sanctions for those organisations that do not comply with the law (Hega 1998: 12).

Sexual harassment is common in the corporate sector. According to the Labor Secretary, Bienvenido Laguesma, the incidence of sexual harassment of women is higher in banks, hotels and restaurants, and in the media and entertainment industries. Perhaps this is because 'these are the kind of workplaces, which put a premium on physical attributes' (Lacuarta 2000a). In the previously mentioned survey conducted by Lopez, Borromeo and Maravillas-Salim (May 2000), the respondents were asked if they were aware of any incidences of sexual harassment that had happened in their previous and present workplace. Forty per cent of respondents answered 'yes'. In response to a question about whether their employer has a specific policy on sexual harassment, about half of the respondents answered 'yes'.

The mass media have been strongly advocating the abolition of sexual harassment in the workplace. The root of women's victimisation or vulnerability, according to Rina Jimenez-David, a well-known newspaper columnist, is women's status in Philippine society. She states that women are often seen to be inferior and less important and exist merely for propagation. She goes on to say that they, in fact, contribute to the quality of the lives of those boys and men who are responsible for discrimination, harassment, abuse and exploitation of women and girls (Jiminez-David 2000b).

According to the Center for Women's Studies, from 1992 to 2000 an estimated 2300 sexual harassment cases were filed to the Department of Justice (DOJ). In September 1998, one such case was filed against a health officer in Central Visayas who was found guilty of violating at least two provisions of the Anti-Sexual Harassment Act. He was sentenced to a maximum penalty of six months' imprisonment and was ordered to pay a fine of P20 000 and to pay the complainant a total of P500 000 in moral and exemplary damages. He was also found guilty of administrative offences, which resulted in the order for his dismissal from government service and other penalties (Jiminez-David 1999).

In November 1998, a sexual harassment case was filed by a National Labor Relations Commission's (NLRC) stenographer against an NLRC chairman for allegedly squeezing her shoulders while she took dictation inside his office. The Committee on Decorum and Investigation that was created by the Department of Labor and Employment found the assailant guilty of making sexual advances, thus violating

the Anti-Sexual Harassment Act. A six-month suspension was recommended considering that it was his first offence. However, President Joseph Estrada later dismissed the NLRC chairman saying that 'he had shown an attitude, a frame of mind, a disgraceful conduct, which renders him unfit to remain in the service' (Lacuarta 2000b).

In spite of the fact there are highly publicised sexual harassment cases such as those mentioned above, in reality, filing a sexual harassment case is not easy. Although some assailants were convicted of violating the Anti-Sexual Harassment Act, there are a number of cases in which victims did not get support from their agency or organisation. The victims were not only discouraged from pursuing their cases, but their organisation implied that nothing really happened. In the worst cases, victims of sexual harassment were told to drop their complaints (Guanzon 1999).

One example is the case of a clerk who worked in a municipal trial court and who filed a case against her superior judge. She was approached by another judge who advised her to drop the charges. Another is a case of three women, a physician, a nurse, and a medical technologist, of the Medico Legal Division of the National Bureau of Investigation. They filed a sexual harassment case against their chief doctor and they were scolded for 'embarrassing the bureau'. Soon after, retaliation suits were filed against them (Guanzon 1999).

Expatriates working in the Philippines need to pay particular attention to the issue of sexual harassment. Although male expatriates, who are usually employed in senior positions, may not intend to sexually harass employees, their behaviour can be perceived as such in a different cultural context. While official cases of sexual harassment involving expatriates rarely surface, some claims of sexual harassment have been made by Philippine women subordinates against their expatriate employers in a number of multinational corporations. Because claims of sexual harassment by foreigners against women tend to get more sympathy from Filipinos, multinational corporations have sometimes been forced to move some expatriate managers to other countries in order to protect their corporate image.

There are several reasons why the issue of sexual harassment involving foreigners arises. The expatriates are often male and they usually occupy senior positions over locals. On the other hand, the Filipinos, both male and female, are very friendly and pleasant, and in general, they avoid saying no to others, especially to their superiors and in particular to foreigners. Instead, Filipinos have subtle ways of expressing their disagreement that sometimes leads to misunderstanding by the foreigners who are not familiar with the Philippine cultural context. When incidents like this happen, the expatriates usually find it difficult to continue to work in the Philippines.

Overseas workers

During the 1970s, the Philippines was subjected to a severe and sustained economic crisis with the result that Filipinos began migrating and working overseas. In 1975, 12 per cent of the total population of Overseas Filipino Workers (OFWs) were women. This rose to 47 per cent in 1987 and reached a height of 52 per cent in 1995 (see table 10.2) (Illo 1997: 28). In 1998, there was an estimated 2.4 million legally documented Filipino OFWs in more than 130 countries around the world. Male migrant workers comprised 52 per cent of the total population and female migrant workers 48 per cent (NSO 1999).

Table 10.2: ***Distribution of overseas contract workers, by occupation and sex, 1995***

Occupation	September 1995 (new hires and rehires)		
	Total workers ('000)	Per cent female OFWs to all OFWs	Per cent to total female
Professional, technical, and related workers	**94**	**47**	**12**
Architects and engineers	20	5	*
Medical, dental, and related workers	34	82	7
Composers and performing artists	12	92	3
Others	28	2	1
Administrative, executive, and managerial	**3**	**33**	*
Clerical and related workers	**21**	**48**	**3**
Sales workers	**15**	**60**	**2**
Service workers	**323**	**85**	**73**
Cooks, waiters, and bartenders	22	18	1
Helpers and housekeeping workers	276	95	69
Others	25	3	3
Agricultural and related workers	**11**	**9**	**—**
Production and related workers	**321**	**11**	**9**
Total	**721.2**	**52**	**100**

* Less than one per cent.

Sources: Derived from data from the Bureau of Labor and Employment Statistics (BLES), *1995 Yearbook on Labor Statistics* and personal communications with officials of the Philippine Overseas Employment Administration.

Workers had little choice but to migrate. This was necessitated by the lack of employment opportunities in the Philippines and their need to provide food and education for the families. By the early 1990s, 16 per cent of Philippine households were receiving remittances from abroad (ILO 1997a). This money was used to feed the families of OFWs and send their own and relatives' children to school. OFWs contributed about seven per cent of the Philippines gross domestic product in 1995 and women workers played a very significant role since they made up half of the OFW population (Illo 1997: 28–9).

In 1999, most of the female OFWs were in the 25–29 age bracket, while the biggest portion of male OFWs were 30–34 years old. The biggest portion of female OFWs (83 per cent, compared with 73 per cent in 1995) were service workers who were predominantly employed as domestic helpers and in the entertainment industry, while 92 per cent of male OFWs were production workers, transport equipment operators and labourers (NSO 1999).

To promote the welfare of OFWs and to protect their rights, President Fidel Ramos signed the Republic Act 8042 or the *Migrant Workers and Overseas Filipinos Act 1995* (Pazzibugan 1999). This was in reaction to the highly publicised case of a Philippine domestic helper in Singapore who was hanged for murder. In spite of their contribution to the economy, Filipino migrant workers still remain unprotected and

their basic rights are sometimes violated abroad. Many workers, especially women migrants, continue to experience abuse and exploitation worldwide (Philippine Australia Network 1997). Between 1990 and 2000, different institutions and organisations recorded a continuing pattern of rampant abuse against Filipinos working abroad. For example, an average of 12 300 complaints were being processed every year by the Overseas Workers Welfare Administration during this period. Maltreatment, contract violation, non-payment of salaries, underpayment, physical abuse, rape, sexual harassment and sex trafficking are among the most common complaints of women workers (Philippine Australia Network, 1997). Moreover, OFWs suffer the consequences of working overseas to support their families — cultural disorientation, breakdown of marriages, and children being raised in a single parent environment. Today, the interests and rights of the OFWs are neglected and the government has yet to prove that it can protect the welfare of Filipinos who work overseas.

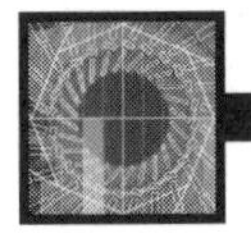

Child labour

Child labour is defined by the United Nations Children's Fund (UNICEF) as 'employing children below 15 years old in factories and industries where they are not directly under the supervision of their parents'. It also includes the prohibition of the employment of children below 18 years old to work in hazardous jobs.

In 1995, child workers aged 5–17 years old numbered 3.7 million in the Philippines (NSO 1995). Of this figure, 2.2 million, mostly boys, were engaged in hazardous work usually involving noxious fumes and machinery, and about 50 000 to 60 000 children were prostituted. On the other hand, one-third of child labourers are girls and many of them are working in rural areas. Many girls (79 per cent) work as domestic helpers and about 65 per cent of the total population of working girls live away from home (Illo 1997: 30–31).

To protect these children, the Philippines has signed United Nations Conventions and enacted two specific national laws to protect their welfare. The first of these laws is the Republic Act No. 7610, which protects against child abuse, exploitation and discrimination, and there are severe penalties for its violation. It states the rules and regulations governing the employment of children. The second law is the Republic Act No. 7658, which prohibits public and private employment of children younger than 15 years of age. However, implementation of these laws is not easy. Many of the working children are 'invisible' or hidden behind factory walls, prostitution dens, and in many homes in Manila, which is the reason why law enforcers have difficulty in finding them (Arroyo 1999).

While child labour practices are prevalent in Philippine society, children's voices are rarely heard. It is reported that children as young as eight are employed as domestic workers and many of them are subjected to physical and verbal abuse (Ramos 1999). At a forum at the University of the Philippines, young people told how they were exploited and abused. One of the victims said that he was recruited from a province by an agency that promised him a job, but he found himself working in a cannery without pay. Another child was promised an education by the agency but ended up working in a bleach company without pay. Most of these children who were 'recruited' by the agencies were from Visayas and Mindanao. According to UNICEF, 'these rescued child labourers complained that they were put in shelters unfit for humans, fed inadequate food, forced to work long hours without pay, and subjected to verbal abuse'

(Arroyo 1999). UNICEF also noted that the issue of child labour becomes more complicated because some parents, for reasons of poverty, ask their children to work.

In 1992, the ILO launched a major program known as the International Programme on the Elimination of Child Labour (IPEC), which the Philippines joined in 1994 (ILO 1996). IPEC programs concentrate on the eradication of the most hazardous and exploitative forms of child labour, and on the progressive elimination of child labour by strengthening national capacities for addressing this problem. The program also serves, in cooperation with trade unions and employer organisations, other UN agencies and NGOs in promoting a worldwide movement against child labour. According to IPEC, 'little is known about child domestic workers as an occupational group'. They are widely dispersed, hidden and largely ignored, which is why they are called invisible workers. However, the NGO Consultation on Child Domestic Workers has shown that a growing number of services to these children are now being developed by NGOs with the help of IPEC. Today, many NGOs provide legal assistance in specific cases as well as campaigning generally for children's legal rights. They are also lobbying for improvements in national legislation relating to domestic service (ILO 1997b).

Workers with disabilities

Workers with disabilities constitute a negligible percentage of the Philippines' total labour force population. Though the law declares the equal rights of disabled workers, in a low employment economy such as the Philippines they are not as readily hired as regular employees.

The issue of protection of disabled workers was highlighted in a Supreme Court ruling on the money sorters of a prominent Philippine commercial bank in July 1999. Given that the bank is a highly regarded corporation, this case illustrates the low level of awareness of the rights of disabled workers in the Philippines.

Since regular employees were no longer willing to perform the tiresome task of sorting paper bills and coins, deaf workers were hired as money sorters and the bank found them to be a cheap, compliant and focused workforce. In the Philippines, if workers are employed for more than six months, they have the right to be hired as regular employees; however, this did not apply to the deaf workers at the bank. Most of these workers had worked for three to six years, but the bank did not pay them the minimal wage and readily dismissed them. They had to work in the backrooms, which were locked and tightly guarded, probably to prevent theft. The case between the bank and workers began when the workers complained about sexual harassment by the bank's security guards. The disabled workers initially brought their complaints to their supervisors but they were told to ignore the guards and concentrate on their work. However, the problem became worse and they brought their complaints to a federation of people with disabilities which insisted that the bank take full responsibility and institute measures to protect the deaf workers from sexual harassment. The bank's management reacted by dismissing not just the complainants but all deaf workers.

The court ordered the bank to pay the difference in wages owing, separation pay and other benefits to which the workers were entitled. The court argued that, as regular employees, people with disabilities are entitled to the same security of tenure as able-bodied employees, and their services could only be terminated for just reasons within the law. Employers are coming to realise that hiring disabled workers is not an act of charity which obviates the need to follow appropriate labour laws.

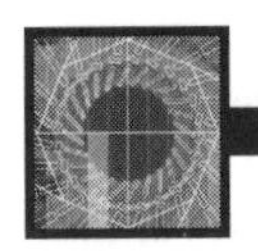

Conclusions

The Philippines has the appearance of being a well-developed meritocracy with a sound legal system, both of which have developed from its association with the United States. The Philippines has an excellent legal system, to the point where it is one among the few countries in Asia, which has laws on sexual harassment. Yet, there are other systems and factors that interplay with these formal systems. For example, the gender issue in the Philippines is very complex and other factors impact on it, such as the pre-Hispanic tradition, ethnicity, religion, class, poverty, pressure of urbanisation, child labour, sexual harassment, and the pressure for migration to foreign countries.

For expatriates who work in the Philippines, it appears that the country is easy to work in. The people are nice, fluent in English, and systems are similar to that of the West. However, this first impression is somewhat deceiving. The reality of the Philippines, which has been discussed in this chapter by focusing on the issue of gender, is much more complex. It is important for expatriates to examine and understand these complexities, to avoid making the wrong decisions and jeopardising their careers and the good name of their employers.

References

Arroyo, D. M. 1999. 'Child Labor in the Philippines: Exploiting Innocence'. *Philippine Daily Inquirer*, 28 November.

Aeberhard-Hodges, J. 1996. 'Sexual Harassment in Employment: Recent Judicial and Arbitral Trends'. *International Labour Review* 135(5). http://www.ilo.org

Aeberhard-Hodges, J. 1997. 'Unwelcome, Unwanted, and Increasingly Illegal: Sexual Harassment in the Workplace'. In *World of Work*, No. 19. International Labour Organisation, March. http://www.ilo.org

Ariff, M. 1991. *Islam and Economic Development of Southeast Asia: The Muslim Private Sector in Southeast Asia*. Singapore Institute of Southeast Asian Studies.

Bonvillain, N. 1998. *Women and Men: Cultural Constructs of Gender*. Upper Saddle River, NJ: Prentice Hall.

Center for Women's Studies. 2000. Interview, September, University of the Philippines, Diliman, Quezon City.

Chant, S. & McIlwaine, C. 1995. *Women of a Lesser Cost: Female Labour, Foreign Exchange and Philippine Development*. Ateneo de Manila University Press.

Foz, V. B. 1999. *The Labor Code of the Philippines*. Pp. 523–89, 15–38, 119–21, 181–3, 217–23, 524–6, 578–89, 97, 69.

Gastardo-Conaco, M. C. & Ramos-Jimenez, P. 1986. *Ethnicity and Fertility in the Philippines*. Singapore Institute of Southeast Asian Studies.

Guanzon, R. V. 1999. 'Brave Women and Their Stories'. *Philippine Daily Inquirer*, 27 May.

Guerrero, M. C. 1992. 'Sources of Women's Roles in Philippine History: Texts and Counter-texts'. A paper presented at the Fourth International Philippine Studies Conference, Australian National University, Canberra, Australia, 1–3 July: 1490–1983.

Hega, M. D. 1998. *Women and Trade Unions: The Context, the Gains and the Road Ahead: The Philippine Experiences*. Project Group for Development Policy, Division for International Development Cooperation.

Human Development Report Office. 1999. *Human Development Indicators*. http://www.un.or.id/undp-update/office/national.htm

Illo, J. F. I. 1997. *Women in the Philippines*. Manila Asian Development Bank: 1–38.
International Labour Organisation. 1996. 'International Action: Standards Need Reinforcing'. http://www.ilo.org
International Labour Organisation. 1997a. 'Emigration Pressures and Structural Change: Case Study of the Philippines'. September. http://www.ilo.org
International Labour Organisation. 1997b. 'International Programme on the Elimination of Child Labour'. *Children and Work*. No. 4. http://www.ilo.org
International Labour Organisation. 1998. 'Recruitment Policies and Options'. Labour Administrative Branch. http://www.ilo.org
International Labour Organisation. 1999. 'International Labour Standards'. http://www.ilo.org
Institute for Labor Studies. 1997. *Adolescence in the Labor Force*. Monograph Series No. 3.
Institute for Labor Studies. 1997. *Effects of Globalization on Child Work in Selected Philippine Industries*. Monograph Series No. 5.
Institute for Labor Studies. 1997. *Selected Papers on the Work Improvement in Small Enterprises (WISE) Program*. Monograph Series No. 7.
Institute for Small-scale Industries. 1991. *Filipino Women in Business: A Casebook*. Small Enterprises Research and Development Foundation Inc. Quezon City: University of the Philippines.
Jiminez-David, R. 1999. 'One Man's Comeuppance'. *Philippine Daily Inquirer*, 10 November.
Jiminez-David, R. 2000a. 'Linking Issues and Allies'. *Philippine Daily Inquirer*, 24 February.
Jiminez-David, R. 2000b. 'Women in Islam, Confront Gender'. *Philippine Daily Inquirer*, 20 May.
Jocano, F. L. 1999. *Management by Culture: Fine Tuning Modern Management to Filipino Culture*. Manila: Punlad Research House.
Lacuarta, G.G. 2000a. 'Touching Hair, Texting May Draw Sex Raps'. *Philippine Daily Inquirer*, 23 April.
Lacuarta, G.G. 2000b. 'Estrada Sacks Labor Exec for Sexual Harassment'. *Philippine Daily Inquirer*, 17 May.
Manila Institute of Women's Studies. 1992. *LILA: Asia Pacific Women's Studies Journal Number 1*. Malate: St. Scholastica's College.
Manila Institute of Women's Studies. 1992. *LILA: Asia Pacific Women's Studies Journal Number 2*. Malate: St. Scholastica's College.
National Statistics Office. 1999. Press Release on the 1996 Overseas Filipino Workers. http://www.census.gov.ph
National Statistics Office. 2000. *NSO–Quickstat*. http://www.census.gov.ph
Ordoñez, M. A. 1985. *Guidance in Philippine Setting*. Quezon City: Vermar Printing Press.
Paderanga, C. 1988. *Employment in Philippine Development*. Quezon City: School of Economics, University of the Philippines.
Pazzibugan, D. 1999. 'Migrant Workers' Act a Failure, Says Study'. *Philippine Daily Inquirer*, 17 August.
Philippine Australia Network. 1997. 'Another Bad Year for Filipino OCWs'. *KASAMA* 11(1): January–March.
Ramos, M.P. 1999. 'The Many Faces of Child Labor'. *Philippine Daily Inquirer*, 27 November.
Reid, A. 1988. *Southeast Asia in the Age of Commerce: The Lands Below the Winds*. New Haven & London: Yale University Press.
Salinas, A. & Liamzon, T. 1985. *Too Little, Too Late: An Alternative Philippine Report on Government Initiatives for Women*. Philippine Women's Research Collective.
Smith, C. R. & Hutchinson, J. 1995. *Gender: A Strategic Management Issue*, Sydney: Business & Professional Publishing.
Wolters, O. W. 1999. *History, Culture, and Region in Southeast Asian Perspective*. Ithaca, NY: Cornell University, Southeast Asia Program Publications.

Chapter 11

Singapore

Jacqueline Landau and Chung Yuen Kay

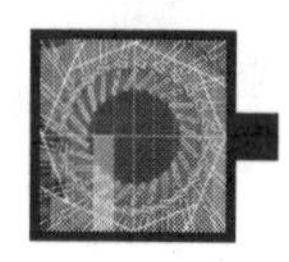

Introduction

Singapore is one of the world's smallest countries, having a land area of only 62.4 square kilometres. Despite its small size, the population is quite diverse, consisting of 76.8 per cent Chinese, 13.9 per cent Malays, 7.9 per cent Indians, and 1.4 per cent other (Singapore Census of Population 2000). In addition, over 596 000 expatriates live in Singapore including Americans, Europeans, and other Asians. Malaysians make up the majority of the latter group, but there are also many workers from Indonesia, the Philippines and India.

Singapore is in a unique position. The country has only been independent for 34 years and has almost no natural resources. Even water has to be transported from neighbouring Malaysia. Despite these conditions, Singapore is one of the most economically prosperous countries in Asia, and is in the enviable position of having an almost non-existent unemployment rate (averaging two per cent pre-crisis). Even at the height of the Asian crisis, the unemployment rate was only 4.4 per cent, a rate that has not been seen in Europe for a long time, and a rate the United States has only recently achieved. Due to this tight labour market, job mobility is extremely high compared to many other countries. In fact, during the two-year period of 1997 and 1998, nearly one in five employed persons changed jobs. Therefore, the search for qualified, skilled employees is a constant uphill battle.

Another unique aspect of Singapore is that its various ethnic groups have never been under pressure to assimilate. Singapore, as part of its official policy, is committed to multiracialism and multiculturalism. The four main racial categories, as officially designated, are Chinese, Malay, Indian, and Other (composed of Europeans, Eurasians and other groups who do not fit into the first three categories), and the major religions are Buddhism, Christianity, Taoism, Hinduism, and Islam. Public holidays have been established for Hindu, Muslim and Chinese festivals. Christmas and Good Friday are also public holidays.

There are four official languages in Singapore: Mandarin, English, Malay, and Tamil. Singaporeans are encouraged to learn English (to be able to compete globally and communicate with each other), as well as their so-called 'mother tongue' (in order to preserve their cultural heritage). Thus, for those of Chinese ancestry, Mandarin has been designated as the mother tongue, for those of Malay ancestry the designated mother tongue is Malay, and for those of Indian ancestry the language is Tamil. This matching of 'mother tongues' for the three communities, however, belies a much more complex reality of diversity within the communities. (For a discussion of some of these issues, see PuruShotam 1989; Siddique 1989.)

In this chapter, we frame our discussion of cultural diversity in Singapore by first providing an overview of Singapore's historical and economic development, and its industrial relations system. Then we present information on Singapore's changing labour force, followed by a discussion of legislation and policies in regards to discrimination in the workplace. Next, issues of gender, age, ethnicity and disability will be discussed in detail, and finally, we will highlight some aspects of diversity that expatriate managers should be aware of, and sensitive to, in order to enhance their effectiveness.

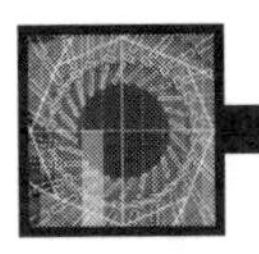

Singapore's historical and economic development

Although Singapore is believed to have been a thriving port in the seventh century, when the British arrived under Sir Stamford Raffles in 1819, it was inhabited only by a small Malay community. In the 1800s, Singapore grew into a thriving trading port for the Malayan hinterland and much of the region. In 1959 Singapore became internally self-governing, and was actually part of Malaysia from 1963 to 65. However, irreconcilable differences with Malaysia led to eventual separation and, on 22 December 1965, Singapore was declared an independent republic. Since 1959 the nation has been ruled by the People's Action Party (PAP), led until 1993, by Lee Kuan Yew. He was succeeded by the current Prime Minister, Goh Chok Tong.

Since 1960, Singapore has been propelled into the ranks of the newly industrialised countries in Asia. Singapore's economic growth has been characterised by its commitment to exports, and a reliance on foreign investments, coinciding with the multinationals shifting of their labour intensive, low-skilled factory work to 'off-shore' sites in South-east Asia, Central and South America. Singapore has been a favoured location because of its strategic geographical location, relatively literate population, and efficiently organised transportation and banking systems.

Since 1997, when US disk-drive companies channelled millions into computer hardware, the growth of the electronic products and components industry has been phenomenal, making Singapore a world-wide disk-drive exporter. Even in the midst of the regional crisis, the electronics industry maintained its strong performance in 1999, with robust exports of semiconductors and telecommunication equipment. There were retrenchments, however, particularly in the disk-drive industry. In recent years, the republic has also emphasised development of the chemicals industry.

Since 1993, Singapore has embarked on the globalisation of its economy, going beyond encouraging foreign investments to encouraging locally based companies to develop a 'second-wing' by expanding overseas. Despite the regional economic crisis, the drive to develop its external wing continues (Chin 1999), and Singapore's cultural diversity is noted as one of its competitive advantages in expanding overseas. In 1996, Singapore was reclassified by the OECD, from a developing country to an advanced developing country.

The republic is currently concerned with meeting the demands of a knowledge economy. While the government and other institutions have been active in building the necessary physical infrastructure and supportive facilities, Singapore acknowledges that a stronger culture of innovation and a larger skilled workforce need to be developed (Low 1999). There is a shortage of information workers in research and development (R&D) and, therefore, a need to tap foreign talent. It is to this end that Singapore and India have recently agreed to set up a task force to boost cooperation between their information and communication industries.

Simultaneously, the government is trying to create an environment that encourages and nurtures young entrepreneurs. While three decades of orchestration and planning have catapulted the republic to first world levels of affluence, the planning has also made it overly dependent on two main sources of business enterprise: multinationals and government-linked firms. Thus, the government has liberalised finance and telecommunications in an effort to bring in more business. Also, the education curriculum has been revamped to encourage more creativity among students, more money has been pumped in to the arts and censorship relaxed, with the intention of making Singapore a more attractive place to live. If local businesses are to grow beyond their home markets, they require a new breed of leaders — people who move rapidly and are not afraid to take risks. The results, thus far, seem encouraging, with many small companies carving out space in the hi-tech world and providing business services over the Internet (Dolven 2000).

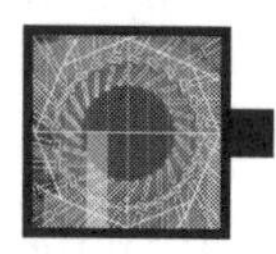

The industrial relations system

Two factors have been central to the success of Singapore's industrial strategy: first, the institutionalisation of wage restraints and second, the development of a cooperative labour force. Following the separation of Singapore from Malaysia, government leaders focused on requirements for the survival of the small, independent city-state. The 'ideology of survival' (quoted in Rodan 1989: 88) postulated that economic prosperity was a necessary pre-condition for political stability, and vice versa, and that all other considerations would have to be subsumed under this overarching ideal. Workers, in particular, would have to be very disciplined if Singapore was to be successful in highly competitive world export markets. A succession of legislative measures remoulded the traditional roles of trade unions. The National Trade Union Congress (NTUC) was to become a junior partner with the government in national development. Thus, NTUC became a partner in a tripartite relationship with the government and employers (SNEF or the Singapore National Employers Federation), on the National Wage Council (NWC), set up in 1972 to recommend annual wage increase guidelines (and these are largely respected and adhered to by employers and unions). To ensure that the symbiotic relationship between the government and trade unions would endure, a program of 'cross-fertilisation' was also implemented whereby union leaders were co-opted into the PAP leadership and elected as Members of Parliament (MPs), while non-unionist PAP MPs were deputised to work with unions. The previous Secretary-General, of the NTUC, Ong Teng Cheong, was also the Deputy Prime Minister of Singapore, while the current Secretary-General, Lim Boon Heng, is also the Minister Without Portfolio.

Towards the end of 1980, the government addressed what it saw as the problem of workers' poor attitudes (as signified by the common practice of job-hopping). The then Prime Minister, Lee Kuan Yew, prescribed that Singapore should model itself on the Japanese system of industrial relations. Greater team spirit was identified as the key to success in the next stage of economic development. Singaporeans were exhorted to learn to become team achievers, and a comprehensive campaign to imbue the populace with this message was carried out. This was not an easy lesson for workers to internalise, as previously, Singaporeans had been urged to be competitive, and there was an obvious contradiction between the notions of 'teamwork' and 'meritocracy'. Lim Chee Onn, then Secretary-General of NTUC, addressed this issue in his address to the Fourth Triennial Delegates' Conference in 1982 when he spoke of the need to maintain 'a careful balance between developing individual skills and encouraging group performance' (Lim 1982, as quoted in Chung 1994). Lim also focused on the issue of the advent of new production technology, and the importance of a skilled, high-performance workforce to meet the challenge, necessitating the training and upgrading of workers at all levels. To criticisms that the various legislative measures had whittled away workers' rights and changed the traditional roles

of unions, the government's response has been, 'but have they not benefited from economic growth?' (Chua 1995).

There are 79 registered employee unions in Singapore today. Of these, 70 are affiliated with the NTUC. The profile of unions reflects key public sector institutions, industries, and occupations in the manufacturing, service, and financial sectors. Many of these unions were established during colonial times (for a profile and history of the trade unions, see Chung 1995). Trade unionists themselves feel that they have some way to go in improving public perceptions of the constructive role that trade unions play in Singapore. As Wong puts it:

> . . . on the one hand the conventional perception existed among many employers that unions were adversarial and a hindrance. On the other hand, the unions cooperative approach and symbiotic relationship with the PAP resulted in some public suspicion, held by both employers and workers that workers were ineffective in representing workers' interests (Wong 1992: 154, cited in Chung 1994).

More recently, NTUC Secretary-General Lim Boon Heng has called on trade unions to play their part in ensuring that workers are suitably trained, and not left behind in the transition to the knowledge economy (*Straits Times* 2000).

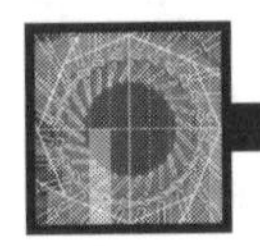

The labour force

According to the June 1998 Labour Force Survey, 64 per cent of the population aged 15 and above were in the labour force. The labour force has been growing at an average rate of 3.4 per cent over the past ten years, and the growth rate has been higher for females (4.3 per cent) than for males (2.9 per cent) (Singapore Ministry of Manpower 1998). Table 11.1 shows the number and percentage of males and females in the labour force as at 1997.

Table 11.1: ***Employed males and females by occupation in 1997***

	Males		Females	
	Below 40	40 & over	Below 40	40 & over
Administrative and Managerial	13.1	20.8	6.0	8.3
Professionals and Technicals	33.4	19.8	29.2	17.8
Clerical	6.0	5.7	32.8	20.3
Sales and Service	10.9	13.1	10.0	19.2
Production and Related	27.0	39.6	21.4	34.0
Others	9.7	0.9	0.2	0.3

Source: Adapted from Singapore Ministry of Manpower (1998).

In recent years, the Singapore workforce has become more highly educated and skilled. The government's Manpower 21 report emphasised the need for even more

training and education. Table 11.2 shows the educational profile of the current workforce compared to the workforce in 1995.

Table 11.2: ***Educational profile of labour force (%), 1995 and 1999***

	1995	1999
Primary and Below	24.8	22.0
Lower Secondary	11.5	15.5
Secondary	30.4	27.9
Post Secondary	12.0	9.7
Diploma	8.0	10.3
Degree	13.4	14.7

Source: Adapted from Key Manpower Statistics (2000).

In the past ten years, due to economic restructuring and the development of a more highly educated workforce, the occupational profile has been shifting. As shown in table 11.3, there has been a significant increase in professionals and technicals, and associate professionals, and a decrease in service and sales, craft and factory positions.

Table 11.3: ***Comparison of employed persons aged 15 years and over by occupation in 1988 and 1998***

Occupation	June 1988		June 1998	
	Number	%	Number	%
Legislators, Senior Officials and Managers	104 900	7.9	239 100	12.8
Professionals	61 700	4.6	172 000	9.2
Technicians and Associate Professionals	153 000	11.5	332 400	17.8
Clerical Workers	186 500	14.0	278 800	14.9
Service and Sales Workers	201 000	15.1	236 300	12.6
Production Craftsmen and Related Workers	194 500	14.6	144 300	7.7
Plant and Machine Operators and Assemblers	255 000	19.2	224 500	12.0
Cleaners, Labourers and Related Workers	104 600	7.9	178 700	9.6
Others*	70 500	5.3	63 700	3.4
Total	**1 333 600**	**100.0**	**1 869 700**	**100.0**

*Includes agricultural and fishery workers not classifiable by occupation.
Source: Adapted from Singapore Ministry of Manpower (1998).

Table 11.4 shows the breakdown of occupation by ethnicity according to the 1990 census. Although the vast majority of Singaporeans are of Chinese origin, the Chinese are not an integrated group. They include the Cantonese, Hokkiens, the Hainanese, and the Teochows. They all speak different dialects, and at one time each group had its own cantonment.

Table 11.4: ***Percentage employed by ethnicity and occupation 1990***

	Total	Chinese	Malays	Indians	Others
Professional and Technical	15.7	17.3	9.7	12.5	10.6
Administrative and Managerial	8.6	10.0	1.1	5.8	10.4
Clerical	13.1	13.8	15.4	11.7	2.6
Sales and Services	13.8	14.5	14.0	14.8	3.3
Agriculture and Fishery	0.3	0.3	0.3	0.1	—
Production and Related	44.5	39.7	57.0	50.4	72.3
Not Classified	4.0	4.4	2.5	4.7	0.8

Source: Adapted from Singapore Census of Population (1990).

The expatriates in Singapore generally fall into two different categories: those who are highly-educated and skilled and work as professionals or managers; and those who are unskilled and come to Singapore to take the labour intensive and low-level service jobs that Singaporeans do not want. Thus, there is a clear distinction between the higher-educated, skilled 'foreign talent' and the lowly-paid, unskilled 'foreign workers' also referred to as 'migrant workers'.

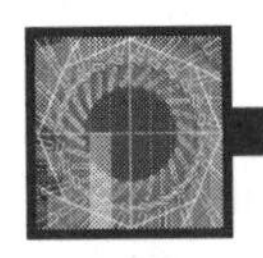

Employment law

Singapore's Constitution states that all persons are equal before the law and entitled to the equal protection of the law, and that there shall be no discrimination against citizens of Singapore on the grounds of religion, race, descent, or place of birth in any law or in the appointment to any office or employment under a public authority. There are no specific laws addressing gender, age, or disability discrimination. Generally, the Singaporean government prefers to deal with issues of diversity and discrimination through policy and education rather than law. For example, recently a female Caucasian expatriate who was looking for a job noticed that many of the job advertisements in the newspapers specified age, gender, and sometimes even ethnicity requirements. She questioned the merits of such criteria in a country that proclaims itself to be a meritocracy. Her letter to the Editor of the *Straits Times* stirred up quite a controversy. Many individuals and organisations wrote in to the *Straits Times* with their opinions. Articles were written and TV shows were aired about Malays and Indians who had felt that they had not been able to find employment because of their ethnicity. A debate arose over whether more legislation was necessary to prevent discrimination. The government took the stand that the Constitution already prohibited discrimination and what was needed was education, not legislation. In March 1999 the Ministry of Manpower, SNEF, and NTUC launched the Tripartite Guidelines on Non-discriminatory Advertisements. This document describes what constitutes 'acceptable' and 'unacceptable' job advertisements. The tripartite partners stated that employers should hire the most suitable candidates based on merit, experience, skills, and other relevant job requirements. They posted the guidelines on a web site, and from February to April 1999 the percentage of advertisements stipulating discriminatory criteria dropped from 30 per cent to one per cent (Report on Discriminatory Job Advertisements 2000).

Given Singapore's emphasis on multiculturalism, and its law prohibiting discrimination, Westerners coming to work in Singapore, and particularly Americans, might be quite surprised by the questions asked on many job application forms such as: what is your religion? what is your marital status? and, what does your father do for a living? All job candidates are required to submit a recent photograph with their applications.

Since Singapore relies so heavily on foreign workers, there are many laws and regulations regarding the employment of these workers. Foreign workers are classified into three categories:

- *P work pass holders* (professionals, managers, administrators, investors, entrepreneurs, top artists, musicians)
- *Q work pass holders* (skilled workers, technicians, and those with specialised skills)
- *R work pass holders* (semi-skilled and unskilled workers).[1]

All P work pass holders can bring their children and spouses with them to Singapore, and receive long-term visit passes for parents and parents-in-law. R pass holders cannot bring their families to live with them.

Prior to July 1999, work passes were issued only to workers who had already found employment in Singapore. The government recognised, however, that this excluded foreigners interested in starting up technopreneurial businesses. Therefore, the Ministry of Manpower and the Ministry of Home Affairs, in consultation with other agencies, have developed guidelines for issuing Long Social Visit Passes and Work Passes for foreign talent and technopreneurs.

Singapore has many other laws to promote industrial peace and balance the interests of workers and employers. The *Employment Act 1968* (and its amendments) cover conditions of employment and basic rights and responsibilities of employers and employees. The *Industrial Relations Act* spells out the rights and duties between employers and employees who are represented by unions (see C. H. Tan 1999).

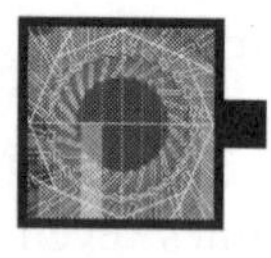

Diversity in the workplace

Gender

As mentioned earlier, Singapore has a very small workforce that needs constantly to replace itself. This creates a dilemma regarding the role of women in society. On the one hand, Singaporean women are encouraged to get an education and be active members of the workforce for most of their adult lives. On the other hand, women are urged not to neglect their roles as wives and mothers, and the government has put programs into place to encourage educated women to marry and preferably to have more than two children. This emphasis on both work and family has led to some policy contradictions (see Lee, Campbell & Chia 1999).

At the ideological level, the non-waged and often 'hidden' work that goes into the maintenance of such roles (i.e. 'wife' and 'mother') in the 'private' domain of the home are not considered to be work in the narrow economic sense of the word. This undermines the social value of these traditional roles. Also, married women workers in Singapore may be perceived to be more committed to their family than their work role (see PuruShotam & Chung 1992).

In 1998, the labour force participation rate for women in Singapore was 51.3 per cent (Key Labour Statistics 1999), greater than in most other Asian countries. However, the labour force participation rate of women is still far below that of males. In 1997, the overall labour force participation rate for married women was 48 per cent compared to 86 per cent for married men (Singapore Department of Statistics 1998). The participation rate of single women was 66 per cent, almost the same as the rate of 67 per cent for single men (Singapore Department of Statistics 1998).

Since 1987 there has been an increasing number of women in administrative and managerial, and professional and technical jobs, particularly for women under 40. As shown in table 11.1, however, similar to most other countries, there is a much higher percentage of men in these positions, and a dearth of women in upper management. Women earn less than men, on average, and in recent years, the gap has increased rather than narrowed (see Chan 2000). Table 11.1 shows that many occupations are sex-segregated.

'Singapore is not a signatory to the three United Nations Conventions which call for equality of the sexes in employment opportunities, remuneration for work of equal value, and institutional treatments in all forms. In addition, there is no specific legislation prohibiting sexual discrimination' (Lee et al. 1999: p. 52). However, in order to induce more women to enter and remain in the workforce the government has instituted several policies. As early as 1962, the government accepted a proposal of equal pay for equal work in the civil service. Prior to that date, female civil servants were paid only 80 per cent of men's salaries, and were only temporary staff who were denied pension rights once they married (Lee et al. 1999). In 1999, the first female Permanent Secretary (of the Ministry of Community Development) was appointed. In an interview with the press, the (then) new Permanent Secretary said that she had never experienced any discrimination in the workplace and that her appointment was evidence that the civil service was 'gender-blind' (i.e. egalitarian) (*Straits Times* 1999a). One could query why, if the civil service was indeed 'gender-blind', it had taken so long before a woman was appointed to the post.

Policies to support women's dual roles of labour force participants and mothers include maternity and childcare leave, and the foreign domestic maid scheme. According to the Employment Act, which covers most employees earning a salary of S$1500 or less per month, a female employee who has worked for her employer for no fewer than 180 days before the day of confinement is entitled to four weeks' paid maternity leave before delivery of the child and four weeks after. With the consent of her employer, she can choose to take less pre-confinement and more post-confinement leave. This Act applies, however, only if the female employee has had no more than one child at the time of confinement.

Although the *Employment Act 1968* does not include a provision for childcare leave, starting in 1987 the government made provisions for female civil servants to take up to four years of unpaid childcare leave. This leave must be taken within four years of the birth of the child. In practice, however, anecdotal evidence suggests that women who do apply for this leave may meet with some resistance from their immediate superiors who may cite understaffing as a reason for their reluctance to approve the leave. Women may also be 'persuaded' to put in applications for a shorter period (such as six months) than they originally intended.

In addition, each female civil servant is entitled to a maximum of five days unrecorded leave per year for each child below six years old, subject to a maximum of three children. There are no provisions for paternity leave. It has been argued, however, that this policy, which many employers in the private sector also observe, may be a disadvantage as well as a privilege, because it further biases employers against hiring and/or promoting married female workers. Furthermore, insofar as the sick child leave scheme only applies to women, it entrenches traditional gender roles and relations and places the onus and responsibility of childcare on women (Chung 1999).

The Foreign Domestic Maid Scheme, introduced in 1978, allowed Singaporean women to hire a full-time live-in foreign maid (usually from the Philippines or Indonesia, but also from Sri Lanka and India), for an initial payment of about S$1500, and subsequent costs of S$200 to S$400 a month for the maid and a monthly government levy of S$345 (1 April 1998) (Lee et al. 1999). Together with board and lodging and medical expenses (which include a compulsory medical examination every six months) a foreign maid could cost an employer up to $1000 a month. Since this is prohibitively expensive for many families, the government also encouraged the establishment of more childcare centres. Even so, childcare centre numbers are not increasing fast enough. Furthermore, most centres generally take in children aged two and above, which still leaves a void in the care of younger children. Alternative arrangements for childcare may be available for some women (such as the use of the services of relatives or other women — housewives in the housing estate[2] who 'do not work'), but such private and informal arrangements reinforce the social invisibility of the problem, and perpetuate the sexual division of labour.

Despite the government's efforts to aid women in their pursuit of careers, there are still some policies and practices that would appear to be discriminatory, reinforcing women's traditional role as wife and mother. One example is the issue of healthcare benefits. Since men are still considered to be the heads of households, the family members of male civil servants, but not female civil servants, are entitled to medical benefits. However, medical benefits are provided to the children of women who are widowed, divorced, or separated. This policy makes the reversal of traditional roles, where the husband stays home to care for children, and the wife goes to work, almost impossible.

Women also do not have completely equal access to education. Since 1979 there has been a quota that no more than one-third the class entering the National University of Singapore Medical School can be female. The reasoning behind this decision was that most women would not be willing to work the long hours required as a physician because of their demanding and time-consuming family responsibilities (Lee et al. 1999). This reinforcement of traditional sex roles may be one factor contributing to the inability of women to progress to top-level management and government positions. For instance, only five out of the top 100 public sector posts in the republic are held by women. In a survey of female business graduates, Yuen (1992) found that while most of the high performing females managed to get good jobs

initially, after their stint as trainee managers, they were often assigned to supporting functions or to areas such as personnel. At the second stage (about four or five years after graduation) the respondents reported a lack of training and upgrading opportunities, as well as inadequate career guidance. Later in their careers, women cited problems of limited interorganisational mobility and a dearth of mentors available to them (Yuen 1992).

Some work practices, meant to improve the quality of work and family life, which are commonplace in the US and Western European countries have yet to be implemented in Singapore. Very few organisations have childcare facilities, flexible work schedules, job sharing, parental leave, or even a 5-day work week.[3]

Age

Although issues of race and gender at the workplace are rarely openly discussed, age issues are at the forefront of the government's effort to increase labour force participation rates. Currently, the participation rate of older workers is comparable to Hong Kong, but lags behind Japan, Korea, Taiwan, and the United States (Ministry of Manpower 1999). Similar to other countries, the population in Singapore is ageing rapidly. In 1998, 14 per cent of the resident population were age 55 and above, but this figure is expected to increase to 27 per cent by the year 2020 (Ministry of Manpower 1999). Encouraging older individuals to remain in the workforce will ameliorate the economic and social burdens of old-age reliance, and reduce the dependency on foreign workers.

In Singapore, individuals 50 years and over often have great difficulty in obtaining and retaining a job. Indeed, in the manufacturing sector, some companies require job applicants over the age of 40 to undergo certain 'tests' for dexterity. Until recently, many job advertisements specified upper age limits. This can be attributed to the higher cost of hiring older workers, their lower levels of education compared with younger workers, and the perception among some employers that they are less productive and receptive to new ideas (Ministry of Manpower 1999). In an effort to avoid rampant age discrimination and ensure the labour participation of older workers, the government has implemented various measures.

First, the retirement age of 60 years (instituted in 1993) has been raised to 62, and will eventually be raised to 67 (however, contracts for academic positions still end at 55). Also, a non-statutory Code of Good Practice on Age Discrimination has been adapted to provide advice and educate employers and employees about age stereotyping. In 1996, a Back-To-Work program was launched to encourage housewives and retirees to return to the workforce. Companies are encouraged to employ older workers and to promote friendly human resource practices such as flexible hours and part-time work. Individuals are encouraged to enrol in training programs run by government bodies to upgrade their skills and prepare for the new knowledge-based economy. To motivate companies to retain and hire older workers, the employer's CPF[4] contribution for older workers has been reduced, and employers can cut the compensation package of employees aged 60 and above by up to 10 per cent. This may be in the form of reduced wages or it could be from fringe benefits, annual leave, or medical leave. Cuts would have to be negotiated by employers and unions.

As with gender and race discrimination, the government has largely relied on a program of education and enlightenment rather than legislation to end age discrimination. Numerous articles have been published in the *Straits Times* recently about the potential contributions of older workers. Examples are given of organisations that have successfully employed the elderly, such as McDonald's, Walmarts, and 3Com Technologies. Articles also publicise the government's proposed Silver Manpower centres. These centres will be located in housing estates and will function as one-step training, counselling, and job placement centres.

Despite all that the government has done, attitudes are hard to change. The government campaign has been geared to protect persons 55 years and older. However, prior to April 1999 and the job advertisement situation described previously, the cut-off age for many positions was posted at 30. Perhaps even to a greater extent than in the United States, Singapore has a culture that promotes youth.

Ethnicity

The last communal riots in Singapore occurred in the 1960s. In July/August 1964, and again in September of that year, Chinese and Malays fought in the streets. Twenty-two people were killed and 481 were injured. In May 1969, there was an escalation of tension and some violence in Singapore as a spillover of the Malaysian riots of 13 May. However, today, Singapore is often considered as a fine example of a society where different ethnic groups live together peacefully. Siddique has argued that while the CMIO (Chinese, Malay, Indian, Other) model of multiracialism has caused certain internal contradictions and tensions within each of the constituent ethnic groups, given the complexity of Singaporean society, the government chose the only model which could have ensured such a lengthy period of stability. She feels that 'multiracialism' as a concept acknowledges social heterogeneity and also implies that the 'races' are intrinsically equal (Siddique 1989).

However, the issue of ethnic relations in Singapore is quite complex. On the one hand, credit for the harmonious ethnic relations that have existed thus far must go to the government's espousal of the ideology of multiracialism — the accordance of equal status to the cultures and ethnic identities of the various 'races'. On the other hand, a multiracial ideology serves to define such a population as divided into a particular array of 'races'. As Benjamin puts it, 'the constant reiteration of the Chinese-Malay-Indian-Eurasian categorisation in national censuses, in the reports of government departments concerned with social policy, and the schools put considerable pressure on people to see themselves as ethnically defined' (Benjamin 1976: 121). A consequence, according to Ong, was that 'one could not deal with individuals without due regard for their communal attributes . . . As a result, other communities were taken as aggregates, and the assumption was that all individuals were cast in the same mould and had the same predispositions to act' (Ong 1989: 932). PuruShotam suggests that although race in contemporary Singapore is anchored in the morality of equality, as promised by the model of meritocratic multiracialism, the inherited colonial logic of divide-and-rule still exists. There is a contradiction between the practice of a multiracial policy and the claim to be a meritocratic society, given that race as discourse is principally founded on judgemental differentiation (PuruShotam 1998b).

To ameliorate the problems of the poor, the government has supported the creation of ethnically based self-help groups. In 1981, the Majlis Pendidikan Anak-Anak Islam/Council on Education for Malay (Muslim) children, or Mendaki as it is better known, was formed. Then in 1991, the Singapore Indian Development Association, or Sinda, was created, followed in 1992 by the establishment of the Chinese Development Assistance Council, CDAC. The funding for these organisations comes from a small sum of money deducted from the compulsory monthly social security savings of every working person. The funds are used to conduct remedial classes for

children, or upgrade the skills of adults of needy families. Although there has been some controversy regarding this policy, Senior Minister Lee Kuan Yew believes that this is the best approach for Singapore:

> When a Malay leader goes down to a Malay parent and says, 'Look, you've got to do something about your child's mathematics ... we're running these evening classes so that you can catch up', I think the response will be different if a Chinese community leader were to do that. There would be 'automatic bristling' and the Malay parent would say, 'Why, do you think I am that weak?' Because the realities are such, we have found that these community-based self-help organizations work best because the motivation is there, the empathy is there, the trust is there (Ng & Lim 1999).

The government discourages one racial group from comparing itself to another racial group, or the disadvantaged from comparing themselves to the advantaged, because this breeds conflict and unrest. The community based self-help organisations encourage each group to look within themselves and strive for improvement over time. PuruShotam has pointed out, however, that the government is not unaware that the critique of racially based self-help groups is compounded by 'suspicions and friction', especially considering the enormous potential of self-help that the Chinese could render themselves, vis-à-vis the Malays and the Indians (PuruShotam 1998b).

In a 1998 paper, PuruShotam argues that the government's emphasis on multiculturalism in almost every organised national event may simply be reinforcing stereotypes and delineating differences that no longer exist in the everyday life of most Singaporeans. PuruShotam describes a pictorial depiction that was highlighted during the 1994 National Day Parade:

> The Chinese are represented in yellow-ochre skin tones, with just a touch of pink that gives them a peasant rosiness. The man will be dressed in trousers and a shirt, but the woman will be clothed in a cheongsam; her children have some varying items that are commonly identified as Chinese; such as guazi'mao. The Malays are always warmly browned, and dressed up in appropriate clothes, viz. in baju kurong, with kain samping around the waist and songkok on the heads of the males, and slendang hanging down one shoulder of the females. The Indians are given a richer, darker brown — closer to milk chocolate; the woman invariably in a sari and a bindhi between her eyebrows; the man, quite often, in a Sikh turban; the girl child in a long silk skirt and the boy child in salwaar khameez. 'Others' are one or two shades pinker than the Chinese, and in what would be described, in everyday language as formal Western dress (PuruShotam 1998a: 52).

PuruShotam argues that this contrasts sharply with what a visitor could be expected to see on the streets of Singapore today:

> ... women and children in Singapore are attired in the latest fashions of Hong Kong garment factories, produced for the American and European markets. Most Indians in Singapore are not turbaned, unless they are Sikh practitioners; and while many women still hang a cheongsam, sari, sarong kebaya or two in their wardrobe and also actually wear them on a daily basis, any casual observer would notice at once that for most women daily dress in not a marker of their ethnicities (PuruShotam 1998b: 52).

In everyday life, the cultural boundaries are more fluid, and societal traditions are often a hybrid of customs from different religious or ethnic groups. This hybrid is signified by the local term 'rojak', which refers to a mixture of disparate elements (Chua 1998). Rojak is a popular Singaporean dish, the Chinese version of which includes:

> ... deep-fried dried bean curd, slices of raw pineapple, turnip and cucumber, a handful of cooked local vegetables ... bean sprouts, a pinch of banana flower ... all tossed thoroughly with a dressing made of dense, strong smelling shrimp paste, tamarind sauce, and heaped spoons of crushed peanuts, sugar and chili (Chua 1998: 187–8).

Ethnicity in the workplace, however, is less of an issue of concern and discussion. Singapore views itself as a meritocracy, and any economic or occupational segregation is seen as a problem of inadequate education rather than discrimination. Therefore, the emphasis has been on ensuring that all citizens, regardless of their backgrounds, have the opportunity to acquire the skills necessary to find employment in a knowledge-based economy. There are, however, anecdotal accounts of discrimination along ethnic lines in hiring practices. An executive search firm, for example, revealed that they were instructed by their corporate client not to consider Indian candidates in their search. Non-Chinese job seekers tell of how they would be informed that they were unsuitable for a position because they did not 'speak Mandarin' even though it did not appear that that was a requirement of the post.

At the workplace there is general consensus that social relations among the different ethnic groups are convivial and relaxed. Chinese, Malays and Indians help each other out at work, intermingle socially in the workplace, share jokes, trade office gossip, and may be familiar with the details of each other's life circumstances. They may or may not lunch together, however, as the dietary considerations of say, Malays, who are Muslims, and may only eat at 'halal' (food prepared according to Islamic practices) outlets, may preclude them from eating with Chinese colleagues. Whatever the stereotypes that each ethnic group may have of the others (and these stereotypes certainly do exist, and may occasionally be encountered in everyday life) ethnic consciousness, when it occurs in the workplace, is subtle rather than overt (see Chung 1989). People are more likely to be prejudiced towards people they have little interaction with, than those they see on a regular basis at the workplace.

Disability

No laws in Singapore expressly protect the disabled against discrimination. Anecdotal evidence suggests that the disabled may have a difficult time finding employment. Many employers in Singapore worry that they lack the expertise to handle a handicapped person (*Straits Times* 25 April 1999). Also, the majority of buildings in Singapore are not well equipped to accommodate the disabled. (One of the authors of this chapter discovered this when she broke her foot and needed to get around on crutches for a few weeks.) Efforts are being made, however, to change the situation. In 1998 the National Council of Social Service commissioned a survey to investigate the employment problems of the handicapped, and increase their chances of finding a job. Bizlink, a job placement service for the disabled, offers a centralised information and referral service. Again, major efforts to combat discrimination are being made through education, rather than legislation.

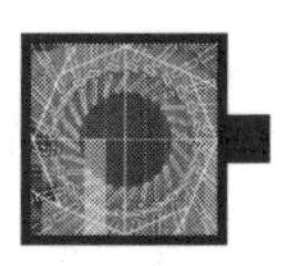

Managing diversity in the Singapore workplace

Given the previous discussion, this section presents some aspects of culture that an expatriate manager might find 'different' in the Singapore workplace. Much of this information is based on interviews conducted with expatriates currently living and working in Singapore. The points raised here should not be taken as 'general truths' applicable to all workplaces in Singapore. Each workplace is different, and as discussed previously, Singaporeans themselves come from many different ethnic backgrounds, and have various religious affiliations. Singaporeans may also differ in terms of stage of life, biographical experiences, and family and educational backgrounds. The following discussion may be applicable to some Singaporeans in some workplaces, but certainly not to all Singaporeans in all workplaces.

Sense of self and space

The Singaporean's sense of space is probably not too different from that of Americans. Both Americans and Singaporeans feel comfortable standing about an arm's length from one another when engaging in a conversation. This distance will be more strictly observed in cross-gender interactions. A closer distance is reserved for contact with family members or good friends. The handshake is the common greeting in Singapore. Among friends, and particularly among the more 'westernised' younger women, the typical greeting might be a hug and the ritual kiss on each cheek.

These physical aspects of the Singaporeans' respect for an individual's sense of self and space is complemented by a degree of formality, particularly in newer relationships. New acquaintances, bosses, and older individuals are commonly addressed as Mr, Mrs, Ms and other titles, as a sign of respect. First names are generally not used, unless one has been given permission to do so by the individual being addressed. The expatriate manager also needs to keep in mind that for the Chinese, the family name is listed first. For Malays, the given names are placed first, followed by the father's name — thus, Suriani bte Ismail tells us that the person's first name is Suriani, and she is the daughter of (binte) Ismail, while her brother could be Ahmad bin Ismail — 'bin' meaning 'son of'.

Among Indians, traditionally, a person's name would comprise a given name, the name of his/her lineage and the father's name, although with emigration, differences have cropped up over time. Still, a general practice is that the given name comes first, followed by just the father's name in some cases, or the lineage name and the father's name (or the order of this may be reversed) together, in other cases. For Singaporeans with Western first names, the surname may come after the Western name, even if they are Chinese.

Language differences and styles of communication

While English is spoken widely in Singapore, and prevalent in the workplace, the expatriate manager is likely to encounter several different accents (including Australian, American, British and Singaporean). Pronunciations, language use, and tonal inflections may take some getting used to. A current concern with language-use in the republic is the prevalence of Singlish, an ubiquitous local patois that combines English with words or phrases from Malay and Chinese dialects, in vivid, but non-grammatical ways. Although Singlish has been around for a long time, it has only

recently been identified as contributing to lowering English standards. Popular television characters who had been speaking Singlish in a local sitcom have been 'rehabilitated' by the show's producers, and will be speaking grammatically correct English in future. At the same time, the government has instituted a 'Speak English' campaign (*Straits Times* 2000).

The expatriates should also recognise that the Singaporeans with whom they are working might experience difficulties understanding their accents. One of the expatriate interviewees commented that she found some of her colleagues a little aloof in the beginning as they often did not speak (to her) unless spoken to. When the interviewer suggested that this could be because the Singaporeans may have difficulty understanding some of her spoken English, and do not want to risk the embarrassment of miscomprehension by initiating conversations, the interviewee conceded that this was a possibility which had not occurred to her. Some simple strategies to improve communication include becoming more aware of one's own communication style, to speak slowly if one senses incomprehension or confusion, to practise active listening skills, and to paraphrase if necessary.

In recent years, the 'Speak Mandarin' campaign has led to the prevalence of Mandarin as a common spoken language among those of Chinese ancestry. Thus, in the workplace, Mandarin speakers may sometimes switch from speaking English to Mandarin, even when non-Mandarin speakers may be around. Speakers may not be conscious of this as an exclusionary practice, and there may indeed be no intent to exclude, but non-Mandarin speakers, including expatriates, may find this disconcerting.

Expatriates have also commented on how the formal communication styles of some Singaporean colleagues at times seem abrupt and task-oriented, devoid of such polite expressions as 'please' and 'thank you'. A Thai expatriate said that when she first came to Singapore, it took her some time to get used to the lack of eye contact and the unsmiling countenance of Singaporeans. She felt as if people had 'no time' to be pleasant or sociable. This phenomenon has been noted by Singaporeans themselves, and there have been government campaigns to promote 'courtesy' and urge Singaporeans to be more polite, gracious, and courteous in their interactions with others. All the interviewees did note, however, that with time and more frequent interaction, they did find their colleagues to be friendly and helpful. Singaporeans, however, tend to be more formal and less outgoing than Americans, and may not divulge personal information to people they do not know well. They may also appear to be more hierarchical.

Singaporeans may also be less direct than Westerners, and may communicate their opposition to a proposal in a roundabout way. Instead of saying 'no' a Singaporean may indicate that he/she will 'think about it', or 'get back to you'. A fellow Singaporean will know that he/she is denying a request, but an American might think that the issue is still being considered. There can be many different ways of expressing a refusal or turning down a request both verbally and non-verbally. A Singaporean may avoid a direct 'no' to prevent causing loss of face and therefore embarrassment, to the other party.

Dress and appearance

In recent years, the term 'dressing for success' has gathered some currency in the Singapore workplace, particularly with reference to women, depending on their level and the industry in which they work. Executive women generally wear skirt suits,

stockings and high-heels, but for men the dress is generally less formal, given the hot and humid climate. A formal suit is usually only worn for important functions and meetings. For men in senior executive positions in multinational firms and professions such as law, banking, and commerce, the long-sleeved shirt and the tie are de rigueur. Some companies may still have dress codes that forbid women from wearing pants to work, but this is changing. Staff in more junior positions and in what are considered 'the arts' or 'creative' fields may dress in a more relaxed and casual fashion. Causal dressing such as jeans and tee shirts may be allowed in some companies on Saturdays. As for headdress, Muslim women may be seen wearing the 'tudong' (which covers their hair and ears) with their traditional Malay costumes, while Sikh males may wear a turban. More 'exotic' hairstyles like dreadlocks, ponytails on men and mohawks are likely to raise eyebrows in the more mainstream industries, and are seldom seen on the streets.

Time consciousness

Wedding dinners in Singapore usually start about one to one and a half hours later than originally designated because most of the guests arrive late! Notions of time can be somewhat stretched, when applied to social occasions, events, or appointments. Fortunately, however, this elastic sense of time does not apply to the workplace. Workers generally get to work on time, superiors frown on tardiness, and meetings start on time, particularly when they are chaired or attended by superior officers and bosses (meetings of officers of equal rank, however, may sometimes be subject to some delay). Deadlines for work are usually taken seriously and met.

Values and norms

The topic of values and norms is extremely complex, but a book chapter on diversity in Singapore would hardly be complete without a discussion of 'Asian values'. The question of whether there are specific Asian values and what these values might be has been hotly debated during the past decade. There has been continuing discourse in Singapore, juxtaposing a reinvented 'Asian' culture and values with a homogenised 'Western' culture. The former, which is seen as 'good' and 'wholesome', is depicted as a bulwark against the 'decadence' of the latter. And yet, it has been pointed out, values such as hard work, the worth of education, pragmatism, self-discipline, and familial orientation, can all be translated into Western values, either present, or lost, but recoverable (Chua 1995). Thus it would be fair to say that while these are values that many Singaporeans subscribe to, they are not uniquely Asian!

Much has also been made of the Singaporean's aspiration to the five Cs — cash, credit card, car, club (membership in a private club) and condominium. While it would be ridiculous to say that all Singaporeans embrace the five Cs, nonetheless, for some who live in this dense metropolis, the 'good things in life' are also the material things and the sense of security that money can buy. Chua notes examples of ostentatious consumption in terms of fashion, related consumer products, and particularly housing (i.e. private housing as opposed to public housing where the majority of the population dwells) at the expense of other aspects of daily life (Chua 1999). It would be fair to say that there is a culture of consumption (albeit one that is class-differentiated). As one interviewee succinctly expressed herself, she found her Singaporean colleagues 'work-oriented and money-oriented' with a great deal of social talk focusing on shares and investment.

The ideology of meritocracy has served Singapore well. The belief that any individual, regardless of socio-economic background, can get to where he/she wants, on the basis of sheer merit/capability has fostered a competitive spirit, often referred to in the local context as 'kiasuism' ('kiasu' is a word from the Hokkien dialect meaning 'scared to lose'). Driven by kiasuism, therefore, Singaporeans makes sure that they are at the head of a queue for tickets for a concert, for 'free gifts' from department stores, and such things as for places for their children in good schools.

In 1991, Parliament adopted a set of 'shared values' for the purpose of enabling its citizenry 'to evolve and anchor a Singaporean identity, incorporating the relevant parts of our varied cultural heritage, and the attitudes and values which have helped us to survive and succeed as a nation' (White Paper on Shared Values 1991: 1).

These values were:

1. Nation before community and society above self.
2. Family as the basic unit of society.
3. Community support and respect for the individual.
4. Consensus, not conflict.
5. Racial and religious harmony.

The Shared Values have institutional and ideological significance (but do not possess any legal or Constitutional power (as, say, in the case of Indonesia's national ideology, the Pancasila). The extent to which Singaporeans, as an entity, subscribe to this set of shared values is unknown. There is, for example, a contradiction between the call to place 'society above self' and the ideology of meritocracy, which we discussed earlier on. More recently, Prime Minister Goh Chok Tong, in spelling out his vision for Singapore in the twenty-first century, pointed to the need to develop 'heartware' — namely meeting the spiritual, emotional, intellectual, cultural and social needs of Singaporeans.

In terms of Hofstede's cultural dimensions, Singapore has been identified as high in collectivism, high on power distance, low on uncertainty avoidance, and medium on masculinity. We should point out, however, that it has been some two decades since Hofstede's study was conducted, and cultures, as we know, do not remain static and unchanging. Therefore, the extent to which these rankings still hold true for Singapore needs to be validated.

While Singaporeans tend to be less individualistic than Americans, British or Australians, they are probably more individualistic than people in other South-east Asian cultures. Singaporean managers who have worked in Malaysia, for example, have commented on their surprise at having to deal with staff more as members of groups than as individuals, something they were less accustomed to in the Singapore context. It is also possible that Singaporeans have become more individualistic in the past two decades in response to the fast-paced challenges of rapid economic growth. Furthermore, the need for achievement as tied to the ideology of meritocracy may also have shifted Singaporeans away from a more collectivist mentality.

According to our observations and experience we concur that Singapore is still high in power distance. Managers are expected to be very familiar with the nature of subordinates' work, and to provide a sense of direction with regard to both desired outcomes of work and methods to carry out tasks. This could be a challenge for managers who come from small power-distance countries and prefer a more consultative and participative style. Some Singaporean employees may be resistant to participating in decision-making, and may perceive that a participative manager is indecisive or lacks technical expertise. Managers are hired to tell other people what

to do and are expected to act the part — in terms of how they dress, carry themselves, and interact with others. This depends, however, on the organisational culture, the nature of the industry, and the hierarchical level of the employee.

From our experience and observation, we would not rank Singapore particularly low on uncertainty avoidance. Singaporeans tend to like order and structure, and are less disposed to deviate from precedent and rules than are many Westerners. Innovation and change will be accepted, however, when they are imposed from higher up the organisational ladder. The government's current emphasis on creativity and innovation may result in a population that is becoming decreasingly risk averse over time.

Singapore ranks medium on masculinity because it is more of a 'doing' culture — that is, assertive, somewhat aggressive, materialistic and achievement-oriented, at least in the workplace. At the same time, the increased participation of women in the workforce in the past four decades has meant that the distinctions of traditional gender roles have become blurred. While we would argue that Singapore has some way to go in achieving true gender equality, women in the workplace are, in the main, treated in an appropriately professional manner, so the female expatriate manager should not encounter any problems.

Religious beliefs

An English expatriate commented that she found religion to be more important in the Singapore workplace than in her own country. In any organisation in Singapore it is common to encounter Christians, Buddhists, Muslims and Hindus. In general, people are tolerant of, and sensitive to, each other's religious beliefs. Thus, in one office, the Chinese staff do not use the microwave in the pantry, because the Muslim staff use it to heat up their meals, and Chinese food may contain pork or lard which is taboo for Muslims. Generally Singaporeans are also sensitive to the fact that during Ramadan (the ninth month of the Islamic calendar when followers are enjoined to fast from dawn till sunset) Muslims fast on a daily basis, and so apart from not offering food or snacks to Muslim colleagues, or holding office lunches during that period, they may try to avoid assigning demanding tasks to Muslims for this period. In some offices, where there may be more Muslim staff, a room may be set aside for Muslims to pray, and Muslims may take certain prayer breaks during the workday. But management policy on this can vary. Some companies in the manufacturing sector, for example, do not allow such prayer breaks, as this would disrupt the production flow.

Conclusions

A common and popular image of Singapore is that it is a highly regimented society, with penalties for such innocuous behaviour as littering and gum chewing. Readers may also have heard of the widely publicised case of the American teenager Michael Fay, who was arrested for vandalism, and then caned for his offence. Such images are merely 'snapshots', representing a particular aspect of Singapore at a given point. Unfortunately, people often form stereotypes from these images, with little knowledge of the context of the situation. What we have done in this paper is to approach culture and society in Singapore in a more holistic manner, with all its nuances and complexities.

Anyone managing in Singapore must be attuned to its cultural complexity. The values, rules and norms may vary considerably, depending not only on the demographic make-up of the labour force, but also the culture of each organisation and the organisation's home country. The multinational corporations in Singapore originate from many different countries, for example, Germany, Japan, the United States, and the Netherlands. Each of these entities has profoundly different ways of doing business and this will have an impact on everyday practices and behaviour, Singapore's culture notwithstanding.

Some of the general lessons about effective cross-cultural management apply here — first, the need to be aware of one's cultural baggage, realising when one is being ethnocentric (judging people of other cultures according to the standards of one's own), and second, the need to rid oneself of parochialism and ignorance by genuinely wanting to learn about the host culture. The best advice we can give to any expatriate manager in Singapore is to keep your eyes and ears open, and refrain from making judgements and conclusions too rapidly. Perhaps one of the biggest mistakes an expatriate can make is to assume that Singapore is more 'Western' than 'Asian'. While the country may certainly appear to be 'Westernised' on the surface, considerable differences do exist behind the facade, and it takes time and effort to uncover and understand these differences.

References

Chan, J. 2000. 'The Status of Women in a Patriarchal State: The Case of Singapore'. In Edwards, L & Roces, M. (Eds). *Women in Asia: Tradition, Modernity and Globalization*. Allen and Unwin.

Chin K. W. 1999. 'Singapore: Towards Developed Country Status — The Security Dimension'. In Low, L. (Ed.). *Singapore: Towards a Developed Status*. Singapore: Oxford University Press/ Centre for Advanced Studies.

Benjamin, G. 1976. 'The Cultural Logic of Singapore's "Multiracialism"'. In Hassan, R. (Ed.). *Singapore: Society in Transition*. Kuala Lumpur: Oxford University Press.

Chua, B. H. 1995. *Communitarian Ideology and Democracy in Singapore*. London: Routledge.

Chua, B. H. 1998. 'Culture, Multiracialism, and National Identity'. In Chen, K. H. (Ed.). *Trajectories: Inter-asia Cultural Studies*. London: Routledge.

Chua, B. H. 1999. 'The Attendant Consumer Society of a Developed Singapore'. In Low, L. (Ed.). *Singapore: Towards a Developed Status*. Singapore: Oxford University Press/Centre for Advanced Studies.

Chung, Y. K. 1989. 'Gender, Work and Ethnicity: An Ethnography of Female Factory Workers in Singapore'. Unpublished PhD thesis. Department of Sociology, National University of Singapore.

Chung, Y. K. 1994. 'Conflict and Compliance: Workplace Politics of a Disk-drive Factory in Singapore'. In Belanger, J., Edwards, P. K. & Haiven, L. (Eds). *Workplace Industrial Relations and the Global Challenge*. New York: ILR Press.

Chung, Y. K. 1995. 'Trade Unions Over 50 Years'. *NTUC News Weekly,* 17 Nov: 10–20.

Chung, Y. K. 1999. 'It's More Than Nine to Five'. Paper presented at the forum Take Back the Future: Blueprint for Action for Women Now, hosted by The Working Committee for Civil Society, Singapore, 28 August.

Craig, J. M. 1996. *Culture Shock, Singapore*. Oregon: Graphic Arts Center Publishing Company.

Dolven, B. 2000. 'Go On, Take a Risk'. *Far Eastern Economic Review.* Hong Kong, 4 May: 16–18.

Eusofe, O. H. 1995. 'Malay Participation in the Labour Market: Challenges and Opportunities'. Department of Malay Studies, National University of Singapore.

Key Labour Statistics. 1999. Singapore.

Key Manpower Statistics. April 2000. Singapore.

Khalik, S. 1999. 'Start Planning for Older Workforce'. *Strait Times*. Singapore: 1 September.

Koh, L. 1999. 'Workers Get Better with Age'. *Strait Times*. Singapore: 18 September.

Lee, J., Campbell, K., & Chia, A. 1999. *The Three Paradoxes: Working Women in Singapore*. Singapore: Association of Women for Action and Research.

Manpower News. 1999. 'Tripartite Partners Launch Guidelines on Non-discriminatory Job Advertisements'. Singapore.

Ng, I. & Lim, L. 1999. 'Reality is Race Bonds Exist: SM'. *Strait Times*. Singapore: 19 September.

Ong, J. H. 1989. 'Community Security'. In Sandhu, K. S. & Wheatley, P. (Eds). *Management of Success: The Moulding of Singapore*. Singapore: Institute of Southeast Asian Studies (ISEAS).

Osman, A. 1999. 'Better with Age'. *Strait Times*. Singapore: 16 August.

PuruShotam, N. 1989. 'Language and Linguistic Policies'. In Sandhu, K. S. & Wheatley, P. (Eds). *Management of Success: The Moulding of Singapore*. Singapore: Institute of Southeast Asian Studies (ISEAS).

PuruShotam, N. 1998a. 'Disciplining Difference: Race in Singapore'. In Kahn, J. (Ed.). *Southeast Asian Identities: Culture and the Politics of Representation in Indonesia, Malaysia, Singapore and Thailand*. New York: St. Martin's Press.

PuruShotam, N. 1998b. *Negotiating Language, Constructing Race: Disciplining Difference in Singapore*. Berlin: Mouton de Gruyter.

PuruShotam, N. 1999. 'It's Not a "Woman" Problem'. Paper presented at the forum Take Back the Future: Blueprint for Action for Women Now, hosted by The Working Committee for Civil Society, Singapore, 28 August.

PuruShotam, N. & Chung Y. K. 1992. 'Double Trouble: The Work of Women Wage Earners in Singapore'. Paper presented for Industrialisation and Women's Health: A Regional Workshop for the ASEAN Countries, Singapore, 22–25 April.

Ministry of Manpower. 2000. 'Report on Discriminatory Job Advertisements'. Singapore, April.

Rodan, G. 1989. *The Political Economy of Singapore's Industrialisation*. London: Macmillan.

Scarborough, J. 1998. *The Origins of Cultural Differences and Their Impact on Management*. Connecticut: Quorum Books.

Siddique S. 1989. 'Singaporean Identity'. In Sandhu, K. S. & Wheatley, P. (Eds). *Management of Success: The Moulding of Singapore*. Singapore: Institute of Southeast Asian Studies (ISEAS).

Singapore Census of Population. 2000. *A Quick Count*. Singapore.

Singapore Department of Statistics. 1998. 'Social Progress of Singaporean Women: A Statistical Assessment'.

Singapore Ministry of Manpower. 1998. 'Report on the Labour Force Survey of Singapore'. Manpower Research and Statistics Department.

Singapore Ministry of Labour. 1997. 'Women Returning to Work'. Singapore: Research and Statistics Department.

Singapore Ministry of Manpower. 1999. *Annual Report*. Singapore.

Singapore Ministry of Manpower. 1999. 'Older Workers'. Singapore: Manpower Research and Statistics Department.

Straight Times. 2000. 31 March.

Straight Times. 1999a. 17 August.

Straight Times. 1999b. 25 April.

Tan, A. 1999. 'Change Attitudes Towards Hiring Older Workers, Employers Urged'. *Business Times*. Singapore: 16 August.

Tan, C. H. 1995. *Labour Management Relations in Singapore*. New York: Prentice Hall.

Tan, C. H. 1999. *Employment Relations in Singapore: Concepts and Perspective*. Singapore: Prentice-Hall.

Tham, S. C. 1996. 'Cultural Forces and Counter Forces in Contemporary Singapore'. Unpublished. Department of Malay Studies, National University of Singapore.

White Paper on Shared Values. 1991. Singapore.

Yuen, E. 1992. 'Perceptions of External Barriers and the Career Success of Female Managers in Singapore. *The Journal of Social Psychology* 132(5): 661–74.

End notes

1. For further details refer to the Ministry of Manpower website.
2. Over 85 per cent of Singapore's population lives in subsidised government housing. These are high-rise apartment buildings called 'housing estates'.
3. All government employees and many private employers have a $5^1/_2$ day work week. In 1999 employees worked an average of 42.7 hours a week.
4. The Central Provident Fund (CPF) was set up in 1955 to provide financial security for workers upon retirement or when they are no longer able to work. It has evolved into a comprehensive social security plan.

Chapter 12

Taiwan

Cheng Soo-May

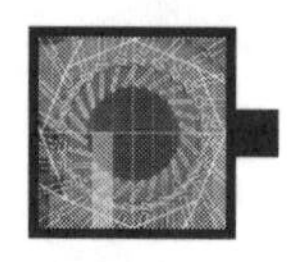

Introduction

This chapter discusses several labour-related issues confronting Taiwan as it undergoes political transition and economic restructuring. Its political liberalisation culminating in the recent election of the first non-Kuomintang president, and the preparation of the economy for entry into the World Trade Organisation (WTO), both present particular challenges for Taiwan to balance the diverse interests of local and foreign workers, older workers, and female workers.

As one of Asia's 'Little Dragon' economies (others being Singapore, Hong Kong and South Korea), Taiwan enjoyed international acclaim for its economic 'miracle' until the Asian economic turmoil of 1997 which put an end to the double-digit growth rates of these economies during the past decade. Fortunately for Taiwan, it has emerged from the crisis relatively unscathed, and is carefully balancing three sets of paradoxes: unemployment versus labour shortage, information technology development versus the needs of older workers, and the satisfaction of changing expectations of women versus the preservation of family values. Before these issues are considered, a review of Taiwan's historical and contemporary scenarios leading to these paradoxes follows.

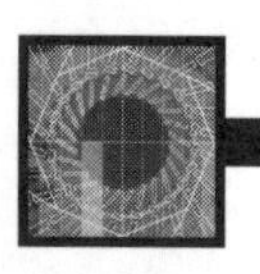

Historical background

Originally an island province off the coast of mainland China, Taiwan was ceded to Japan at the end of the Sino–Japanese War of 1894–95. Its economy was first orientated to supporting the Japanese war effort, as a consequence of which the Taiwanese–Japanese relationship has remained cordial until the present day. After World War II, Taiwan was given back to China, at a time when the nationalist Kuomintang party and the communists were at civil war on the mainland. In 1949, Taiwan was founded as the Republic of China (ROC) on Taiwan when the nationalists under General Chiang Kai-shek retreated there after the communists declared the People's Republic of China (PRC) on the mainland. When the Korean War broke out in 1950, Taiwan received American aid of over US$1.5 billion to develop its agricultural sector to support America's war effort. This early relationship with the United States put Taiwan on the road to economic and political development that has turned it into one of the world's most formidable economies; today it is the thirteenth-largest trading nation and third-largest producer of personal computers and accessories. In getting to where it is today, Taiwan has moved through a number of phases: import-substitution (1950–62); export orientation (1962–80); original equipment manufacturing (OEM), when it established its reputation as a manufacturing centre for well-known international companies; and original design manufacturing (ODM), when it progressed to developing its own designs and products for the world market (1980–95). Today, according to a government blueprint, Taiwan is being developed into an Asia–Pacific Regional Operations Centre (APROC) servicing the needs of multinationals with interests in the large markets of the PRC and South-east Asia (Maguire 1999). Its location on the major trading routes to Japan, China and Korea has aided its development.

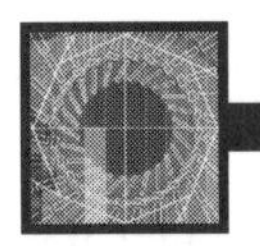

Contemporary Taiwan

Population and labour force

The last influx of mainland Han–Chinese people to Taiwan in 1949 immediately swelled the population of about one million indigenous aborigines and 500 000 earlier Chinese Hakka and Fukienese migrants on the island to 7.39 million (Government Information Office 1999a: 23). By 1998, the aboriginal population numbered just over 390 000. They may be classified into nine major ethnicities: Atayal, Saisiyat, Bunun, Tsou, Paiwan, Rukai, Puyuma, Ami and Yami. Their integration into mainstream Han lifestyle and modernisation meant a diminishing of the aboriginal languages and lifestyles (*Brief Introduction to ROC* 1999: 10–11).

Today, Taiwan's population has surpassed 22 million, 60 per cent of which is concentrated in the four metropolises of Taipei, Kaoshiung, Taichung and Tainan. It is also a greying population; in 1998, the number of people over 65 years of age exceeded eight per cent of the population, and is expected to rise (*Brief Introduction to ROC* 1999: 10–11). The gender ratio in 1997 was 105 boys to every 100 girls, reflecting the traditional preference among Asian parents for boys over girls to carry the family name (Government Information Office 1999a: 24). Over 91 per cent of the population is literate, as primary education is provided free by the government for nine years, extendable to 12 years. Twenty-six per cent of the population is in school or university. Thirty-four per cent of secondary school students go on to attend university. As an example of the serious pursuit of education in this Confucian society, in 1989 over 25 000 students from ROC were studying in universities in the United States. This resulted in an extremely well-educated labour force that experienced underemployment, that is, people working in jobs for which they are over-qualified (Griffin 1989: 112).

National consciousness

'New Taiwanese' is the term popularly used by Taiwan people to identify themselves, as distinct from the traditional 'Mainlanders' and 'Taiwan-born'. The indigenous people's (*yuan chu min*) ancestry pre-dates modern Taiwan, while the Hakka and Fukienese migrants had settled there from southern China 100 years prior to Chiang Kai-shek's arrival. But the Mainlanders formed the new government-in-exile, and from then on instituted language and cultural policies to promote the Han–Chinese culture in anticipation of eventually returning to the Mainland. Half a century later, the tide has turned. A whole generation of Taiwanese born on the island nation, assured of their own identity, no longer looked towards reunification with the Mainland. Resistance to previous government policies that marginalised non-Mandarin languages has grown. The election of former president Lee Teng-hui, and recently of President Chen Shui-bian, both Taiwan-born, is evidence of this change of heart. The post-Chiang governments and other institutions are consciously changing policies to promote the New Taiwan consciousness (GIO 1999a).

Signs of this new consciousness and the blurring of ethnic divisions may be found in several developments:

- Taiwanese or Southern Min language is now spoken widely alongside Mandarin, and by government officials hoping to get closer to the citizenry. Hakka and aboriginal languages are now taught in elementary schools.

- Military personnel and their dependants previously housed in segregated villages are now integrated into areas with Taiwanese-speaking residents, in a move to reduce the potential for conflict between the pro-Mandarin military and local communities.
- The identification card carried by all ROC citizens living in Taiwan no longer has a blank stating the cardholder's 'native place', meaning the birthplace of his/her father, previously a criterion distinguishing Mainlanders from locals. In its place is a space for the cardholder's own place of birth, implying a de-emphasis of ties to the Mainland and a closer linking of personal identity with Taiwan.
- Some companies have practised reverse discrimination by hiring only people born in Taiwan, or who speak Taiwanese, though these policies are unofficial and not readily admitted to (GIO 1999a).

If Taiwanese were to be described in behavioural terms, they would be known for a great propensity to save money, primarily for a 'rainy day', and secondarily for their children's education. Such thriftiness and investment in their children's future are traits of the Confucian character that would typify a majority of the Taiwanese today. The high national savings rate explains to a large extent the country's economic resilience and wealth today. Other traits like capacity for hard work, flexibility and competitiveness have also produced a nation of workers and small business people who have turned the country into a leading newly industrialised economy (NIE) (Wu 1985: 114–30). Confucianism also explains the power of the family as the basis of the business structures in Taiwan. On the flipside of these Confucian leanings, however, is a tendency to subjugate women to their menfolk, relegating them to traditional roles of mother and homemaker.

Political scenario

The Taiwanese made history on 18 March 2000 by electing to the presidency the Democratic Progressive Party's (DPP) Chen Shui-bian, thus ending the Kuomintang's (KMT) half-century domination of the central government. While the last years of KMT rule under former president Lee Teng-hui were known more for social disintegration, corruption and underworld influence, there is no denying that it was also a period of economic growth and political liberalisation. Lee was the first Taiwan-born president, ascending from the vice-presidency upon the death of Chiang Ching-kuo, son of Chiang Kai-shek. Inspired by his predecessor's liberal ideals, and under increasing pressure from the opposing DPP, Lee initiated reforms including the lifting of emergency rule and widening of elections. He also oversaw the first efforts to assuage China's claims of sovereignty over Taiwan through cross-straits negotiations, by allowing Taiwanese to visit their relatives on the mainland, and by allowing — albeit gradually — Taiwan investments in China (Lu 2000: 1). Voter turnout at elections had consistently been around 70 per cent of eligible voters (higher than in the US) and political parties and other grassroots organisations have flourished (Government Information Office 1999a: 104). Chen's government now faces the daunting challenges of tense relations with Mainland China, economic opportunities and threats with Taiwan's imminent entry into the WTO, and the management of political liberalisation (Wu 1985: 41).

Internationalising the economy through WTO membership

Since 1971 when it lost its seat at the United Nations, Taiwan has endured diplomatic isolation internationally, but has persisted in being one of the world's leading newly industrialised economies (NIEs), returning an average of 8.63 per cent growth per year from 1952 through 1995 (Yu 2000: 19).

Beginning its modern history as an agricultural economy servicing the Korean War needs of the United States between 1952 and 1962, the economy has successfully shifted gears several times to accommodate external and internal environmental changes. Taiwan's industrial era started in 1962, moving steadily from light to heavy industry, and from labour- to capital-intensive industry. From 1981 through 1995, industrialisation was accompanied by the rapid growth of the service and trading sectors. During this period, the landmark year of 1987 saw the lifting of the Emergency Decree which had put Taiwan under martial law since its inception. This, on one hand, allowed the venting of pent-up frustration and grievances but, on the other hand, released much entrepreneurial energy, both of which worked to encourage the relocation of businesses away from Taiwan. It was also the year when civilian visits between Taiwan and the Chinese mainland were allowed, leading to growing private exchanges and business transactions culminating in a massive flow of Taiwanese investments into the Mainland. By 1996, it was estimated by the ROC Government that such investments had topped US$6 billion, though Beijing statistics put them closer to US$20 billion (Yu 2000: 17).

The financial economy that had taken shape in East Asia in the late 1990s was heartily embraced by Taiwan as it furthered the internationalisation of its economy. Along with its neighbours, it launched into futures and stocks trading, credit transactions, and electronic commerce via the Internet. Unhappily, increasing financial liberalisation and globalisation had locked the region into one interdependent economy so much so that when the financial crisis broke out in early July 1997, one country after another experienced sharp currency devaluation and near collapse of their stock markets. Luckily, the damage to Taiwan was relatively minor, signs of which included:

- a slowdown in economic growth from 6.8 per cent in 1997 to 4.8 per cent in 1998
- a drop in industrial production from 6.9 per cent to 4.4 per cent in the same period
- negative growth in foreign exports
- depreciation of 24.4 per cent of the New Taiwan (NT) Dollar against the US dollar
- a fall in the stock index of 16.4 per cent
- a rise in unemployment.

Taiwan was cushioned from the crisis by various structural conditions and fiscal measures. The country had no foreign debt and its SME-based (i.e. small to medium enterprises) economy was flexible and adaptable. Prudent and conservative financial management had led to the banking sector having only four per cent of bad loans compared with some of the Asian neighbours (e.g. 18 per cent for Thailand, 16 per cent for Indonesia, 15 per cent for Malaysia). Stabilising action taken by the government included using its large reserves for foreign exchange to stop the slide of the NT Dollar and the stock market, increasing high-tech capabilities, diversifying its portfolio of trading partners, and restructuring financial institutions (Yu 2000: 24–6; Wong 2000: 3–15).

Nevertheless, Taiwan is cautious about being a part of the global economy even as it stands on the brink of entry into the World Trade Organisation after successfully completing bilateral and multilateral negotiations in Seattle in December 1999. After eight years of lobbying, Taiwan will once again have a voice in the international community as a 'developed' nation WTO member. It is cognisant of having to bear more responsibilities and obligations, including adopting higher labour standards in pay and benefits, health and safety, and employment equity (Chen 2000: 44). It will thus have to manage effectively the increasing diversity of interests in the labour force, created by the presence of foreign workers, the changing age composition of the workforce, and the increasing labour participation of women. These issues are discussed below in terms of several socio-economic paradoxes.

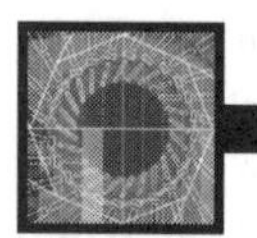

Paradox 1: Unemployment versus labour shortage: The foreign labour issue

Unemployment had gone up to 2.92 per cent in 1999, which compares favourably with Singapore's 3.5 per cent, Japan's 4.7 per cent, South Korea's 6.3 per cent (Chiu 2000a: 3). Yet it is a cause for concern because it had never risen above the two per cent mark prior to 1995 (Chiu 2000b: 3). Moreover, the increasing presence of foreign workers in various sectors of the economy has given rise to protests about inadequate government action to address the unemployment problem. Therein lies a paradox which requires careful human resource management.

Taiwan's economic prosperity and ensuing high wages have cost the nation its competitive advantage as a labour-intensive manufacturing economy. The 'nouveau riche' mentality of an affluent population also threatened to erode the work ethic, with young people preferring white-collar jobs in comfortable surroundings to the '3-D' (dirty, difficult and dangerous) jobs. Such jobs would typically be in textile dyeing, basic metal casting, metal processing, mechanical and electrical maintenance, and machine operation.

Since the mid-seventies, many foreign workers have arrived on tourist visas from Thailand, Malaysia and the Philippines, and have overstayed to work illegally, but were tolerated by authorities (Griffin 1989: 112). In the eighties, the first foreign workers were brought in for the construction industry to supplement local labour. In 1989, needing to overcome a shortage of labour for national infrastructure developments, the ROC Government's Executive Yuan approved a package of measures legalising the presence of overseas workers on these and other important projects. In 1992, the Employment Services Act was passed to regulate the employment of foreign workers. The Act prescribes the same minimum wage and working conditions for foreign workers that local workers have, as stipulated in the Labor Standards Act; it prohibits employers from hiring foreign labourers without prior government authorisation. Foreign workers can apply for working visas of up to two years, which may be extended for another year if their contracts are renewed (Chao 1992: 159). However, according to Robert Kuo Kuo-wen, secretary-general of the Taiwan Labour Front (founded in 1984 as the first organised labour movement group) the Act did not quite serve the purpose as foreign labour, legal and otherwise, continues to pour in (Jin 2000: 46–7).

By 2000, there were over 290 000 foreign workers in Taiwan, forming about five per cent of the population and increasing the island's cultural diversity. They represented several nationalities: Thai — 138 347 (47.4 per cent), Filipino — 116 709 (40 per cent), Indonesian — 36 198 (12.4 per cent), and Malaysian — 183 (0.06 per cent). They were employed in specific industries, namely, construction — 48 752 (16.7 per cent), manufacturing — 171 744 (58.9 per cent), and domestic duties — 69 982 (24 per cent) (Statistics from Employment & Vocational Training Administration [EVTA], Council for Labour Affairs, cited in Lu 2000).

Local job losses

These workers provide temporary relief for the labour shortage but are also blamed for undermining the local job market, putting a brake on the pace of industrial upgrading, and triggering social problems. According to Hsin Ping-lung, a researcher at the Chung-Hua Institution for Economic Research, wages for foreign labourers are currently around 70-80 per cent of the pay of local workers, and employers use this to leverage against local job applicants. Even if foreign workers are paid the minimum wage of US$511 per month, that is more than double what Filipinos can earn at home, and enough to keep attracting them to Taiwan (Jan 2000: 4). Labour groups tend to blame local job losses on foreign workers. For example, Robert Kuo Kuo-wen of the Taiwan Labour Front thinks that by allowing the importation of foreign labour for the high-tech industries as an incentive for major investments worth over NT$200 million, highly coveted jobs in the high-tech sector are being given to workers from overseas. Aborigines are the worst hit, at 10–30 per cent unemployment compared with the national average of almost three per cent. On 1 May 2000, International Labour Day, over 1000 aborigines took part in a demonstration to protest job losses to foreign labourers; this marked an unprecedented level of mobilisation among aborigines.

Supervision problems

Communication problems and unclear responsibility for the supervision of workers often lead to conflict. For example, in September 1999 at Formosa Plastics' naphtha cracker plant at Mailiao, where hundreds of workers from Philippines, Indonesia and Thailand were housed in shared quarters, minor clashes blew up into bloody rioting for two weeks in the streets of Mailiao. Formosa Plastics, which applied for the importation of more than 10 000 workers, was seen to be responsible, but it blamed the subcontracting firms for not managing the foreign labourers as specified in their contract. The Council for Labour Affairs (CLA) itself was partly to blame for not monitoring the supervision of foreign workers.

Social problems and crime

Another problem is the social impact of foreign labour on Taiwan. Foreign workers can have a monotonous life, being cooped up in cramped quarters and working long hours with little diversion. Frustration and depression can set in, spread through the quarters, and trigger off violence and crime. Thefts have gone up, with 100–200 reported cases every month linked to foreign workers, or around one for every 1000 workers. Serious crime among these workers has included rape. Prostitution — and its attendant risk of sexually transmitted diseases — is a problem at some worksites. Extramarital affairs (called FTO — For Taiwan Only, or TLA — Taiwan Love Affair) are not uncommon.

Government and community groups are eager to help reduce some of these social problems associated with foreign workers. The Employment and Vocational Training Administration (EVTA), churches and broadcast stations all promote cultural programs and events for foreign workers. For instance, Taipei Mayor Ma Ying-jeou announced that the city is drawing up plans for a park and an activity centre to be dedicated to overseas workers (Jan 2000: 4). Many have intermarried with locals, and show concern for the society they work in, for example, by helping to raise funds for victims of the 21 September earthquake. A degree of cultural fusion appears to have been forged, but their integration has never been an official goal.

Absconding and illegal workers

Illegal and exploitative labour importation also gives the Taiwanese extra cause to take issue with the presence of foreign workers. The Taipei Association of Manpower Agencies is an association of brokers responsible for the arrival of most foreign labourers in Taiwan. They collaborate with agencies in supplying countries. The contract labourer pays a total of NT$60 000–70 000 in fees to both agents, who are expected to facilitate contacts and arbitrate in disputes between employers and workers. Some agents do not fulfil their obligations, and workers' rights may be violated.

Some workers also run away just before their contracts expire, to go 'underground' to work illegally. According to CLA, about 24 per cent of foreign labourers run away from their contracted jobs; and an estimated 6000 runaways are working illegally on the island. Missing person advertisements appear regularly in Taiwan's English-language newspapers, with rewards of between US$323 and US$968 being offered for information leading to their whereabouts. There is always a demand for illegal workers because the rules for hiring legally can be draconian, for example, the government rule that only families with a dependant over 70 or two children aged six or under can apply for a foreign domestic helper. Some employers are willing to pay the higher fee of NT$20 000 for an illegal worker as it works out about the same as a legal one after additional expenses and costs. But this underground trade undermines official regulations and encourages underworld exploitation of foreign labour.

To manage some of these problems, the CLA has taken measures such as: encouraging people to report recalcitrant employers, making it mandatory to declare fair terms of employment, restricting the ratio of foreign to local employees, and approving recruitment of a foreign worker only after the company has copied relevant correspondence to the union for confirmation that no local worker wants the job (Jan 2000: 4). The CLA will also raise the minimum capital requirement for major manufacturing companies applying to import foreign labourers to US$16.23 million from the current US$6.49 million. Further, only families with a seriously disabled member will be allowed to hire foreign domestic helpers. The penalty for employers who hire illegal foreign labourers will be raised from the current maximum of US$974 to US$2922 (*Taipei Journal* 2000: 3).

To encourage the employment of local workers, the CLA has announced plans to cut quotas of foreign workers by 15 000 a year, to raise their minimum wage and the hiring companies' vocational stabilisation fee. However, at the time of writing, no dates have been set for these measures to be implemented, as a possible impact could be to push businesses to relocate overseas for cheap labour. The restructuring of industry from labour- to capital-intensive has to be sped up first. In order to allow businesses sufficient time to adjust, the government will reduce the number of foreign workers gradually, by 60 000 over a six-year period, and may allow a grace period for introducing a shorter working week (Chiu 2000c: 3).

Such policies are in keeping with the principles which guide the foreign labour policy, as articulated by former chairman of the CLA, Chao Shou-po (1992: 161–3):

1. *Citizen's right to work must be protected at all cost.* Before a job is opened to foreign recruitment, the employer must first prove that all means to recruit a local worker have been exhausted.
2. *All foreign workers must not become migrant settlers.* Taiwan cannot afford to take in foreign workers as migrants.

3. *To contain the social differences created by the foreign workers.* Basically Taiwan is known for its homogeneous and exclusive culture. Foreign workers from diverse social, religious and language backgrounds will have difficulty integrating with the local community. Taiwan has no experience or tolerance to accommodate foreign customs, and so prejudice against foreign workers is not unexpected.
4. *Importing labour should not become a liability for industrial and economic restructuring.* The importation of foreign workers should only be regarded as a temporary solution until firms can upgrade their operations to embrace higher technology.
5. *Must maintain the principle of equity.* The admission of foreign workers is not an open policy for all economic sectors, but a contingency for several categories of industry whose survival could be jeopardised by severe labour shortage. It is therefore equitable that the lower labour cost they enjoy is compensated by a mandatory foreign worker tax that can be redistributed among all industrial and economic sectors.

So long as the economic gap between the foreign workers' home countries and Taiwan continues to be significant, and Taiwan's labour shortage persists, the issue of foreign labour importation will remain unresolved. Foreign labour is acceptable as a peripheral workforce so long as their economic and social impact on Taiwan is positive, but they remain very visible 'outsiders' (Lin, E. 2000). Another strategy that has been considered for the temporary alleviation of the labour shortage in Taiwan is the importation of workers from Mainland China. This issue is discussed next.

Mainland China as a source of labour supply

Whether or not Mainland China should be considered a labour supply source has been a subject of debate. A compelling argument for importing Chinese workers is that they are culturally and historically similar, if not identical, to the Taiwanese. However, the rocky political relationship between China and Taiwan remains a hurdle, and the admission of Chinese workers into Taiwan will have political and social complications no less serious than the hiring of foreign workers from other countries (Chao 1992: 173–4).

Positives

The ROC Government has identified several advantages in looking to China for labour. China has an abundant supply of workers. There would be little social cost in assimilating such workers into the local community, and thus is a more long-term solution to the labour shortage problem. Alternatively, if these workers return home, they could continue to facilitate communication and cultural exchange with Taiwan, and be the witnesses to their own people of the Taiwan way of life, paving the way for closer political ties across the China Straits.

Negatives

On the negative side, labourers engaging in espionage would be a breach of national security. Also, 50 years of political estrangement has produced different value systems and behavioral patterns that could hinder the Chinese workers' adaptation to life in Taiwan. Any prejudicial treatment or administrative inconvenience towards the workers would invite hostile criticism from the Mainland government, and thus worsen the political atmosphere. There would also be difficulty in determining the jurisdiction of laws, as the terms 'Chinese national' (referring to the imported workers) and 'Chinese citizen' (meaning citizens of Taiwan) could be easily confused. It would be difficult also to repatriate Chinese workers at the end of their contracts, particularly if they married local residents and had their status changed to citizen. Current quota restrictions on travel between China and Taiwan are strictly imposed. Foreign workers filling these quotas would displace other potential travellers. Because of these difficulties, Taiwanese are not exactly eager to receive workers from China, as an opinion poll in 1991 showed. Nevertheless, as a goodwill gesture to the Mainland government, the Labour Council opened a sea-going category for Chinese sailors. Sailors are expected to work offshore and would have very limited time or opportunity to spend time on land (Chao 1992: 174–6).

Conditions

Hence, the official position at this stage is not to allow Chinese workers into Taiwan, though the CLA keeps it open as a possibility for the future, subject to constant review of policy, and the presence of specific pre-conditions. Crucially, the cross-straits relationship must be conducive towards such a policy, and domestic public opinion in Taiwan is receptive. Legislation appropriate to the management of such workers must be instituted, as must the same considerations as are applied to other foreign workers (Chao 1992: 176–8).

It is therefore paradoxical that at a time when Taiwan is grappling with insufficient labour for both high- and low-tech ends of its industrial development, and with the difficulties of importing foreign labour, more of its local workers are becoming unemployed. Most of the unemployed are middle-aged workers, and most of them are victims of Taiwan's high-tech drive. The next section deals with this second paradox, that is, that the needs of Taiwan's industry have prevailed over the needs of ageing workers in a Confucian society which has traditionally valued hard workers and revered older people.

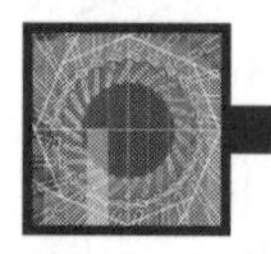

Paradox 2: IT development versus problems of the SMEs: The issue of an ageing workforce

Because of the predominance of small and medium enterprises (SMEs) in Taiwan, the unemployment problem is uniquely linked to the fortunes of these SMEs which run the gamut from hardware information technology manufacture to agricultural processing. SMEs constitute close to 98 per cent of all firms in Taiwan, employ 80 per cent of the total workforce, and account for half of the island's aggregate export value (Government Information Office 1999a: 172; Government Information Office 1999b: 5).

SMEs emerged after World War II when the Japanese conglomerates withdrew from Taiwan. Squeezed out of the local market by state-run and large private companies, SMEs focused on foreign markets to survive. The export-oriented economic policy of the 1960s and infrastructural development supporting it were conducive to the rapid growth of SMEs. The tendency of these firms to pass from one generation to the next also ensures their survival.

The official definition of SMEs goes by sector, paid-in capital/annual turnover, and the number of employees. In industries like manufacturing, construction, mining and quarrying, firms that have a paid-in capital of less than NT$60 million (US$1.76 million) or that hire less than 200 regular workers are classified as SMEs. In commercial, services and transportation sectors, firms with an annual turnover not exceeding NT$80 million (US$2.35 million) or that hire less than 50 workers are also considered SMEs. Sixty per cent of Taiwan's SMEs are in the commercial sector, while 15 per cent are in manufacturing (Government Information Office 1999a: 172).

SMEs are undoubtedly the backbone of the economy, particularly in producing hardware for the IT industry which is the ROC's most important foreign exchange earner. In 1997, some 900 computer hardware suppliers hired 100 000 employees, and turned over a total of US$30 billion. Currently Taiwan ranks third behind the US and Japan as a supplier of high-tech products to the world, dominating in notebook computers, scanners and motherboards. However, the acceleration of the knowledge industry spearheaded by the government is still challenged by the fact that the SMEs are mostly producing designs from multinationals; they have neither the key technologies required nor the capital to invest in research and development. Moreover, the human resources required in the IT sector are inadequate in both numbers and skills. While labour productivity in the IT hardware manufacturing sector has been growing at about seven per cent per year, it still lags behind the overall industry growth rate of about 15 per cent per year. The skill demands of the industry have also left behind workers — particularly ageing workers — unable to adapt to the new technologies. Almost 43 per cent of the unemployed at the end of June 2000 were basic-level workers (Chiu 2000d: 3).

Among the problems faced by SMEs are the shortage of labour, increase in wages, prohibitive land prices, fluctuating exchange rates and strong competition from other countries. The ROC Ministry of Finance figure put wages and salaries as accounting for nearly 19 per cent of operating costs for local SMEs, more than double the 8.92 per cent for large enterprises. Among the labour-related problems encountered by SMEs, that of rising wages is most serious, followed by costly pension plans, an ageing domestic work force and the need to pay labour insurance and national health insurance expenses. SMEs spend only 0.05 per cent of their operating budget on training, and do not tend to apply for government training incentives (Cheng 2000: 3).

Changing demographics

Over the past 30 years, Taiwan's population growth rate has dropped sharply. Statistics compiled by Farh (1995) based on government data show that growth rates had declined steadily from about three per cent during the 1960s, to two per cent in the 1970s, and 1.3 per cent during the 1980s (table 12.1). By 1997, growth had dropped to 1.01 per cent (Government Information Office 1999a: 23). Meanwhile, the proportion of people aged 55 and above had grown steadily from 6.6 per cent in 1960 to 13.6 per cent in 1990. Likewise, the age group of 35–54 had also grown from 18 per cent to 22.5 per cent during the same period (Farh 1995: 274).

A combination of factors accounts for the changing demographics. A falling death rate and higher life expectancy, longer education, delayed marriages, and tendency towards smaller families have resulted in a greying population. On the average, Taiwanese men live until 72 years of age, and women until 78 years. With 8.06 per cent of the population being over 65 years of age in 1997, up from 7.86 per cent in 1996, Taiwan now stands midway among other 'older' countries like Great Britain (16 per cent), France (15 per cent), Japan (13 per cent), and the United States (13 per cent), and 'younger' nations like mainland China and Korea (6 per cent each), and Thailand and Philippines (4 per cent each) (Government Information Office, 1999a: p. 23).

Table 12.1: *Distribution of population in Taiwan by age group, 1960–90*

End of year	Total population (m)	Percentage of population			
		Under age 20	Age 20–34	Age 35–54	Age 55 & above
1960	10.79	54.1	21.3	18.0	6.6
1970	14.68	51.6	20.7	19.8	7.9
1980	17.81	43.3	27.1	19.2	10.4
1990	20.36	35.9	28.2	22.5	13.6

Source: Adapted from Farh (1995: 274).

Costs of employing older workers

The Directorate General of Budget, Accounting and Statistics reported that of the 274 000 (2.83 per cent) people out of work in March 2000, 94 000 were in the 35–55 age group. The changing industrial structure, with the shift from traditional industries to high-tech manufacturing, the relocation of labour-intensive businesses overseas, and the downsizing of government administration, have largely been responsible. A recent survey indicates that 95 per cent of employers in Taiwan are unwilling to hire middle-aged people, and many recruitment advertisements specify age limits (Lin, J. 2000a: 4).

Under Taiwan's labour laws, SMEs generally find it costly to keep on middle-aged workers. According to the Labor Standards Act and the Rules for the Allocation and Management of Workers' Retirement Fund, a retiree is entitled to a maximum pension equal to 45 times his average wage in the six months prior to retirement. Each month, employers must pay between 2 and 15 per cent of their employees' total monthly wage aggregate into the wage retirement fund. This fund is monitored by a supervisory committee which is made up of labour and management representatives (Government Information Office 1999a: 350). Under current regulations, employers can receive a monthly subsidy of US$165 for one year for each new person hired aged between 50 and 65, as long as these labourers are recommended by government-registered vocational training institutes. However, few companies take advantage of this measure as a basis for hiring middle-aged citizens. Companies prefer young workers because they are more easily trained, they demand lower salaries, and they turn in more work years before requiring retirement pay (Lin, J. 2000a: 4).

In addition to retirement benefits, companies are required under the Labour Insurance Act (1988) to provide insurance coverage for two categories of benefits: (a) ordinary insurance covering maternity, injury and sickness, disability, old age, and death; (b) occupational injury insurance, providing four kinds of benefits, that is, injury and sickness, medical care, disability, and death. The responsibility of paying for the premium of ordinary insurance is shared by the employee, employer and government in the proportions 2:7:1. Employees usually contribute between 6.5–11 per cent of their salaries towards the premium. Injury insurance premiums are paid entirely by the employer (Government Information Office 1999a: 346).

As older workers are more prone to sickness and injury, particularly in the manufacturing sector, age-related payouts can become substantial enough to jack up premiums. Some employers attempt to save premium by deliberately under-reporting workers' salary (Farh 1995: 283), or by laying off older workers. Hence the government has to provide a broader national insurance scheme to protect the interests of specific groups of citizens such as retirees and civil servants. Interestingly, the government policy of extending national health insurance to policy-holders' spouses and parents before their children reflects a Chinese cultural value that one's first and foremost responsibility is to take care of one's elderly parents (Farh 1995: 284).

There is higher compliance with the Wage Arrears Repayment Fund to which employers are required to pay 0.025 per cent of the wages for each employee to ensure that workers receive due wages in the event of company closures. As of June 1998, nearly 94 per cent of eligible firms in Taiwan were contributing to the fund (Government Information Office 1999a: 351).

The government also provides a safety net in the form of unemployment insurance for laid off workers; labourers covered for at least two years can apply for subsidies equal to 60 per cent of former monthly salaries, with payments granted for 6–16 months (Lin, J. 2000a: 4). According to the Taiwan Labour Front, unemployment insurance currently covers only 10 000 of the 300 000 unemployed (Jin 2000: 46–47).

Early voluntary retirement

For companies retaining their operations in Taiwan, the best hope of cutting labour costs may be in the voluntary early retirement of older workers. SMEs are traditionally familistic in their hiring policies, often recruiting family members and friends, which makes it difficult for them to lay off workers. Their small training budget would also make it non-viable to put displaced older workers through retraining. It would therefore be of interest to examine the findings of a study by Raymo and Cornman (1999) on the propensity of Taiwan workers to retire earlier.

The authors conducted a cohort study to see if, over a 20-year period, older Taiwanese workers exhibit a trend toward earlier retirement, as in the Western advanced nations, and why. They found three possible determinants of earlier retirement: the eligibility for social security and private pension plans, changing occupational structure, and economic growth.

- Social security and private pension plans are found to be inadequate to induce much early retirement. Substantial proportions of workers are not covered by either of the two public pension provisions in Taiwan and those who are covered receive retirement benefits that are generally smaller than those received by retirees in the US, Europe and Japan (Raymo & Cornman 1999: 362). The Civil Servant Retirement Regulation (CSRR) has covered civil servants since 1943 and the Labor Standards Act (LSL) has covered private sector employees other than those in finance, service and commerce only since 1985. In 1990, 53 per cent of the labour force was covered by these two pension plans. 'Although they cover more than half of the labour force, neither of these programs provides benefits of a level sufficient for financing more than a brief period of retirement' (Raymo & Cornman 1999: 362). The CSRR pays a lump sum at the time of retirement; benefits are determined by length of employment and last drawn salary with maximum benefits set at 61 months' wages. Those with more than 15 years' service may opt to receive a monthly payment rather than a lump sum. The LSL pays those who have been in the same company for more than 15 years, at age 60 for men, and 55 for women and miners. The lump sum LSL benefit is equivalent to two months' wages per year of service for each year beyond 15 years with a maximum benefit of 45 months' wages. No mandatory retirement age is associated with receipt of LSL pensions. Both programs therefore provide a maximum of only four to five years' worth of wages. In the context of increased longevity, it does not seem that early retirement is promoted by pension receipt in Taiwan (Raymo & Cornman 1999: 362–3).
- Changing occupational structure and technology. When the agricultural sector and traditional industries diminished in importance, it would have been reasonable to

expect the early retirement of less skilled workers in these industries. The agricultural labour force declined from 36.7 per cent in 1970, to 12.8 per cent in 1990 (Raymo & Cornman 1999: 363), and 10.1 per cent in 1999 (Government Information Office 1999a: 196). But a substantial proportion of the non-agricultural labour force is self-employed and thus not eligible for pension receipt. In fact, the number of self-employed increased from 11–14 per cent between 1970 and 1990, indicating no real increase in aged people leaving the workforce. It appears that, despite changing industrial structure, the new conditions were still not conducive to workers withdrawing from labour participation altogether. Those conditions appear to encourage entrepreneurship instead, which is in keeping with the Chinese belief that 'it is better to be the head of a cockerel than the tail of a bullock', a saying signifying the importance placed on being one's own boss, no matter how small the business.

- Economic growth. Taiwan's economy saw a five-fold increase between 1970 and 1990, with growth rates averaging 8.2 per cent. Wage increases, on one hand, may induce workers to stay longer in the labour force. On the other hand, higher income meant greater accumulation of personal assets to finance retirement, which would be a disincentive to continue working. Financial well-being has changed the perception of retirement to that of being desirable, rather than an enforced loss of productivity, economic security and social interaction. In Taiwan, where the most important source of income for the elderly continues to be transfers from children (Raymo & Cornman 1999: 361), children's financial well-being and consequently their increased ability to support their ageing parents to stop working are important determinant of earlier retirement.

For men, the highest rate of exit from the workforce still occurs between the ages 55 and 65 when most mandatory retirement limits are reached. Further research will be needed to investigate if such exit constitutes a complete withdrawal from labour force participation, or simply a change of status from being employee to self-employed. In a society where hard work is respected, where wisdom and experience of the elderly are valued, and where small business start-up is the norm rather than the exception, it would be reasonable to expect that retirement does not mean the end of working.

For existing SME employers of older workers to cope better with the rising wage costs, or for displaced older workers to successfully start up new SMEs, more governmental support is seen to be necessary. Day Sheng-tong, chairman of the National Association of Small and Medium Enterprises, considers the present level of development funding and business and management advice as provided under the Small and Medium-sized Enterprise Guidance Regulations (1967) and its various revisions, as inadequate. He would like to see the Chen administration develop Taiwan as a regional manufacturing centre, focusing on a range of industries instead of just IT. The IT sector, while leading spectacularly, is also getting too much of the nation's resources, Day feels, while contributions of the SME-based traditional manufacturing industries are neglected. Traditional industries like textiles have been the roots of the Taiwan economy, and he believes — with the country's vast human and natural resources — they can continue to flourish alongside newer industries like IT and financial services (Jin 2000: 41–43).

Balancing the needs of the IT drive in the nation with the limited financial, technological and human resource capabilities of SMEs will continue to be a challenge. Caught in this transition will be a generation of older workers whose productive capabilities are still employable, albeit less so in the IT sector which requires completely new knowledge, skills and speed. How to utilise this human resource pool at time of labour shortage would require a practical and socially conscionable solution.

Another resource pool that has been under-utilised is women. In male-dominant Taiwanese society, women's role has traditionally been that of dutiful daughter-in-law, wife and mother, hence the paucity of professional aged care and childcare facilities. This situation has bound women to the home, even at a time when labour for high-tech development is in short supply, and when women themselves are eager and ready to participate. However, there is a perception that the potential erosion of Chinese family values would be an inevitable outcome of women's emancipation. The management of women as workers, then, is a third paradox to be discussed in this paper.

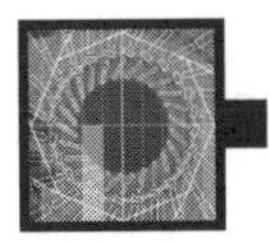

Paradox 3: Satisfaction of changing expectations of women versus traditional family roles: The issue of women workers

The Taiwanese made history twice over on 18 March 2000 by electing to office the Democratic Progressive Party's Chen Shui-bian and his female running mate Annette Lu. This was a significant victory for the DPP because, not only did they oust the Kuomintang which had ruled Taiwan since its inception in 1949 in favour of an untried opposition promising to hold China's reunification overtures at bay, they also put into office the first-ever woman vice-president. In her victory speech, 'The Birth of a New Taiwan', Lu declared, 'Taiwan today became the first country in the world with a Confucian cultural heritage to elect a woman vice-president. This election victory ... is not just a triumph for democracy, but also a milestone for gender equality in government' (Her 2000: 16).

Despite such a dramatic statement of women's 'arrival' on the political scene, the gender gap remains wide in most fields. The labour participation rate of Taiwan women has remained around 45 per cent over the past 10 years. In the United States, it is about 60 per cent, and in Singapore, 51 per cent (Hsu 2000: 2). Education and technology have created greater opportunities for women to enter the workforce, but more direct measures are needed to redress the imbalance. Chen's DPP platform on gender equality and his pledge to appoint women to one-fourth of the cabinet positions have won many supporters. But even in government, female ministers are perceived to be suitable for portfolios like 'education, culture, community development, conservation of natural resources, and social welfare', whereas male ministers might be given the portfolios of finance or foreign relations (Her 2000: 17). It remains to be seen if Chen's promise to push for passage of a stronger law on gender equality to encourage women to pursue careers and secure their rights would be translated into workplace changes in the near future.

For thousands of years, Chinese women were expected to marry, and all married women had to give birth and take care of children and parents-in-law. Taiwanese women share this cultural heritage. Hence at one time, the policies formulated for 'women's welfare' were directed at helping them to fulfil these traditional obligations, such as in providing subsidies for daycare, medical expenses, and education of children. However, increasing domestic violence and divorce rates have forced the authorities to consider more far-reaching protection of women's interests (Government Information Office 1999a: 329). Today, the Council for Labour Affairs has a policy on female workers which emphasises their protection from employment discrimination and their vocational upskilling, which recognises the increasing labour participation of women (Chao 1992). Based on the Constitution and the Labor Standards Act, the policy pertains to the regulation of:

- health and safety at work, the administrative details of the welfare system for women workers

- the education of women and their employers in their rights and obligations
- the establishment of flexible working hours and childcare facilities to allow female workers to manage their time between work and family commitments
- the provision of employment opportunities, equal pay for equal work, employment advice, and vocational training in the services sector specifically tailored to capitalise on available women workers entering or re-entering the workforce, or moving from traditional industries.

In spite of such provisions, implementation often falls short. Farh (1995: 287) points out that Article 25 of the Labor Standards Act simply states that, 'An employer shall not show discrimination in the payment of wages based on gender; workers shall receive equal wages for equal work of equal efficiency'. The law is silent about other aspects of employment rights, and it has not been rigorously enforced. In practice, women employees are subject to various forms of unfair treatment, which can be illustrated by examples such as (a) employers stating gender preferences in hiring for high paying jobs; (b) lower starting pay for women with equal qualifications and experience as men; (c) before hiring, women are made to sign a contract that requires them to quit their jobs when they are married or become pregnant. A CLA survey in 1990 supports these observations as it found that the average female worker's wage was about 65 per cent of the male's, that 50 per cent of employers applied different selection criteria for new male and female hires, and that many employers would not consider women for technical training (45 per cent) or training to prepare women for entry into managerial jobs (70 per cent) (Farh 1995: 288). It is therefore not surprising that the same survey reported very low career aspirations and work motivation among women, compared to men. Fewer than five per cent of female workers considered a managerial position their ultimate goal, compared to 46.7 per cent male workers. While 37.5 per cent of the men reported a desire to work harder than their peers, only 17.3 per cent of the women indicated so (Farh 1995: 288).

In the 10 years since the CLA survey, social conditions have changed sufficiently in Taiwan to suggest some differences in the perception of women's role. According to the Ministry of the Interior (Government Information Office 1999a: 329), at the end of 1997, women constituted 47 per cent of junior college graduates, 43 per cent of university and college graduates, and 28 per cent of graduate school graduates. More women are resisting the traditional view that women are inferior to men, and that in male–female relationships a woman should be submissive. As more women enter the workforce, many complain that they are unfairly burdened with both traditional roles of good mothers, dutiful daughters-in-law and wives, and the modern role of wage earner. This resistance is reflected in the later average age of women getting married for the first time. In 1990, it was 25.8 years; in 1997, it had gone up to 28.1 years. Moreover, the marriage rate has hardly increased, rising from 7.5 per 1000 people in 1970 to 9.68 in 1980, and then falling back to 7.68 by 1997. In contrast, the divorce rate has quadrupled in the last 25 years, standing at 18 per cent in 1997 compared to 3.7 per cent in 1970 (Fahr 1995: 332).

However, the employment situation of Taiwanese women does not seem to have changed as dramatically. Manpower reports from the Directorate General of Budget, Accounting and Statistics indicate that in 1999, 52 per cent of local single women held jobs. However, less than half of married women did so. In 1998, another survey found that 37.4 per cent of the women who left their jobs in that year did so to care for children at home, while 28.7 per cent left for marriage. Of the 30 per cent of local single women who quit work in the 1982–9 period to get married or have children, only 20 per cent have resumed employment. The biggest hurdle appears to be a lack

of skills currently in demand, such as IT skills. A host of public and private women's services networks, many catering to providing appropriate training courses, have been established in the last 15 years. The government's 1994 Female Employment Promotion Measures target gender equality, vocational training of women, childcare centres for working mothers, and daycare of the elderly, to give women more time for employment. The Employment and Vocational Training Administration of the CLA reports that between 1997 and 1998, some 1739 women had graduated from Taiwan's 13 government-supported vocational training centres as full-time students, and 3466 as evening-class students. Another 6115 completed vocational programs organised by local county or city governments (Government Information Office 1999a: 331). However, the measures are seen as too general and lacking teeth (Lin, J. 2000b: 4).

Recent research has confirmed that the wage gap still exists between men and women workers (Huang 1999a, 1999b), that women's need for different employee benefits to that of men are not met adequately (Hong et al. 1995), and that women still occupy lower job levels and have lower job satisfaction than men despite having the same job values like task-orientation and team-spiritedness (Cheung & Scherling 1999). There appears to be agreement with the conclusion that 'Taiwan is a patriarchal society that leaves women at a disadvantage', that 'man's superiority over the woman is also a teaching of Confucianism which is the ideology sponsored by the Taiwan government' (Cheung & Scherling 1999), and that 'traditional values are deeply rooted and will take a long time for society to change' (Farh 1995). Moreover, 'women in power', like politicians Annette Lu and independent rival Chu Hui-liang who came fourth in the recent elections, are still an anomaly, and the fact they are unmarried at the time of their success highlights the difficulties women face on the road to true gender equality (Her 2000).

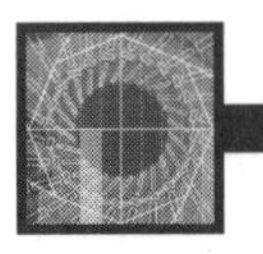

Conclusions

The fact that newly elected President Chen Shui-bian and Vice-president Annette Lu decided against having the huge election victory party originally planned for their supporters, settling instead on a more subdued celebration (Chung 2000: 4), signifies a realisation of the enormity of their win. Having overturned 50 years of Kuomintang rule, the responsibility of ruling now lies squarely on their untested shoulders. The opportunities presented by strong economic growth and imminent entry into the WTO are great to inherit, but the challenges of restructuring the political, economic and social fabrics of the country to optimise its resource utilisation are daunting. Domestically, the needs of diverse groups of people who provide the labour power to propel the engine of progress will need to be met. Women and elderly workers are valuable resource pools that unfortunately appear to be inadequately galvanised in the cross-fire between tradition and modernisation, between pragmatic, short-term cost considerations and more strategic human resource planning, particularly in the dominant SME-sector. The interests of other minorities like the indigenous peoples and the disabled have fallen outside the scope of this paper, but certainly would warrant further discussion elsewhere. Foreign workers offer a stop-gap measure, but they present yet another set of challenges in the management of diversity. As Taiwanese increasingly assert their identity, they draw ever further from the cultural heritage they inherited from mainland China, making their relationship with their mainland compatriots still another source of challenge in political and social diversity. Hence, Taiwan in the coming decades should be a fascinating subject of study in the field of diversity management.

References

Chao, Shou-po. 1992. *Labour Policy and Labour Issues*. Taiwan (translated): China Productivity Centre.

Chen, Ya-hueh. 2000. 'Free to Trade'. *Taipei Review*, April, p. 44 (translated).

Cheng, Brian. 2000. 'SMEs Doing It Themselves'. *Taipei Journal*, June: 3.

Cheung, Chau-Kiu & Scherling, Steven A. 1999. 'Job Satisfaction, Work Values, and Sex Differences in Taiwan's Orgnaizations'. *The Journal of Psychology* 33(5) 563–75.

Chiu, Yueh-wen. 2000a. 'Downsizing Workweek a Laborious Process'. *Taipei Journal*, 30 June: 3.

Chiu, Yueh-wen. 2000b. 'Technology Key to the Economy', *Taipei Journal*, 18 August: 3.

Chiu, Yueh-wen. 2000c. 'Council Labors to Improve Welfare of Taiwan's workers'. *Taipei Journal*, 9 June: 3.

Chiu, Yueh-wen. 2000d. 'Technology Key to the Economy'. *Taipei Journal*, 18 August: 3.

Chung, Oscar. 2000. 'Island of Uncertainties'. *Taipei Review*, May, 4–13.

Farh, Jing-Lih. 1995. 'Human Resource Management in Taiwan, the Republic of China.' In Moore, L. F. & Jennings, P. D. *Human Resource Management on the Pacific Rim*. Walter de Gruyter: 265–92.

Government Information Office. 1999. *Brief Introduction to ROC*. Taipei.

Government Information Office. 1999a. *ROC 1999 Yearbook*. Taipei.

Government Information Office. 1999b. *Small and Medium Enterprises: The Driving Force of Taiwan's Economy*. Taipei: 5.

Griffin, T. J. 1989. *Taiwan Republic of China: Opening Up to the World*. Taipei: Euromoney Books.

Her, Kelly. 2000. 'The New Office Ladies'. *Taipei Review*, May: 16.

Hong, Jon-Chao et al. 1995. 'Impact of Employee Benefits on Work Motivation and Productivity'. *International Journal of Career Management* 7(6): http://www.emerald-library.com/brev/07607fb1.htm

Hsu, Joe. 2000. 'Women Are Making Their Mark'. *Taipei Journal*. 18 August: 2.

Huang, Tung-Chun. 1999a. 'Gender Differences in Company Training: The Case of Taiwanese High-tech Firms'. *Employee Relations* 21(5): http://www.emerald-library.com/brev/01921ed1.htm

Huang, Tung-Chun. 1999b. 'The Impact of Education and Seniority on the Male-Female Wage Gap: Is More Education the Answer?'. *International Journal of Manpower* 20(6): http://www.emerald-library.com/brev/01620fb1.htm

Jan, Tracy. 2000. 'Filipinos Make Ends Meet by Working in Taiwan'. *Taipei Journal*, 9 June: 4.

Jin, Yang. 2000. 'Great Expectations'. *Taipei Review*, May: 40–7.

Lin, Eric. 2000. 'The Outsiders: Foreign Labour Changes the Face of Taiwan'. *Sinorama* 25(1): January (translated).

Lin, Joyce. 2000. 'Middle-aged Women Sing Employment Re-entry Blues'. *Taipei Journal*, 28 July: 4.

Lin, Joyce. 2000a. 'Skills Upgrading the Key for Older Workers'. *Taipei Journal*, 19 May: 4.

Lu, Myra. 2000. 'Lee's Legacy: Pursue the Public Good', *Taipei Journal*, 9 June: 1.

Maguire, K. 1999. 'Taiwan: From Sub-contractor to Regional Operations Centre'. *European Business Review* 99(3): http://www.emerald-library.com/brev/05599cd1.htm

Taipei Journal. 2000. 'Business This Week', 2 June: 3.

Raymo, J. M. & Cornman, J. C. 1999. 'Trends in Labour Force Status Across the Life Course in Taiwan: 1970–1990'. In Chaonan Chen (Ed.). *Emerging Social Economic Welfare Programs for Aging in Taiwan in a World Context*. Institute of Economics, Academia Sinica.

Wong, Yim-Yu et al. 2000. 'Taiwan: A Tiger Increasingly at Bay But Still Ferocious'. *Managerial Finance* 26(4): 3–15.

Wu, Yuan-li. 1985. *Becoming an Industrialized Nation: ROC's Development on Taiwan*. New York: Praeger Special Studies: 114–130.

Yu Tzong-shian. 2000. *The Story of Taiwan: Economy*. ROC Government Information Office: 19.

Chapter 13

Thailand

Niti Dubey-Villinger

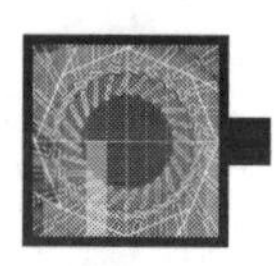

Introduction

Diversity has special meaning in Thailand, a country which has recently experienced one of its most serious economic crises in decades. Thailand is a country rich in terms of its human resources potential, and its labour market can be viewed as diverse in terms of ethnic diversity, the visibility of women, and forms of employment enterprise in the economy. One finds diversity in the workplace setting with respect to the ethnic and national origins of participants in the workforce. In particular, communities of ethnic Chinese, Indians, workers from neighbouring south-east Asian nations and other 'guest workers' are in evidence, along with a local indigenous workforce of 33 million Thais, who, among themselves form a diverse population. Women's participation in the workforce is notable, for example, in areas which are often not covered in official statistics — domestic work, petty or informal trade and services.

This chapter attempts to address these diverse elements of the Thai workforce in light of how organisations within the country — and certainly the Thai Government — have supported and shaped the cause of diversity through specific policies and practices. This paper looks at diversity in the Thai labour market from five different perspectives:

1. basic labour force composition;
2. education and skills development;
3. diversity in the workplace;
4. the relevant legal framework;
5. the impact of Thai culture.

The strong social impact of the recent economic crisis in the country, particularly on the labour force, has meant that this analysis of the labour market is viewed from the perspective of an economy having experienced tumultuous change. The level of diversity in the Thai workforce in principle, however, remains unchanged.

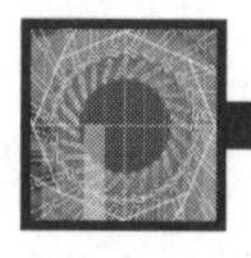

Labour force composition

The impact of the Asian economic crisis has been felt in Thailand. Though the crisis appears to have had a greater social impact in urban areas, namely in the construction and manufacturing sectors in terms of unemployment, the rural economy also experienced growing unemployment particularly in the north-east where the return migration of workers occurred. The Thailand Development Research Institute (TDRI) estimates that of the 1.48 million unemployed persons (4.6 per cent of the labour force) in February 1998, about 33.8 per cent previously worked in construction and manufacturing and 27 per cent in agriculture.

According to the National Statistical Office (NSO), unemployment in February 1998 increased from about 2.2 per cent to 4.6 per cent over the previous year. The economic crisis also resulted in the growth of the informal[1] sector and self-employment as employees were forced to migrate from formal sector unemployment. Underemployment, or work under 20 hours per week, has also been prevalent, partly resulting from the economic crisis. According to the ILO, 'the reliance of many Thais on the traditional safety net of the extended family' following the crisis may have resulted in a four to five fold increase in underemployment (ILO 1998b). The Labour

Force Survey conducted in November 1998 found that about 3.2 per cent of the labour force worked under 20 hours a week and about 10.6 per cent worked under 35 hours per week.

Table 13.1: ***Estimated labour force and employment: Kingdom of Thailand, 1992–1999***

	1992 %	1993 %	1994 %	1995 %	1996 %	1997 %	1998 %	1999 %
Population ('000)	57 404	58 236	59 035	59 113	59 750	60 351	60 949	61 551
Total labour force	54.80	54.32	52.60	53.03	53.39	53.02	52.74	53.31
Current labour force	53.26	52.20	49.93	50.38	51.45	51.31	50.69	51.57
Employed persons (as percentage of current labour force)	95.52	96.08	95.78	97.57	97.91	97.75	95.21	94.59
Unemployed persons (as percentage of current labour force)	4.48	3.92	4.22	2.43	2.08	2.25	4.79	5.41
Seasonally inactive labour force (percentage of total labour force)	2.82	3.91	5.06	5.01	3.63	3.24	3.89	3.26
Persons not in labour force (of which):	17.97	19.05	21.58	22.99	23.00	23.75	24.43	24.25
— Household work	NA	31.77	30.33	29.20	29.16	29.26	29.16	28.26
— Studies	NA	38.74	39.92	38.78	39.82	40.54	40.90	41.95
— Too young, too old or incapable of work	23.86	23.23	21.92	25.89	24.59	24.16	24.59	24.75
Others	NA	6.26	7.83	6.12	6.44	6.01	5.35	5.04
Persons under age 13	27.22	26.63	25.83	23.98	23.61	23.22	22.83	22.45

Source: Derived from *Yearbook of Labour Statistics 1998* (Department of Labour Protection and Welfare, Ministry of Labour and Social Welfare and National Statistical Office's Labour Force Survey.

* Note: The National Statistical Office carries out The Labour Force Survey four times a year. The figures vary by season: first round is in February, the non-agricultural season, the second in May, at the end of the school year when new members of the labour force are entering the labour market, the third round is in August, when the agricultural season has peak employment, and the fourth round is in November, during the harvest season. Hence, figures vary.

In a country of over 61 million inhabitants in 1999, 53 per cent or close to 33 million people form the labour force in Thailand (table 13.1). Of this figure, close to 92 per cent are actually engaged in work, the remainder comprising those displaced or unemployed. The gradual increase in population has not been met with an increase in persons in the labour force. Part of this may be due to an increasing number of people choosing to remain in school for higher studies — enrolment in primary and secondary school, on the other hand, may have actually decreased as the result of the crisis — and there has been the suggestion that a disproportionate number of women who have been displaced from work form the 'uncounted' home or domestic workers in the population. On the whole, the very youthful Thai market (with about 25 per cent of the population under the age of 15 years) is struggling to come to terms with the crisis that forced one in 10 employed people to have to change jobs and where approximately half of employed persons who did not change jobs experienced some reduction in income, bonus and benefits (LFS 1998).

In general, a gradual trend away from an agriculture-focused orientation in the economy can be observed in Thailand (table 13.2).

Table 13.2: ***Number of employed persons in agriculture and non-agriculture, 1992–1999***

Year	Agriculture		Non-agriculture	
	Peak season %	Off-peak season %	Peak season %	Off-peak season %
1992	60.8	51.0	39.2	49.0
1993	56.7	48.9	43.3	51.1
1994	56.0	43.9	44.0	56.1
1995	52.0	40.8	48.0	59.2
1996	50.00	40.4	50.0	59.6
1997	50.3	39.4	49.7	60.6
1998	51.3	39.6	48.7	60.4
1999	48.5	41.8	51.5	58.2

Sources: Derived from *Yearbook of Labour Statistics 1998* (Department of Labour Protection and Welfare, Ministry of Labour and Social Welfare) and National Statistical Office's Labour Force survey.
Note: Peak season indicates Round 3 (agricultural season with peak employment) of the LFS, while Off-Peak indicates Round 1 (non-agricultural season) of the LFS.

In terms of occupational groups, craftsmen and labourers formed the largest group of unemployed people following the crisis — many worked in the non-agricultural sectors but were later absorbed by the agricultural sector following a return migration from the city to the rural north-east (table 13.3).

The large stream of migration of labourers, particularly from Bangkok to the rural north-east, was also affected by diminishing employment prospects in the city. Of those unemployed following the crisis, close to 80 per cent were former workers, the remainder comprised of new entrants to the workforce — those never having been previously employed. Thailand historically has been a strongly agricultural-oriented economy. Even today, the country is a strong net exporter of food (such as rice and tapioca).

Table 13.3: ***Unemployed workers by their last jobs (industry), August 1996–1998***

Previous job/industry	1996	1997	1998
Unemployed population (in 000's)	354	293	1138
Never worked/new entrant (%)	26.5	31.1	19.0
Agriculture (%)	48.3	24.7	32.3
Non-agriculture, of which: (%)	51.7	75.3	67.7
— Manufacturing	17.6	24.6	33.0
— Construction	32.6	30.2	27.7
—Commerce	10.8	22.7	17.9
— Transport	3.6	3.2	4.2
— Service	16.4	19.2	16.4
— Others	2.5	(—)	(—)

Sources: Derived from *Yearbook of Labour Statistics 1998* (Department of Labour Protection and Welfare, Ministry of Labour and Social Welfare) and National Statistical Office's Labour Force survey.

Table 13.4 shows the breakdown of employment by occupation during 1992–1998. The most notable changes or trends seem to be in the increase of the share of professional and technical workers in the country and other administrative, executive and managerial workers.

Table 13.5 divides employees in terms of their work status — differentiated among those occupied as employers, government employees, private employees, own account workers and unpaid family workers.

The public sector continues to be a major employer in Thailand though its ability to absorb a wide unemployed educated workforce has been diminished during the last two decades. There are over two million civil servants in Thailand and an additional 250 000 working in state enterprises according to the American Embassy (1996). The public sector is facing a challenge with the migration of qualified workers into the private sector.

While the private sector continues to attract workers, particularly in the areas of services and general commerce (table 13.6), its overall share in terms of the work status of those employed decreased in 1998 (table 13.5). The NSO has a special name for small family business enterprises: 'Own account workers'. These are persons who run businesses by themselves or cooperate with others for the purpose of profit or sharing of profit without wages or non-wage employment by employees. Their business may also occasionally be assisted by relatives without payment, according to the NSO. Own account workers comprised 32 per cent of the labour force during 1997 and 1998. Not surprisingly, the number of unpaid family workers increased in 1998 (table 13.5).

Table 13.4: ***Employed individuals by occupation, 1992–1998***

	1992 %	1993 %	1994 %	1995 %	1996 %	1997 %	1998 %
Farmers, fishermen, hunters, minders, quarrymen and related workers	53.3	53.1	48.2	46.9	45.4	45.3	44.6
Craftsmen, production process workers and labourers	18.7	18.0	20.8	20.5	22.1	21.0	19.0
Sales workers	10.7	10.8	11.5	12.1	12.3	12.7	14.0
Professional, technical and workers	4.1	4.3	4.8	5.0	4.8	5.4	6.2
Services, sports and recreation workers	4.2	4.4	4.6	4.7	4.6	4.8	5.1
Workers in transport and communication	3.4	3.5	3.8	4.2	4.1	4.2	4.1
Clerical workers	3.4	3.7	3.9	4.0	3.9	3.9	4.1
Administrative, executive and managerial workers	2.1	2.2	2.3	2.5	2.6	2.6	3.0
TOTAL (000)*	29 885	30 679	29 763	30 815	31 166	31 714	30 260

Sources: Derived from *Yearbook of Labour Statistics 1998* (Department of Labour Protection and Welfare, Ministry of Labour and Social Welfare) and National Statistical Office's Labour Force survey.
* Workers not classifiable by occupation comprise less than one per cent.

Table 13.5: ***Employed individuals by work status, 1992–1998***

	1991 %	1992 %	1993 %	1994 %	1995 %	1996 %	1997 %	1998 %
Employer	1.93	2.32	2.06	2.02	2.64	2.65	2.39	2.55
Government employee	6.84	6.96	7.09	7.83	7.86	7.40	7.63	8.91
Private employee	28.82	29.88	30.32	32.37	32.32	34.54	34.21	32.29
Own account worker	31.22	30.12	30.02	31.18	31.34	30.97	30.23	32.18
Unpaid family worker	31.19	26.98	30.51	26.60	25.84	24.43	25.54	24.07
TOTAL (000)	28 859	29 885	30 679	29 763	30 815	31 166	31 714	30 260

Sources: Derived from *Yearbook of Labour Statistics 1998* (Department of Labour Protection and Welfare, Ministry of Labour and Social Welfare) and National Statistical Office's Labour Force survey.

Table 13.6: ***Employed individuals by industry, 1992–1998***

	1992 %	1993 %	1994 %	1995 %	1996 %	1997 %
Agriculture, forestry, hunting and fishing	53.34	53.03	48.06	46.70	45.36	45.14
Mining and quarrying	—	—	—	—	—	—
Manufacturing	13.57	13.62	14.61	14.95	14.92	14.64
Construction, repair and demolition	5.90	5.26	7.35	7.29	8.50	7.89
Electricity, gas, water and sanitary services	—	—	—	—	—	—
Commerce	12.06	12.41	13.00	13.58	14.11	14.51
Transport, storage and communication	2.87	2.96	3.15	3.27	3.19	3.28
Service	2.87	11.98	13.03	13.41	13.15	13.78
Activities not adequately described	—	—	—	—	—	—
TOTAL (000)*	29 885	30 679	29 763	30 815	31 166	31 714

Sources: Derived from *Yearbook of Labour Statistics 1998* (Department of Labour Protection and Welfare, Ministry of Labour and Social Welfare) and National Statistical Office's Labour Force Survey.
Note: Mining and quarrying, electricity, gas, water, and sanitary services, and 'Activities not adequately described' are less than one per cent for the years 1992–1998.

A recent Labour Force Survey found 44 per cent of all women to be employed compared with 56 per cent of all men (table 13.7). Women have been said to be particularly adversely affected by the economic crisis (*The Nation* 2000) though actual figures suggest that the impact of the crisis in terms of resulting unemployment has been equally dispersed in terms of gender breakdown according to TDRI (table 13.8).

Table 13.7: ***Population by sex and employment status, 1998***

	Male	Female
Total population (000)	30 626.6	30 773.3
Employed	56.30	44.62
Unemployed	2.56	2.20
Seasonally inactive labour force	*	*
Persons not in labour force	17.66	30.09
Persons under 13 years of age	23.18	22.48

Sources: Derived from *Yearbook of Labour Statistics 1998* (Department of Labour Protection and Welfare, Ministry of Labour and Social Welfare) and National Statistical Office's Labour Force Survey.
* Less than one per cent.

Table 13.8: ***Distribution and incidence of the unemployed, February 1997 and February 1998***

Unemployed persons by region	Number (000)				Percentage distribution				Percentage of labour force			
	Male		Female		Male		Female		Male		Female	
	97	98	97	98	97	98	97	98	97	98	97	98
Rural Central	35	96	39	73	10.2	11.4	10.9	11.5	1.3	3.5	1.7	3.3
Rural North	46	123	58	199	13.4	14.5	16.4	12	1.6	4.4	2.7	3.7
Rural North-east	159	430	151	308	46.5	50.6	42.6	48.8	3.1	8.1	4	8.2
Rural South	18	39	255	26	5.2	4.6	7	4.2	1	2.1	1.7	1.8
Bangkok	31	53	255	70	9.2	6.2	6.9	11.2	1.5	2.5	1.4	3.6
Other Urban	54	107	57	78	15.6	12.6	16.2	12.3	1.6	3.3	2.1	2.9

Source: Adapted from Thailand Development Research Institute 1999.

Females comprised a higher share of 'unpaid family workers' (65 per cent; table 13.9) with the distinction between municipal and non-municipal areas (urban versus rural) slight (66 per cent versus 65 per cent).

Table 13.9: ***Employed persons by work status and sex (both municipal and non-municipal areas*) 1998***

	Male %	Female %
Employer	3.22	0.98
Government employee	9.61	7.88
Private employee	30.15	30.28
Own account worker	40.38	21.67
Unpaid family worker	16.65	39.18
TOTAL (000)	17 242	13 732

Sources: Derived from *Yearbook of Labour Statistics 1998* (Department of Labour Protection and Welfare, Ministry of Labour and Social Welfare) and National Statistical Office's Labour Force Survey.
* Roughly defined as municipal (urban) and non-municipal (rural) areas.

When considering industry and gender, females comprise a higher share of employees in manufacturing, commerce and services (table 13.10). For example, this is consistent with research which has concluded that employers in the export processing zones situated across the country and especially in the north, favour female employees (Ungpakorn 1999). It is difficult to estimate female employment in the informal sector, though research has suggested that women comprise a high share of workers in this area, particularly as petty traders and merchants. Also, domestic workers such as household help, sex trade workers, hawkers and vendors, who primarily comprise women, are often not included in official statistics. Again, it must be emphasised that statistics for these sectors are difficult to obtain, estimate and verify.

Table 13.10: ***Employment by industry and gender in municipal and non-municipal areas, 1998***

	Male %	Female %	Total (000)
Agriculture, forestry, hunting and fishing	57.08	47.92	15 047.8
Mining and quarrying	79.89	20.11	36.8
Manufacturing	49.57	50.43	4 419.8
Construction, repair and demolition	85.85	14.23	1 285.1
Electricity, gas, water and sanitary services	83.41	16.59	184.4
Commerce	47.70	52.30	4 463.8
Transport, storage and communication	87.69	12.31	996.3
Services	47.83	52.17	4 523.5
Activities not adequately described	54.11	45.89	14.6
TOTAL			30 973.1

Sources: Derived from *Yearbook of Labour Statistics 1998* (Department of Labour Protection and Welfare, Ministry of Labour and Social Welfare) and National Statistical Office's Labour Force Survey.

Table 13.11 summarises gender and age differences in terms of the last Labour Force Survey of 1998. A majority of those over 59 and under 14 do not participate in the labour force. One finds peak unemployment in the 20–24 age group which is consistent with other research on unemployment of fresh (university) graduates and recent hires in the Thai workforce. Education and skills development are considered to be important barometers of social and economic development of a labour force. The next section looks at this aspect in more detail.

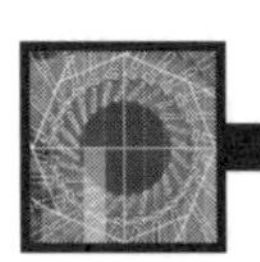

Education and skills development

The economic crisis has also had an impact on human resource development in Thailand. There is some evidence that enrolment in schools has decreased following the crisis. Because of the erosion in family income, poor parents are unable to send children to school for higher education. According to the Ministry of Education, school dropouts in 1998 were estimated to be about 100 000 from primary schools, and 90 000 from junior secondary schools. This represents an increase in school

Table 13.11: *Population by age group, sex and labour force status, 1998*

	Male (%)				Female (%)			
	Employed	Unem- ployed	Seasonal inactive	Not in labour force	Employed	Unem- ployed	Seasonal inactive	Not in labour force
13–14	8.6	1	<1	90.3	7.6	<1	<1	92
15–19	33.8	4.8	<1	60.8	30	2.5	<1	67
20–24	69.5	8.4	<1	21.4	60	6.1	<1	32.8
25–29	87	5.5	1.1	6.4	72.5	4.3	<1	22.6
30–34	92.5	3	<1	3.9	75.5	3.4	1.3	19.9
35–39	94.8	2	<1	2.9	78.7	2.8	<1	17.5
40–49	95.7	1.8	<1	2.4	77.2	2.5	<1	19.4
50–59	90.9	1	<1	8	62.8	2	<1	34.4
Over 59	45.5	4	0	54.2	22	<1	<1	77.1

Sources: Derived from *Yearbook of Labour Statistics 1998* (Department of Labour Protection and Welfare, Ministry of Labour and Social Welfare) and National Statistical Office's Labour Force survey.

dropouts and has two major implications: it contributes to an increase in child labour and reduces the level of education of the workforce. According to one estimate, between 200 000 and 400 000 children still work in conditions of potential abuse (American Embassy 1996). The Thailand Development and Research Institute found that education at higher levels was also affected by the crisis. It noted reduced budgets for governmental departments connected with education and a reduction in the number of scholarships available for higher education. Data (table 13.12) reveal unemployment rates by education levels. Workers with primary and lower education formed the largest number of unemployed while workers with upper secondary level education had the highest relative unemployment rate.

The oversupply of an educated workforce — primarily in the social sciences and liberal arts — is the result of some fundamental changes in Thai educational institutions since the 1970s. Thailand's rapid economic growth had encouraged the demand for higher education. The governmental response to this increase in demand was to increase its expenditure on education in the country. The resulting explosion in new degree and certificate-granting institutions, along with increases in enrolment, caused the large flow of graduates in the marketplace during the late 1970s. The public sector, which cannot absorb all of these graduates, has been trying to formulate policy which deals effectively with manpower planning and the training of a workforce to meet the requirements of a changing marketplace. Skills development, the 'right' skills development, has been the priority of labour planners for low- and semi-skilled labour, while other initiatives have included developing labour in skills areas for export to overseas markets (Torrington & Tan 1994) and the promotion of foreign investment in Thailand for rapid technology transfer.

Table 13.12: *Unemployment by level of educational attainment, 1994–1998*

	1994		1995		1996		1997		1998	
	Unemployed %	Total labour force	Unemployed %	Total labour force	Unemployed %	Total labour force	Unemployed %	Total labour force	Unemployed %	Total labour force
Primary and lower	4.06	24 892 951	2.31	24 238 544	1.98	24 509 724	2.02	23 974 463	4.46	23 071 788
Lower secondary	3.85	2 347 737	2.46	2 768 645	2.57	3 029 801	3.13	3 167 750	5.83	3 676 227
Upper secondary	3.35	877 865	3.03	1 087 725	2.10	1 031 834	2.23	1 201 093	6.03	413 407
Vocational and others	2.49	1 542 768	2.63	1 511 491	1.61	1 507 168	2.75	1 582 407	3.58	1 664 144
University	2.29	1 515 980	1.35	1 630 654	1.86	1 703 619	2.21	1 976 788	4.03	2 259 548
TOTAL	3.86	31 177 301	2.31	31 237 059	2.02	31 782 146	2.19	31 902 501	4.61	32 085 114
Over 59	45.5	4	0	54.2	22	<1	<1	77.1		

Sources: Derived from *Yearbook of Labour Statistics 1998* (Department of Labour Protection and Welfare, Ministry of Labour and Social Welfare) and National Statistical Office's Labour Force Survey.

There are several issues concerning the quality of labour supply in Thailand according to a recent summary report ('Direction for Manpower Development for Long-Term Industrial Development') prepared on behalf of the Ministry of Industry. The first issue deals with the lack of incentives for continuing higher education given the fact that the expenses for higher education are rather high in the country. Secondly, educational institutions are considered slow when adapting to employment demands in the labour market. They are said to produce a high number of graduates in 'outdated' fields. Finally, the rapid expansion of certain sectors in the economy has brought about a severe shortage of technicians and engineers. Often, companies have attempted to train primary or vocational graduates to do the work of engineers but this has resulted in low product quality.

The government has been trying to encourage Thai students to pursue science and engineering degrees. Thailand has faced a shortage of technical workers — the Thailand Development Research Institute (TDRI) projects that by the year 2001 there will be a severe shortage of engineers in the country (9300 engineers up from 6400 in 1996). According to the Ministry of University Affairs and the Ministry of Edu cation, Thai universities produce about 3000 engineering graduates a year (Tan & Torrington 1998). Kirivong (1988) found that Thailand has a ratio of 50 engineers to every million persons, compared to Malaysia, Taiwan and South Korea which have ratios of 82, 425 and 679 respectively.

The Department of Skill Development (DSD) (Ministry of Labour and Social Welfare) estimates that 75 per cent of the present labour force of 33 million workers are unskilled workers with an average of 5.1 years of education. In its projection of the labour force, TDRI found a greater demand for workers with medium and higher educational levels than is currently available in the primary-education dominated labour force. This is in line with the conclusions of the Thai Skills Development Project, an ADB financed project at the Department of Skill Development, Ministry of Labour and Social Welfare. One policy move being considered is to increase the compulsory education of workers from the current system of six years to nine years.

In conjunction with this professional training system, the DSD has encouraged the participation of the private sector in stimulating the achievement of its labour force objectives. The private sector is to benefit from skill development in a number of ways:

- employers who register as professional trainers are exempt, under the *Vocational Training Promotion Act 1994*, from labour and private institution law and are allowed to deduct additional expenses from income tax (50 per cent deduction of training expenses)
- employers who provide training for employees in the workplace are able to deduct additional expenses from taxes (50 per cent)
- also, employers help support the Skill Standards Testing Centers with the DSD controlling the standard and issuing licences.

In addition, the DSD is encouraging the private sector to become more responsible in skill development by improving the law under the *Promoting Professional Training Act 1994*, in two main areas: one, requiring employers to develop the skills of some of their employees or contribute to the Skill Development Fund; and two, offering loans to businesses to help them provide skill development for their employees. The Skill Development Fund offers loans at a one per cent interest rate to new entrants to the labour market, laid off workers and those wishing to upgrade their skills. Those eligible for the loan must be poor Thai nationals, aged 15–45 years, who will use the

loan for training expenses. Following the economic crisis of 1997, this Fund has enabled many to continue their professional development.

When progress in basic education is considered on a historical basis, though, Thailand can be viewed as a success story. Thailand has made substantial progress in this area during the past few decades. Primary school enrolment has been substantial and Thailand experienced universal enrolment (Sussangkarn & Chalamwong 1994) during the 1980s. Considering its population explosion during the 1960s and 1970s, this is an accomplishment. In particular, when adult literacy rates are evaluated (table 13.13) in a regional comparison, Thailand's 1990 rate of 93 per cent was just short of those found in more developed countries like South Korea (96 per cent), for example.

Table 13.13: ***Adult literacy rates for selected Asian countries, 1960–1990***

Country	1960 %	1970 %	1980 %	1990 %
Thailand	67.7	78.6	86.0	93.0
Hong Kong	70.4	77.3[a]	90.0[b]	n.a.
India	27.8[C]	34.1[a]	36.0[d]	48.0
Indonesia	39.0[C]	56.6[a]	62.0[e]	74.0
Malaysia	52.8[f]	58.5	60.0	78.0
Philippines	71.9	82.6	75.0[b]	90.0
Singapore	n.a.	68.9	83.0	n.a.
South Korea	70.6	87.6	93.0	96.0
Sri Lanka	75.0[f]	77.6[a]	85.0[b]	88.0

Sources: (adapted from Sussangkarn and Chalamwong, 1994: 4); IBRD, *World Tables 1983*, and *World Development Report 1991, 1994*.
Notes: a=1971, b=1979, c=1961, d=1981, e=1978, f=1962.

The National Plans subsequently reflect the need for *continued* human resources development in Thailand where a skilled and semi-skilled labour force is needed to satisfy the demands of a rapidly industrialising market.

Diversity in the workplace

Some legislation in the Thai Constitution addresses the issue of discrimination, which, like the US, Title VII of the *Civil Rights Act 1964*, calls for the elimination of employment and union practices that discriminate against employment and job applicants on the basis of race, colour, religion, sex or national origin. In practice, however, there is little discussion in working circles about practices such as sexual harassment, disability and employee privacy as they exist in the West. The revised *Labour Protection Act 1998* also stipulates that there should be no discrimination among the sexes in terms of how they are treated (Section 15) and that sexual harassment by a 'chief of staff, supervisor, or inspector' against employees who are women or children is prohibited (Section 16).

Under the new Thai Constitution, enacted on 11 October 1997, Section 5 states 'the Thai people, irrespective of their origins, sexes or religions, shall enjoy equal protection' (under the Constitution). The Thai Constitution is the 'supreme law of the State'. It also asserts the following provisions:

Section 30 All persons are equal before the law and shall enjoy equal protection under the law. Men and women shall enjoy equal rights. Unjust discrimination against a person on the grounds of the difference in origin, race, language, sex, age, physical or health condition, personal status, economic or social standing, religious belief, education or constitutionally political view, shall not be permitted.

Section 34 A person's family rights, dignity, reputation or the right of privacy shall be protected.

Section 38 A person shall enjoy full liberty to profess a religion, a religious sect or creed, and observe religious precepts or exercise a form of worship in accordance with his or her belief; provided that it is not contrary to his or her civic duties, public order or good morals.

Section 45 A person shall enjoy the liberty to unite and form an association, a union, league, cooperative, farmer group, private organisation or any other group.

Additional statutes address the issues of: protection of the interests of children and youth (Section 53), the disabled (Section 55), and the elderly and the underprivileged (Section 80). The state is also responsible for the promotion of 'people of working age to obtain employment, protect labour, especially child and women labour, and provide for the system of labour relations, social security and fair wages' (Section 86). Section 83 of the Constitution furthermore states that the state 'shall implement fair distribution of incomes'. In practice, however, the issue of diversity or equity is not a common underlying theme in the Thai workforce. It is unclear whether the legislation behind the support for the weaker or under-represented elements of the Thai workforce has been put to the test.

In some cases, it has been argued, culture and repression have played a role in undermining the potential enforcement of any legislation dealing with discrimination (Ungpakorn 1999). For example, religious beliefs might mean that a worker does not see a boss as an exploiter (or vice-versa). Limqueco et al. (1989) have argued that repression has halted the development of unions towards Western standards — union organisers are often fired for their activities (Ungpakorn 1999) which is in violation of Section 45 of the Constitution.

Gardenwartz and Rowe's (1998) 'Diversity Related Performance Standards for Managers' provides a checklist of best practices in terms of maintaining a diverse workforce:

- hiring, retaining and promoting individuals from diverse backgrounds
- coaching and grooming diverse individuals for advancement
- resolving diversity-related conflicts between staff members
- maintaining a low rate of discrimination and harassment complaints
- developing staff through delegation
- planning and leading effective meetings with diverse staff
- learning about the cultural norms and values of employees
- helping new employees acculturate to the organisation's norms

- providing cultural sensitivity training for staff
- attending cultural awareness training and applying learning with own staff.

In Thailand there is no overt awareness of diversity related issues. Diversity in the American sense does exist when one looks carefully at a sampling of the workforce. At Thai located companies it is not uncommon to find ethnic Thais working side by side with ethnic Chinese and Indians. The Chinese in particular have a longer relationship with Thailand, having arrived during the eighteenth century from the southern provinces of China. Some characterise modern Thailand business environment as being dominated by the 'Sino–Thai merchant culture' (Reynolds 1998). Indeed, the ethnic Chinese are said to dominate the business landscape today, certainly as far as ownership of the largest corporate entities are concerned (Backman 1999).

Religious diversity is evident in Thai companies with Sikhs, Hindus, Christians and Muslims working together. Given this setting, one might expect a tendency to promote or cultivate a diverse image in the public view such as that found in ASEAN neighbour Singapore, for example. In companies located in Malaysia and Singapore, for example, employers adopt the diverse holiday schedules prescribed by the various religious groups represented in their companies. Holidays such as Chinese New Year or the Hindu holiday Deepavali are celebrated and observed in these countries. In Thailand, only Thai or Buddhist holidays are celebrated and observed and most employees who choose to celebrate other holidays do so informally. In Thailand, assimilation is encouraged and expected (Reynolds 1998). The ethnic Chinese, for example, faced decades of racist policies during the early part of this century. This forced assimilation was evident in overt ways: speaking Thai, dressing Thai and pledging loyalty to the King and Buddhism (Kasian 1992; Skinner 1957, Reynolds 1998).

Linguistic diversity might present another facet of the diversity issue. Unlike Malaysia or Singapore, where knowledge of other languages is promoted even in the workplace, employers in Thailand, certainly in the larger corporations, expect competency in Thai, the local language. Thai is the country's official language. Job advertisements, for example, may specify Thai language skills as a requirement. Thailand is said to have maintained a one-language policy 'for the solidarity and unity of the country' (*The Nation* 2000) and does not have a policy specifically on teaching English. Ethnic Chinese and Indians continue to use their native languages, especially in smaller and family establishments. For the most part, they use Thai in daily life and when working for larger organisations. Section 30 of the Constitution addresses the issue of discrimination as it relates to language 'unjust discrimination against a person on the grounds of the difference [in] ... language shall not be permitted'.

English usage is becoming more widespread. Certainly in the large hospitality and tourism sector, it is viewed as a valuable skill but one that can still be improved upon. There has been some consensus recently regarding the possible adoption of English as a second language. Officials from the National Education Reform Board have recognised the importance of English being a lingua franca of the world. The private sector is considered to be an effective harbinger for the use of English. With English being compulsory in the Thai educational system, Thailand may one day achieve the levels of adoption found in countries such as Malaysia, Singapore and the Philippines.

The following sections will address in more detail some key elements of the Thai workforce which contribute to diversity. Gender-related aspects of diversity will be addressed as well as the three major categories of non-ethnic Thai workers representing Thailand's diverse workforce: the entrepreneurs, primarily the ethnic Chinese and Indian business communities; the 'guest workers', those from predominantly neighbouring South-east Asian nations; and the expatriates, skilled foreign labour in Thailand. Some mention will also be made of Thais as expatriates and their impact on the labour market.

The 'second' sex

The present Thai Constitution asserts that the state will promote gender equality in the country. Women constitute for more than 50 per cent of the population but form less than 10 per cent of public decision-makers at the national level. While figures on female representation in management at Thai firms are difficult to obtain, female representation in government has been documented (*The Nation* 2000). The proportion of female representation at senior levels in local government is: provincial governors (less than three per cent); district officers (0.1 per cent — prior to 1996 women were barred from this position); sub-district heads (1.8 per cent); and village heads (2.4 per cent). At the more senior MP level, female representation is six per cent. Female representation in the Cabinet was four per cent in 1998, up from no representation in 1995.

Appold et al. (1998) have presented the most recent analysis of the employment of women managers and professionals in Thailand. Their investigation found the most current estimates of female economic presence in the marketplace using three countries as a basis for comparison, the US, Japan and Thailand. Women formed 40.1 per cent of those economically active in Japan, 45.0 per cent in the US and 46.7 per cent in Thailand. However, when looking more closely at the occupation of administrative and management positions in the three countries, the figures are 7.5 per cent, 39.3 per cent, and 22.2 per cent respectively.

Interestingly, Appold et al. (1998) found 'no evidence for the effect of deeply-rooted cultural forces on the employment of women' in their sampled firms. Chinese 'patriarchal' practices and Japanese 'closed' mentality towards women were not evident. In practice, Japanese firms operating in Thailand, for example, are more likely to attract female employment in job categories which are not traditionally held by women (Lawler 1994) than either American or Thai firms. It is unclear whether these female employees reach upper managerial positions but it was found that Japanese firms provide support mechanisms for women by assisting them in raising their families (Galenson & Odaka 1976; Ono 1980) — a practice few others choose to emulate.

Culture may still play a role in terms of how female employees are perceived by employers in Thailand. Thanachaisethavut and Chouwilai (1998: 75), in their study of a Thai export processing industrial estate, argue that 'women are [viewed as] more docile and easier to manage than men' and they imply that this is the reason why foreign investors prefer to hire female workers (Ungpakorn 1999). The Asia Monitor Resources Center (1998) found that women in these export processing zones suffered from long working hours, forced overtime, unsafe conditions, underpayment of wages and job insecurity due to increased casualisation of labour.

Ungpakorn (1999: 70) notes, citing Phananiramai (1996):

> Despite the indication that women gain a better standard of living from working in factories, rather than working in the fields, women do suffer from discrimination

> with regard to men. Women's monthly earnings in 1989 were on average, 80 per cent of men's earnings. Only 30 per cent of this wage differential between men and women could be explained by average differences in age, education and marital status between men and women, and even these factors are related to sex discrimination.

Appold et al. (1998) noted that Thai women were more heavily represented both at the bottom and at the top of the organisational hierarchy in Thai firms. They concluded: 'the greater representation of women at the top in Thai firms implies that gender is only one of a number of distinctions contributing to social distance in organisations'. Critics, particularly in the area of sustainable development, argue that the status of Thai women still lags behind that of women in more industrialised countries. Far too often careers are sidelined during child-bearing years when women in Thailand are expected to sacrifice their career interests for the sake of family. Recently, in conjunction with International Women's Day, leading representatives from non-governmental groups concerned with labour welfare promotion presented the government of Prime Minister Chuan Leekpai with a five-point demand. These points include:

- accelerating the issuing of a Royal decree to put the employment insurance scheme into effect by the end of 2000
- establishing an independent institute to protect workers' health and safety and to reduce hazards in the workplace
- make 8 March a public holiday (International Women's Day) so that both male and female workers might participate in gender-related activities of the day
- formulate a policy to help fund and promote the establishment of preschool childcare centres in industrial and community areas for low-income families
- the government should set a clear policy on promoting and supporting female workers' participation in national committees that set policy and legislation affecting the well-being, rights, liberty and interests of workers.

The recent crisis had a detrimental impact on women according to the Working Committee of the International Women's Day campaign in Thailand (comprised of the Labour Federation, State Enterprise Worker Relations Federation, Labour Congress of Thailand and labour unions in several industrial sectors). Female workers have suffered under worsening working conditions following the crisis. Because they are said to have less bargaining power in the labour market, they are often treated unfairly and not protected by labour laws. Many women hold temporary and unsafe jobs, work long hours and often are paid less than the minimum wage.

The current *Labour Protection Act 1998* (Section 15) states that an employer is to treat male and female employees equally 'except where the nature or conditions of the work does not allow the employer to do so'. Women are to refrain from hazardous and strenuous work (Section 38–40) and are not to be discriminated against during pregnancy (Section 43).

Business enterprise in Thailand is dominated by small-scale family enterprise. The 'informal' sector of petty trade and services and handicraft and cottage industries has been traditionally dominated by women who were considered the first entrepreneurs in the country and indeed, in the region as a whole (Lim 1985). When farming was still mainly for subsistence and before agriculture became substantially commercialised, all market activity — both buying and selling — was conducted by women. The small-scale business enterprise activity found in all corners of the country — market sales, hawking and small stallholders are often controlled by women, some having acquired the necessary capital for such enterprises through initial employment in the country's notorious 'informal' sectors.

The entrepreneurs

> Since the numbers of ethnic Chinese are few, and many prefer to be entrepreneurs rather than employees[2], Southeast Asian Chinese companies must employ many non-Chinese, who also form the bulk of their customers. Thus they need to develop ethnically-neutral business practices (Lim 1996: 67).

Chinese migration to Thailand began during the early nineteenth century when labour supplies were becoming scarce in the Kingdom. The common practice of *phrai*, the use of indentured servants by the King or noblemen, was greatly reduced during the 1850s. This combined with the expansion of the agrarian frontier and to some extent the expansion of private trade, drove the Siamese court to import labour from China. During the early period, Chinese labourers arrived in Siam to work on major infrastructure projects. Most labourers stayed for shorter periods of time and subsequently returned home. Some, however, settled in the country during an era which saw the Kingdom, particularly its urban centres, expand rapidly.

Partly resulting from political disorder in southern China and largely the consequence of Thailand's labour shortage, the Chinese numbered around 40 000 to 60 000 in Bangkok by the 1850s (Phongpaichit & Baker 1995). During the latter decades of the nineteenth century, with the growth of the tin and timber trades and the development of urban areas on all fronts (streets, buildings, markets, road and railway networks), Chinese labour satisfied increased requirements. By some accounts, there were over 600 000 ethnic Chinese in Thailand by the turn of the century (Skinner 1957: 74).

Of Thailand's current population of about 61 million inhabitants, 12 per cent are ethnic Chinese (EIU 1998). However, this relatively small share of the population controls approximately 75 per cent of private, corporate and domestic capital in the country according to one estimate (Backman 1999). Chinese-managed conglomerates are dominant in the Thai landscape, forming an essential part of the business community.

A number of Thailand's largest corporations are managed by Thais of Chinese origin. The Charoen Pokphand (CP) Group, Thailand's largest business group in terms of domestic and overseas combined revenues is a prominent Chinese family-run conglomerate. Chinese control the two leading private banks, the Bangkok Bank and Thai Farmers Bank. Countless other enterprises, particularly small family businesses are Chinese-owned.

The Chinese are said to have astutely used their economic strength and network associations in Thailand's tumultuous political landscape in recent years. The leading corporations which are Chinese-run and managed regularly make financial and leadership contributions to the country's main political parties (Backman 1999). Individual parties have strong links to Thai big business which are rewarded with their own representation in the government. These government-industry linkages fostered the exchanges between the corporate boardroom and the Cabinet which were reminiscent of the US Government during the 1980s. It is unclear whether this close relationship has supported the cause for diversity in labour policy and practices.

Ethnic Indians form another minority group in Thailand which can best be described as entrepreneurial. Indians, notably Sikhs, are a vibrant community with significant presence in the real estate and textile businesses. They are also recognised for their contributions in small-scale enterprises such as tailoring services, restaurant and other hospitality services. While many Indians are engaged in private enterprise, younger generations are choosing to pursue higher education both in the country and, increasingly, abroad. There is little information available on Indians in Thailand though their presence is felt. They maintain their community networks like the Chinese, though their complete integration into Thai society may not be viewed as unproblematic by insiders as well as outsiders alike. Indians are visible but form a much smaller proportion of the population than the ethnic Chinese.

There is no specific legislation which addresses discrimination against a particular minority group such as the Chinese or Indians, but Section 30 of the Constitution does address the issue of discrimination. Section 14 of the Labour Protection Act states 'unless otherwise provided for in this Act, the employer shall treat the employees properly according to the rights and duties as provided for in the Civil and Commercial Code'. The Act does not apply to various governmental institutions including central administration, provincial administration, local administration and state enterprises. There are no figures on the ethnic origin of employees in these departments of the government but one can assume that Thai nationality is required. The concept of discrimination against a particular ethnic group is a foreign one in the Thai setting given Thai culture and the Buddhist religion which stresses the 'middle path' (see also, Sussangkarn & Chalamwong 1994). In other words, Thais are said to be unaware of such a concept because there is a propensity for harmonious relationships in the workplace, according to one lawyer familiar with the Thai Constitution. This lawyer has also noted that there are no well-known cases involving the issue of discrimination against a particular minority in Thailand.

Given historical considerations and intermarriage, many ethnic Chinese consider themselves Thai. Employers in Thailand do have a lot of latitude in terms of hiring, however. It is not uncommon, for example, to find a job advertisement in Thailand specifying nationality, age and/or sex. Employers are allowed to be specific in making their requirements known, according to the Thailand Board of Investment. When a company asks for a Thai, they are likely to mean a Thai national who is either an ethnic Thai or ethnic Chinese/Indian raised in Thailand (and a naturalised citizen).

The 'guest' workers

Diversity in terms of the promotion of people of foreign backgrounds is a debatable topic in business circles. First, one must specify the level of staff concerned. It is clear that in many family-owned businesses, senior positions penetrated by managers of foreign origin are rare. However, there are exceptions and the trend is towards recruiting capable managers, in some cases, even from abroad.

At the worker level, there is acknowledgement that numerous SMEs (small- and medium-sized enterprises) and larger-sized (over 250 employees) companies retain a share of foreign employees who are *illegal* workers. Given the nature of this practice, it is difficult to get actual figures. The Department of the Interior recently estimated that there are over 206 000 illegal aliens working in Thailand but other estimates suggest that the figure is much higher (up to 1 000 000) (Chalamwong & Sevilla 1996; Wut 1995; American Embassy 1996). Many illegal workers come from Myanmar and other neighbouring countries. The migratory flow of illegal workers has been attributed to an internal labour market tightening. Due to the relatively low levels of open unemployment and increases in wage rates in both Bangkok and the provinces illegal workers primarily from neighbouring countries have been drawn to work in Thailand (Chalamwong & Sevilla 1996; see table 13.14). This is particularly true with respect to the agricultural sector during peak seasons.

Table 13.14: ***Estimates of undocumented (illegal) workers in major border provinces,* 1995–1996***

Provinces	1994	1995	Sector (sub-sectors)
Chiang Rai, Chiang Mai, Mae Hong Son	30 000	40 000	Agriculture, construction, housework (maids), gem cutting, etc.
Tak	20 000	24 000	Same as above, small industries, prostitution
Kanchanaburi, Ratchaburi	16 000	41 000	Agriculture, construction, wood factories, mining, gas stations, golf courses, food shops, etc.
Ranong	34 000	32 000	Fishing boats, fish processing, construction, housework (maids), food shops, etc.
Chumporn, Surat Thani	6 000	13 000	Fishing boats, rubber plantation, palm oil, coffee, shrimp farm, etc.
Other border provinces and coastal provinces	100 000	60 000	Fishing boats, food processing, housework (maids), food shops, etc.
TOTAL	206 000	210 000	

Source: Ministry of Interior (1995), adapted from Chalamwong and Sevilla (1996).
* Workers mainly from Myanmar.

The Thai Government on the one hand recognises the need for attracting a highly-skilled workforce to Thailand. On the other hand, it cautiously observes the influx of illegal migrants from countries in the South Asian subcontinent, China and neighbouring countries such as Myanmar, Laos and Vietnam. In some cases, skilled workers from these countries migrate to Thailand and work in areas where higher domestic unemployment exists. Others enter the country on tourist visas and set up businesses jointly with Thais. Most are political and economic refugees who the Thai Government has begun to monitor, viewing these groups as a genuine threat to national security and interests.

The National Economics and Social Development Board (NESDB) and the Secretariat of the National Security Council (SNSC) influence labour market policy development and human resource development in Thailand. For example, when the SNSC observed a rise in the number of South Asian tourists overstaying their visas during the late 1980s, they announced a policy requiring application for visas prior to arrival in Thailand for those specific countries (Chalamwong & Sevilla 1996). The Ministry of Labour and Social Welfare, established in 1993, also works to facilitate policy making in the area of labour and social welfare. Other objectives of the Ministry include the promotion of employment both domestically and abroad for Thai nationals and the continual improvement in the vocational skills of workers.

The Thai Government has made numerous attempts to estimate the number of illegal workers in its borders. On the one hand, the government realises that these workers occupy positions which many Thais are presently unwilling to engage in. On the other hand, their low wages have further deteriorated the bargaining position of Thai workers. And there is always the constant threat of political upheaval with an influx of foreigners to Thailand.

These communities of foreigners tend to segregate themselves from Thais in daily life. Thais may engage in behaviours which might constitute 'harassment'[3] in the Western sense: little or no integration of workers and what is considered teasing or derogatory remarks about these illegal foreigners who have made Thailand their home. The Labour Protection Act and other legislation, it must be noted, applies to foreigners — but only those who are legally permitted to work in Thailand. A varied group of resident foreigners (table 13.15) does exist in the country and will be discussed in more detail in the following section.

The expatriates

The legal migration of skilled labour into Thailand has followed some distinct patterns over the years. The *Investment Promotion Act 1977*, the *Alien Act 1978*, and the *Immigration Act 1978* enabled skilled labour to temporarily migrate into the country. During 1979 to 1991, the number of skilled foreign workers given permission to temporarily work in the country increased by 270 per cent. This figure tripled to 36 623 by 1994 (Poapongsakorn & Taethiengtam 1992). According to the *Yearbook of Labour Statistics* (various issues), a large number of foreigners who were granted temporary permits[4] worked in Thailand as: engineers and technical specialists; administrative and managerial workers; and production supervisors/general foremen. In recent years, the majority of workers receiving work permits were Japanese, Chinese (Hong Kong and Taiwan), and American, (Chalamwong & Sevilla 1996; Torrington & Tan 1994), reflecting the major foreign investors in the country.

The Alien Occupation Division (Department of Labour and Social Welfare) determines which occupations are to be reserved for Thai citizens (see figure 13.1 for a detailed description of occupations forbidden to foreigners) and controls and inspects foreigners who come to work in Thailand under the Alien Occupations Act.

The government has attempted to solve the skilled labour shortage resulting from rapid industrialisation by allowing foreign investors to bring their own staff from overseas. According to some observers, the duration of their stay is dependent upon a review of effective technology transfer to local workers (Pitayanon 1988). There has been some concern about the influx of skilled labour in Thailand. In some quarters arguments have been made about the displacement of skilled Thai labour. Along with the rising unemployed ranks from vocational and technical institutions, the government has been under pressure from unions and professional associations to require that foreign companies accelerate the transfer of skills to local employees (Torrington & Tan 1994).

According to some accounts of foreign presence and participation in the Thai economy, Thais view foreigners in a positive manner (Cooper 1994). Foreigners are said to be welcome and appreciated for their expertise. There appears to be some preference for foreigners originating from Western countries — indeed, the United States, for example, has received preferential treatment as an investor nation by some accounts — and there may even be a hierarchy of foreigners. Western or white foreigners are perhaps viewed more favourably than others (Cooper 1994).

Table 13.15: ***Resident immigration population by citizenship, Thailand 1993–1996***

Country of origin	1993		1994		1995		1996	
	% of all immigrants	Total number from country	% of all immigrants	Total number from country	% of all immigrants	Total number from country	% of all immigrants	Total number from country
China	86.4	236 703	85.3	232 677	84.6	229 184	84.2	226 065
India	2.2	6 089	2.2	6 099	2.3	6 105	2.3	6 118
United Kingdom	1.9	5 285	1.9	5 272	2.0	5 290	2.0	5 333
Vietnam	1.2	3 281	1.2	3 216	1.2	3 163	1.1	3 077
Japan	1.0	2 574	1.0	2 570	1.0	2 578	1.0	2 568

Source: *Key Statistics of Thailand* (National Statistical Office), also found in International Labour Migration Database of the ILO.

Agricultural Businesses:
- Rice farming
- Salt farming, including salt mining except rock salt

Commercial Businesses:
- Internal trade in local agricultural products
- Land trade

Service Businesses:
- Accounting
- Law
- Architecture
- Advertising
- Brokerage or agency
- Auctioning
- Barbering, hair dressing and beauty shop ownership

Other businesses:
- Construction

Agricultural Businesses:
- Cultivation
- Orchard farming
- Animal husbandry, including silk worm raising
- Timber
- Fishing

Industrial and Handicraft Businesses:
- Rice milling
- Flour making from rice and other cash crops
- Sugar milling
- Manufacturing of alcoholic and non-alcoholic drinks and beverages
- Ice making
- Manufacturing of pharmaceuticals
- Cold storage
- Timber processing
- Manufacturing of gold, silver, nielloware and stone inlaid products
- Manufacturing of casting of Buddha images and bowls
- Wood carving
- Lacquer-ware making
- Match manufacturing
- Manufacturing of white cement, portland cement and cement finished products
- Dynamiting or quarrying of rocks
- Manufacturing of plywood, veneer wood, chipboard or hardboard
- Manufacturing of garments or footwear except to export
- Printing
- Newspaper publishing
- Silk spinning, or weaving of silk fabric
- Manufacturing of finished products from silk fabric, silk yarn or silk cocoons

Commercial Businesses:
- All retailing except for items included in Category 'C'
- Ore trading except for items included in Category 'C'
- Selling of food and drinks except for items included in Category 'C'
- Trading of antique, heirloom or fine arts objects

Service Businesses:
- Tour Agency
- Hotel, except hotel management
- All businesses under the law governing places of service
- Photography, photographic processing and printing
- Laundering
- Dressmaking

Other Businesses:
- Land, water, and air transportation in Thailand

Categories (open to foreigners)

Commercial Businesses:
- All wholesale trade except in items included in Category 'A'
- All exporting
- Retailing of machinery, equipment and tools
- Selling of food or beverages for promotion of tourism

Industrial and Handicraft Businesses:
- Manufacturing of animal feeds
- Vegetable oil refining
- Textile manufacturing including yarn spinning, dyeing and fabric printing
- Manufacturing of glassware including light bulbs
- Manufacturing of food bowls and plates
- Manufacturing of stationery and printing paper
- Rock salt mining
- Mining

Service Businesses:
- Service businesses not included in Category 'A' or Category 'B'

Other Businesses:

Other construction not included in Category 'A'

Figure 13.1: *Occupations forbidden to foreigners*

Foreign skilled labour is a growing phenomenon in a country experiencing a shortage of skilled expertise. While an indigenous community of trained and skilled labour exists — partly the result of overseas periods of study and occasionally work experience — it has not satisfied the growing demands for such expertise in wake of the country's rapid industrialisation. The pool of Thai skilled labour has also diminished somewhat through the decades with the migration of Thai professionals to (largely) Western countries beginning in the 1970s. This was followed with migration to other regions including the Middle East and ASEAN countries since the late 1970s.

The international migration of Thai workers is another outcome of the imbalance of the Thai labour market. Workers are attracted to higher wage levels and the ease of migration to foreign lands. According to Chalamwong and Sevilla (1996), this migration has been the result of: persisting income inequalities in Thailand; a labour policy that has encouraged the export of labour; and abundant job opportunities abroad. A large concentration of Thai labour out-flow has been to the Middle East and ASEAN countries where Thai workers participate in labour-intensive industries. Most Thai workers in Singapore, for example, are unskilled. In Malaysia, most Thai workers are occupied in the construction industry though in recent years an increasing number of Thai professionals including engineers, doctors and technical specialists have made Malaysia a temporary home (Torrington & Tan 1994).

The Office of Overseas Employment Administration is responsible for a number of tasks connected with Thai overseas employment including: policy making, planning and directing overseas employment services (certifying and controlling private employment service agencies, processing foreign demands for Thai workers to work abroad; certifying skills of workers; examining grievances of job seekers; and processing court cases on behalf of those who do not follow the law properly) (Torrington & Tan 1994). It also manages the overseas workers' welfare fund in accordance with the *Employment Services and Job Seekers' Protection Law 1985*.

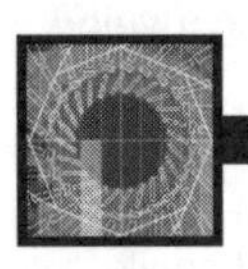

A legislative overview

In addition to the new Thai Constitution (Chandler & Thong-ek 1997) which addresses the issue of discrimination, there are a number of major laws governing labour and employment in Thailand including: the Civil and Commercial Code; the Labour Protection Act; the Labour Relations Act; and the Labour Procedures Act. This section will summarise their major points.

The Civil and Commercial Code describes the rights and duties of an employee and employer regarding their employment contract (and termination thereof) which can be made either verbally or in writing. The contract stipulates the terms and conditions, duties and responsibilities of employment between both parties.

Employees are also entitled to additional protection under the Labour Protection Laws. These laws cover the basic levels of protection which an employee is to be provided during employment and primarily cover the minimum standards concerning: working hours, rest periods, holidays, wages, employment of women and children, severance pay and compensation:

- *Working hours*. Normal working hours are 48 hours per week for industrial work; not more than eight hours per day for transportation work; not more than 42 hours per week for work potentially harmful to the health or physique of the employee; and not more than 54 hours per week for commercial work.
- *Holidays and time off*. At least one day per week off from work and at least 13 days per year for the observation of traditional holidays. Employees are also entitled to an annual leave of at least six working days following completion of one year's service. Military and/or monkhood leaves are accorded by organisations in Thailand to male employees.

- *Minimum Wage.*[5] This rate depends upon the location and types of employment activities. As of 1 January 1998, the minimum wage in Zone A is 162 baht/day, in Zone B 137 baht/day and for the remaining provinces 128 baht/day. The average minimum wage[6] has increased since it inception in 1973 (table 13.16) and tends to be higher in the services industry than other sectors of the economy. Wages also tend to be higher in Bangkok and Board of Investment Zone 1 than in other areas (table 13.17).

Table 13.16: ***Minimum wage per day (Bangkok) since its inception***

Effective date	Minimum wage per day
17 April 1973	12 baht/day
16 January 1975	25 baht/day
1 September 1980	54 baht/day
1 January 1985	70 baht/day
1 April 1990	90 baht/day
1 January 1998	162 baht/day

Sources: Derived from *Handbook of Labour Statistics*, Ministry of Interior 1989 and *Yearbook of Labour Statistics*, Ministry of Labour and Social Welfare 1998.

- *Children and women.* It is forbidden to hire children under 13 years for employment and females are to be given three months paid maternity leave. Women should also not participate in hazardous or strenuous work. Actual practices differ from what is expected of employers. While figures are hard to obtain, numerous companies employ underage workers. Women are also said to face uncertain job prospects following marriage and children though there are a number of prominent women occupying senior-level positions in companies.

The *Labour Relations Act 1975* provides for a resolution of conflicts for promoting a harmonious relationship between employees and employers in Thailand. The Act outlines the rules and regulations concerning: the formation and operation of labour unions and federations; employee committees; employers' associations; employee federations; labour relations committees; employment conditions agreements; procedures for the settlement of labour disputes and unfair practices; protection measures and the rights and procedures to be made by employees in relation to unfair practices. When examined in detail, there is one significant qualification in the Act in terms of the establishment of committees, associations or federations and representation: they require Thai nationality thereby disqualifying all foreigners from participation. Sections 56 and 69 (2), establishment of an 'Employers' Association' and membership in committees; Section 88, establishment of a labour union; and Section 101 (2), membership of a labour union committee or sub-committee, all stipulate Thai nationality, in some cases, by birth. The Act also details extensive unfair practices which broadly concern the unfair termination of employees by virtue of their membership in unions or labour federations. Penalties are also discussed in the Act, the majority comprising of fines and imprisonment for limited periods of time.

Table 13.17: ***Minimum wage per day in baht by province and effective date, 1994–1998***

Work status	BOI investment zone	1 April 1994	1 October 1994	1 July 1995	1 October 1996	1 January 1998
Bangkok	1	132	135	145	157	162
Nakhon Pathom	1	132	135	145	157	162
Nonthaburi	1	132	135	145	157	162
Pathum Thani	1	132	135	145	157	162
Samut Prakan	1	132	135	145	157	162
Samut Sakhon	1	132	135	145	157	162
Phuket	1	132	135	145	157	162
Saraburi	2	116	118	126	137	140
Chon Buri	2	116	118	126	137	140
Nakhon Ratchasima	3	116	118	126	137	140
Chiang Mai	3	116	118	126	137	140
Phangnga	3	116	118	126	137	140
Ranong	3	116	118	126	137	140
Other provinces	2 and 3	108	110	118	128	130

Sources: Derived from *Yearbook of Labour Statistics 1998* (Department of Labour Protection and Welfare, Ministry of Labour and Social Welfare) and National Statistical Office's Labour Force survey.

The *Labour Protection Act 1998*, as discussed above, addresses a number of points including: uses of female and child labour; wages, overtime pay, holidays; the wage committee and welfare; safety, sanitation and environment of working; control; suspension from work and severance pay; submission of complaints and considerations thereof; the employee welfare fund; and penalties. While the Act is considered to benefit employees, particularly women and children, it has drawn some criticism in certain quarters. The Federation of Thai Industries, the Thai Bankers Association and the Board of Trade view the law as 'impractical' saying it will hurt small and medium-sized industries. Laws concerning hours of work and the issue of increased severance pay for laid-off workers are considered impractical by some in the business community.

The *Labour Court Procedure Act 1979* stipulates that a labour case 'arising out of any dispute, controversy or claim relating to the employment between employer and employee must be conducted in a simple and speedy manner' (Price Waterhouse

1997). Thailand's system of dispute settlement is tripartite: candidacies of judges and an equal number of associate judges are proposed respectively by workers' and employers' organisations. The labour court system has played an important role in safeguarding labour protection during worsening economic conditions. According to the ILO (1998) by September 1997, the system's nine-month caseload numbered 12 073, already exceeding all annual totals in its 17-year history. Over 80 per cent of cases in 1997, moreover, concerned severance pay entitlements (in 1985, this issue accounted for 52 per cent of disputes heard).

Thailand is not considered to be a strongly unionised country. The level of trade union organisation is extremely low with approximately 245 000 union members according to the ILO. There are perhaps 1000 unions representing approximately 3.5 per cent of the seven million or so workers in the industrial workforce (ILO 1998). These unions aspire to improve the lot of Thailand's working population in a number of ways (figure 13.2).

Figure 13.2: ***Trade Union wishes***

Trade Union Wishes from Labour Day demands, 1997:

- Social Security compensation
- Medical treatment of social security cardholders
- Nursery centres in all workplaces
- Making the labour relations law a subject in the high school curriculum
- Abolition of the minimum wage and introduction of a workers' pay scale
- Controlling the price of consumer goods
- Affordable accommodation for workers
- Halting the privatisation plan for state enterprises
- Allowing state enterprise workers to set up unions
- An amendment of the election law to make migrant workers eligible to vote in the constituencies where their workplaces are located
- Amendment of labour related laws to ensure fair treatment
- Allowing workers' representatives to sit on the tripartite committee of the Board of Investment and Joint Public-Private Consultative Committee
- Controlling the influx of illegal workers

Source: Adapted from Toews and McGregor, 1998: 154.

Thai labour legislation provides for two main channels through which labour–management dialogue can occur. One is through collective bargaining at workplaces in which a trade union has been recognised. The meagre level of workplace organisation in Thailand means that collective bargaining applies only to a small minority of the Thai workforce. The other formal channel is labour–management dialogue through Employee Committees (ECs) in enterprises employing more than 50 persons. To date, however, ECs remain underdeveloped, existing in only 500 enterprises (ILO 1998).

Foreign companies are said to be discriminated against when it comes to the interests of Thai labour. Following a large-scale lay-off in the textile industry in 1997, the Ministry of Labour and Social Welfare formed a committee to oversee the interests of Thai labour. The Committee legislates to protect Thai employees from massive lay-offs.

Thailand does have a social security program (covering cases of sickness, childbirth, death and disability), under the *Social Security Act 1994*[7] which affects those engaged in private sector employment and self-employment but not the unemployed. The Act insures employees between 15–60 years old only.

The law also requires an employer or the Workmen's Compensation Fund to provide compensation to an employee (or the dependant) upon injury, sickness, absence or death as a result of service to an employer. The Act applies to every employer except government and state enterprise employees, private schools, not-for-profit enterprises, among other employers as prescribed by Ministerial regulations (Bangkok Legal Consultant 1995). The compensation paid by an employer due to injury or sickness includes: compensation expenses, medical expenses, rehabilitation costs and funeral expenses.

The lack of social insurance has been widely criticised following the economic crisis. The National Labour Development Advisory Council (NLDAC), an advisory board influencing government decisions, established a subcommittee on the social effects of the economic crisis in October 1997 (ILO 1998). Its report documented the potential consequences of the crisis: unemployment figures; the negative effects on family, educational system, personal health; the impact on the crime rate and political stability in the country. It called for the expansion of the public welfare system, in particular, an amendment of the Social Insurance Act to cover the cost of school fees and to extend free medical treatment to the unemployed. In addition, it expounds such measures as the expansion of credit options for self-employment, further training opportunities and the promotion of job fairs and other labour exchanges.

What is considered a strong 'safety net' thus far in Thailand is severance pay though it works only in the formal sector on behalf of laid-off workers. The government has also set up a fund to aid unemployed workers and a centre for assistance to laid-off workers, in addition to numerous committees addressing the unemployment situation as well as training for the unemployed and fresh graduates (TDRI 1999).

On the whole, the legal and institutional framework for labour in Thailand is considered extensive[8]. A national minimum wage structure exists, an extensive system of labour courts, and a number of tripartite committees and councils dedicated to labour issues. Enforcement, however, is considered weak. The country is slowly expanding social security and public welfare benefits.

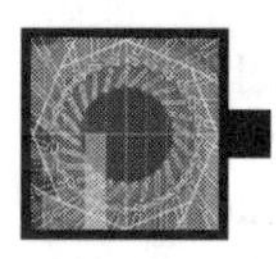

Building diversity in Thai culture

One means for encouraging diversity is to build an awareness of it through training programs. Western companies in Thailand have taken the lead in this area. Supported in part by the commercial office of the US Embassy, which established relationships with various training companies in the country, leading Western firms have engaged their employees in cross-cultural training programs and seminars. This cross-cultural training is offered to both foreign and Thai employees for the improvement of their cross-cultural understanding. The outcomes of the training are said to encourage cultural sensitivity and an appreciation for diversity in the workplace. Given its potential impact, training is considered to be the single most important issue facing Thai labour (Hall 1996).

The Department of Public Welfare (DPW), which has responsibility for looking after underprivileged target groups, including people with disabilities, women, the elderly, children and beggars, noted that the crisis resulted in a large number of individuals who might be socially excluded. The DPW manages a 2000 baht grant

scheme, as well as the 10 000 baht loan scheme, under which one day of enterprise training is provided for borrowers (ILO 1998).

Thai cultural values and traits also shape management practices and behaviours. An example of how culture shapes behaviour might be seen in how local employees react to a performance appraisal. Local employees may, according to Gardenwartz and Rowe (1998):

- avoid appraisals due to 'loss of face'
- emphasise harmony rather than conflict which may result as an outcome of an appraisal
- show respect for authority
- show fear of the repercussions
- reveal a lack of understanding of what an appraisal means
- side towards the relationship aspect versus the task aspect of what an appraisal actually represents.

The preceding are examples of culture's role in shaping both practices and perceptions to managing in a diverse setting — one perhaps made more diverse by virtue of a cross-border business relationship or a culturally diverse workforce.

A number of features of Thai culture can be described with respect to diversity and its promotion in the workplace. In the following paragraphs, Thai cultural practices are presented, followed by potential responses of firms seeking to promote or encourage 'best practices' (desired Thai practices for employers and resulting diversity responses).

- *Avoidance of conflict.* Thais are said to favour harmony over conflict in work as well as private settings (Holmes & Tangtongtavy 1997). Both academic and practitioner research have pointed to behaviour where an avoidance of conflict is viewed in diverse settings, most notably in the cross-border business situation (see Manusphaibool n.d.). This is perhaps the most difficult response to formulate. In a Western setting, conflict is sometimes viewed as constructive behaviour, a vehicle for the improvement of a situation. Conflict in other societal settings such as that found in Thailand is avoided. In attempting to foster diversity in the Thai work environment, the Western[9] manager, in particular, may first develop an understanding of why conflict is seen as an inappropriate response to a problem or concern. The manager may learn to respect the wishes of a work team. Finally, he or she may see that an avoidance of conflict may, with patience, result in more effective team processes as the concern for harmony hopefully has overcome any disruptive effects of conflict. Diversity in this sense is maintained.
- *Work in groups or collectivism.* There appears to be a predilection for group formation approaches to work, though Thais may be considered more individualistic than other Asian neighbours (Hofstede 1980). A group approach to work is viewed more favourably by Thais. It is considered inappropriate, even ill advised to expect Thai colleagues to work alone, on their own, irrespective of their personal ability to do so. Diverse organisations are not always the best in terms of integration unless there is a strong corporate vision or guiding principle which urges otherwise. Corporate culture and/or a leadership vision (by a company manager or founder, for example) can foster an approach to work which does not exclude anyone or isolate one from the group as a whole. The contribution of every employee is valued for its own merits. A good employer recognises the potential for isolation before an employee realises it himself.

- *Provide incentives.* Incentives can be provided in many ways. A small bonus, a company vacation retreat, or even good snacks at work are said to be effective incentives for Thais (Cooper 1994)[10]. It is said that Thais are very incentive driven and are even more effective when given the proper incentives to complete tasks. Companies that do not provide such incentives grapple with an unproductive and unhappy workforce. Incentives are provided in many ways. They can be monetary — that is often most appreciated — or in the form of conveniences which make work and life more comfortable for employees. In dealing with a diverse workforce, or even to promote a diverse workforce, employers can attempt to tailor-make incentives for the varying groups within their organisation. It was suggested, for example, that Thai organisations start providing on-site day-care centres for employees with children. Employees without access to transportation to and from work could be provided with a shuttle service to work. Vegetarians can receive appropriate meals at the company cafeteria. There are numerous ways to promote diversity through incentives.
- *Concern for staff or reciprocity.* A boss or employer has certain roles according to Thai employees. Their employer, whether a family business owner or a salaried manager is often viewed as holding the responsibility for caring for all employees. In the traditionally rural society which often characterises Thailand, workers bring expectations of reciprocity between 'master' and worker which, in former times, formed the norms of labour relations (Phongpaichit & Baker 1995). Concern for staff can be revealed in many ways, such as providing incentives and making tasks manageable. Of primary importance is showing that they care. Care can be accorded to all employees. One must factor in concern with the rules of Thailand's labour laws. Employees, depending upon their specific roles and backgrounds, often form a diverse group in terms of ethnicity, education, contribution to the organisation, and the like. This varies by industry so the employer needs to look at his organisation carefully and work out his responses in an appropriate manner.
- *Observe relationships and hierarchies carefully.* Related to the previous point, a caring boss/employer is someone who should ideally be well-informed of the nuances of relationship management which are so essential in the Thai setting (Cooper 1994; Holmes & Tangtongtavy 1997; Hall 1996). The boss or manager is: aware of the respect due to certain members of Thai society (those with titles) such as the Royal family; those with honours; membership in clubs; religious figures such as monks) and the network of relationships and hierarchies which govern business conduct and life. A caveat must be made about the issue of hierarchy's importance in Thai society. Academic study of this issue has been somewhat inconclusive. On the one hand, for example. a strong hierarchy is acknowledged with respect to the importance placed on respecting the monarchy and Buddhist clergy (both incidentally are also stipulated under the Constitution). On the other hand, some have noted a strong Thai sense of confidence and self-esteem which translates into a more egalitarian view of others within society (Lim 1985). Ungpakorn (1999) found that many working Thais, who would normally be classified as white-collar workers in other societies, actually describe themselves as working class. Hence, one must be careful to weigh these diverging perspectives. Another example: outsiders are said to be welcomed and embraced in Thai society. However, there is some hesitation in certain quarters to describe Thais as being open, particularly towards ethnic groups which are not viewed

favourably (e.g. illegal workers from other South-east Asian countries, people from the South Asian subcontinent). Nonetheless, firms should be aware of such distinctions and nuances in relationships when observing employees.

It is important to show an understanding of deeply imbued traditions and practices. However, it is equally important to show concern for all members of one's work team. While foreigners in Thailand, for example, are generally welcomed (Cooper 1994) and shown respect, they are expected to display some knowledge of local practices and customs however rudimentary. In a business context, it is expected to be known and acknowledged that certain members of society belong to a more favourable position in the societal hierarchy. Those forming the other parts of this hierarchy are still accorded respect and integrated in a way appropriate to the fulfilment of mutual objectives.

While the actual practices of organisations in Thailand in terms of encouraging diversity are varied, their patterns suggest that they have acknowledged the concept but do not accord it the overt importance which countries like the United States have accorded it in terms of policy and practice. Cultural factors have played a role in terms of how the notion of diversity is perceived and whether participants in the labour force have rewarded it with prominence in terms of how they might formulate their agendas. The popular view can be summarised as follows: 'We follow the "middle path" [Buddhism]; we are guided in our behaviour [by this] and diversity is implicitly recognised and supported'.

References

American Embassy. 1996. *Foreign Labor Trends: Thailand*. US Department of Labor, Bureau of International Labor Affairs, Bangkok, American Embassy, FLT 96–10.

Appold, S. J., Siengthai, S. & Kasarda, J. D. 1998. 'The Employment of Women Managers and Professionals in an Emerging Economy: Gender Inequality as an Organizational Practice'. *Administrative Science Quarterly* 43: 538–65.

Asia Monitor Resources Center. 1998. *We in the Zone: Women Workers in Asia's Export Processing Zones*. Hong Kong: Asia Monitor Resources Center.

Backman, M. 1999. *Asian Eclipse: Exposing the Dark Side of Business in Asia*. Singapore: John Wiley and Sons.

Bangkok Legal Consultant. 1995. *Doing Business in Thailand*. Bangkok: Bangkok Legal Consultant.

Chalamwong, Y. & Sevilla, R. C. 1996. 'Dilemmas of Rapid Growth: International Migration and Border Flows: The Case of Thailand. Workshop paper. Bangkok: Thailand Development Research Institute.

Chandler & Thong-ek Law Offices. Working copy of the *Labour Relations Act 1975* with amendments.

Chandler & Thong-ek Law Offices. 1997. Unpublished translation of the new Thai Constitution.

Chandler & Thong-ek Law Offices. 1998. *Labour Protection Act A.D. 1998* (English translation). Bangkok: Nititham Publishing House.

Cooper, R. 1994. *Thais Mean Business*. Singapore: Times Books International.

Economist Intelligence Unit (EIU). 1998. *Country Report: Thailand*. London: Economist Intelligence Unit.

Galenson, W. & Odaka, K. 1976. 'The Japanese Labour Market'. In Patrick, H. & Rosovsky, H. 1976. *Asia's New Giant: How the Japanese Economy Works*. Washington, DC: Brookings Institution, 587–671.

Gardenwartz, L. & Rowe, A. 1998. *Managing Diversity: A Complete Desk Reference and Planning Guide*. Revised Edition. New York: McGraw-Hill.

Hall, D. 1996) *Business Prospects in Thailand*. Singapore: Prentice Hall.

Hofstede, G. 1980. *Culture's Consequences*. London: Sage.

Holmes, H. & Tangtongtavy, S. 1997. *Working with the Thais*. Bangkok: White Lotus.

International Labour Organisation. 1998. 'The Social Impact of the Asian Financial Crisis, a Technical Report of the Cross-departmental Analysis and Reports Team'. Bangkok: ILO Regional Office for Asia and the Pacific.

International Labour Organisation. 1998a. 'When Working Becomes Hazardous'. In *World of Work*. No. 26, September/October 1998. http://www.ilo.org.

International Labour Organisation. 1998b. 'Grim and Getting Grimmer'. (In *World Employment Report 1998–99*), *World of Work*, No. 27, December 1998. http://www.ilo.org.

Kasian, T. 1992. 'Pigtail: A Pre-history of Chineseness in Siam. In *SOJOURN* 7(1): 95–122.

Kirivong, N. 1988. 'The Shortage of Engineers and Technicians is at Crisis Level'. In *Business Review (Thailand)*. 1 December, 25–50.

Labour Force Survey. 1998. 'The Impact of the Economic Crisis on Employment, Unemployment and Labour Migration'. August 1998. Bangkok: National Statistical Office, Office of the Prime Minister.

Lawler, J. J. 1994. 'Overt Gender Discrimination in Multinational and Local Firms: The Case of Thailand'. Paper presented to the International Conference on Managing Human Resources/Labour Relations Diversity for Global Competitiveness, Hamilton, Ontario, 22–24 May.

Lim, L. 1985. 'An Introduction to Business in Southeast Asia. In *Southeast Asia Business*. Ann Arbor, MI: Center for South and Southeast Asian Studies 5: 31–42.

Lim, L. Y. C. 1996. 'The Evolution of Southeast Asian Business Systems'. *Journal of Asian Business* 12(1): 51–74.

Limqueco, P., McFarlane, B. & Odhnoff, J. 1989 'Industrialisation and the Labour Process: The Bangkok Area'. In *Labour and Industry in ASEAN*. Journal of Contemporary Asia Publishers.

Manusphaibool, S. n.d. 'Cross Cultural Problems in the Management of Human Resources in Thailand'. In *Legal, Socio-cultural Problems in the Management of Human Resources in Thai Industries*. Bangkok: Board of Investment.

Ministry of Industry (Office of Industrial Economics). 1998. Direction for Manpower Development for Long-term Industrial Development (Executive Summary). Bangkok: Ministry of Industry.

National Statistical Office. 1997. Key Statistics of Thailand.

Ono, T. 1980. 'Postwar Changes in the Japanese Wage System'. In Nishikawa, S. 1980. *The Labor Market in Japan*. Tokyo: University of Tokyo Press, 145–76.

Phananiramai, M. 1996. 'Changes in Women's Economic Role in Thailand'. In Horton, S. (Ed.). *Women and Industrialization in Asia*. Routledge: London.

Phongpaichit, P. & Baker, C. 1995. *Thailand Economy and Politics*. New York: Oxford University Press.

Pitayanon, S. 1988. 'Labour Market Changes and Economic Development in Thailand'. In Pang, E. F. (Ed.). *Labour Market Developments and Structural Change: The Experience of ASEAN and Australia*. Singapore: Singapore University Press: 243–77.

Poapongsakorn, N. & Taethiengtam, A. 1992. 'Foreign Workers and Labour Laws in Thailand'. Paper presented at the Symposium on Law and Social Sciences (organised by the Center for Advanced Studies) National University of Singapore, 6–8 August.

Price Waterhouse. 1997. *Thailand: A Guide for the Investor*. Bangkok: Price Waterhouse.

Reynolds, C. J. 1998. 'Globalization and Cultural Nationalism in Modern Thailand'. In Kahn, J. S. 1998. *Southeast Asian Identities*. Singapore: Institute of Southeast Asian Studies, 115–45.

Skinner, W. G. 1957. *Chinese Society in Thailand: An Analytical History*. Ithaca: Cornell University Press.

Sussangkarn, C., Ashakul, T. & Myers, C. 1986. 'Human Resources Management'. Research paper, Bangkok: Thailand Development Research Institute.

Sussangkarn, C. & Chalamwong, Y. 1994. Development Strategies and Their Impacts on Labour Market and Migration: Thai Case Study, Bangkok: Thailand Development Research Institute.

Tan, C. H. & Torrington, D. 1998. *Human Resource Management for Southeast Asia and Hong Kong*. Singapore: Prentice-Hall.

Thailand Development Research Institute. 1999. *Social Impacts of the Asian Economic Crisis in Thailand, Indonesia, Malaysia and the Philippines*. Bangkok: Thailand Development Research Institute.

Thanachaisethavut, B. & Chouwilai, J. 1998. 'Women Workers in Export Processing Zones: A Case Study of the Northern Region Industrial Estate in Thailand'. In *We in the Zone. Women Workers in Asia's Export Processing Zones*. Hong Kong: Asia Monitor Resources Center.

The Nation. 2000. 8 March, 25 (48898.1).

Toews, B. & McGregor, R. 1998. *Succeed in Business Thailand*. Singapore: Times Books International.

Torrington, D. & Tan, C. H. 1994. *Human Resource Management for Southeast Asia*. Singapore: Prentice-Hall.

Ungpakorn, J. G. 1999. *Thailand: Class Struggle in an Era of Economic Crisis*. Bangkok and Hong Kong: Asia Monitor Resources Center and Workers Democracy Book Club.

Wut, N. 1995. 'Cheap and Vulnerable'. *Bangkok Post*, 17 December.

End notes

1. According to the labour market segmentation view, the labour market can be broadly defined into two parts — the informal and formal sectors, a conceptual distinction in terms of the way the two markets operate. According to Sussangkarn et al. (1986: 121), in the formal sector: wages are not determined according to the standard textbook demand and supply analysis; entry is difficult but those with access can earn more than what they would get in the informal sectors, and job security is better (jobs in government and larger firms are examples especially where unionisation exists). In the informal sector, 'entry is easy, but wages are low and there is little job security ... the sector is made up mostly of small firms, and also includes most of the self-employed such as hawkers and peddlers, but excluding the major professions such as doctors and lawyers. The key to the informal sector is that it can act as the employer of last resort for those who cannot get jobs in the formal sector ...'
2. According to Lim (1996: 71), 'This is a rational choice in fast-growing economies where new market opportunities are plentiful and competition often limited, and where upward mobility as an employee is limited either because monopoly of top management by family owners, or government-mandated ethnic quotas, impose a glass ceiling on the career advancement of ethnic Chinese employees'. This is in reference to ethnic Chinese in south-east Asia as a whole.
3. The ILO (1998a) notes that in recent years psychological violence is emerging as a growing problem in the workplace in various Western countries.

4. A foreigner who wishes to work in Thailand must first obtain a work permit. This involves submitting an application to the Labour Department of the Ministry of the Interior. A foreigner applying for a work permit must either be permitted to stay temporarily in Thailand (non-immigrant) or have residence in Thailand according to Immigration Law. The Labour Department assesses the size and type of business prior to granting a work permit (e.g. a smaller company with 10 employees may have a quota for just one alien).
5. Average rate of exchange to the dollar in 1999 was 37.5 bt; 1998–41.58; 1997–31.48; 1996–25.39.
6. Thai manufacturers have been undercut by even lower cost exporters in the Asian region following an increase of the minimum wage to 157 bt per day in Bangkok (approximately $6.20). As a result companies are struggling to compete with other regional manufacturers. The Thai Board of Investment (BOI) has tried to encourage manufacturers to move from the capital to the provinces — enticing them with a package of tax holidays to set up business in the rural north-east instead of the increasingly expensive capital, Bangkok.
7. The Act became effective on 30 March 1995. The penalty for not registering with the Social Security fund for employers is imprisonment of not more than six months or a fine not exceeding 20 000 bt or both. Those failing to maintain a register of insured employees will be subject to one month imprisonment or a fine not exceeding 10 000 bt or both.
8. This is a view shared by the American Embassy which has periodically monitored labour trends in the country.
9. In this case, Western can be ascribed also to certain non-Western cultures where conflict is not avoided.
10. There is some disagreement on this point, however. Manusphaibool (p. 9), in his article for the Board of Investment, states that one of the negative aspects of Thai employees is that 'they cannot be easily motivated by offering more money in exchange for more work'.

Chapter 14

Insiders and outsiders

Peter W. OBrien

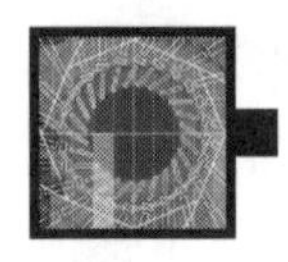

Introduction

As Patrickson points out in chapter 1, there is no widely accepted definition of diversity. Nor is there any widely accepted way of managing diversity. The various contributors to this book have each addressed the issue of managing diversity from the perspective of different societies. In the course of doing so, they have illustrated that diversity (and its management) mean different things in the societies in the region.

The authors themselves represent diverse backgrounds and bring to their chapters perspectives derived from these backgrounds. Most of the authors in this book are female, and many are writing about societies other than in their country of origin. For example, Kondo writes about managing diversity in the Philippines from the perspective of a Japanese woman resident in Manila, Renshaw writes about Japan from the perspective of woman holding American citizenship, while Dubey-Villinger writes about Thailand from the perspective of a United States citizen of Indian origin. Authors like Muthaly have been able to write about their country of origin from the perspective of an expatriate. In this book, diversity is seen not only from the perspective of citizens but also through alien eyes. In addition, while the majority of contributors to this book are academics, others, such as Burns and McNaughton who come from other occupational backgrounds, add another perspective.

Several contributors to this book note that managing diversity is not a concept indigenous to the region. Bennington and Mariappanadar comment that managing diversity is not an issue of concern to Indians. It is seen as an American issue and, even in US-based firms operating in India, it is perceived as a business issue rather than a human rights one. Renshaw cites the traditional Japanese view that diversity is to be controlled and contained, while Dubey-Villinger comments that in Thailand there is no overt awareness of diversity related issues.

Indeed, what constitutes diversity differs across the societies reviewed in this book. Diversity has a broad meaning in Australia, New Zealand and Thailand, for example, but a much narrower definition in Hong Kong and Japan. The other societies fall somewhere between these polar extremes.

All societies are diverse in terms of their histories, politico-legal and economic systems, cultures, and religious and ethnic make-up. These factors play important roles in the way in which diversity is defined and managed. In attempting to manage diversity in the societies covered in this book, expatriate managers should be aware of these underlying factors.

Managing diversity can be seen as the management of the 'insider–outsider' phenomenon, as Renshaw notes so cogently in her chapter on Japan. Renshaw uses the expression to refer to the distinction made between those who are part of the ethnic Japanese in-group and those who are not. But the term can be extended to refer to those who form part of the dominant group in any society and to those who do not. Simon (1999) and Bloom (2000) demonstrate the corrosive effect on a society that can result from differences between those who form the dominant group and people who come from outside. In this chapter, managing diversity is seen as the process of managing the insider–outsider division.

This insider–outsider distinction is built into some of the languages of the region. Tagalog and Bahasa Indonesia, for example, have different pronouns for the inclusive 'we', meaning 'all of us together', and the exclusive 'we', meaning 'us but not you'. In

Bahasa Indonesia, the forms are *kami* and *kita* respectively. Expatriate managers, by and large, are part of the exclusive 'we' — part of the educated able-bodied, often urban, males — neither too young nor too old, who become 'insiders' as part of the dominant managerial caste in their host country. The challenge for them is in learning how to manage the 'outsiders' — women, children, the uneducated and the undereducated, the disabled, older workers, and members of 'lesser' ethnic groups or social castes.

In this concluding chapter, attention is drawn to five specific areas of difference in an effort to help understand the ways in which this insider–outsider divide is managed in the societies covered in this book. These specific areas are factors in the societies' histories and cultural (in the broadest sense) environments; legal and constitutional provisions; management of gender diversity; management of ethnic and social diversity; and the management of age and disability diversity. The final section deals with what expatriate managers can do in managing diversity.

The approach, of necessity, highlights similarities and dissimilarities in order to compare and contrast practices in a way that will help expatriate managers understand, and cope with, ways of managing diversity that may differ from those with which they are familiar. There is no claim to cover all the issues addressed in the preceding chapters, and users of this book are encouraged to read the chapters on those societies which interest them. Previous chapters have included discussions of discrimination in education, political representation, and public sector employment. This chapter focuses on the situation in private sector employment, the area in which expatriate managers are most likely to encounter host country workers.

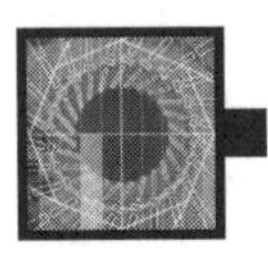

Different histories, different values

Two of the societies — Australia and New Zealand — may be seen as transplanted Christian Western European states. Historically, they have drawn heavily on their British roots for their political and legal systems and for many (if not most) of their cultural values. More recent exposure to wider sources of migrants, particularly in the case of Australia, as well as the pervasive influence of mass communications, has softened the British influence and opened the societies to new ideas and new values. Australia and New Zealand share membership of the British Commonwealth with India, Malaysia and Singapore, a membership shared until 1997 by Hong Kong. As a consequence, these societies have similar systems of government and law. Indeed, as Kramar points out, the relevant legislation in Hong Kong is based on British and Australian precedents.

Though largely Hindu in religion but with significant non-Hindu minorities, India is a secular state with constitutionally guaranteed freedom of religion. In Malaysia, on the other hand, Islam is the official religion although freedom of religion is guaranteed in the constitution. Though there are three main ethnic groups in Malaysia (i.e. ethnic Malays or *bumiputras*, Chinese and Indians), India has a larger number of ethnolinguistic groups and 18 constitutionally recognised languages.

Both societies, like Australia, are constitutionally federations with certain powers residing in the constituent states and territories. Each was established with some bloodshed. India was born out of the dissolution of the old British *Raj* into the two separate sovereign states of India and Pakistan when massive population dislocations occurred. The modern Federation of Malaysia faced *konfrontasi* (confrontation) with

Indonesia over the inclusion of Sabah and Sarawak, just as its predecessor faced a communist insurgency in the 1950s.

Singapore's foundation is attributed to the British East India Company and Sir Stamford Raffles, the man after whom much in the country is still named. Formerly a constituent state of the Federation of Malaysia, it was established as an independent parliamentary republic in 1965. Since independence a single party has governed it and, for most of the period since independence, Lee Kuan Yew ruled it. Like its neighbour, Malaysia, Singapore has the same three main ethnic groups (Chinese, Malays and Indians in order of population percentages) but it has no established state religion. It has a substantial expatriate population, however, just as Malaysia has a substantial number of foreign or guest workers.

Two other societies — Indonesia and the Philippines — share a history of colonisation by European powers. The Netherlands was the colonial power in the case of Indonesia, while the Philippines was colonised by Spain before becoming a possession of the United States in 1898. Both societies, however, are constitutionally secular states and each has a large number of ethnic and linguistic groups in its population. While Dutch influence was strongest in Java and the Spice Islands, the Dutch legacy can still be found in Indonesian law. The Spanish occupation of the Philippines bequeathed Catholicism to the country as well as a certain Hispanic character to the cultural values. The occupation of the country by the United States till Independence in 1946 left an indelible mark on the Philippines that caused one observer to liken it to Southern California (Sheridan, 1998).

The three Chinese societies — the People's Republic of China, Hong Kong and Taiwan — covered in this book share a common heritage of Confucianism though, more recently, they have experienced the influence of other philosophies as well. At various times, the British secured the cession of Hong Kong, the Portuguese the cession of Macau, the Japanese the cession of the island of Formosa (now Taiwan) and the occupation of Manchuria. Other powers, including the French, the Germans and the United States, competed to wring privileges in cities such as Shanghai. From the fall of the Qing Dynasty in 1912 until after World War II, Mainland China was a series of quasi-colonies and the fiefdoms of competing warlords. Not until 1949 was the greater part of mainland China united under one central government. The Communist People's Republic of China, established on the mainland in 1949 after the defeat of the Kuomintang, has experienced both the Cultural Revolution of Mao and the economic reforms of Deng in the past 40 years. Officially, however, it remains committed to communism although with a capitalist face.

Hong Kong was ceded in perpetuity to Great Britain at the end of the first Sino–British Opium War in 1842, the Kowloon Peninsula was ceded at the end of the second Sino–British Opium War in 1858, and the New Territories were leased for 99 years in 1898. The whole territory, however, reverted to the sovereignty of the mainland Chinese state in 1997 when the lease on the New Territories expired. Before that time, the economic system had been one of unfettered capitalism and the system of government had been largely one of benevolent despotism, with the participation of the local Chinese inhabitants limited to voting for the Urban Councils which controlled street names, street peddlers and garbage collection. Not until 1991 were free elections to the Legislative Council permitted. For 50 years from 1997 Hong Kong will enjoy the status of a Special Autonomous Region under the 'One State, Two Systems' policy.

Taiwan, the third Chinese society, is regarded as a renegade province by the central government in Beijing. Like Hong Kong, the island was ceded to a foreign power at the end of a war. In this case, however, Taiwan was ceded to Japan at the end of the Sino–Japanese War of 1894–95. It remained under Japanese control until the end of World War II when it was retroceded to China. Taiwan came under the control of the defeated Kuomintang (KMT) in 1949 at the end of the civil war and was reborn as the Republic of China. It remained under KMT control till the election of President Chen Shui-bian of the opposition Democratic Progressive Party.

The last two societies covered — Japan and Thailand — share three things in common. They share, first, their geographic location on the Asia–Pacific Rim and, second, the fact that neither was ever colonised by a foreign power. During World War II, however, Thailand was effectively occupied by the Japanese. In turn, after World War II, Japan was occupied by the victorious Allies, effectively by the United States. Throughout their histories, however, both societies have been influenced by their neighbours and more recent Western influence is a thin veneer over deeper cultural values, customs and mores. Each country also shares the fact that during the last part of the nineteenth and first part of the twenthieth centuries they were exposed to Western influences during the reigns of enlightened monarchs — the Meiji Emperor in Japan and Kings Mongkut (Rama IV) and Chulalongkorn (Rama V) in Thailand.

The two societies are dissimilar, however, in religion (Thailand is officially Buddhist whereas Shinto is the traditional religion in Japan) and in ethnic composition (Thailand has large numbers of ethnic minority peoples whereas Japan is ethnically much more homogeneous).

A common thread linking Indonesia, Malaysia, the Philippines, Singapore and Thailand with Hong Kong, Taiwan and the PRC is the dominance in commercial life by ethnic Chinese.

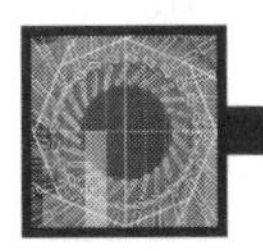

Constitutional and legal frameworks for managing diversity

It is clear, from the preceding chapters in this book, that there are differences in the constitutional and legal frameworks for managing diversity in the Asian and Pacific region. For example, constitutional provisions may be more or less inclusive or (as in the case of Australia) non-existent. Domestic legislation may or may not have been enacted to prohibit discrimination against particular groups within society. Countries may or may not have ratified UN and/or ILO conventions on issues such as ending discrimination against women or the disabled. Some societies may have enacted specific legislation concerning the employment of foreign 'guest' workers, while others may be more concerned over the treatment of their citizens working abroad. Permitted exceptions to the law may also differ, as is the situation in Hong Kong where being male may be a genuine occupational requirement. Knowledge of the constitutional and legal provisions governing discrimination and diversity is surely a requirement for expatriate managers in working with local labour forces.

As De Cieri and Olekalns point out, it is Australian state and federal legislation (not the federal Constitution) that recognises a wide range of forms of diversity. It is legislation that prohibits discrimination on the grounds of age, race or national extraction, colour, ethnic or social origin, religious or political affiliation, sex or sexual preference, marital status, pregnancy, mental record, criminal record, trade

union activity or political opinion, or physical or intellectual or psychiatric disability characteristics in appointment, promotion or transfer of employees. Commonwealth legislation covers direct and indirect discrimination in employment, while state and territory legislation prescribes minimum conditions of employment notwithstanding specific conditions in employment contracts. Certain Commonwealth legislation, such as the *Human Rights and Equal Opportunity Commission Act 1986*, enacts provisions of international conventions that Australia has ratified (in this instance, International Labour Organisation [ILO] Convention 111). The legislation applies to employment in both the private and the public sector.

In New Zealand Burns and McNaughton outline a legal framework for managing diversity which comes from both domestic and international law. In terms of domestic law, discrimination and diversity are covered by such laws as *The Race Relations Act 1971*, *The Equal Pay Act 1972*, the *Human Rights Commission Act 1977*, *The Labour Relations Act 1987*, *The Employment Contracts Act 1991*, and *The Human Rights Act 1993* which collectively prohibit discrimination on grounds of gender, race, colour and national or ethnic origin, marital status, religious or ethical belief, sexual orientation, age, disability, family status, employment status, political opinion and trade union involvement. In terms of international law, New Zealand is a signatory to the United Nations Convention on the Elimination of All Forms of Discrimination Against Women (CEDAW).

Australia and New Zealand rely on specific laws governing discrimination and diversity, and prohibit discrimination in both public and private sector employment. The situation is different in other societies and, even when there are constitutional guarantees of equal treatment, this equality may be limited to public sector employment only. For example, Bennington and Mariappanadar draw attention to the centrality of the Indian Constitution in providing the legislative authority for equal opportunity legislation and programs. The Indian Constitution guarantees the fundamental rights of citizens, including equality before the law, and commands that the State shall not discriminate against any person on grounds of any or all of religion, caste, sex or place of birth. The Constitution also prohibits private persons from discriminating against people on these grounds in the use of certain specified facilities (such as wells, shops, restaurants and accommodation). It does not prohibit discrimination in employment by private persons, however. The employment of children under the age of 14 years is prohibited, equal pay for equal work for men and women is mandated, and other clauses deal with preserving the health and strength of adult workers and children.

Bennington and Mariappanadar found the Indian Constitution is silent on general age discrimination, the rights of the disabled, of carers and those of 'alternative sexual orientations'. Other Indian domestic legislation, however, protects the rights of minorities, provides for the investigation of human rights abuses by public servants, and provides for equal opportunities, full participation and the protection of the rights of persons with disabilities (defined to include persons with vision or hearing loss, locomotor disability, mental retardation or mental illness, or who have recovered from Hansen's Disease (leprosy).

Like the Indian Constitution, the Constitution of Singapore states that all citizens are equal before the law and that there shall be no discrimination on grounds of religion, race, descent or place of birth in any law or in appointment to any office or employment under a public authority. Landau and Chung found that there are no laws addressing gender, age or disability discrimination in Singapore. The republic,

however, has ratified 21 clauses of the ILO's Labour Rights Convention but it has not ratified three UN Conventions (on equality between the sexes in employment opportunities, remuneration for work of equal value, and institutional treatments in all forms). Nor is there any specific legislation outlawing sexual discrimination (Landau & Chung).

As Burgess and Muthaly note, the Malaysian Constitution provides 'the usual guarantees' of protection of life and property, and freedom of expression and religion. They also comment, however, that other sections of the constitution and other legislation (such as the *Internal Security Act, 1960*) restrict such rights. Consequently, Malaysia has no legislation mandating equal employment opportunities nor any outlawing discrimination, child labour, or sexual harassment (though for Muslims, this may be covered in part by laws against outraging the modesty of women). Affirmative action for ethnic Malays (or *bumiputras*), enshrined in the constitution, affects only public sector employees. There are strict regulations on trade union organisation and activity. While child labour is not illegal, the *Child and Young Persons' Employment Act, 1967* governs types of work and hours of work for children. There is also special legislation governing foreign workers. Like Thailand (see below), Malaysia is a signatory to only 11 clauses of the ILO's Labour Rights Convention.

The Thai Constitution of 1997 provides for the equal treatment for Thai citizens and outlaws discrimination on grounds of origin, race, language, age, sex, physical or health condition, personal status, economic or social standing, religious belief, education or political beliefs. Clauses in the constitution also provide for the protection of children and youth, the disabled, the elderly and the underprivileged (see Villinger). The revised *Labour Protection Act, 1998* also prohibits discrimination between the sexes in how they are treated and outlaws sexual harassment by superiors against women and children but it permits employers to discriminate against women because of the nature of the work to be performed, for example, hazardous and strenuous work. Although Thailand, like the Philippines, has a large number of its citizens working abroad, it has enacted no legislation to protect their rights (Vanijaka 2000). In the three Chinese societies, the legal and constitutional frameworks for managing diversity are markedly different. In the People's Republic of China (PRC), specific constitutional and legal provisions have been made for women, the disabled and for ethnic minorities. Under the terms of the 1982 Constitution of the PRC, women are guaranteed equal rights with men in all spheres of life, including in business. Women have the right to work outside the home and to have equal pay with men for equal work. In 1992, a law protecting women's rights and interests was adopted, which was intended to ensure the protection of women's special rights and interests granted by law. Specific constitutional provisions and domestic legislation at both the national and the provincial, regional and municipal levels guarantee that the disabled may enjoy the same civic rights as the able-bodied in employment (as well as in education, political participation, inheritance, marriage, civil and criminal procedures). Moreover, in 1987, the PRC became a signatory to the Convention Concerning Vocational Rehabilitation and Employment (Disabled Persons) (which had been adopted at the International Labor Conference in 1983.

The present Constitution of the PRC recognises the equality of national minorities and prohibits discrimination against, and oppression of, any nationality. Minorities are guaranteed equal rights to vote and stand for election, freedom of religious belief, the right to education, to use and develop their own language, and have the freedom to preserve or reform their own folkways and customs and be assisted in economic development. The PRC is also a signatory to international conventions outlawing racial discrimination, apartheid, and genocide.

Kramar finds that anti-discrimination legislation in Hong Kong is narrower in focus than in some of the other societies covered in this book but is, at the same time, broader in its coverage. Hong Kong anti-discrimination legislation comprises three ordinances (The Sex Discrimination Ordinance, The Disability Ordinance and the Family Status Ordinance) which prohibit discrimination on grounds of gender, marital status, pregnancy or disability and which also prohibit victimisation, sexual harassment and vilification. These three ordinances were all introduced prior to the return of the territory to the sovereignty of the Chinese state in 1997. The Hong Kong legislation, however, also makes illegal both direct and indirect discrimination (i.e. applying the same treatment to people that is in practice discriminatory) as well as discrimination on the basis of association (e.g. on the basis of a spouse's disability) in recruitment, training, promotion and dismissal. The Hong Kong ordinances cover not only public sector employment but also private sector employment and such areas as the employment of contract workers, employment-related training, the conferral of professional or trade qualifications or authorisations, the provision of services by employment agencies, the appointment of commission agents, and the selection of partners in partnerships. Permitted exceptions under the Sex Discrimination Ordinance include where being male is a genuine occupational qualification for a job or when the job is performed inside a private home. Hong Kong legislation, however, does not prohibit discrimination on the basis of age, race, religious beliefs or sexual orientation.

In Taiwan, where labour relations are governed largely by the Labour Standards Law, managing diversity focuses on managing foreign workers, as Cheng highlighted. *The Employment Services Act, 1992* prescribes the same minimum wages and working conditions for foreign workers as for local workers, though the Labour Standard Law prohibits employers from hiring foreign workers without prior government approval. Under the Labour Standards Act, women are entitled to 'equal wages for equal work of equal efficiency' but the law is silent on other aspects of employment rights. As Kondo notes, Filipino constitutional and legal attention to managing diversity has focused on gender issues but it has also addressed the issues of Overseas Contract Workers, the disabled and child labour. Filipino society holds deeply rooted beliefs regarding the role of both men and women at home and in work. The *Constitution of the Philippines*, adopted after the EDSA People's Power revolution in 1986, contains two specific provisions relating to women. Article II, Section 14, recognises the role of women in nation building and ensures the equality of men and women under the law. Article XIII, Section 14, requires the State to protect working women by proving safe and healthful working conditions, 'taking into account their maternal functions', and to ensure that 'such facilities and opportunities that will enhance their welfare and enable them to realise their full potential in the service of the nation' (Sabilano 1986: 63). Both domestic and international laws govern the treatment of women in employment and other areas of life. Like several of the societies covered in this book, the Philippines has ratified ILO and UN conventions prohibiting discrimination against women with respect to equal pay, employment and occupation. The Philippines has also enacted domestic legislation prohibiting gender-based discrimination in such areas as employment, wages, salaries and fringe benefits, training and promotion opportunities. Specific legislation outlaws discrimination based on marital and maternal status, and well as outlawing sexual harassment. Other specific legislation addresses the issue of child labour and the treatment of Overseas Contract Workers (OCWs) in the Philippines. While this latter law will not interest expatriate managers working in the Philippines, it may be of interest to expatriate managers in situations where large numbers of Filipinos are employed, as in Hong Kong, Malaysia and Singapore.

In Indonesia, as Bennington notes, the legal and constitutional situation is less clear-cut. The recent political changes consequent upon the downfall of President Suharto and the installation of the country's fourth President since formal Independence from the Dutch make the legal framework more ambiguous. The legal and industrial relations context arises from numerous sources, is both extremely complicated and somewhat vague, and much is left of the discretion of government authorities. Constitutionally the country is a secular unitary republic with the usual rights guaranteed to, and obligations imposed on, its citizens (both native and naturalised), but the Constitution does not explicitly forbid discrimination based on gender, race, disability, language or social status. While the 1993 Guidelines of State Policy (legal statutes) explicitly state that women have the same rights, obligations and opportunities as men, previous guidelines make it clear that women's participation in national development should be subordinated to their role of improving family welfare and the education of the younger generation.

The Employment Law regulates types of employment, and penalties exist for infringing its requirements. Labour laws also apply to Export Processing Zones (EPZs) where expatriate managers would encounter local workers. Legislation governs minimum wages (which differ by region), annual vacation leave, sick leave, social insurance, accident and sick leave, severance and service pay, and protection of employment for the sick. Forced and bonded labour by children is prohibited. While employers may hire child labour, children must be given access to education, socialisation and mental and spiritual guidance and they may not work more than four hours a day. Specific regulations govern the employment of children under the age of 14 who must work to contribute to family income.

If the legal and constitutional situation in Indonesia is ambiguous and confused, the situation in Japan is crystal clear — at least on the surface. The Constitution of Japan 1947, which was essentially imposed on Japan by the occupying powers after World War II, is based on the Constitution of the United States. The constitution provides for equality under the law and the unfettered rights of people to life, liberty and the pursuit of happiness. It provides that there shall be no discrimination in political, economic or social relations on the basis of race, creed, sex, social status or family origin. Articles in the constitution also prohibit employers from discriminating against or for employees by reason of nationality, creed or social status in wages, working conditions or working hours. The Labour Standards Act also prohibits discrimination against women and minorities in wages, and requires protective measure in favour of women in some areas.

In theory, citizens in all the societies covered in this book are guaranteed by national constitutions or by domestic or international laws, a certain measure of equal treatment. But while constitutions and laws mandate one set of behaviours and actions, in practice human beings implement these constitutional and legal frameworks. Their actions and behaviours reflect their interpretation of the legal and constitutional frameworks and, as the preceding chapters show, practices in the workplace either breach the spirit of constitutional and legal provisions or blatantly ignore them altogether.

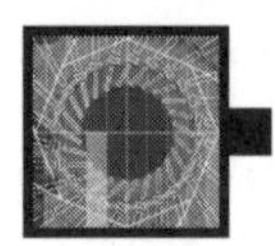

Managing gender equality

In many societies, entrenched social values override legal requirements and few people or organisations fully comply with the law. This is particularly the case with workplace gender diversity. Gender equality is explicitly constitutionally or legally mandated in most of the societies covered in this book. In many of the societies, however, women are expected to conform to rigid gender–role stereotypes. Indeed, in Indonesia and the Philippines, the legal framework reinforces the role of women as wives and mothers. While women may actually comprise more than half the population in most of the societies in the region, they are a social 'minority'. Throughout the region, women's labour force participation rates are lower than those of their male peers, they receive lower wages and salaries than do their peers, and they may be subjected to sexual harassment or violence in the workplace.

Bennington and Mariappanadar cite evidence that employers in India evade their legal responsibilities. Women are paid less than men, not promoted to senior management levels, and are still subjected to violence in the workplace. Bennington notes that in Indonesia, not only are jobs gender stereotyped but women also receive lower wages than men and may be hired as day labourers rather than full-time employees (thus not becoming eligible for benefits such as maternity leave or head-of-household benefits). Women employees may be illegally dismissed or replaced while on maternity leave. As in other societies, women employees in Indonesia may be subjected to sexual harassment.

Kondo notes that both Christian and Muslim women in the Philippines are expected to conform to gender role stereotypes that cast them in the role of wife and mother. She points out, however, that there are differences between the gender role models to which Muslim and Christian women are expected to conform, thus emphasising that diverse expectations exist even within a country. Kondo, moreover, draws attention to social class differences that help upperclass Philippine women reduce the effect on them of social expectations by passing domestic chores on to hired helpers. Occupational gender stereotyping, however, influences employment choices and job advertisements in newspapers such as the *Philippine Daily Inquirer* will specify the sex of preferred candidates. While job advertisements may specify age limits for men, for women they may also specify preferred height limits and other characteristics such as 'a pleasing personality'. Despite legislation, such as Republic Act 6725, women in management do not have access to the promotion and training opportunities made available to men. Married women workers are discriminated against by practices such as little or no maternity benefits or leave.

The writers on the three Chinese societies, covered in this book (the PRC, Hong Kong and Taiwan) draw attention to the continuing traditional (Confucian) patriarchal values in which women are responsible for running the household and men are in charge of running the outside world. Millennia of tradition have influenced social beliefs about the role of women and the centrality of the family. Compared with many other societies, women in the PRC have a high labour force participation rate but they still receive lower wages than males. As elsewhere, women are not equally represented in employment and, as elsewhere, the glass ceiling seems to exist. Even in enterprises where 50 per cent of the employees are female, women are clustered in the lower paid, lower status positions. Although government policy may declare equality between men and women, men have more power and de facto

inequality still exists. The careers of Chinese women managers are strongly influenced by central government planning and the patriarchal tradition. Female managers are seen as less effective in time management than their male counterparts and are thought to work fewer hours. Where women are successful, their success is more often attributed to their 'performance beneath the sheets' than to their skill, luck or ability (Kwang 2000).

Although private sector business does provide opportunities for Chinese women, these opportunities, and whether women choose to take advantage of them, are constrained by their social and political environment. Both urban and rural women face unequal employment opportunities. Organisational change in the state sector is disadvantaging women. In the urban areas, opportunities for women in the State Owned Enterprises (SOEs) are declining. In the current drive to reform bankrupt enterprises, men are retired at 40 years of age but women are retired at 35 (Kwang 2000). Women are a primary target for state enterprise downsizing because industries dominated by women (such as textiles) are the first to go. Women are not recruited because they bear and rear children, care for the elderly and have to do the housework, all of which makes them less productive than men according to Chinese male managers. Also the necessary welfare provisions such as maternity leave make the enterprise less profitable.

Chinese women also encounter discrimination in the urban private sector. While large foreign-owned and joint venture private factories employ large numbers of women, this female labour force is comprised almost exclusively of the young, unmarried, frequently rural migrant workers. Factory management is almost exclusively male and women employees may experience exploitation, overwork, harmful working conditions, poor living conditions and no proper labour contracts and harassment. Women have died when locked doors prevented escape from fires in factories or dormitories.

Kitching also draws attention to the continuing influence of traditional social customs in rural areas that for the most part excludes women from management unless they are politically well connected, and that defines each job as one for a certain gender and age. Although few expatriate managers are likely to venture into rural areas, they should be aware that in such regions there are as yet few signs of organisational change with respect to gender equality of opportunity.

Kramar notes that local firms in Hong Kong continue to prefer men to women in managerial and supervisory positions and that cases of sex-based discrimination are brought before the Equal Opportunities Commission. She draws attention to the fact, however, that discrimination on grounds of gender is focused on Hong Kong women and that expatriate women employees do not face the same situation. Cheng's chapter on Taiwan points to the policies adopted by the Council for Labour Affairs which, based on the Constitution of the Republic of China and the Labour Standards Act, are intended to regulate the system for the employment of women. She notes that, under the Labour Standards Act, women are entitled to 'equal wages for equal work *of equal efficiency*' [emphasis added] but the law is silent on other aspects of employment rights. Cheng further comments that the law is not rigorously enforced and that women workers are subjected to various forms of unfair treatment. In Taiwan, as in Thailand and the Philippines, employers state gender preferences in hiring for (high paying) jobs. They also start women workers with equal qualifications and equal experience on lower salaries than their male counterparts, and require women to sign contracts by which they agree to resign if they marry or become pregnant.

In Singapore, which also has a majority Chinese population, Landau and Chung note that women are urged to fulfil the role of wife and mother, and the government has put in place programs to encourage educated women to marry and to have at least two children. In Singapore, women earn less than their male peers do, many occupations are sex-segregated and overall female participation rates in the workforce are lower than for males.

Dubey-Villinger cites evidence drawing attention to the fact that, despite its large ethnic Chinese minority, there is no evidence that Chinese patriarchal practices influence the employment of women in Thailand. Nevertheless, in Thailand, women's wages are not equal to men's. Thai women are seen as more docile and easier to manage than men. Job advertisements in newspapers such as *The Bangkok Post* specify not only educational and age requirements but also the gender of preferred job applicants.

In Japan, women comprise 51 per cent of the population and 41 per cent of the total workforce but they are confined to lower levels of employment and are paid, on average, only two-thirds of male wages. As Renshaw points out, however, both the Japanese Constitution and Japanese law are read with Japanese eyes and interpreted in Japanese ways. The courts' interpretation of the laws as they relate to the employment of women (and other minorities) has been to rule that only *unreasonable* discrimination is prohibited and employers have learned to justify their actions as reasonable.

Burns and McNaughton, in their chapter on Aotearoa New Zealand, add their voice to the chorus of authors in this book who point out differences in male and female labour force participation rates. They also point out that women make up a higher proportion of the part-time workforce than do men. Their chapter suggests that, as with the other societies surveyed, women's participation in the workforce is strongly influenced by their role as mother (if not as wife) and by the absence of childcare and opportunities for early childhood education. Burns and McNaughton note, too, that occupational segregation is a feature for both Maori and Pakeha women, with such women's work force participation being confined to a narrower range of occupations than that of men.

Last, as with the situation in the other societies surveyed in this book, female labour force participation rates in Australia are not equal to those of men, and women continue to have fewer opportunities for promotion than do their male colleagues. De Cieri and Olekalns point out, for example, that women comprise only eight per cent of executive managers. Despite equal opportunity and affirmative action legislation in Australia, social and cultural expectations discourage women from entering professions such as engineering. Organisational practices and hostile work environments may deny them promotion opportunities or drive them from the job and profession.

In sum, therefore, while the great majority of societies surveyed in this book have in place constitutional and/or legal frameworks mandating equal treatment for all workers in employment, wages, training and promotion, in practice discrimination in work place treatment continues in all of them. The discrimination may be direct or indirect, overt or covert, subtle or in the form of sexual harassment or workplace violence, but some degree of discrimination between the sexes in conditions of employment persists in the societies surveyed in this book. While such discrimination results from the interaction of actions, social attitudes, decisions, regulations, practices and policies, women will continue to be outsiders in the workplace.

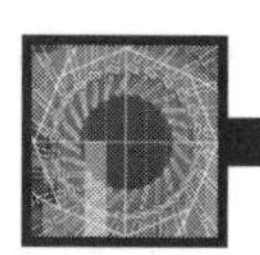

Managing ethnic and social diversity

Do ethnic and social minorities who are seen as 'outsiders' fare better in practice than women when it comes to managing diversity in the workplace? 'Outsiders', in this context, refers not only to members of minority immigrant communities but also to members of indigenous ethnic minority groups. It is used also to refer to people whose ethnic origin is identical to that of the majority population but who are perceived as 'outsiders' by the wider society. In this latter group are members of the Scheduled Castes and Scheduled Tribes in India, and the *burakumin* in Japan.

The 'insider–outsider' dichotomy is particularly noticeable in Japan, as Renshaw shows. Special terms, many of them derogatory, are applied to non-Japanese minorities as well as to the descendants of Japanese who migrated to other societies and who have now re-migrated to Japan. These derogatory terms are applied to both legal and illegal resident foreigners. Japanese law is highly protective of citizens and citizenship is rarely granted to persons who are not ethnically Japanese. Resident aliens are required to register with the police and to carry their registration cards with them at all times, irrespective of the length of their residency.

There is considerable social and organisational prejudice against resident Koreans who, until 1991, had to be fingerprinted. As Renshaw shows, this prejudice is carried over into the operation of Japanese multinational corporations in other societies. A similar prejudice is held towards resident Chinese, though they did not have to be fingerprinted. Japanese society also sees as outsiders several Japanese minorities. These include the indigenous Ainu people (now mostly confined to the northern islands of Hokkaido and Sakhalin) who were the original inhabitants of the islands, the Okinawans (whose Ryukyu kingdom was not formally incorporated into Japan until the end of the nineteenth century), the *burakumin* (descendants of the 'Untouchables' in the caste system that was abolished in 1871 under the Meiji Emperor) and the *nikkeijin* (descended from Japanese who migrated to other societies). Along with people of mixed race ancestry, members of all these groups face social and legal discrimination and prejudice. Sometimes this involves checking a job applicant's ancestry to determine if he or she belongs to one of the 'outsider' minority groups and, if so, the applicant may not be hired. Like Japanese women, however, members of ethnic minorities are speaking out against inequities in employment and working conditions.

Like Japan, India has officially abolished its caste system and it also prohibits discrimination on the grounds of untouchability. While there is an affirmative action policy with respect to public sector employment, the principles do not apply to private sector employment and, as Bennington and Mariappanadar note, they are not known to be applied by any private sector enterprises.

While current government policy sees China as having been a united multinationality country since ancient times and describes the country as a united multinationality state founded jointly by the peoples of all nationalities, the 55 groups which are officially designated as National Minorities comprise only nine per cent of the population. It seems that people are now readier than they were in the past to identify with their ethnic group. Kitching notes that those ethnic minority nationality people employed in SOEs share the same problems as women and the disabled as these enterprises are restructured on to a profit basis.

Despite the numbers of expatriate workers in Hong Kong Kramar does not see there being an ethnic 'insider–outsider' problem. In Taiwan, Cheng sees the ethnic and social 'insider–outsider' issue as an evolving one. It involves not only the Han Chinese population (both the post-1949 immigrants and also descendants of earlier Hakka and Fukien migrants) but also members of the nine major ethnic minority tribes as well as large numbers of legal and illegal foreign workers (including Chinese from the mainland). The rise of the self-descriptor 'New Taiwanese' to describe Taiwanese born on the island as distinct from 'Mainlanders' and 'Taiwan-born' Chinese, and resistance to the marginalising of non-Mandarin languages is giving rise to a new consciousness of identity. If, and how, this sense of identity will affect business operations remains unclear.

In Malaysia, the ethnic Malays, or *bumiputras*, enjoy special privileges in business licences and share-ownership in new companies under Section 153 of the Malaysian Constitution. This constitutionally-sanctioned, privileged position was adopted in order to incorporate ethnic Malays into the economy and to help resolve some of the conflict arising from the dominance of the economy by the ethnic Chinese minority. This conflict had erupted into communal violence between the two communities. As noted earlier, the affirmative action provisions of the Constitution are limited to the public sector only and do not reach into the private sector.

Although communal riots occurred in 1964 and 1969 in Singapore (when Chinese and Malays fought in the streets), there is today a policy of harmonious multiracialism. Singapore considers itself to be a meritocracy and ethnic origin is not an issue of concern or discussion in the workplace. Economic or occupational segregation is seen as a consequence of inadequate education in a knowledge-based economy rather than of ethnic discrimination.

In Indonesia, the 'outsiders' are the ethnic Chinese minority, members of whom are identified by a special symbol on their identity cards. Communal violence between the ethnic Chinese community and others has occurred in the past in Indonesia, most recently at the time of the downfall of former President Suharto. Government regulations prohibit them the right to run businesses in rural Indonesia although they may (and do) own and operate businesses in urban and metropolitan Indonesia. There are restrictions exclusive trade associations and on the public display of Chinese written characters. While ethnic Chinese are prohibited from joining the public service, Bennington does not cite evidence that systematic discrimination is practised in private sector employment.

At the present moment, however, inter-communal violence in Indonesia between groups such as the ethnic Malays, the Madurese, the Ambonese and so on, many of whom are internal transmigrants, suggests unpleasant parallels with the situation in the former Yugoslavia and draws attention to the continued strength of the 'insider–outsider' phenomenon.

Kondo does not suggest, either implicitly or explicitly, that there was any awareness of the 'insider–outsider' phenomenon in employment in the Philippines, despite the presence of economically important ethnic Chinese and Spanish *mestizo* minorities. Filipinos of Chinese ancestry have played, and continue to play, important roles in public life, including figures such as Jaime Cardinal Sin (the Archbishop of Manila), former President Corazon Cojuangco Aquino, the politically powerful Osmena clan (of Chinese ancestry despite the Spanish family name) from Cebu, and businessmen Lucio Tan and Henry Sy. Spanish-descended families such as the Zobels and the Ayalas continue to dominate commercial life. Overt discrimination occurs only among the criminal classes in that they target wealthy ethnic Chinese business people for kidnap and ransom.

Like Malaysia and Singapore, Thailand has large ethnic Indian and Chinese minorities. In the early years of the twentieth century, ethnic Chinese were subjected to forced assimilation, being required to take Thai names, dress in Thai fashion and speak Thai, as well as pledge loyalty to the King and to Buddhism. Dubey-Villinger found that, while the ethnic Chinese now comprise about 12 per cent of the total population, they control around three-quarters of private, corporate and domestic capital. Dubey-Villinger however, explicitly notes that there is no overt awareness of ethnic diversity issues in Thailand, pointing out that in Thai companies it is common to see ethnic Thais, ethnic Chinese and ethnic Indians working side by side. The 'insider–outsider' phenomenon is apparent, however, in the Thai language proficiency requirement that appears in job advertisements.

The 'insider–outsider' phenomenon is extended to illegal foreign workers in Thailand, who may be subjected to behaviour that is tantamount to harassment. The provisions of legislation such as the Labour Protection Act do not cover such workers, however, and foreign workers legally in Thailand are not subjected to such harassing behaviour. Thailand, in common with societies such as the Philippines, does legally prohibit foreigners from practising a range of occupations and professions. Such overt examples of the 'insider–outsider' phenomenon may be contrasted with the covert actions of bodies that regulate the practice of some professions in, say, Australia where foreign-born and/or foreign-trained personnel are required to undertake retraining and/or to take professional examinations that will enable them to practise their profession.

In New Zealand, as Burns and McNaughton illustrate, non-European New Zealanders face disadvantages in employment and working conditions. Included in this group are not only Maori and other Pacific Islanders (e.g. Samoans, Tongans and Cook Islanders) but also members of non-European immigrant groups. There is evidence of employer prejudice against non-European New Zealanders even when they may be better qualified and more experienced than their Pakeha counterparts.

Ethnic diversity is a characteristic of Australian society but that country, too, has 'insiders' and 'outsiders'. The groups of 'outsiders' that receive the most attention are the first Australians — the Aborigines and Torres Straits Islanders. Census figures indicate that they form around two per cent of the population. The indigenous Australian population is disadvantaged in employment. Australia has also received immigrants from around 160 societies. Around 25 per cent of the population is overseas-born (and about 46 per cent of these came from the United Kingdom, Ireland or North America), and around 40 per cent of the population is either migrant or first-generation Australian-born. Workforce participation rates of overseas-born migrants from societies where English is not the main spoken language are 54 per cent. De Cieri and Olekalns note that, while overseas-born workers from non-English speaking backgrounds are likely to be as well qualified educationally as all workers, they are less likely to participate in on-the-job or external training than the general worker population.

As in George Orwell's *1984*, it is clear that even if constitutions and laws mandate the equality of all citizens, some citizens are more equal than others. Members of ethnic and social minorities face the same, sometimes subtle and sometimes overt, discrimination in employment and workplace conditions that is directed against women.

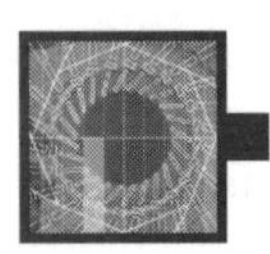

Managing disability and age diversity

The old (and the evidence cited in the chapters in this book suggests that people are being seen as 'old' at younger ages!) and the young, as well as those with a disability, are clearly as much 'outsiders' as women and members of ethnic and social minorities in terms of managing diversity. These groups are all subjected to discrimination in the form of unequal employment opportunities as well as to discrimination in the form of lower wages, unequal working conditions and, often, physical, verbal or sexual violence. Despite legal and constitutional guarantees of equal treatment, it is clear that these groups do not receive 'a fair go'.

In some societies covered in this book, social stigma and embarrassment are attached to being disabled, as Kitching notes for the PRC, Kondo points out for the Philippines, and as Bennington comments on for Indonesia. Families hide disabled members, and the disabled face discrimination in employment. In Indonesia, while there is legislation requiring companies with more than 100 employees to give one per cent of their jobs to disabled workers, there are no implementing regulations and the effect of the law remains unclear. As Kramar points out, complaints on grounds of disability account for 61 per cent of complaints referred to the Equal Opportunity Commission in Hong Kong, compared with only 36 per cent for sex discrimination and three per cent for family status discrimination. Complaints of discrimination on grounds of disability were resolved by conciliation in only 43 per cent of the cases, compared with 60 per cent in the case of family status and over two-thirds in sex discrimination complaints.

In the Philippines, Kondo notes that having a physical disability becomes an excuse for employers not to pay workers minimum wages, for able-bodied workers to refuse to work in the same room with disabled workers, and for security guards to sexually harass such employees. Landau and Chung find that here no legislation exists to prohibit discrimination on grounds of disability, as in Singapore, employers may not hire the disabled either because they perceive themselves as not possessing the expertise to deal with such employees or because buildings do not possess appropriate and adequate facilities to accommodate them. To Landau and Chung's list of reasons, McCoy (2000) adds that Singaporean employers discriminate against persons with disabilities because of the need to make changes to work schedules, the perceived lower ability of the disabled, and the possibility of negative reactions from other employees.

In the PRC, as elsewhere, there is a gap between the law and social attitudes. Disabled people employed in the regular workforce can face discrimination and behaviour tantamount to harassment. Persons with a disability employed in government departments, SOEs and private businesses now face some of the same problems faced by women in the rapidly changing economic system. With the loss of jobs in the state sector and both state-owned and private businesses emphasising profit, unemployment among the disabled is increasing.

Discrimination on grounds of age affects both the old and the young. Both groups are 'outsiders' as the young have yet to reach maturity and the old are deemed to have passed some organisationally or socially determined 'use by' date. Despite the commonly held perception that Asian societies revere age, it is clear that to be old is to be disadvantaged in the workforce. In Indonesia, as elsewhere, job advertisements specify not only the gender but also the age of preferred applicants. In Taiwan, companies prefer younger workers and hire them in preference to older, middle-aged, ones despite government subsidies for employing workers between the ages of 50 and 65 years. The cost of retirement and other benefits is used to under-report employee wages (thus reducing entitlements) or to lay-off older workers. In Singapore, the participation rates of older workers are a concern for government. The participation rates are below those in Japan, South Korea and Taiwan but comparable to those in Hong Kong. As Landau and Chung comment, Singapore is a youth-oriented society where individuals over 50 years of age have difficulty obtaining and retaining a job, and individuals over 40 years of age may be required to demonstrate their dexterity. In New Zealand, too, older workers face discrimination, as Burns and McNaughton show. There, labour force participation rates for those older than 45 years of age are diminishing. In part, such discrimination can be attributed to the higher costs of hiring older workers, their lower levels of education compared with younger workers, and the perception that they are less productive, possess obsolete skills (see Bennington and Mariappanadar, chapter 5), are less receptive to new ideas, and are more often ill or sick. Being old is valued only in advisory positions for the wisdom, experience, knowledge and connections age brings.

While in many societies children work to supplement family incomes, almost all the societies surveyed in this book place restrictions on the use of child labour. It is apparent, however, that in most cases these regulations are neither observed nor enforced. Children are recruited as workers because they provide cheap labour, are docile, agile and quick, less status conscious than older workers, and less expensive to feed and house. In Indonesia, as Bennington notes, children work long hours, receive no pay, have little information about their rights, and are often far from their families. In some cases, they are virtual prisoners, and many are subjected to physical, verbal and sexual abuse. In the Philippines, despite laws to protect their welfare, working children are exploited and abused, and are usually hidden away behind factory walls or in family compounds where law enforcers are unable to locate them. In India, the real number of child workers is unknown because much of it is illegal and the true figures are concealed. The *Child Labour Act 1986* focuses only on children in hazardous industries and so ignores 92 per cent of all children working in industry. In the PRC, as elsewhere, the laws are routinely flouted or ignored and children as young as 14 years of age are alleged to be illegally employed in sweatshops to make toys sold in McDonald's stores in Hong Kong (*Bangkok Post* 2000a).

The practice of using child labour has continued because of a lack of popular pressure to end it. Irawat Chanprasert, the permanent secretary of the Thai Labour and Social Welfare Ministry, believes that child exploitation will be cited in the next few years as a reason for the world community to impose trade tariffs (*Bangkok Post* 2000b). The ILO Convention on the Worst Forms of Child Labour (C.182), adopted in 1999, lays down exact definitions of what are unacceptable practices for any child anywhere in the world. These worst forms of child labour are fourfold: all forms of slavery, forced labour and armed conflict; prostitution and pornography; illicit activities, especially the drug trade; and work likely to harm the health, safety or morals of children. Knowledge of this international convention is important to expatriate managers for two reasons. First, it provides a definition of the worst forms of child labour that is acceptable to those coming from an Asian or from a Western perspective. Second, the convention provides a graded scale of punishments for states found to be transgressing the dictates of the convention, up to and including being black-listed. For the first time, trading rights are linked to human rights. The implementation of Convention 182 will significantly affect child labourers in the societies discussed in this book. The threat of sanctions or trade embargoes against industries (such as the garment or toy industries) where child labour is found should concern not only expatriate managers but also to those who import products made by exploited children.

Managing gender diversity well allows corporations to make use of the skills of more than half the population. Managing ethnic diversity well allows corporations to draw on the experiences of wider, more culturally diverse, groups in developing new products and services. Managing discrimination on grounds of advanced age well allows corporations to draw on experience and mature expertise. Managing disability diversity well allows corporations to display a humane face. Managing child labour well could become a commercial and political necessity.

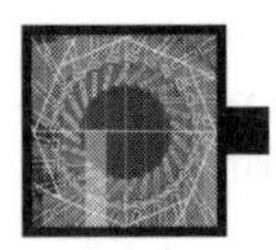

Multinational companies and managing diversity

For multinational companies and expatriate managers the issue of managing diversity can be summed up as a series of questions. Is diversity management a constitutional and legal issue given that, by and large, the societies covered in chapters in this book have provisions in their constitutions or legal codes dealing with human rights issues of equality before the law, equal rights to employment and so on? Should multinational companies and their expatriate managers be good corporate citizens in their host societies and insist on obeying the law even if, or most likely when, this conflicts with local practice?

Or is diversity management a business issue? Should multinational companies and expatriate managers adopt, or adapt to, recruitment and selection practices based on nepotism, corruption, and other forms of overt and covert discrimination? Should they turn the proverbial blind eye, in their own work place or in those of suppliers, to discriminatory and/or exploitative practices? Should MNCs customise their policies and practices according to local cultural beliefs and practices if this includes practices such as the use of child labour, the firing of pregnant women, discrimination against members of despised social minorities, or the use of physical, sexual or emotional violence? If indigenous companies and corporations permit such practices, and if the law is enforced so poorly that they can get away with it, what incentives are there for expatriate managers, safely ensconced behind high walls and security guards in compounds such as Metro Manila's Forbes Park, to enforce non-discriminatory workplace practices, particularly when workers report themselves as satisfied with their wages and working conditions?

There is evidence in this book to suggest that some MNCs and expatriate managers see diversity management as a business issue. Bennington cites evidence, for example, that neither Australian nor Japanese nor Taiwanese firms operating in Indonesia treat their workers with humaneness and a respect for their human dignity. Bennington and Mariappanadar cite evidence to suggest that, where firms have adopted diversity management programs, diversity management is seen as critical to business success. The last section of Renshaw's chapter on Japan draws attention to the more recent Japanese view that diversity is to be expanded and used for creativity and innovation, inherent in which are new and diverse perspectives that can lead to increased business success.

Is the issue of managing diversity a cultural one? As noted earlier, in several societies managing diversity is not seen as an indigenous issue but one imported from Western, and particularly American, sources. Is the challenge that faces expatriate managers and MNCs one of successfully reducing the 'insider–outsider' gap in ways that do not conflict too much with traditional values but which lead to more egalitarian workplaces?

It may be that the issue of managing diversity will boil down to one of commercial self-preservation. The adoption of the ILO Convention on the Worst Forms of Child Labour (C.182) may be seen as a portent of things to come. For the first time, it links trading rights to human rights and, moreover, provides, to those coming from both Western and Asian perspectives, an acceptable definition of the worst forms of the exploitation of the weak and defenceless. As the world becomes a small place, as websites spring up throughout the Asian–Pacific region, firms will no longer be able to hide human rights abuses, and pleading ignorance will become harder to defend. Ignoring human rights will mean that firms and managers will face internationally-sanctioned penalties. Those who ignore human rights will have nowhere to run.

References

Bangkok Post. 2000a. 'McDonald's toys made in sweatshop', 28 August p. 1.

Bangkok Post. 2000b. 'Child workers to get workplace learning', 31 August p. 2.

Bloom, S. J. 2000. *Postville: A Clash of Cultures in Heartland America*. Harcourt.

Kwang, M. 2000. 'Behind Every Successful (China) Man is a . . . Mistress?' *The Sunday Times* (Singapore), 12 November, p. 44.

McCoy, P. 2000. 'She Wants a Job, But is Likely to get Rejected'. *The Sunday Times* (Singapore), 12 November p. 31.

Sabilano, A. A. 1986. 'The Status of Women Workers in Philippine Industrial Relations'. *Philippine Journal of Industrial Relations* 7, 2/8: 1, 56–64.

Sheridan, G. 1998. 'Asian By The (Story) Book'. *The Australian*, 9 January 13.

Simon, S. 1999. 'Diversity's Arrival in Tiny Iowa Town Makes for Uneasy Mixing of Cultures. *Los Angeles Times*, 21 February. http://webusers.anet-stl.com/~civil/dv-ethnic-poisoning-postville-iowa.html

Vanijaka, V. 2000. 'Thai Workers Tread Tough Road in Search of Better Incomes. *Bangkok Post*, 2 October, Business section, p. 8.

Index